Endowment Asset Management

Endowment Asset Management

Investment Strategies in Oxford and Cambridge

Shanta Acharya and Elroy Dimson

OXFORD

UNIVERSITY PRESS

Great Clarendon Street, Oxford ox2 6DP

Oxford University Press is a department of the University of Oxford.
It furthers the University's objective of excellence in research, scholarship,
and education by publishing worldwide in

Oxford New York

Auckland Cape Town Dar es Salaam Hong Kong Karachi
Kuala Lumpur Madrid Melbourne Mexico City Nairobi
New Delhi Shanghai Taipei Toronto

With offices in

Argentina Austria Brazil Chile Czech Republic France Greece
Guatemala Hungary Italy Japan Poland Portugal Singapore
South Korea Switzerland Thailand Turkey Ukraine Vietnam

Oxford is a registered trade mark of Oxford University Press
in the UK and in certain other countries

Published in the United States
by Oxford University Press Inc., New York

British Library Cataloguing in Publication Data

Data available

Library of Congress Cataloging in Publication Data

Data available

Typeset by SPI Publisher Services, Pondicherry, India
Printed in Great Britain
on acid-free paper by
Biddles Ltd., King's Lynn Norfolk

ISBN 978–0–19–921091–6

1 3 5 7 9 10 8 6 4 2

To our parents

Contents

Acknowledgements   ix
List of Tables   xii

1. Endowment definition   1

2. The investment committee   50

3. Investment objective   69

4. Spending policy   98

5. Asset allocation   121

6. Investing in property   160

7. Issues in portfolio management   185

8. Portfolio risk   208

9. Consultant selection and monitoring   233

10. Manager selection and monitoring   244

11. Socially responsible investment   270

12. Performance measurement   284

13. Endowment management cost   301

14. Fund-raising: Role of gifts   314

15. Concluding observations   325

Notes   343
Bibliography   351
Index   355

Acknowledgements

We wish to thank the many individuals whose encouragement and continued guidance convinced us to work on this book. Especially noteworthy were Sir Alan Budd, Dick Brealey, Dr Jeremy Fairbrother, Will Goetzmann, Michael Gwinnell, Barry Hedley, John Kay, and Tom Seaman to whom we are very grateful. The bursarial committees at Oxford and Cambridge Universities, led respectively by Frank Marshall and Christopher Pratt, supported us generously with time, interest, and thoughtful feedback.

In the course of our research numerous Oxford and Cambridge bursars and investment committee members spent time answering our questions, allowing us to record and analyse their responses in detail, and reviewing our meeting notes after each interview. Many of them commented on successive extracts and draft chapters, which was of particular help in developing and wording our analysis. We had valuable meetings with Professor Alison Richard and Dr John Hood, the Vice Chancellors of Cambridge and Oxford Universities, and their respective colleagues.

We would particularly like to express our gratitude to Stephen Barton (Jesus College), Nick Baskey (Pembroke College), Peter Brindle (Darwin College), Gale Bryan (Homerton College), Charles Crawford* (St Catharine's College), Nick Downer (Selwyn College), Chris Ewbank (St John's College), Dr Michael Gross (Emmanuel College), Donald Hearn (Clare College), Dr Peter Hutchinson (Trinity Hall), Dhiru Karia (Homerton College), David Kerr* (Robinson College), Charles Larkum (Sidney Sussex College), Dr Sue Lintott (Downing College), Deborah Lowther (Girton College), Dr Simon Mitton (St Edmund's College), Andrew Murison* (Peterhouse), John Pegler* (Trinity Hall), Ian Du Quesnay (Newnham College), Dr George Reid* (St John's College), Jennifer Rigby (Churchill College), Dr John Seagrave (Wolfson College), Andrew Thompson (Magdalene College), Joanna Womack (Clare Hall), Nick Wright (New Hall), and Dr Nigel Yandell (Corpus Christi College) in Cambridge.

In Oxford, we would particularly like to express our gratitude to Roger Boden (Keble College), Dr Anthony Boyce (St John's College), John Church

---

* These individuals were in post at the time of our meetings with investment bursars in Oxford and Cambridge; they have now retired or moved on to other positions.

(Pembroke College), Tim Cockburn (St Anne's College), Brigadier Clendon Daukes (St Peter's College), Fram Dinshaw (St Catherine's College), Brigadier Alan Gordon (Wolfson College), Dr Alexander Hardie (Oriel College), Dr Hilkka Helevuo (St Hilda's College), Ian Honeyman* (St Hugh's College), Ian Jewitt* (Nuffield College), Professor John Knight (St Edmund Hall), Dr John Knowland (Brasenose College), Tim Knowles (Lincoln College), James Lawrie (Christ Church), Dr Patrick Martineau (Wadham College), John Martyn (Trinity College), John Montgomery (St John's College), Helen Morton (Somerville College), Roger van Noorden (Hertford College), David Palfreyman (New College), Alan Parsons (The Queen's College), Glyn Pritchard (Templeton College), Alison Reid (Linacre College), Hugh Richardson* (Christ Church), Mark Robson (Lady Margaret Hall), Ben Ruck Keene (Corpus Christi College), Richard Smethurst (Worcester College), Dr Brian Stewart (Exeter College), Allan Taylor (St Antony's College), Marten van der Veen* (Balliol College), Dr Graham Vincent-Smith (Oriel College), Stephen Waterman (Mansfield College), and Clifford Webb (Merton College).

We are grateful to Peter Agar and Andrew Reid at the University of Cambridge along with John Clements, Sue Cunningham, Steve Howarth, and Giles Kerr at the University of Oxford for their patience in dealing with our questions and requests for data.

We also had useful conversations with and/or received helpful contributions from John Bailey, Philip Coates, Freddie Cross, Peter Davies, John Griswold, Dr Ian Kennedy, Col David King, Howard Lake, Colin Mayer, Simon Pennington, Cathy Pharoah, Richard Robinson, Chris Russell, Stefano Sacchetto, Pedro Saffi, Peter Stanyer, Gary Steinberg, Lindsay Tomlinson, Karl Sternberg, Adriene Williams, and others. We apologise to individuals who guided us or responded to our questions who may inadvertently have been omitted from this list.

We wish to thank participants at seminars where we showcased preliminary findings and received valuable comments on our study. There were presentations at Cambridge University, London Business School, Oxford University, the Yale University School of Management, conferences in the UK and internationally, and in-house seminars at several foundations, consultancies, and asset managers. The reviews of our manuscript, provided through Oxford University Press, contained invaluable suggestions to guide successive drafts of our study, and we are extremely grateful to OUP's anonymous referees.

Our indebtedness is great. However, we would like to emphasize that our research was entirely independent; it was not sponsored nor endorsed by our interviewees, their organizations, or any third parties. While individuals at the two Universities cooperated generously, all observations and interpretations are our own, and we are responsible for any errors, omissions, or misinterpretations.

The Atlantic Philanthropies, Barclays Global Investors, and London Business School provided financial support, as well as encouragement to undertake this study. In addition to information published by the Colleges and Universities of Oxford and Cambridge, we made extensive use of data from the Commonfund Institute and the National Association of College and University Business Officers (NACUBO) in the United States, for which we are grateful.

We appreciate the careful proof-reading of our manuscript by Ashutosh Aman, Rajat Bhattacharya, Bruce Clibborn, Cristina Nunziata, and James Schappelle. Oxford University Press has been highly professional in all aspects of commissioning, guiding, and preparing our manuscript, and we especially wish to express our appreciation to our editor, Sarah Caro. We are grateful to Natasha Antunes, Carol Bestley, and Jennifer Wilkinson, also at Oxford University Press, for their unstinting support.

Finally, we wish to thank our colleagues, notably Paul Marsh and Mike Staunton, friends, and families for their understanding and support over the three years that we have been working on this project.[1]

List of Tables

1.1. Distribution of endowment assets in per cent, 2003–4   12

1.2. Size of top 10 US educational endowments in $ billions   13

1.3. Size of top 10 US endowments held by public institutions in $ billions   14

1.4. Largest educational endowments: Oxbridge versus Ivy league   15

1.5. Oxbridge compared with top US public institutions   15

1.6. Value of endowment and assets per FTE student, 2003–4   16

1.7. Endowment assets per FTE student, 2004–5   17

1.8. Size of top 10 university endowment assets in the UK, 2004   19

1.9. Higher education funding in the UK: sources of income in per cent   20

1.10. Sources of income: Universities of Cambridge and Oxford in per cent   20

1.11. Contribution of endowment income and gifts to total income, 2004   26

1.12. Sources of income: Harvard and Yale in per cent   27

1.13. Sources of income: Oxford colleges in per cent   28

1.14. Foundation dates of colleges and size of endowment assets   41

1.15. Wealthiest colleges in Cambridge and Oxford   42

2.1. Name of committee charged with investment management   51

2.2. Who chairs the investment committee?   56

2.3. Number of members in Oxbridge investment committees   56

2.4. Number of members in US investment committees   57

2.5. Percentage of investment committee members who are external   60

2.6. Investment experience in committees with no external members   60

2.7. Percentage of investment committee members with professional experience   61

2.8. Number of investment committee meetings per year   63

3.1. Frequency distribution of alternative investment objectives   75

3.2. Investment objectives (from Table 3.1) versus endowment size   76

3.3. Investment return targets and endowment size   82

3.4. Frequency of citing total return versus income-oriented policy, in per cent   85

3.5. Proportion of total income derived from endowment, in per cent   89

3.6. Endowment and interest income as percentage of total income   90

3.7. Importance of endowment income, in per cent   91

3.8. Peterhouse College revenues and expenditures, as per cent of total
     income   92

4.1. Date when the current spending policy was established   101

4.2. Relationship between spending policy and endowment income   105

4.3. Spending rate and endowment size   107

4.4. Interval over which spending rate is smoothed, in per cent   111

4.5. Frequency of spending rules within US educational institutions   112

4.6. Linkage between spending rate and inflation, in per cent   115

4.7. Distribution of spending rates, in per cent   118

5.1. Asset allocation of Oxford colleges, in per cent   124

5.2. Asset allocation of Cambridge colleges, in per cent   126

5.3. Comparison of average Oxford and Cambridge allocations, in per cent   128

5.4. Comparison of highest and lowest allocations to each asset, in per cent   129

5.5. Comparison of asset allocations with WM and NACUBO, in per cent   130

5.6. Asset allocation and endowment size, in per cent   132

5.7. Oxbridge asset allocation by size of endowment, in per cent   132

5.8. Asset allocation: institutional groups in the United States, 2003, in
     per cent   134

5.9. Comparison of Harvard and Yale asset allocations, 2002, in per cent   135

5.10. Harvard, Yale, and large US educational endowments, 2004, in per cent   135

5.11. Asset allocation of various sized US institutions, 2004, in per cent   137

5.12. US educational endowment asset allocation percentages, dollar-weighted   138

5.13. Total allocation to listed equity investments, in per cent   140

5.14. Allocation to domestic equities, in per cent   140

5.15. Allocation to overseas (OS) equities, in per cent   141

5.16. Five-year comparison of US asset allocation percentages   144

5.17. Oxbridge endowment size versus allocation to alternative assets   145

5.18. Oxbridge endowment size versus allocation to property   151

5.19. Allocation to property versus size of endowment, 2004   152

5.20. Date of foundation versus property allocation in 2004   153

6.1. Range of allocation to property within the endowment, in per cent   164

6.2. Peterhouse College endowment asset allocation, in per cent   165

6.3. Asset allocation: Colleges with no property assets, in per cent   167

6.4. Proportion of endowment income from property, in per cent   169

6.5. Nature of property holdings in the endowment, in per cent   171

6.6. Use of external managers in property management, in per cent   172

6.7. Distribution of mandates among external property managers	174
6.8. Impact of property on asset allocation	178
7.1. Percentage of portfolio indexed	189
7.2. Allocation to various strategies by colleges that hold alternatives assets	191
7.3. Allocation to various strategies by colleges with large index holdings	192
7.4. Percentage of assets managed passively by US educational endowments	193
7.5. Proportion of US educational institutions with a rebalancing policy	195
7.6. Adoption of portfolio rebalancing policies within Oxbridge	198
7.7. Examples of rebalancing cited by Oxbridge colleges	202
7.8. Relative importance of motives for changes in asset allocation	202
8.1. Degree of risk in institutional investment pool	211
8.2. Oxbridge perceptions of market risk	212
8.3. Oxbridge perceptions of risk relative to benchmark	214
8.4. Oxbridge perceptions of liquidity risk	216
8.5. Oxbridge perceptions of fiduciary risk	218
8.6. Oxbridge perceptions of other risk factors	219
8.7. Instructions to investment manager regarding risk	225
8.8. Extent to which the IMA defines accountability and authority	227
8.9. Extent to which the IMA identifies permissible investments and limits	227
8.10. Extent to which the IMA includes guidelines on use of derivatives	229
8.11. Extent to which the IMA specifies tracking error and downside risk	229
8.12. Defined performance targets and required actions if target is missed	230
8.13. Consistency of application of investment management guidelines	231
8.14. Extent to which investment management guidelines are agreed in writing	231
9.1. Extent to which external investment consultants are used	236
9.2. Investment consultants used by Oxbridge colleges	238
9.3. Length of appointment of investment consultants	241
10.1. Percentage of endowment assets managed externally	247
10.2. Size of endowment and assets managed externally, in per cent	249
10.3. US educational endowments: distribution of assets managed internally versus externally (dollar-weighted)	250
10.4. Responsibility for selection of assets managers	251
10.5. Oxbridge manager monitoring process	254
10.6. Frequency of asset manager review	256
10.7. Changes in the appointment of asset managers	257
10.8. Number of asset managers	260

10.9. Number of asset managers for US educational endowments, 2003
and 2004   261

10.10. Number of mandates cited   262

10.11. Number of managers versus endowment value   264

10.12. Number of mandates per asset manager   267

10.13. Number of managers versus asset allocation   267

11.1. Extent to which SRI issues influence allocation, in per cent   275

11.2. Extent to which SRI features in the asset management process, in per cent   278

11.3. Methods for implementing SRI Policy in Oxbridge colleges, in per cent   280

11.4. US endowments: Social responsibility criteria followed, in per cent   282

12.1. Organization responsible for undertaking performance measurement   287

12.2. Criteria for appraising endowment performance   293

12.3. Percentage total returns reported by Oxbridge colleges   294

12.4. Endowment performance of Oxford colleges, FY 2003, in per cent   294

12.5. Endowment performance of Oxford colleges, FY 2004, in per cent   295

12.6. Oxford college endowment returns versus size of endowment   298

13.1. Oxford endowment management costs, 2003–4, in per cent   305

13.2. Oxford endowment management costs, 2004, per cent of total
expenditure   307

13.3. Cambridge endowment management costs, 2003–4, in per cent   308

13.4. Cambridge endowment management costs, 2004, per cent of total
expenditure   310

13.5. Endowment management costs for US educational institutions, in
per cent   311

14.1. Additions to endowment assets in the United States, 2003, in per cent   315

14.2. Distribution of Oxford Colleges' funds raised, 2004, as percentage of
endowment assets   319

14.3. Additions to endowment assets among US educational institutions   323

1

Endowment definition

Introduction

In this study we examine endowments within the educational sector, focusing on some of the oldest Colleges in the United Kingdom (UK), with a view to capturing investment perspectives among institutions with ostensibly similar objectives. Colleges in Oxford and Cambridge, popularly referred to as Oxbridge, are eleemosynary corporations. The term eleemosynary means that their support comes from charitable giving. The universities of Oxford and Cambridge, however, are not eleemosynary but civil corporations created by Statute. When the Colleges were founded, benefactions made to these institutions were for the sustenance of the Colleges, not for passing on to others. It was the work of the College—achieving the purposes of the Head of the College and its appointed Fellows—that fulfilled the objective of the charity. Thus, the Head of the College and Fellows acted like trustees but were also the beneficiaries of the foundation.

Unlike charitable institutions, Colleges did not bear responsibility for collecting funds and distributing them among needy students. Nor were the students meant to be beneficiaries of the College unless they were appointed as Scholars, as opposed to Commoners who paid their way. The corporate endowment was never meant to benefit students, though the Governing Body of each College had, and still has, the power to spend the funds as it sees fit, as long as the activity supports the objects of the College. The purposes that endowments are created to serve also determine the manner in which they are invested.

Today the endowments of the Colleges and the Universities of Cambridge and Oxford consist of funds generally regarded as for the long term, and which fundamentally underpin and sustain the operation of these institutions at their desired level of activity. While educational organizations have common objectives, individual Colleges interpret their investment objectives as being slightly different to that of other Colleges, often resulting in remarkably dissimilar asset allocation decisions. Colleges consistently make long-term

1

commitments, such as the appointment of faculty members, to maintain their regular activities, but the level of individualism and diversity manifested in their investment approaches is remarkably engaging. When viewed as a cohesive unit or collegiate university, their combined assets and their asset allocation are closer than one might expect to those of educational endowments in the United States with pioneering investment strategies.

In broad terms, educational endowments share many features of other foundations and charities. Most enjoy favourable tax status and operate within a time horizon that is perpetual. For some foundations, the perpetual nature of their mission may not be an obligation. The Atlantic Philanthropies, a Bermuda-based entity with several affiliate organizations in the United States, Britain and Ireland, redefined their purpose in early 2002, opting to spend down their $4 billion endowment by 2020. The decision to do so was based on the Founder's belief in the importance of 'Giving-while-Living', and that the next generation of philanthropists are best left to address the issues of the future. Atlantic's limited life helped drive their decision to concentrate resources on targeted programmes to fulfil their stated purpose 'to bring about lasting changes in the lives of disadvantaged and vulnerable people'.

Even without a time-bound horizon, spending at rates that wipe out endowed assets may constitute a legitimate option for some trustees, if the nature of their current spending is considered urgent; for example, funding research to cure a certain type of ailment or some killer epidemic. Educational institutions, particularly ones that have been around for centuries, would be failing their fiduciary obligations if they followed the same strategy.

Universities in the UK generally derive their income from a combination of student fees, research grants, residential, catering and conference charges, donations and legacies, in addition to income from endowment investments. In contrast to foundations, public universities receive a substantial transfer of resources from the government sector. While educational institutions generally have multiple sources of income, foundations often derive the bulk of their income from their endowment assets.

The largest foundations in the world derive a significant portion of their resources from their investment-related activities, with gifts and donations very occasionally boosting capital inflows. At the current time, the Bill and Melinda Gates Foundation is an exception, receiving huge infusions of capital from its founders and from the Foundation's co-contributor, Warren Buffet. Founders of large endowments, such as Henry Wellcome, Andrew Carnegie, John D. Rockefeller, or Joseph Rowntree, are not around to make such donations. It is worth mentioning that the new generation of philanthropists, such as Intel's co-founder, Gordon Moore and his wife Betty, or Pierre Omidyar, the founder of eBay, are actively engaged in doing good. Many of the philanthropists of today are as imaginative in their giving as their predecessors were a century ago. But the current generation of philanthropists believe more in

Giving-while-Living. Many of the older foundations do not accept gifts as a matter of policy. This means that these foundations require relatively stable income flows to sustain their established level of grant-making.

Educational institutions, on the other hand, receive annual gifts and donations in addition to the fees they receive from the government or directly from their students. As they are not entirely reliant on endowment income for operations, any disruption in such flows does not immediately threaten their existence. The impact of annual giving on endowment assets may appear insubstantial, but it plays a major role in boosting asset values over the long term, as well as on spending on educational objectives and enhancing new initiatives. The experiences of Harvard, Yale, and the Carnegie Institution over the course of the twentieth century provide insight into the importance of donor support. While differences in investment policies no doubt account for some of the gap in the assets of these institutions today, the absence of continuing gift inflows constitutes the fundamental reason for Carnegie's failure to keep pace with the wealth of Harvard and Yale.[1] Oxford and Cambridge may struggle to match the endowment assets built up by their transatlantic Ivy League peers, such as Harvard, Yale, Stanford, and Princeton, as differences in approaches to investments and fund-raising play a critical role in determining objectives, policies, and performance within the endowed sector.

While theories of endowment asset management have evolved more recently, College endowments in Oxford and Cambridge have been in existence for centuries. The manner in which these institutions have come to embrace modern approaches to investment management provides useful insights for other institutions facing similar dilemmas. Though the focus is on the challenges and rewards of investment management by educational endowments, particularly Oxbridge ones, the issues raised concern all long-term investors whose ultimate aim is real capital growth and sustainable (or increasing) spending power. Investment success improves with better understanding of dilemmas that may arise at various stages of the asset management process. Attempting to understand the nature of risks associated with such a process can be educational for all investors.

Oxford and Cambridge: A brief background

Oxford and Cambridge are independent and self-governing institutions, consisting of the central University and the Colleges. Today, there are 39 Colleges in Oxford and 31 in Cambridge. The Colleges, independent and self-governing institutions, form a core element of each University, to which they are related in a federal system, not unlike those in the United States of America. Through their collective body, the Conference of Colleges in

Oxford, for example, they engage in discussion and debate on key strategic academic decisions within the University.

In Oxford, the ultimate body of the University is the Congregation. Congregation has responsibility for approving changes in or additions to the Statutes and Regulations of the University, which define the corporate governance structure. Under Oxford's governance structure, the principal policymaking body, introduced in 2000, is Council. Council comprises 26 members, including those elected by Congregation, representatives of the Colleges and four members from outside the University. Council reports upwards to Congregation, which comprises over 3,700 members of the academic, senior research, library, museum, and administrative staff, and which decides on resolutions put by Council and is the ultimate decision-making body of the University. Council is responsible for the academic policy and strategic direction of the University, and operates through major committees. Council is responsible to the Higher Education Funding Council for England for meeting the conditions of the financial memorandum between the Funding Council and the University. The Council is chaired by the Vice-Chancellor and advised by a range of committees, including the Investment Committee, which is responsible for the management of the University's investment portfolio.

Cambridge is similarly a confederation of Colleges, Faculties, and other institutions. The Regent House is the governing body and principal electoral constituency of the University. It has more than 3,800 members, comprising University Officers, Heads and Fellows of Colleges, and certain other categories of individuals defined by Ordinance. The Regent House has important responsibilities in electing members to the Council and the Board of Scrutiny, as well as in making appointments to a number of University bodies. Cambridge's Council is the principal executive and policymaking body, consisting of 21 members of whom 19 are elected members of the University. It has overall responsibility for the administration of the University, for defining its mission, for planning its work, and for the management of its resources. The Council has many standing committees, but among the most important committees with executive responsibilities is the Finance Committee, whose main obligations are to account to the Council for the receipts and payments of the University and all its Departments and subsidiaries; to budget and advise the Council on the trends in University income and expenditure; to control the University's investments; and to maintain and care for all University sites and buildings.

Each College in Oxford or Cambridge, on the other hand, is a charitable corporation established by Royal Charter and governed by a Head and a Governing Body comprising of a number of Fellows, many of whom also hold University posts. The Governing Body is responsible for the strategic decisions of the College, and for its overall management of finances and assets. Governed by Statutes under the Universities of Oxford and Cambridge Act 1923, the Colleges are exempt charities under the Charities Act 1993. They are subject to the jurisdiction of the court but are exempt from all supervisory or regulatory powers of the Charity Commissioners, though the degree of exemption may change once impending charity legislation passes into law. Thus, Colleges are autonomous, self-governing institutions with their own property, endowment, and income.

There is no clear date of foundation for Oxford or Cambridge but teaching existed at Oxford in some form in 1096 and developed rapidly from 1167, when King Henry II banned English students from attending the University of Paris. By 1201 Oxford University was headed by a *magister scolarum Oxonie*, on whom the title of Chancellor was conferred in 1214, and in 1231 the Masters were recognized as a *universitas* or corporation. The University of Cambridge was established in 1209 when scholars taking refuge from hostile townsmen in Oxford migrated to Cambridge. They were numerous enough by 1226 to have set up an organization, represented by an official called a Chancellor, and they arranged regular courses of study, taught by their own members. King Henry III took them under his protection as early as 1231. The two universities were formally incorporated by Act of Parliament in 1571. Oxford and Cambridge thus have no founders and no charters. Their common law powers to enact rules for the regulation of their internal affairs are supplemented by the power to make Statutes which was conferred upon them by the Universities of Oxford and Cambridge Act 1923.

For the purpose of this study, the 36 Colleges listed in the *University of Oxford Accounts of the Colleges*, and the 30 in the *Cambridge University Reporter* were approached. For accounting purposes, the three Colleges in Oxford which do not have Royal Charters (Green, Kellogg, and St Cross) are departments of the University and their annual financial figures are included in the main University accounts. The College Accounts discussed here are therefore those of the University's 36 Chartered Colleges. Similarly, in Cambridge, Homerton College, which does not have a Royal Charter, is not included in the University's 30 Chartered Colleges. Homerton College was invited to participate as we wished to include in our study an example of a College actively engaged in building its endowment.

Among the Colleges invited to participate, 33 in Oxford and 26 in Cambridge accepted. The Investment Committees of the two Universities also participated. When we conducted our interviews in 2003, we met Sir Alan Budd, Chairman of the University of Oxford's Investment Committee, and his team. As Cambridge was in the midst of considerable restructuring, we were unable to meet Sir Alan's equivalent. We met Joanna Womack, a long-time member of Cambridge University's Investment Committee. As we go to press, the recently appointed Chief Investment Officer (CIO) for Cambridge University, Nick Cavalla, had not joined; and Oxford University had announced the appointment of Richard Oldfield as Chairman of its Investment Committee, which had been reconstituted. This committee had decided to appoint a CIO to oversee its investment office. We have endeavoured as far as possible to reflect the rapid changes taking place in the endowment management of these institutions.

In total, 61 responses were received from 69 institutions (a participation rate of 88 per cent). The Colleges that declined to participate were Christ's, Hughes Hall, King's, Lucy Cavendish, and Queens' in Cambridge, along with Harris Manchester, Jesus, and Magdalen in Oxford. Apart from Harris Manchester and Hughes Hall, deemed too small for our survey, the other Colleges did not provide any reason for their lack of participation. Other associated bodies, such as the Gates Trust (Cambridge) or the Rhodes Trust (Oxford), were not included in the study; nor were Oxford University Press (OUP) and Cambridge University Press (CUP), though these organizations make an important contribution to the activities of the universities to which they are attached. OUP, for example, contributes 4 per cent of the total income of Oxford University.

Most of the participating institutions responded to a detailed questionnaire, which required specific responses with qualitative nuances, and were interviewed in depth. The interviews took place in 2003–4. The transcriptions of the interviews were subsequently sent to the participants for verification. The Investment Bursars of Colleges and relevant members of the Investment Committee of the two Universities were the main participants. The study benefited from the frank and forthcoming observations of participants.

The study also benefited from the publication of financial statements of the Colleges in the recommended format, known as SORP (Statement of Recommended Practice). The first set of accounts in the new format for the Cambridge Colleges appeared in 2004, reflecting data for the financial year ending June 2004. Colleges in Oxford started reporting in the new format the previous year. The second set of accounts for Oxford Colleges in the new format, for the year ending July 2004, contained a higher level of disclosure for all the Colleges compared to the first set of accounts issued by Cambridge Colleges. When the 2003–4 accounts were published, five Colleges in Cambridge failed to report in the new format. In the 2004–5 accounts, two Colleges in Cambridge continued to report in the old format. Thus, aggregate data for Cambridge Colleges are not available for comparison with Oxford Colleges. Data in the public domain contributed to our analysis.

For the sake of convenience, participating institutions, including the two universities, are referred to as Colleges. The data presented in our study are intended to provide an overview of the management of endowed assets of institutions in Oxford and Cambridge at the cusp of change. Little information was, and still is, in the public domain. Information given to us on asset allocation, for example, at the end of financial year 2002–3, is most likely to have altered by the time of publication. Financial market conditions have changed in addition to the process of internal changes in management approaches, such as the move towards total return among all Oxbridge institutions. Gonville and Caius College in Cambridge, for example, had 5 per cent in hedge funds and private equity in 2002–3; this allocation had risen to 13 per cent in hedge funds by March 2006 with a target allocation of 20 per cent of the endowment portfolio in hedge funds. As Colleges do not disclose detailed asset allocation in their annual reports, the data collected during the course of our interviews are intended to provide a snapshot of the way things were in 2003.

As annual asset allocation data are not publicly available, it has not been possible to analyse such information over a longer period. Even the distribution between property and other investment assets was only made available with the publication of the new accounts. More information will hopefully become available in future as a change in the status of these institutions is anticipated, once the impending Charities' Bill, due to be passed into law in late 2006, has had an effect. Schools, for example, operating under the superintendence of the Charity Commission in the UK commonly provide an elaborate review of their activities. Oxbridge institutions will most probably need to move towards such a review over the next several years. Much of the information in the published accounts today on subjects as diverse as asset allocation, investment performance, costs, or fund-raising is incomplete or inconsistent. Hence, any analysis is subject to the limitations inherent in the available data.

Comparison has been drawn frequently with contemporary US practice, particularly among peer group institutions such as Yale and Harvard, reflecting their pioneering efforts at addressing investment issues faced by independent educational institutions with substantial endowments. The authors do not seek to recommend US practice; the objective of this study is to provide an understanding of alternative approaches to critical aspects of endowment asset management. As information on endowment asset management, especially among educational endowments in Europe and Asia, is not in the public domain, this study is limited to comparative data from the United States, where the sector is more evolved, more transparent, and under greater public scrutiny. As foundations and endowments face similar dilemmas, institutions can learn from the American experience and develop individual strategies without repeating old errors and without slavish adherence to what Harvard, Yale, and Princeton did a decade or more ago.

Restricted versus Unrestricted funds

Endowments typically consist of Specific (or restricted) and General (or unrestricted) funds, managed on a pooled or segregated basis by each institution. Most Colleges have a main portfolio of assets such as a General Endowment

Fund, also known variously as the Consolidated, Amalgamated, Unrestricted, or Corporate Fund. General endowments represent the corporate capital of Colleges and include bequests and gifts where the use of the capital and income, or only the income, is for the general purposes of the Colleges. At Oxford, 80 per cent of the Colleges' endowment assets are designated for the 'general' purposes of these institutions.

Universities, on the other hand, receive funds that are designated for a 'specific' purpose. In 2005, for example, 99 per cent of Cambridge University's endowment funds were for 'specific' purposes. The corresponding proportion for Oxford University was 79 per cent.

While the University funds are more specific, the Governing Body of a College has greater flexibility in choosing to designate part of its unrestricted endowment funds for a particular purpose. Notwithstanding the Universities and College Estates Act 1925 (amended 1964), there are no significant external regulatory constraints imposed today on how the permanent endowment assets are invested, save the ones imposed by the institutions themselves— such as specific income requirements or socially responsible investment (SRI) constraints. Oxford and Cambridge institutions have recently embraced a 'total return' approach in managing their assets.

Some College endowments are held in Trust Funds, also called Specific or Restricted Funds, which are constrained to the extent that these funds are required to be spent in a certain way to retain their Trust status. Specific Endowments are those bequests and gifts where the use of the capital and income, or only the income, is for a specific purpose or activity designated by the donor and which can only be used for that purpose or activity. Sometimes, the income generated from such endowments may be directed towards activities that lie outside the current objects of the College. There appear to be no substantive limits on the way in which these assets are invested.

'We are constrained by what these specific endowment funds can be spent on,' explained one bursar, 'not what they are invested in. That said, it can be argued that our investment decisions are constrained as certain of the Trust Funds have to be spent in a certain way.' Most Colleges, regardless of their age, have a large number of such funds amalgamated into a pool. To illustrate, in Cambridge, Gonville and Caius has some 120 specific Trust funds within its Consolidated Trust Fund, a unitized collective vehicle within the endowment. Newnham, also in Cambridge, has some 280 such funds. In Oxford, Christ Church reports 95; and Balliol and Somerville respectively have about 175 and 110 funds.

Individual trusts managed by the Universities tend to be numerous: Oxford University, for example, has over 630 trust funds. The total number of Specific Trusts within each university would therefore run to thousands. The picture is similar in the United States; the endowments at Yale and Harvard are composed of thousands of specific funds with a diverse range of designated purposes and restrictions. Harvard University's endowment consists of 10,700 separate funds, the majority of which are restricted for specific purposes similar to those in the universities of Cambridge or Oxford.

Individual endowments for specific purposes are usually pooled, creating a vehicle similar to a mutual fund or unit trust. This enables broad diversification of investments among asset classes, thereby providing an appropriate balance between return and volatility. Pooling also permits economies in oversight, investment management, and accounting costs. Though endowment assets are invested as a pool, each College maintains the identity of each component fund in their accounting record. Most university or college endowments consist of an investment pool composed of several individual funds with a wide variety of purposes and restrictions. Donors frequently specify a particular purpose for their gifts, creating endowments to fund professorships, scholarships, fellowships, prizes, books, libraries, buildings, and other miscellaneous purposes.

Depending on the institution, endowment funds usually consist of gifts, some of which are restricted by donors to provide long-term funding for designated purposes, along with others that are unrestricted, which the endowed institution is free to invest and spend as it sees fit. According to the notes to the 2003–4 accounts of Girton College, Cambridge, for example, the policy on management of reserves sums up how these institutions treat their various endowment assets:

The income or expendable capital of restricted funds is used only for the purposes for which the funds were originally given or bequeathed to the College. The income or expendable capital of unrestricted funds may be used either for the general educational purposes of the College or for a particular purpose designated by Council. The Council may designate or re-designate unrestricted funds as it deems appropriate depending on the College's financial situation. The permanent capital of restricted and unrestricted funds is invested for the long-term with a view to maintaining its real value. Expendable capital is also invested for the long term unless expenditure is planned. Expendable capital required for specific projects is held in the form of cash.

It is only within the last 50 years or so that, along with other philanthropic institutions, Oxford and Cambridge Colleges have been able to exercise freedom of choice in their investment decision-making. Even that discretion was fairly limited as, until 2000, UK universities' tax-exempt status limited them to spending only income earned from their endowment investments, not via capital gains. Thus, many of these institutions operated under mandatory 'income only' spending rules, which meant that assets were managed to produce the requisite cash flow via dividend income which was tax free. Many foundations, endowments, and charities in the UK continue to invest for income in high-yielding companies long after these tax incentives were withdrawn.

Funds constrained by asset mix have diminished following the Trustee Act 2000, though an income-oriented asset allocation influenced manager selection. From 1945, when Oxford University's Trust Pool was established, the Trust's investments were managed by a single manager within a balanced fund. It was only in 1997, when the Investment Committee decided that the returns obtained from their balanced mandate were suboptimal that a more diversified structure was adopted, and a wider range of financial assets and specialist managers were considered. There was a major shift in the investment strategy of the University of Oxford's Trusts Pool as a result of its review. As implementation of a new asset allocation takes time, the University was until recently in the process of doing so.

Prior to this restructuring, the University of Oxford obtained legal advice on the spending rules pertaining to income and capital and it became evident that a 'total return' approach could be used, implying that expenditure could be financed from the sale of assets and that the University need not secure its expenditure only through income. This significant decision enabled the University to move away from an income-oriented investment policy towards a total return one, enabling the Trust to restructure its management arrangements. This had profound consequences on the University Investment Committee's ability to alter asset allocation and, with it, manager selection. Ten years ago, the Trusts Pool had two managers; today it has over 20 managers. It also has exposure to investments in private equity and hedge funds, in addition to equity, fixed income, and property.

The endowment of Cambridge University was similarly managed by a single asset manager, F&C Asset Management, from January 1981. Before then, the University's Amalgamated Fund set up in 1956 (now known as the 'Cambridge University Endowment Fund') was managed by an individual, Oliver Dawson, who was with stockbrokers Buckmaster & Moore, which was taken over by F&C. Thus, the Cambridge University endowment was effectively managed by a single individual followed by a single asset manager since 1956. The establishment of an Investment Office in 2006, with a CIO, for the management of the University's endowment and the investments of its related bodies therefore marks a new direction in the history of Cambridge University.

Many Oxbridge Colleges have Trust funds, which are registered charities in their own right, and are typically engaged in fund-raising for the institution concerned. These funds support the educational and related activities of the Colleges. But, the Trust assets do not form part of the Endowment. The Trust funds are sometimes invested differently and have diverse asset allocation policies, reflecting their individual aims and objectives. These charities, also with permanent endowments, exist to support the operations of the Colleges, although their assets are kept quite distinct from that of the College endowment assets. A few examples of such College Trust funds are Balliol's

Appeal Trustees Fund, Magdalen College Development Trust, the New College Development Fund, the Perse Trust (Gonville and Caius, Cambridge) or The Isaac Newton Trust (Trinity College, Cambridge).

Similarly, the two University endowments exclude individual Trust funds and related endowments that are not invested in the University's Trust or Deposit pools managed by the University Investment Committee. Until 2004–5, for example, the University of Cambridge's Endowment, represented by the Amalgamated Fund and the Deposit Pool were managed separately from the Gates Cambridge Trust (worth £150 million in 2004–5). The Gates Cambridge Trust, like the Rhodes Trust in Oxford, is an international scholarship programme; but unlike the Rhodes Trust it is now part of the University's Endowment. So is the University of Cambridge's Learning and Examination Scheme, renamed Cambridge Assessment (worth £85 million), which was managed separately along with the Associated Trusts (worth £92 million). CUP's assets (worth £25 million) were not part of the University endowment pool. Cambridge pooled these assets (with CUP being deferred until 2005–6 for operational reasons) making its 2004–5 consolidated Endowment worth over £1 billion. This also enabled Cambridge to establish an Investment Office with full-time professional management staff.

Oxford has not taken this route in aggregating its various endowments into a single unit for efficient management. The James Martin 21st Century Foundation, worth £69 million for example, is currently managed externally to the University's Trust and Deposit Pool. The amount is included as a 'Specific' endowment in its consolidated accounts. The Rhodes Trust, with assets worth around £150 million, is also managed separately from the University's; but its assets are not consolidated into the University's Endowment. The Rhodes Trust, based in Oxford is an educational charity whose principal activity is to support scholars selected from various countries to study at the University of Oxford, but it is an independent entity. OUP's investments are also managed separately, though OUP provides direct and significant support to the University's overall revenue.

Size of endowment assets

The endowment assets reported by Cambridge University and its constituent Colleges in 2003–4 amounted to £2.6 billion ($4.6 billion). For collegiate Oxford, endowment assets totalled £2.3 billion ($4.2 billion). The combined value of endowment assets of the 68 institutions (36 Colleges in Oxford, plus 30 in Cambridge along with the two University endowments) at the end of financial year 2004 amounted to £4.8 billion ($8.8 billion), compared with $22 billion for Harvard and $13 billion for Yale. The distribution of

Table 1.1. Distribution of endowment assets in per cent, 2003–4

Endowment	Oxford	Cambridge	Oxbridge
£1–10 m	11	16	13
£10–20 m	22	13	18
£20–30 m	14	13	13
£30–50 m	22	16	19
£50–75 m	8	19	13
£75–100 m	8	13	10
£100–200 m	11	—	6
£200–400 m	3	3	3
£400–600 m	3	—	1
£600–700 m	—	6	3
Total	**100**	**100**	**100**

Source: University of Oxford, Financial Statement of the Colleges 2003–4; Cambridge University Reporter, Accounts of the Colleges 2004–5.

endowment assets among these Oxford and Cambridge institutions is illustrated in Table 1.1.

In 2003–4, most (63 per cent) of the Oxbridge endowments were valued at less than £50 million. Only 13 per cent of endowments contained assets worth more than £100 million; and just 7 per cent of institutions had endowment assets in excess of £200 million. Those worth more than £200 million included Trinity College and St John's College in Cambridge, as well as the University of Cambridge; in Oxford, only St John's College had more than £200 million worth of endowment assets, in addition to the University of Oxford.

The average endowment of a Cambridge College was £65 million compared with Oxford's £52 million. Only two educational institutions in the UK, Trinity College in Cambridge and the University of Cambridge, had endowment assets worth over $1 billion compared with 47 such institutions in the United States, up from 39 institutions in 2003.[2] The two University endowments of Oxford and Cambridge failed to make the $1 billion mark in 2004, despite Oxford University's endowment assets showing a gain for the year. Cambridge University's reported assets declined from £490 million in 2002 to £467 million in 2004.[3] In 2004–5, Cambridge University consolidated the various endowments under its aegis; the dollar value of its restated endowment for 2003–4 rose to just over $1 billion. The value of the consolidated Cambridge endowment by the end of financial year 2005 was over £1 billion.

Comparisons with the size of endowment assets of top universities in the United States are typically made to illustrate the lack of resources available to UK institutions. Size of assets under management can have an impact on some aspects of asset allocation. For example, an endowment's smaller size may restrain its ability to invest in alternative assets and strategies, which tend to

Table 1.2. Size of top 10 US educational endowments in $ billions

Institution	2004	2003	2002
Harvard University	22.1	18.8	17.2
Yale University	12.7	11.0	10.5
University of Texas System	10.3	8.7	8.6
Princeton University	9.9	8.7	8.3
Stanford University	9.9	8.6	7.6
MIT	5.9	5.1	5.4
University of California	4.8	4.4	4.2
Emory University	4.5	4.0	4.5
Columbia University	4.5	4.3	4.2
Texas A&M	4.4	3.8	3.7

Source: 2004 and 2003 National Association of College and University Business Officers (NACUBO) Study.

be illiquid in nature and carry a higher element of risk. Income requirements may also influence asset allocation policy for a small endowment. An endowment's ability to afford independent investment advice and performance analysis may also be a limiting factor. Thus, an institution with less than £10 million of assets under management simply cannot afford to replicate the sort of strategies pursued by institutions with assets above £500 million.

Table 1.2 shows the top 10 university endowment assets in the United States over the past 3 years. Seven of the top 10 largest educational endowments in the United States are independent institutions such as Harvard, Yale, Princeton, and Stanford. The top two, namely Harvard and Yale, have endowments which are significantly larger than that of Cambridge and Oxford, though the collegiate endowments of Cambridge and Oxford are closer to those of MIT and Columbia.

While the University of Texas System was ranked third in the overall US educational endowment league table in 2004, and remains among the largest endowments in the world, the top public universities in the United States have endowments whose assets are closer in size to those of collegiate Oxford and Cambridge. Taking into account the funding structure of universities like Cambridge and Oxford, the size of endowments perhaps needs to be compared with that of the top public institutions in the United States. Table 1.3 shows the top 10 endowments held by public universities in America.

Endowments in Cambridge and Oxford have also grown substantially over the past few years. In 2002–3, inclusive of Colleges and University, Cambridge and Oxford with £2.1 billion ($3.3 billion) and £1.9 billion ($3.0 billion) respectively of endowed assets compared favourably with top public educational endowments in the United States. By 2003–4, Cambridge and Oxford with endowment assets worth £2.6 billion ($4.6 billion) and £2.3 billion ($4.2 billion) respectively compared even better with their institutional peer

Table 1.3. Size of top 10 US endowments held by public institutions in $ billions

Institution	2004	2003	2002
University of Texas System	10.3	8.7	8.6
University of California	4.8	4.4	4.2
Texas A&M	4.4	3.8	3.8
University of Michigan	4.1	3.5	3.4
University of Virginia	2.8	1.8	1.7
University of Minnesota	1.5	1.3	1.3
Ohio State University	1.5	1.2	1.1
University of Pittsburgh	1.4	1.2	1.1
UNC Chapel Hill	1.3	1.1	1.1
University of Washington	1.3	1.1	1.1

Source: 2004 and 2003 NACUBO Study.

group in the United States, though the endowment of the University of Texas System remains significantly larger than that of other public universities worldwide. With Cambridge consolidating its group endowments in 2004–5, the combined value of the endowments of Cambridge University and its constituent Colleges was closer to £3 billion ($5.2 billion), while Oxford's combined endowment assets were worth £2.7 billion ($4.8 billion) in 2005.

Cambridge is richer, with more endowment assets under management; the average value of endowment funds per College is also higher in Cambridge. But there were more Colleges in Oxford with endowment assets over £100 million; in 2003–4, for example, Cambridge University, Trinity College, and St John's College had assets worth over £100 million. In Oxford, in addition to the University, six Colleges had assets over £100 million: St John's, Christ Church, All Souls, Nuffield, Magdalen, and Jesus. By July 2005, a few more Colleges had joined the over £100 million group, such as Merton and The Queen's in Oxford. In Cambridge, Gonville and Caius and Jesus also reported endowment assets worth over £100 million while King's at £99 million worth of endowment funds was virtually a member of this elite group of Oxbridge Colleges.

Table 1.4 shows the size of endowment assets at Cambridge and Oxford compared with that of the top 10 US educational endowments in 2004–5.

Table 1.5 shows the size of endowed assets at Oxford and Cambridge compared with that of the top public educational institutions in the United States in 2004–5.

The size of the endowment may not represent the whole picture. The disparity in funding between public and independent institutions in the United States becomes highly visible when we compare endowment assets per full time equivalent (FTE) student among the top 10 universities with the largest endowments. The differences in endowment assets per FTE student, driven by enrolment numbers, illustrate that students at Princeton, Harvard,

Table 1.4. Largest educational endowments: Oxbridge versus Ivy League

Institution	Endowment $ b
Harvard University	25.5
Yale University	15.2
Stanford University	12.2
University of Texas System	11.6
Princeton University	11.2
MIT	6.7
University of Cambridge*	**5.3**
University of California	5.2
Columbia University	5.2
Texas A&M	5.0
University of Michigan	4.9
University of Oxford**	**4.8**

* Including Colleges and related bodies.
** Including Colleges.
Source: 2005 NACUBO Study; University of Cambridge; University of Oxford.

Table 1.5. Oxbridge compared with top US public institutions

Institution	Endowment $ b
University of Texas System	11.6
University of Cambridge*	**5.3**
University of California	5.2
Texas A&M	5.0
University of Michigan	4.9
University of Oxford**	**4.8**
University of Virginia	3.2
University of Minnesota	2.0
Ohio State University	1.7
University of Pittsburgh	1.5
University of Washington	1.5
UNC Chapel Hill	1.5

* Including Colleges and related bodies.
** Including Colleges.
Source: 2005 NACUBO Study; University of Cambridge; University of Oxford.

and Yale are significantly wealthier compared with their peer group in the University of Texas System. Harvard and Yale had 19,060 and 11,271 FTE students respectively in 2003–4 while the University of Texas System reported 133,039 FTE students.

Endowment assets per FTE student in the United States are even higher in some specialized educational institutions such as The Rockefeller University ($7.7 million per FTE) or the Franklin W. Olin College of Engineering

Table 1.6. Value of endowment and assets per FTE student, 2003–4

Institution	Endowment $ b	Assets per student $000
Harvard University	22.1	1,162
Yale University	12.7	1,131
University of Texas System	10.3	78
Princeton University	9.9	1,476
Stanford University	9.9	686
MIT	5.9	569
University of California	4.8	23
Emory University	4.5	404
Columbia University	4.5	233
Texas A&M	4.4	54

Source: 2004 NACUBO Study.

($2.1 million per FTE) with 193 and 150 students respectively. But these institutions do not have large endowments.[4] Table 1.6 illustrates the size of the total endowment versus endowment assets per FTE student in 2003–4 among universities with the largest endowments in the United States.

It is encouraging that despite significant funding gaps between the top US and UK institutions, endowment assets per FTE student in Oxford ($237,000) and Cambridge ($234,000) were considerably higher in 2003–4 than at wealthier public universities in the United States. By 2004–5, endowment assets per FTE student in Oxford had risen to $269,000. At Cambridge the aggregation of the different endowments into a centralized fund meant that endowment assets per FTE student rose to $296,000 in 2004–5, with Cambridge and Oxford trailing behind Princeton, Yale, Harvard, Stanford, and MIT. Table 1.7 illustrates the comparative size of endowment assets per FTE student in 2004–5 in Oxford and Cambridge compared with the top US institutions.

Oxford and Cambridge feature among the top 10 universities with the largest endowment assets per FTE students in the world. But the difference in endowment assets per FTE student between Oxbridge and the highest ranked US educational establishments is worth emphasizing. Princeton has over five times the amount of endowment assets per FTE student compared with Cambridge, and over six times that of Oxford. Yale and Harvard too have almost five times more endowment assets per FTE student than Cambridge.

What is perhaps not apparent is that, due to the collegiate structure of Oxford and Cambridge, it is possible for a student at a less wealthy College to miss out on the facilities available to a student reading for the same degree at a richer College in the same University. Sometimes, these seemingly minor differences, such as lack of student housing or sporting facilities, impact not only the quality of life but also reflect on academic achievement. Thus, a

Table 1.7. Endowment assets per FTE student, 2004–5

Institution	Endowment/FTE student $000
Princeton University	1,663
Yale University	1,354
Harvard University	1,331
Stanford University	822
MIT	652
University of Cambridge*	**296**
University of Oxford**	**269**
Columbia University	252
University of Michigan	103
University of Texas System	86
Texas A&M	60
University of California	25

* Including Colleges and related bodies.
** Including Colleges.
Source: 2005 NACUBO Study; University of Cambridge; University of Oxford.

student at St John's College, Cambridge, would have significantly higher endowment assets per FTE student ratio (£319,000 in 2004–5) compared with a student at New Hall (£60,000) in the same University. Similarly, a student at Christ Church would have more endowment assets per FTE student (£309,500 in 2004–5) compared with a student at St Edmund Hall (£43,000).

The endowment and its value per full-time student give us an idea of the importance of the endowment within an institution. But two institutions of a similar size may have different objectives with very different costs of operation. It is worth looking at the ratio of the value of the endowment to the expenditure of the institution concerned, as it gives us an idea of the resources available to the institution to support its activities. Thus, Harvard's expenditure in 2003–4 was 11.6 per cent of the value of its endowment while Yale's expenditure was 13.2 per cent. These numbers may vary marginally from year to year, but they have been similar over recent years. Unless the market falls substantially in any one year, such a ratio suggests the stability of the endowment in sustaining operations. To express the same ratio as the endowment to expenditure ratio, it is 8.6 for Harvard and 7.6 for Yale. Princeton has a higher ratio (14.1 in 2003–4), and there are other examples of academic institutions in the United States with high endowment to expenditure ratios among institutions with endowment assets over $1 billion.

In the case of Oxford and Cambridge, it is interesting that collectively the Colleges have an attractive endowment to expenditure ratio of 9.3 and 9.9, respectively, with Colleges like Trinity (Cambridge) and All Souls (Oxford) recording ratios as high as 36.1 and 30.5 respectively in 2003–4. In fact, there are eight Colleges in Cambridge and 12 Colleges in Oxford with higher endowment to expenditure ratios compared with that of Harvard's. The same is not true of the two Universities; both these institutions annually spend more than the total value of their endowment assets. The endowment to expenditure ratios of the universities of Oxford and Cambridge are 0.9 for both institutions. The combined ratio for collegiate Cambridge, that is the Colleges and the University, was 3.0, while that for Oxford was 3.3, compared to 8.6 for Harvard, 7.6 for Yale, and 14.1 for Princeton in financial year 2003–4.

The scale of spending at Cambridge and Oxford may not compare with that of Princeton, Yale, or Harvard, but they are the wealthiest in the UK. The unique historical developments within Oxford and Cambridge resulted in the Colleges having their own endowments, independent and separate from that of the University. If the College endowments are included, then Cambridge and Oxford tower above other educational institutions in the UK in terms of their endowment wealth. An analysis of endowment assets per FTE student in these institutions reveals the extent to which Oxford and Cambridge, thanks to the endowments of their member Colleges, benefit from such support. Endowment assets per student at Trinity College, Cambridge, were estimated to be close to that at Harvard and Yale.

Total endowment assets for the 165 educational institutions or associations in the UK listed in the *Higher Education Financial Yearbook, 2005–6* were £2.5 billion. This is less than half the value of the combined endowments of the individual Colleges and Universities of Cambridge and Oxford. The relative wealth of Cambridge and Oxford in the UK is therefore not in doubt. Excluding the endowment of the Colleges, the universities of Oxford and Cambridge account for over a third (35 per cent) of total educational endowment assets in the UK. The history and wealth of these institutions partly explains why they are in the public eye; and why their actions, be it their admissions policy or medical research using animals, are under constant public scrutiny.

The assets represented in Table 1.8 are the endowment assets held by the universities of Cambridge and Oxford, and do not include those of the Colleges.

Average endowment size in the UK rose from £14.2 million in 2002 to £15.2 million in 2004, with the top 10 endowments representing two-thirds (64 per cent) of assets in the higher education sector. However, only three universities' endowments were worth more than £100 million compared to eight Oxbridge Colleges, not to mention the two Universities. According to the 2004 *NACUBO* Endowment Study, the average endowment size in the United States was $360 million, up from $321 million in 2003.[5] The average size of endowment in the United States at £198 million in 2004 was significantly higher than the average for the Colleges in Cambridge or Oxford. Apart from the two university endowments of Cambridge and Oxford, the remaining endowments did not come close.

Table 1.8. Size of top 10 university endowment assets in the UK, 2004

Institution	Endowment £ m	Assets per student £000 ($000)
University of Cambridge	470	129 (234)
University of Oxford	431	131 (237)
University of Edinburgh	156	8 (15)
University of Glasgow	97	5 (10)
University of Manchester	96	4 (7)
University of Liverpool	89	5 (9)
King's College, London	88	5 (9)
University College, London	78	5 (8)
University of Reading	77	7 (12)
University of Birmingham	60	3 (5)

Source: Higher Education Financial Yearbook, 2005–6; data for Oxford's endowment assets are from the University of Oxford. The HEFY 2005–6 shows Oxford's assets at £406 million, which was the size of the endowment in 2003. Cambridge University's 2005 accounts indicate endowment assets for 2004 at £467 million. Cambridge University has since consolidated its group endowments and the aggregate value for 2005 is closer to £1 billion.

Funding of higher education in the UK

Funding for higher education in the UK is derived largely from the government. While changes are anticipated, the government is expected to remain the major source of financial support for educational institutions. The three principal channels through which institutions receive government funding are: Council funds (which are for the general expenditure of an institution assessed and paid for by the Higher Education Funding Councils), Academic fees (which for UK students are paid for by Local Education Authorities on the basis of number of students and is determined by the academic course; non-EU students are charged directly on a full cost basis), and Research grants (which are paid on the basis of the research carried out by higher education institutions). These variable sources of income represented 79 per cent of the total income of UK academic institutions in 2004.[6]

Recognizing the effects of globalization and the need to redefine sources of comparative advantage in the face of more challenging competition from China and India, in addition to existing challenges from developed economies, the UK government recently conducted a strategic assessment of higher education in consultation with stakeholders. New partnerships, methods of funding, assessment, etc. were included in the agenda for the next five years with a view to providing a more stable funding environment in which institutions can adjust to the new fee arrangements. From 2006–7, for example, universities will have the power to vary the fees they charge directly to students, up to a maximum of £3,000 per year. Other changes in the funding of research in meeting new economic and social challenges, including investing in physical infrastructure, are afoot.

Table 1.9. Higher education funding in the UK: sources of income in per cent

Income source	2004	2003	2002	2001	2000
Funding Council Grants	39	39	40	40	40
Fees and Support Grants	24	24	23	23	23
Research Grants and Contracts	16	16	17	16	15
Other Operating Income	20	19	19	19	19
Endowment Income	1	1	2	2	2
Total Income (£ b)	**17.1**	**15.8**	**14.6**	**13.3**	**12.4**

Source: Higher Education Financial Yearbook, 2005–6.

Table 1.10. Sources of income: Universities of Cambridge and Oxford in per cent

Income source	Breakdown for 2004		Breakdown for 2002	
	Cambridge	Oxford	Cambridge	Oxford
Funding Council Grants	24	29	31	32
Fees and Support Grants	9	12	12	11
Research Grants and Contracts	27	36	33	35
Other Operating Income	35	15	12	15
Endowment Income	4	8	11	7
Total Income (£ m)	**644**	**458**	**447**	**427**

Source: Higher Education Financial Yearbooks, 2005–6, 2003–4.

Table 1.9 depicts sources of income for universities in the UK over the past five years.

The historical distribution pattern of income from public sources—Council funding, Academic fees, and Research grants—which has been stable over the past several years may not be the best guide in forecasting future sources of income. Though small, the contribution from the endowment has failed to keep pace with growth in income from other operating sources, such as residence and catering as well as for conferences and other such events. Institutions have increasingly resorted to using subsidiary companies to carry out non-core activities on a commercial basis or to act as vehicles in the commercial development of businesses that spin out from research functions. The distribution of income received by the universities of Cambridge and Oxford, both of which have substantial endowments in the context of the educational sector in the UK, is significantly different from the sector aggregate. Table 1.10 illustrates this difference.

In 2004, aggregate income received by Oxford and Cambridge from public sources, that is Funding Council grants, Academic fees, and Research grants, was 60 per cent of total income while that for Oxford was significantly higher at 78 per cent. The major difference in such income distribution was the result of income derived from other operations. Cambridge received over a third (35 per cent) of its total income from other operating sources; its examination and assessment services alone contributed £151 million in 2004, compared to £57 million from academic fees and support grants and £37 million from the endowment. Endowment income for both universities remained low at 6 per cent and 4 per cent for Cambridge and Oxford respectively.

When compared with the education sector, the differences in the sourcing of income among these institutions are remarkable. Higher educational institutions received about 80 per cent of their overall income from public sources in 2004 while the endowment's contribution was negligible at 1 per cent. The universities of Cambridge and Oxford, on the other hand, derive considerably more income from their endowments and other operations. The endowments of Cambridge and Oxford thus play a more substantial role in funding their objectives, even if we disregard the Colleges. If the roles of the Oxbridge Colleges are taken into account, the overall significance of the endowment in the context of higher education funding in the UK becomes self-evident.

While Cambridge and Oxford are independent institutions, key differences in the management and funding of higher education in the UK over the past several decades may have constrained institutional ability to build up endowment assets over this period. At the same time, these institutions had to cope with real decline in income from their core activities. Historically, students contributed a much higher proportion of the operational income of the Colleges than is the case today. Until 1978–9, Colleges in Oxford and Cambridge determined tuition fees payable by students; and thus were in a better position to charge for the true cost of their services. Colleges had exercised great restraint in doing so, keeping the increases to below the increases in the University's costs. However, since they lost such control, the University system has been subjected to real cuts, and these cuts were applied to College fees as well.

For Mr Roger Van Noorden, Investments Bursar at Hertford College, Oxford:

College fees as a proportion of the total revenue of Oxford Colleges, for example, declined from 37 per cent of income in 1979–80 to 30 per cent by 2002–3. Though by some definitions, overall student fees may have kept pace with growth in consumer prices, they have not kept up with growth in salaries, which comprise the largest expenditure of the Colleges. Also, as far as fee erosion is concerned, fees per head have declined faster than fees in aggregate for the Colleges. As academic sector salaries in the UK lag significantly behind salaries among Ivy League institutions in the US, there is cause for concern. Colleges have increased their Board and Lodging Charges from their own members (up from 20 per cent in 1979–80 to 24 per cent in 2002–3), and generated income from other sources such as conferences (up from 6.5 per cent to 9.5 per cent) along with private grants and donations (risen from 2 per cent to 5 per cent). The contribution from Endowment income fell from around 35 per cent to 31 per cent of overall income over the same period. There has been an increasing tendency to finance Colleges through higher charges and conference income, and for Colleges to collect grants and donations directly from non-public sources.

Andrew Murison, Senior Bursar of Peterhouse in Cambridge from 1994 to 2003, had a similar take on the subject. According to Murison, 'the Peterhouse Statutes required that its Tuition Fund, an annual income and expenditure account, should not habitually draw on the Endowment. The student body had to pay its own way. Unfortunately, this statutory requirement has fallen into desuetude since the Government has taken responsibility for paying—and therefore limiting—the fees it pays on behalf of students, with the consequence that income from teaching and support has fallen considerably over the years while expenses have soared.'

Today, income received by Colleges in Oxford and Cambridge fails to reflect the true nature of costs. According to one study, educating the average undergraduate was estimated to cost £18,600 per annum, against total income per student of £9,500. The figure for the average graduate student was broadly similar. The annual deficit was calculated at £27.8 million on teaching and £67.7 million on publicly funded research, almost £100 million per annum. Of the estimated total £18,600 cost per student, only 6 per cent was recovered through tuition fees. Of the remaining 94 per cent of the cost, the University contributed roughly half from private sources (principally endowment, earned income and donations) and government contributed the other half.[7] An estimate quoted by a Cambridge College with reference to shortfall in the funding of undergraduate education alone was broadly similar at £24 million.[8]

It is worth pointing out that over the past decade, the cost of attending Harvard College increased by 51 per cent, from $26,700 to $40,450 per year. Tuition costs at Princeton University rose by 77 per cent between 1989–90 and 1999–2000 to $25,430, while total costs rose 68 per cent over the same period, rising to $35,320. Even at government-funded state institutions in the United States, such as Berkeley and Michigan, there is a move to fund higher investment needs of these institutions by the university setting student fees rather than the government while retaining present levels of government funding.[9] In contrast, UK government funding per student has fallen by more than 40 per cent in real terms over the past 15 years. Oxford and Cambridge's endowment assets per FTE student failed to keep pace with that of Harvard and Princeton as a result of this long-term under-funding of education in the UK.

As students at Oxford and Cambridge currently pay around £1,150 (approximately $2,000) in tuition, with total expenses rising to £5,700 (approximately $10,000) annually, top-quality education in the UK is available at bargain prices. This has been secured at the cost of lower compensation for faculty, and lower investments in infrastructure such as its world-class libraries. The median annual salary for a full professor at Cambridge University in the UK is about £53,000 compared to £87,000 at Harvard and £76,000 at Yale, according to the University of Cambridge figures. Oxford starting salaries for lecturers can be as low as £20,000; sometimes, housing and meals are subsidized.

The recently published accounts of Oxford University's Colleges for the year to 31 July 2005 show strong returns on investment and a break-even at the operating level. However, the core activities of teaching, research, accommodating students, and caring for historic buildings remain heavily in deficit, and are subsidized from non-core income. Most significantly academic fees and tuition income fell in real terms by 2.6 per cent. On a combined gross income of £222 million, the Colleges reported an operating surplus of £0.4 million. Surpluses on sales of assets boosted this to £6.6 million. However, Oxford Colleges' core activities (teaching and research; the provision of food and accommodation to College members; and the care of much of the built environment of the University) rely on non-core income to sustain them.

Spending on these core activities during 2004–5 amounted to £195 million, compared with income on core activities (mainly from fees and board and lodging charges) of £104 million. Colleges funded the £91 million annual deficit on core activities through a combination of transfers from endowments; surpluses from conferences; and grants and donations, chiefly from alumni. It is only because of this income from their own resources that the Colleges are able to meet all their commitments: they fund £50 million of the collegiate University's academic staff costs; support a significant proportion of its research activity; provide about 95 per cent of its student accommodation; and are at the heart of the College's intellectual, cultural, sporting, and social life.

Oxford College endowments performed well in 2004–5; on a starting net balance of £1.81 billion, the Colleges achieved a total return of £413 million, an average gain of 23 per cent over the year. Spending from endowments fell slightly to £66 million (3.6 per cent of asset value). Fund-raising contributed £25 million to endowments, £6 million to building projects and £9 million to College bursaries and other operating activities. Commenting on the figures, Sir Michael Scholar, Chairman of the Conference of Colleges in Oxford, said:

The contribution the Colleges are able to make is crucial to the University's academic success. The Colleges managed their finances well in 2004–5, though the financial challenges we face are still significant. Endowments performed particularly well in 2004–5. The Lambert review stated that Oxford and Cambridge 'play a crucial role in the economic as well as the intellectual life of the UK', but would 'need to generate significantly more money than they are likely to get from public funding in order to pay their academics a more competitive wage, to develop their research strengths, to cover their teaching costs, and to subsidise talented students where necessary.' The 2004–5 financial results show that Oxford's Colleges are responding very positively to this challenge.

The gap between the cost of education provided and the fees received by universities in the UK will continue to grow larger unless corrective action is taken urgently. The public debate in the UK about the impact of higher fees—represented as a conflict between opposing views that charging higher fees is a fairer way of securing much needed funding to universities versus the view that higher fees deter students from poorer backgrounds—is being settled by the response to the Higher Education Act, which took effect in 2006.

In addition to recurring annual deficits, demand for capital expenditure remains high. While Oxford and Cambridge have managed to remain more competitive in capital project expenditures than other cost areas on University and College levels, the level of new capital investment cannot be compared with leading US universities. In recent years, Oxford and Cambridge have been successful in garnering public funds for new capital projects. A recent report noted that during 2001 and 2002, taking into account all public and private funding for the University and the Colleges, Oxford invested around £140 million in new capital projects. Harvard University spent a total of $410 million on 'physical renewal, new facilities and acquisitions'. Oxford's spending was nearer Berkeley's at approximately £120 million.[10]

Institutions in Oxford and Cambridge traditionally met costs with a mixture of public funding and external borrowing. They also depended largely on internal resources, often leading to depletion of reserves. Larger American universities regularly use debt to finance large construction projects. This enables them to leverage the value of the initial gift to the university while addressing the cash-flow problem. Universities with large endowments and long operating histories are usually regarded as safe investments by banks in the United States. Not only do universities secure lower rates of interest, they are able to take advantage of US tax exemption rules, throughout the typically 35-year life of the bond. Universities then invest the proceeds of their gifts at rates preferable to those they owe their bondholders. The compounding of the positive differential spread in earnings leads to enhancement of the original gift. Introduction of tax incentives could result in the replication of similar investment strategies among universities in the UK.[11] Some Colleges in Oxford and Cambridge are already resorting to debt financing with larger projects, but to what extent these institutions are in a position to leverage their initial gift is not clear.

Recent achievements of Oxford or Cambridge therefore need to be assessed against a difficult funding environment. Recurrent costs exceed revenues as the core activities of the Colleges lose money. While the 36 Colleges in Oxford may have reported a small operational surplus in 2003–4 and 2004–5, they incurred a deficit in their academic income and expenditure account. The University of Oxford registered a small operational surplus in 2003–4; University income was £493 million compared to expenditure of £491 million. Similarly, Cambridge University spent £693 million while its income for 2004–5 was £695 million.

According to the *University of Oxford, Financial Statement of the Colleges, 2003–4*, the total income of the Colleges exceeded total expenditure by

£4.5 million, up from £1 million in 2002–3; yet over one-quarter (28 per cent) of Colleges recorded a deficit for the year, including richer Colleges such as Christ Church, All Souls and Nuffield. In 2002–3, over one-third (36 per cent) of Oxford Colleges reported operational deficits, again including Colleges with the largest endowments. Over half (54 per cent) the Colleges in Cambridge that published accounts in the new SORP format for 2003–4 also recorded operational deficits; they included Colleges such as Peterhouse, Jesus, and King's.

The operational deficit for individual Colleges in Oxford and Cambridge may appear small in the context of general educational spending, but the constant need to balance accounts must have a detrimental effect on institutional ability to focus on core educational activities, let alone develop new areas of growth. Long-term underinvestment in infrastructure, lower expenditure per student, and lower academic salaries (which are one-third to a half less than at top US universities) must take its toll. While these institutions remain committed to being centres of learning, teaching, and research to stand comparison with any in the world, their aspirations need to be backed by greater resources.

A significant factor influencing overall quality of output is the difference in spending between Oxford and Cambridge and their US counterparts. In 2003–4, for example, the 36 endowed Colleges in Oxford spent a total of £206 million or an average of £5.7 million each. Christ Church spent £16.4 million while St John's expenditure was £12 million. In Cambridge, Trinity's expenditure amounted to £18 million (£5 million of which was donations); St John's spent £22 million while King's expenditure was £12.9 million in 2004. In fact, total expenditure in 2003–4 for all the universities in the UK was £16.8 billion, with an average spending of £102 million.[12] Among the biggest spenders were the University of Cambridge (£660 million or $1.2 billion) and University of Oxford (£486 million or $884 million). The University of Oxford and the 36 Colleges together spent £692 million or $1.3 billion while the University of Cambridge and the 30 Colleges spent £856 million or $1.6 billion.

This compares with Harvard University's expenditure of $2.6 billion in 2003–4 and Yale's $1.7 billion. Other state-funded academic institutions, such as the University of Tokyo, for example, with a faculty of approximately 2,800 and total student enrolment of 28,000, spent about $2 billion. Even the University of Kyoto's expenditure in 2003–4 was over $1 billion. Thus, the challenge faced by universities in the UK is their inability to access the scale of resources that other global institutions command. As academic fees have fallen in real terms, the burden on the endowment to support academic purposes has increased considerably over the years.

Table 1.11 shows the contribution of endowment income and gifts to total income.

Table 1.11. Contribution of endowment income and gifts to total income, 2004

Institution	Endowment income %	Gifts %	Total income $ b
Cambridge University	4	4	1.2
Cambridge Colleges	35	6	0.4
Collegiate Cambridge	**13**	**4**	**1.6**
Oxford University	4	7*	0.9
Oxford Colleges	34	4	0.4
Collegiate Oxford	**13**	**6**	**1.3**
Yale	31	5	1.7
Harvard	31	6	2.6

* Oxford University Press makes a substantial gift (4 per cent of income) in addition to the 3 per cent received from other sources.

Endowment income in Oxford and Cambridge contributes over a third of total income of the Colleges and plays a critical role in sustaining operations while total income from the Colleges' academic activities consists of no more than 30 per cent of income. Oxbridge Colleges currently derive the bulk of their income from non-academic sources. The two universities also derive a substantial sum from non-core operations. As government funding failed to keep pace with the rising cost of operating these world-class institutions, they have successfully diversified their sources of income via fund-raising, improved endowment asset management and other operations.

Funding comparison: Ivy League versus Oxbridge

Twenty-five years ago, the operating resources of Oxford and Cambridge matched those of the best private American universities. Today Oxford can afford to spend half of what Harvard does and Cambridge less than two-thirds. The major difference between the funding of UK undergraduates lies in the assessment of cost-based tuition fees chargeable in the United States coupled with higher levels of financial aid available to students depending on individual financial need.[13] Like others among the very top US universities, admission to Harvard today is blind to the financial circumstances of the applicant; it is based entirely on merit. Deserving candidates receive financial support. While Oxford and Cambridge also admit the best applicants, their inability to charge cost-based tuition fees to students places a greater financial handicap on them.

The funding crisis faced by the top universities in the UK therefore cannot be resolved without enabling them to access substantially greater resources than they are able to command at present. The high level of fixed costs for most Colleges in Oxford and Cambridge means that reducing the number of students will not resolve the crisis, though some Colleges are considering

Table 1.12. Sources of income: Harvard and Yale in per cent

Income source	Harvard	Yale
Endowment income	31	31
Student income	21	13
Sponsored research support	23	30
Other income	14	20
Current use gifts	6	5
Income from other investments	5	1
Total Income ($ b)	**2.6**	**1.6**

Source: Financial Report To The Board of Overseers of Harvard College, Fiscal Year 2003–4; The Yale Endowment Annual Report 2004.

altering the ratio of home to overseas students to be able to charge the higher fees payable by overseas students. The London School of Economics, for example, has shifted its mix of student intake, admitting a higher proportion of applicants from outside the EU. Non-EU students pay fees that are closer to the real cost of their education, though at levels that are still lower than charges at Ivy League institutions.

Table 1.12 summarizes the sources of revenue for Harvard and Yale. The distributions have been standardized for convenience as Yale reports its breakdown slightly differently compared with Harvard. In the fiscal year ending 2004, Yale received $1.63 billion of income, of which 31 per cent was from the endowment, 30 per cent from grants and contracts, 15 per cent from medical services, 13 per cent from net tuition, room and board, 5 per cent from current gifts, 2 per cent from publications income, 1 per cent from other investment income, and 5 per cent from other income.

If one compares the sources of income for the top educational institutions in the UK and the Unites States, it may come as a surprise that Colleges in Oxford and Cambridge (but not the Universities) derive on average a larger proportion of their annual income from the endowment. Also, the income these Colleges derive from gifts and donations does not lag significantly behind Harvard or Yale. Oxford Colleges derived 4.4 per cent of their total income from gifts and donations in 2004 compared with Yale's 5 per cent and Harvard's 6 per cent. As Oxbridge Colleges have recently turned their focus to fund-raising, the level of support they received from their benefactors is hugely encouraging. On a collegiate basis, combining the universities and the colleges, the ratios for income from the endowment and revenue derived from gifts and donations for Oxford and Cambridge look relatively reasonable.

The differences lie mainly in the combined area of student income and sponsored research support (44 per cent for Harvard and 43 per cent for Yale) and 'Other income' (see Tables 1.10 and 1.12). Academic fees and charges inclusive of research grants and contracts for Oxford Colleges are significantly

Table 1.13. Sources of income: Oxford colleges in per cent

Income source	2004	2003
Academic fees and charges*	29.4	30.0
Endowment income	34.1	34.9
Other operating income	36.5	35.1
of which:		
Residential income (from College members)	19.4	19.4
Conferences and functions	9.7	9.2
Donations and benefactions	4.4	3.5
Other income	3.1	3.0
Total income (£ m)	**210.7**	**198.0**

* Inclusive of Research Grants and Contracts.
Source: University of Oxford, Financial Statement of the Colleges, 2003–4.

lower at 30 per cent of overall income. The universities of Oxford and Cambridge, on the other hand, receive a significant proportion of such support from the government: 77 per cent for Oxford in 2003–4, and 60 per cent for Cambridge. The contribution of endowment income as a proportion of total income of the universities of Cambridge and Oxford does not bear comparison with that of their peer group institutions in the United States. The University of Oxford was able to fund just 8 per cent of its operating expenses from endowment income while Cambridge managed at half that level in 2004. Returns on investment and additions to the endowment through fund-raising historically for both institutions have been modest, though both universities are only too aware of their lack in this direction.

The sources of income for the 36 Oxford Colleges are summarized in Table 1.13.[14] Similar comparisons with Cambridge Colleges are not available.

The problem with income for Oxford and Cambridge is not just its distribution and high level of dependence on the government, but also its aggregate level. The total revenue of Oxford Colleges and the University in 2004 was $1.3 billion and that of Cambridge was $1.6 billion compared with $1.7 billion for Yale and $2.6 billion for Harvard. It has become abundantly clear that Oxford and Cambridge need to generate significantly more revenues than they are likely to receive from public sources in order to compensate their academics at a globally competitive rate, to develop and maintain world-class research capabilities, to cover teaching costs, and to attract the best brains in the world. While it could be argued that the distribution of income from various sources for Oxbridge institutions appears balanced, it is the aggregate amount of money available to these institutions that needs to be augmented.

According to an academic strategy paper, published by the University of Oxford: 'Funds raised by Oxford as a whole in 2002–3 were £58 million as compared with £262 million in Harvard and £250 million in Stanford. Allowing for cultural differences in alumni giving, Oxford's fundraising efforts still pale in comparison with those of the leading US universities, where between 40 per cent and 60 per cent of alumni give annually. The best estimate for the figure for Oxford is around 5 per cent.'[15] As both universities plan major fund-raising campaigns over the next few years, it provides an incentive to address weaknesses in the collegiate management system, be it governance arrangements, tax matters, or performance measurement.

Cambridge launched its 800th Anniversary Campaign to raise £1 billion in additional funds across collegiate Cambridge, with many gifts directed towards endowment. The establishment of an Investment Office, with an Investment Board, also represents a significant development in Cambridge University's future approach to endowment asset management. 'This Investment Board is a significant step forward for Cambridge,' said Professor Alison Richard, Vice-Chancellor of the University. 'Building the University's endowment and providing more income to support core activities are crucial elements in our overall strategy to strengthen and reconfigure the University's finances.'

To put higher education funding in perspective, according to figures published by the organization for Economic Cooperation and Development (OECD), the United States spends 2.7 per cent of its GDP on universities, compared with 1.4 per cent in Germany, 1.3 per cent in Britain, and 1.0 per cent in France. In Germany, of the amount spent on higher education, 0.1 per cent comes from the private sector. Students do not pay fees in France, Germany, and in other EU countries. In Britain, the introduction of variable fees chargeable to students remains highly controversial, and they are nowhere near covering the real cost of a student's education. From 2006–7, universities will have the power to vary the fees they charge for courses, up to a maximum of £3,000 per year; in return the universities have to promote wider participation and access.

In their 2003–4 financial statements, many Colleges in Oxford and Cambridge refer to the long-term loss of income. Public funding per undergraduate within higher education has halved in the past two decades, and current plan to increase tuition fees is unlikely to reverse that trend. In December 1998, the Colleges agreed to reduce academic fees by 21.8 per cent (in real terms) over a 10-year period beginning in 1999–2000. While Colleges have the option to charge top-up fees, these fees will not be received directly by them, as the fees will be given to the University. In the past, Colleges received income in the form of a block grant from the Local Authority. In alleviating the problems of the whole collegiate University, some benefit will inevitably accrue to the Colleges.

Another source of income reduction was the government's decision to abolish tax credit on dividends. In one College, it eroded investment income by 20 per cent.[16] Colleges and other institutions with an income-oriented investment policy were the worst affected. Starting in 1998, changes in UK tax rules on the recovery of tax credits affected all sectors of the investment world. Payments of tax credits to pension plans and companies, for example, ceased from July 1997. From April 1999, the amount recoverable by charities in respect of tax credits on ordinary dividends was reduced from 25 per cent of dividend initially to 21 per cent and eventually to zero by April 2004. This was a factor in depressing the income of several endowments, including that of the UK's largest foundation, the Wellcome Trust. Dividends from UK equities for the Trust declined from £205 million in 1997 to £119 million in 2005, declining from 66 per cent of total income to 39 per cent over that period.

While such legislation encouraged investors to move away from an income-oriented investment strategy, the reduction in cash flow put severe pressure on the level of income that these institutions received. The painful adjustments that Colleges had to make as a result of changes in legislation are stated clearly in the 'Report of the Governing Body' for the year ended 30 June 2004 of Sidney Sussex College, Cambridge:

The operating environment remains difficult for Colleges. The phased reduction in the real value of publicly-funded undergraduate College fees, imposed by the government over a 10-year period from 1999/2000, reached its fifth year in 2003/04. The College's publicly-funded undergraduate fee was £2,850 in 2003/04, compared to the fee for students not eligible for public funding of £3,192. The consequent loss of income was of the order of £110,000 in 2003/04. Similarly, the withdrawal of Advance Corporation Tax (ACT) relief on investment income reached its penultimate year in 2003/04 and involved a loss to College's investment income of approximately £60,000 in that year. The disappearance of all ACT relief in 2005/06 will increase the loss to £75,000, which will then be on-going.

...the doubling of College's employer's contribution to the staff pension fund, involving an additional cost of £100,000—a cost also attributable in part to the Chancellor of the Exchequer's earlier decision to withdraw ACT relief from pension funds and charities. The Governing Body is conscious that these income losses and additional costs are permanent, and that the loss associated with the undergraduate fee will worsen over the period to 2009. The College's affairs will accordingly require careful management in the years immediately ahead, in particular to avoid damaging the quality of education provided to undergraduate and graduate students at Sidney Sussex.[17]

The government will, and should, continue to be the major source of funding for universities. But increasing their flexibility to access additional funding streams is critical. To retain their status as leading universities of the world, Oxford and Cambridge, among other UK institutions, need significantly more funds, and not just from private sources. The two universities need increased public funding in addition to their ability to access resources on a global scale. They need to rebalance and strengthen their main sources of income, which includes improving investment returns on endowment while building up endowment wealth by better fund-raising and prudent spending from the endowment; at the same time lobbying government for more funding and attractive tax incentives for donors.

Professor Alison Richard emphasized the need for a greater plurality of support for funding of British universities when she stated in her annual address to the University, on 1 October 2005:

Society provides financial support to universities through five channels: students and their families; alumni and friends; charitable foundations; industry; and Government and its agencies, administering public funds on behalf of society as a whole. This holds for most universities in most countries in the world. In addition, some universities, including this one, develop and manage significant revenues of their own, through endowments, businesses, and intellectual properties.

Heavy dependence on any one of these sources brings institutional risks. A university entirely sustained by student fees would be susceptible to the faddishness of consumerism, as well as putting too much of a burden on students and their families. The demands of donors could open up a route to distortion of the academic purposes of the university. Funding from industry might invite a slide towards research dominated by a quest for results amenable to rapid commercialisation. Exclusive dependence on endowment revenues would expose the university to the roller coaster of the financial markets. And, then there's Government.[18]

Alternative methods in which university financing could be strengthened include an array of sources other than the Government, such as the ability to issue debt or adopt more economic strategies in the management of operating assets, intellectual property assets etc. All this can be achieved by giving the universities and colleges greater freedom in managing their affairs. As Dr John Hood, Oxford's Vice-Chancellor, remarked in his inaugural address with reference to Oxford: 'In essence, the cost of producing a "world-class" university and the revenue available to fund that cost are not in harmony.'[19] As that is indeed the case for Oxford, then other universities in the UK and Europe must find it more than a fair challenge in their aspiration to become world-class institutions.

Governments across Europe have sworn to do something about the parlous state of their universities, which was brought to light in a survey by Shanghai's Jiao Tong University of the world's universities. This ranking gave eight of the top 10 places to American institutions, with only Cambridge (rank 2) and Oxford (rank 10) breaking the American monopoly. In the top 11–20, the only non-American institution was Tokyo University. Imperial College and University College, London, were placed 23rd and 26th, respectively.[20] Not only does the US government spend more on education, there is a well-established tradition of individual giving to one's Alma Mater in America. Such a tradition also flourishes in Oxbridge; the bequests, gifts, pledges, donations, and legacies made to the Colleges amounted to 4 per cent of total income, similar to gifts and donations received by top American universities.

The endowment's share of total income among Oxbridge Colleges continues to rise too. It is the absolute scale of funding and support that needs to be raised.

Endowments in Oxford and Cambridge: Poised for change

There is widespread concern among Oxford and Cambridge Colleges about the question of long-term funding and the need to be more self-reliant in securing their future. Historically, the way in which these institutions were regulated and funded inevitably influenced endowment asset management. In many Colleges internal loans were and in some cases still are outstanding to the endowment. As these loans required only capital to be restored, usually free of any interest charge, the endowment served as an attractive source of borrowing, particularly when the provision of accommodation to students was a loss-making activity.

It needs to be acknowledged that Colleges have the option to spend their endowment capital if it is not permanent or specific capital, rather than merely borrow from it. The critical question is whether it is beneficial in the long-term for the Colleges to do so? The other issue, for institutions adopting a total return investment approach, is what level of annual spending is optimal, though this immediately begs the question, optimal for whom? Many of the examples cited here illustrate that decisions taken by Colleges may have been right from the institutional point of view, but were not beneficial for preserving the endowment's real value in the long-term.

In one relatively poor College, for example, the amount due to the endowment fund represented a significantly high proportion of the value of the endowment. This borrowing from the endowment was in the form of an interest-free internal loan to the College, to be repaid over 30 years. It made sense for a College with a small endowment and restricted ability to raise money cheaply to fund a major capital project in such a manner. If the College had been obliged to borrow from the endowment at the same rate of interest as it would pay for an external bank loan, albeit at a competitive rate, it may have resulted in a different outcome for the College.

The ability to borrow on an interest-free basis from the endowment made it an attractive proposition as the expected stream of income from subsidized student housing could be interpreted as advancing the objective of the College, particularly if market returns were perceived to be relatively unattractive in the short term. It can be argued therefore that assets were diverted from the endowment to fund operations to secure a better return, or a superior revenue stream. Whether that was indeed the case—that is, whether the rental flow was better than market yields—is not evident. Nor was it clear that such a decision was based on hard investment considerations. On the contrary, the endowment's investment policy in this case had to be altered from 'growth-oriented, total return' to 'income-driven.'

In the words of the College's recently appointed bursar:

It used to be a growth fund; and at the peak of the market the College borrowed £8 million from the fund for buildings (thus transferring the investment assets into operational assets), and was left with significantly lower income. Hence, the focus of the existing fund had to be adjusted to yield greater income. The loan is non-interest bearing. The College created a sinking fund and pays back the loan from student rents. However, the income from these operational assets is not good enough. The fallacy in my mind is assuming that the income you get from the buildings is the same that you would get from the market. For example, the yield on these assets at market value is 2.4 per cent. However, the indirect costs are actually a lot higher, often resulting in a negative return. You can put £8 million in the market and have a regular running real yield of 3–4 per cent with no overhead. However, if you convert that into operational assets, then you do not get that sort of a return. It looked like a good idea at the time. But, in reality the College lost out on income. Most operational assets are not run on a commercial basis. So, we have gone from being a small rich College to a large poor College.

Borrowing from the endowment at nil rates of interest not only resulted in depletion of endowment capital, but led to changes in investment policy decisions that were not investment driven. While such practice is relatively uncommon today, such a method of financing capital expenditure was fairly common in the recent past. As a consequence, the investment policy decisions of these institutions remained secondary to operational considerations. Operational decisions dictated endowment asset allocation resulting in lower investment returns for the endowment. Long-term depletion of endowment assets must prove detrimental to achieving the long-term objectives of institutions though the endowment may have sustained the institution in the short term. Some 43 per cent of Colleges in Oxford and Cambridge, about half in Oxford compared with a third in Cambridge, indicated practices that would have resulted in endowment depletion. Taking into account the difficult funding environment in which these institutions operated, budgetary deficits were regularly financed from reserves. Such financing would seem perfectly ordinary if assets were not moved from endowments to reserves.

The majority of bursars today consider such practices as being totally unacceptable. Colleges more dependent on endowment income were more critical of practices that resulted in endowment depletion. There is no conclusive evidence that Colleges resorted to different investment strategies depending on their level of dependency on the endowment. Colleges with larger endowments, being more dependent on the endowment for their operations, were more concerned about preserving the real purchasing power of the endowment over the long term. These institutions also attached greater importance to investment decisions that were most likely to support their stated objectives. Colleges with smaller endowments and lower dependency on the endowment to fund operations typically had access to other sources of income, which may have influenced their decision to borrow from the endowment, particularly when the cost attached to such borrowing was nil. Recent amendments to the way in which the Colleges are taxed internally helped in removing incentives to deplete endowment assets.

Recognizing the need for change, notably because the mispricing of services was clearly unsustainable, the Colleges are implementing more market-oriented policies. As one bursar commented, 'We have to erode the subsidies and charge the students more. We also have to generate more income from conferences and raise more funds from alumni. The reality of the cost of doing business is being appreciated now, and we need to raise more funds in the future as a result.' Radical changes needed to be introduced to a system where the gap between the cost of education provided and the fees received has been steadily widening. According to the *University of Oxford, Financial Statement of the Colleges, 2002–3*, an entry under Review of Operations and Finance of Balliol College stated the dilemma faced by many Colleges:

The College ran a substantial deficit during the year, due to a combination of factors. The steady decline in real terms of the undergraduate capitation fee has become increasingly damaging, as has the College's diminishing ability to reclaim Advance Corporation Tax on its UK equity income. The large fall in the stock market has reduced the amount of money that can be prudently drawn from the endowment. Furthermore, staff costs (both academic and support staff) have continued to outpace the Retail Price Index, due—in part—to the increase in National Insurance Contributions and the further rise of the employer's contribution to the Oxford University Staff Pension Scheme. The Oxford tutorial system—with all its many advantages—is of course costly. This, combined with the expense of maintaining listed buildings, puts a financial burden on colleges like Balliol that other Higher Education establishments do not bear. To counter these adverse trends, the College has agreed to put in place a substantial rise in room rents for 'Freshers' with effect from October 2004. Such a rise will ensure that rental income covers a much greater proportion of the cost of provision, so allowing more of the endowment income to be used for academic purposes and the provision of scholarships and bursaries. These changes, together with a number of economy measures, are designed to bring the College's budget back into balance over the next four years.[21]

The Report of the Governing Body of Balliol College contained a very similar entry in its financial statement for 2003–4, except the College was a year closer to balancing its budget. Several Colleges aim to break even before depreciation on their normal operations, and to build up capital and reserves over time via unrestricted donations and bequests. Sustaining that over the long term would be considered a remarkable achievement. It is worth spending a moment to get a historical perspective on the impact of the ongoing funding crisis on Oxbridge College endowments.

Accounting for endowment and operational assets

Historical rules of accounting and taxation offer some explanation for why endowments in Oxford and Cambridge today do not bear comparison to those built up by independent American universities, most of which were created significantly later but managed to build substantial endowments over the past few decades. Today, an Oxbridge College, with a relatively modest-sized endowment, could own significant property assets that do not appear in the accounts. It may be assumed that any property acquired 25 years prior to 31 July 2002 has a negligible net book value, including the main College buildings. The estimated current market value of property owned by Colleges is thus not to be found from analysing its accounts. While some Colleges have invested in developing surplus land by building up Science Parks, Conference Centres, and other such ventures, the development potential of other existing College property assets cannot be quantified.

Many Colleges own subsidiary trading companies for the management of their property investments. But these companies pay tax as other trading companies do; they also appear in the consolidated accounts. For example, The Lamb and Flag (Oxford) Ltd. is the wholly owned subsidiary of St John's College, in Oxford. This company serves as a vehicle for the trading activities of the Lamb & Flag public house in St Giles', at the heart of Oxford. St John's College applies the profits from this public house towards the financing of graduate studentships.

Endowment and other investment assets are clearly differentiated from operational assets, which in the case of Oxbridge institutions include the main buildings of Colleges that are typically Grade I listed buildings, some dating back to the fourteenth and fifteenth centuries. The Colleges take their collective responsibility for the preservation and maintenance of these buildings seriously. In addition to insuring buildings, some Colleges in the past deemed it prudent to build and maintain reserves equal to a certain percentage of the insured value of buildings. While such provisioning is no longer common, operational assets normally do not appear in the endowment. Also, historic buildings are stated at nil value in the accounts, as it is not possible for the Colleges to ascertain their original cost.

Operational assets include student accommodation, which has seen a considerable rise in investment activity over recent years. The operating income of the 36 Oxford Colleges, derived from rents and other residential charges from members and the income from conferences and other functions for the financial years ending 2004 and 2003, amounted to over one-third

(35–36 per cent) of total income. While these figures are somewhat misleading, as they do not include the costs incurred in generating that income
(expenditure on residencies, catering, and conferences amounted to just over
one-quarter of total expenditure during that period), they give us some measure of their contribution to College operations compared to income derived
from endowment assets, which represented 34–35 per cent of total income.

A word about taxation; the Colleges are exempt charities and thus potentially not liable to pay tax to the Internal Revenue in respect of income or
capital gains as long as such income and gains are applied in support of
purposes which are defined as charitable by law. The subsidiary trading companies of these institutions, however, are liable to Corporation Tax. Typically
profits made by these trading subsidiaries are donated to the College, which
in turn distributes them as determined by its Governing Body. In addition,
Colleges may be liable for contribution under the provisions of an internally
regulated College Contribution scheme, which is made to fund grants and
loans to Colleges on the basis of need.

The constraints that emanate from managing property are also enshrined
in the University Statutes. As one bursar explained it:

A charitable trust has a restraint on property requiring it to be applied to exclu-
sively charitable purposes. The key concept of a permanent endowment stipulates
that all property of the College be treated as such—i.e. if you sell a portion of it
you have to make provisions to replenish it within a limited time—and not treat
it as free money.

An example of this could be if the College, for example, has a Lodging House
for undergraduates, it will also have a housekeeper to look after them. Those
resident housekeepers become part of the endowment. The building is leased to
the housekeeper for a pittance while she collects a market-based rent from the
students. So, she has a commercial contract with the College. Next door we have a
Graduate House. However, as they are adults, graduates do not need housekeepers
to look after them. So the College can pick up the rent directly from them; more
importantly, the building is part of the operational assets. Hence it does not appear
in the accounts. If the housekeeper dies, what the College could do is turn it
into operational property and make it disappear from the accounts. On the other
hand, you could sell some operational property and make that asset appear in the
endowment as a tangible asset.

Whether an asset appeared in the accounts was determined by whether they
were classified as operational or endowment. From the College's standpoint,
operational assets generating tax-free revenues appeared more attractive compared with endowment assets that may not. Thus, there existed an incentive
to transfer assets from the endowment to operations, particularly in an environment where Colleges saw the value of their income being eroded from
all other sectors. In addition, the ability to provide student housing was no

longer considered a competitive advantage for Colleges, as more and more Colleges moved to providing accommodation for all their students.

Colleges in Oxford and Cambridge typically house all their undergraduate students in College. For historical reasons, that accommodation has for many years been charged at rates significantly below both market rents and the economic rents that would be required to cover the full cost to the College of providing the accommodation. In recent years, Colleges have been taking steps to repair that position, but in ways that do not unfairly prejudice the position of the current generation of students. In competing for the best students, the richer Colleges are in a stronger position to subsidize student rents and meals. Historically, the financial returns from such activities were typically negative. In 2003 and 2004, a larger proportion of the wealthier Colleges reported a deficit in their income and expenditure account on residencies, catering, and conferences compared to Colleges with smaller endowments where fewer reported such losses, though the size of losses were not dissimilar. Thus, the size of the endowment was not the main determinant of Colleges' spending on student rents and meals.

Colleges were also able to borrow from their endowment on extremely attractive terms. In the words of the bursar of a newly founded College: 'In the 1980s, the College started acquiring properties immediately around it by borrowing from the endowment. We also raised funds by selling off a few hostels, borrowed from the bank and started building up our non-taxable assets. The College has chosen to invest in operational assets. Over a decade, the College has built a property portfolio, which does not necessarily show in the endowment assets.' There are always exceptions to prove the rule. One College in Cambridge, Pembroke, includes its student houses as part of its investment holdings; these houses were valued at £20 million at end of June 2004 and consisted of a third of its investment portfolio.

The historical status of 'operational' versus 'endowment' assets was fully utilized by Oxbridge institutions. The endowment effectively became a source of subsidizing 'our current generation of students and Fellows quite significantly,' in the words of one bursar. 'If we did not have an endowment, then our rents and charges would be three times higher and salaries would also be lower. So, before long the College would run into deficits. Academic salaries are rising by some 1–2 per cent above inflation. As our student intake is mostly at the graduate level, and we have been subsidizing our students for so long, we are bound to run into funding difficulties. In 1929, for example, in real terms students were being charged twice as much as we charge today. If we were able to do so today, we would be in a much healthier position financially.'

As a result of the ease with which assets could be transferred from the endowment to the operational side of the balance sheet, it was a practice that was widespread among Colleges. These decisions were not whimsical, but driven by a clear need to remain competitive in the field. As Colleges compete with each other in attracting the best students, having to keep up with the Joneses is a grave consideration. As one bursar in Oxford hoping to build up his College endowment explained:

We are trying to reduce the rate of drawdown from the endowment so that we can rebuild it. What I am arguing is that we should be able to make certain economies around the place and while we also work on fundraising, we should be able to depend less on the endowment. Our drawdown used to be a lot higher—it was in some years as high as 10 per cent. What I am trying to do is restore the endowment. Although we will not get there during my lifetime, I believe the endowment needs rebuilding. The spending rate is also relative. If some colleges provide subsidised housing to their students, it does exert pressure on the other colleges to do something similar. There is still a high correlation between the wealth of the colleges and their standing in the Norrington League Table [an annual ranking of Oxford colleges in order of undergraduate performance in each year's final examinations]; the wealthier Colleges get better exam results.

The lack of independence of the endowment and the Colleges' capacity to drawdown from capital led, not infrequently, to inefficient decision-making in endowment terms. While Yale's endowment allows the University to issue debt at attractive rates and on competitive terms for its capital development programmes, Oxbridge institutions have been placed in a situation where it is expedient to borrow from the endowment at a zero rate of interest. Clarification of approaches to capital issues will undoubtedly assist in endowment preservation. Harvard, for example, is in the process of a major redevelopment to expand and improve its physical plant. For the past two decades, Harvard has employed the strategy of financing capital projects with debt, not via internal loan from its endowment.

The size of Oxford and Cambridge Colleges' endowment assets is not reflected in their stated value. The level of understatement is not known, as endowment assets have been used over the years to build or support operational assets. These loans from the endowment do not appear as an investment in the portfolio; they simply disappear from the accounts of the endowment. For example, the endowment assets of Peterhouse in Cambridge were valued at £74.8 million in 2003. This amount, according to Andrew Murison, the College bursar at that time, 'was net of capital expenditures taken out from the endowment to build and continually refurbish the Grade I listed buildings on the home site, and on the estates, over the last 40 years, which amounted to £1.0 million annually during the period of my bursarship, and probably the equivalent of some £35 m in today's terms over the past 30 years. The net amount also excludes the insured value of the buildings within the curtilage of the College, which, if included, would lift the value of the endowment above £150 million. Capital appreciation from the endowment has had to finance this expenditure without help from operating income.'

Financial well-being

Publication of financial statements of all Colleges in Oxford and the majority of Colleges in Cambridge in the recommended format from 2003–4 makes it possible to gain some insight into the accounting practices of these institutions. Among Cambridge Colleges, for example, non-endowment assets appear as 'Investment Assets' in the College accounts. Girton College included 'Antique Furniture, Works of Art, etc.' (worth £3.3 million) as part of its investment assets. Lucy Cavendish included £294,000 worth of 'Works of Art' and Sidney Sussex £177,000 worth of 'Wines and Works of Art' as investment assets. But the Keynes bequest (John Maynard Keynes, Fellow and former Bursar of King's, bequeathed works of art to the College) on loan to the Fitzwilliam Museum in Cambridge has no value put upon it in the accounts of King's College. According to one Cambridge bursar:

We sold a First Folio of Shakespeare for £3.6 million recently. We don't count such existing assets as being part of the endowment portfolio until after they are sold. Assets such as our sports fields, for example, have development potential. But, we do not count them as part of the endowment. Nor do we include in the endowment the student housing we provide to our members. We actually provide accommodation to all our students. However, it does not feature as an endowment asset. Most of our off-campus housing, which is part of our property portfolio within the endowment, is rented out at market-based rents. The definition of our endowment assets includes property assets with debt attached. Works of art and other valuable artefacts that can be regarded as 'inalienable' are not included in the financial statements.

Downing College did not include some £8 million of investment assets, consisting of works of art and silver among other things, in its endowment account, which was worth around £22 million in 2004.[22] Most Colleges do not include in their endowment rare books, works of art, silver, and other assets, which are deemed 'inalienable'. However, these assets can be worth a tidy sum. In the case of New College, for example, they were valued at around £50 million while the functional estate of the College was worth £100 million on top of the endowment assets, which were worth £60 million at the end of July 2004, but whose value had risen to around £118 million by the end of calendar year 2004, thanks to capital infusion as a result of a land sale. These amounts do not reflect the New College Development Fund, which was worth an additional £10 million. The Colleges' and Universities' vast collections of libraries, museums, chapels, and cathedrals housing priceless works of art, literary works, historical treasures, and artefacts, for example, are protected and preserved for current and future generations for the sake of education, research, and public exhibition—in short for the public good. Accordingly such assets are typically not recorded or capitalized for financial statement purposes.

Colleges account for various property interests differently. Girton College remains the joint beneficiary of a trust that owns a number of properties in West London. When tenants vacate the properties, they are sold and the proceeds of the sales (less expenses) are divided equally between the beneficiaries. At 30 June 2004, the College's share in the remaining properties was estimated to be worth £745,000 (gross), which amount was not included in the Investment Assets of Girton.[23] Hughes Hall in Cambridge on the other hand included £800,000 from its disposal of land and buildings as income; so did Trinity Hall (£1.2 million in 2004; £0.9 million in 2003). As stated in Trinity Hall's Bursar's Report for the year ended 30 June 2004:

This is the first year that the accounts have been prepared on the new RCCA [Recommended Cambridge College Accounts] basis being employed by the majority of Cambridge Colleges. The new format more closely resembles General Accounting Standards, and was designed to ensure greater uniformity between the Colleges. The degree of flexibility on accounting for fixed assets, principally buildings, and their depreciation allowed under the RCCA however makes this unlikely. After some debate, we have elected to include and depreciate all College buildings over 50 years down to zero value. The policy choice is to some extent an arbitrary decision, and produces an annual charge of approximately £1.4 million. Another side-effect of the new format is the inclusion of the profit on sale of land and buildings in the income and expenditure account. Over the last few years Trinity Hall has received windfall profits from the extension of the science park. These are included under the Long Term Building Fund on the Income and Expenditure Account (shown as £1,203,681). It distorts the true picture of the College's operating income and would, without the new depreciation charge, have resulted in a completely unrealistic and excessive surplus for the year. These windfall profits are all earmarked either for building the Wychfield accommodation project or invested for academic purposes. As these profits are either spent or invested over the next eighteen months our income position will regularise, the sense of luxury will be lost and our real struggle to balance income and expenditure will be increasingly revealed.[24]

Historical rules of accounting for operational and endowment assets, particularly property, may offer some explanation why College endowments today have failed to keep pace with those built up by independent American universities, most of which were established centuries later. If longevity alone accounted for the wealth of educational endowments, then the Universities of Oxford and Cambridge would be in the top quartile of the rich list of Universities worldwide.

Table 1.14. Foundation dates of colleges and size of endowment assets

Oxford	Founded	AUM	Cambridge	Founded	AUM
University	1249	67.5	Peterhouse	1284	75.5
Balliol	1263	41.3	Clare	1326	53.1
Merton	1264	96.7	Pembroke	1347	59.6
Exeter	1314	30.1	Gonville and Caius	1348	87.8
Oriel	1326	50.3	Trinity Hall	1350	65.6
The Queen's	1341	95.6	Corpus Christi	1352	52.8
New College	1379	62.1	Magdalene	1428	33.6
Lincoln	1427	37.7	King's	1441	90.1
All Souls	1438	155.8	St Catharine's	1473	27.8
Magdalen	1458	108.9	Jesus	1497	77.8

AUM = Assets Under Management (consolidated) at 2004 financial year-end in £ million.
Source: University of Oxford, Financial Statement of the Colleges, 2003–4. Cambridge University Reporter, Accounts of the Colleges 2004.

For Ivy League academic institutions in the United States, other factors such as the ability to charge higher student fees and an active donor programme, in addition to prudent spending rules and astute asset allocation policies, contributed in enabling universities to build their endowments. Gifts and donations not only expand the scope of activities supported by endowments, they also assist in maintaining and growing the real value of the endowment. David Swensen acknowledges the role of gifts to the Yale endowment's growth in these words: 'In the absence of new gifts over the past forty-eight years, Yale's endowment would likely total only about one third of today's value.'[25] While successful investment strategies and prudent spending policies play their part, continuing gift inflows constitute a major contributory factor in generating the wealth of institutions such as Yale or Harvard today. Though the older Colleges in Oxford and Cambridge are better able to attract gifts and donations from benefactors, they are not among the wealthiest today.

Table 1.14 illustrates the size of endowments in 2004 among the 10 oldest Colleges in Oxford and Cambridge.

The top 10 richest Colleges in Oxford and Cambridge today are shown in Table 1.15. The sixteenth century appears to have been a vintage era for the foundation of Oxbridge Colleges that have grown to be among its wealthiest today, followed by those established in the fifteenth and fourteenth centuries. The exception of course is Nuffield College which was founded by William Richard Morris, 1st Viscount Nuffield, under a Deed of Covenant and Trust in 1937.

Despite Oxford and Cambridge being the oldest universities in the UK, a quarter of the Colleges were founded in the twentieth century and a further 20 per cent in the nineteenth century. Sixteen per cent of Colleges were founded in the sixteenth century. These Colleges are among the richest today, and those established in the twentieth century are among the least well off in

Table 1.15. Wealthiest colleges in Cambridge and Oxford

Oxford	Founded	AUM	Cambridge	Founded	AUM
St John's	1555	210.7	Trinity	1546	649.9
Christ Church	1546	180.9	St John's	1511	232.0
All Souls	1438	155.8	King's	1441	90.1
Nuffield	1958	112.4	Gonville and Caius	1348	87.8
Magdalen	1448	108.9	Jesus	1497	77.8
Jesus	1571	99.5	Peterhouse	1284	75.5
Merton	1264	96.7	Trinity Hall	1350	65.6
The Queen's	1341	95.6	Emmanuel	1584	65.5
University	1249	67.5	Pembroke	1347	59.6
Brasenose	1509	62.3	Christ's	1505	59.4

AUM = Assets Under Management (consolidated) at 2004 financial year-end in £ million.
Source: University of Oxford, Financial Statement of the Colleges, 2003–4. Cambridge University Reporter, Accounts of the Colleges 2004.

terms of endowment assets with the exception of the all-graduate institution, Nuffield College. Older Colleges were more successful in their ability to raise funds from alumni and friends compared to their younger counterparts, and that may explain some of the disparity in assets today.

It is a combination of factors that ultimately determines the overall well-being of any higher education institution. As explained in the NACUBO report on 'Endowment Performance and Management Practices in Higher Education':

The overall financial well being of an institution of higher education is influenced by its endowment but only in combination with other important economic and financial characteristics. A significant component related to an institution's financial health is its pricing power in terms of its ability to raise the tuition students pay to help offset increased costs of delivering quality education programs. In addition, the effectiveness of a public institution to attain sufficient state funding weighs significantly on the institution's financial health. An institution's ability to build and sustain a healthy donor base and develop new sources of revenue has become important to counter shifts in the economy and the markets as well as the trend toward declines in federal assistance of college students in real terms.[26]

Such aspects of higher education development and management are increasingly being recognized in Europe as in the UK, not to mention among Oxbridge institutions. Many Colleges have initiated plans to become more efficient by reducing subsidies and raising alternative sources of funding. The inability of academic institutions to influence their pricing power has certainly impacted on their ability to be as successful as their US counterparts. Changes in the way operational and endowment assets are taxed, thereby removing the incentive to switch funds from the endowment to operations, should also assist in endowment preservation. Recent revisions to the College Contributions Scheme, an internal system of redistribution of wealth, may, at least partly, address the disincentive to maintain or increase endowments.

The process of change has begun, albeit recently. In the 'Review of Operations and Finance' provided by New College, in the *University of Oxford, Financial Statement of the Colleges, 2002–3*, we were informed that:

The College continues to operate in difficult conditions. The abolition of tax credit on dividend income has damaged charities such as New College in reducing investment income by some twenty per cent. At the same time, the reduction of the College Fee paid on behalf of undergraduate students represents a loss of a third of fee income over a ten-year period. Since fees had not kept pace with inflation for the previous fifteen years, the loss of a third is difficult to absorb. Where actual damage has not been inflicted by public policy, there is persisting uncertainty about public funding for higher education; the bitterly contested plans for increased tuition fees will in themselves only slightly reduce the extent to which undergraduate education is a loss-making activity.

Given those circumstances, the College has pursued a three-fold policy; first, seeking additional revenue where it can be achieved without threatening its core activities; second, eliminating indiscriminate subsidies and replacing them with more carefully targeted assistance; third, building up funds through the activities of the College's Development Office.[27]

New College along with other Oxbridge Colleges moved away from their previous policy of charging subsidized rents 'towards charging economic rents' and putting a proportion of the money towards supporting students. Over the past three years, in the case of New College, 'the indiscriminate subsidy has been reduced from £300k to £90k per annum, and will be eliminated in 2004–5.' The College has also developed an active fund-raising campaign, which is carried out principally by the New College Development Fund, an independent charitable trust not controlled by the College. Like other institutions, New College receives annual donations from its Development Fund. Total resources transferred to the College from this source amounted to £1 million in 2002 and about £0.5 million in 2003.[28]

The endowment management programmes of these institutions are poised for change; the appointment of new Vice-Chancellors in both Universities has given it greater momentum. Professor Alison Richard brings to Cambridge a wealth of experience from her role as Provost of Yale, responsible for the educational policies, operating and capital budgets and long-range financial plans of this distinguished American University that also nurtured a significant endowment. Dr John Hood, with his engineering, management, and business background, has initiated a major review into endowment management and other practices within Oxford University. He is also the first person in Oxford's 900-year history to be elected to the Vice-Chancellorship from outside the University's current academic body.

The quantum of endowment assets for Oxford and Cambridge therefore does not reflect the full picture. The total assets of these institutions far exceed that of their endowments. While some Colleges may appear to be slow in implementing changes, it is worth noting there have been significant developments in their endowment management practices over recent years—in terms of establishing sensible spending policies, diversifying endowment investments into alternative assets, albeit in a small way, collective employment of consultants, and the current move to establish more centralized form of endowment management among some of these institutions.

Cambridge has amalgamated the investments of the University and related bodies to set up an Investment Office with over £1.2 billion under management. The Colleges are not part of this initiative. Cambridge University has set up a new investment board, ushering in expertise not only from the City of London but from the US endowment world, to oversee the process. Working with a team of analysts, based in an office near the Judge Business School in Cambridge, its CIO can call on the university's expertise to aid investment decisions. While a Harvard or Yale style investment company is not envisioned, the investment process is expected to be a radical departure from the practices of the past half-century.

The establishment of Oxford Investment Partners (OXIP) in 2006, a collective investment scheme, launched by five Oxford Colleges (St Catherine's, Christ Church, Balliol, St John's and New) as majority (60 per cent) shareholders in a new commercial partnership illustrates the kind of financial innovation that some of these institutions are applying. OXIP, with initial funds under management of £120 million, will operate as an independent fund management company and manage a fund dedicated to meeting certain investment objectives of endowments and charities. The fund was set up as a result of the desire of these Colleges to reorganize and diversify their endowments and source appropriate investment products and expertise. The fund will be made available to other investors with similar underlying investment objectives, and is designed to deliver real returns in excess of 5 per cent per annum over rolling five-year periods. Given current asset yields, the Manager believes that this represents a challenging target for any fund. The objective is to offer at least the same long-term returns which should be delivered by public equities, but with considerably less volatility than that experienced from exposure to public equity investment alone.

While support for this venture is currently limited, it clearly illustrates the prospects for greater pooling of resources among these institutions, leading potentially to lower management costs, less volatility of returns, enhanced flexibility when investing in alternative assets and other capacity-constrained strategies, and greater transparency for the investing institutions. Such objectives, however, can best be realized when there is greater consensus among the

Colleges and the University in determining the direction they wish to take as they move forward.

Institutions in Oxford and Cambridge may be partly responsible for their financial plight today, but the legal and regulatory environment in which they operated also conspired against them. Higher education in the UK has been government regulated and supplied largely to local students. Competition and profit were not concepts that were applied to sectors such as education, health, and other public services. With the onset of globalization and emergence of a new economic world order, that environment is changing rapidly. Even Oxford, Britain's oldest university, has to market itself aggressively overseas.

As *The Economist* described it, 'Higher education is now international in a way it has not been since the heyday of Europe's great medieval universities— and on a vastly greater scale.'[29] While private, profit-seeking institutions are a minority, all universities actively compete for talent. Attracting the best brains implies the independence to do so, and that involves financial independence. Private universities in America may have had a head start in growing their endowments and developing strategies to attract the best talent globally while publicly funded universities in Britain, if not in Europe, are waking up to the reality of globalization and competition. As the government's role in higher education declines, British universities will grow to emphasize prudent endowment management and fund-raising to meet their stated objectives.

A point worth making is that the funding of education is a complex issue as it reflects the relationship between society and universities, and the role of finance in mediating that relationship. In the United States, for example, the level of student indebtedness is significantly higher than elsewhere in the world. As American university education is considered among the best in the world, it has been expensive; but in recent decades costs have risen considerably, ahead of inflation. Thus, the burden of financing education has been borne by students and their families, with contributions from alumni and benefactors helping to maintain grants to students. By comparison, students in the UK have benefited enormously from the public funding of higher education. Student indebtedness in the UK will also increase as a result of higher fees after the Higher Education Act takes effect in 2006. But the true cost of educating a full time student in the UK will not be covered by this fee increase. Ultimately, society has to make complex choices in deciding how to pay for services such as education or health where economies of scale may not apply, nor do cost-cutting measures as with other sectors of the economy.

Conclusion

Endowments comprise funds that are regarded as being for the long term and which fundamentally underpin and sustain the operation of the College at its desired level of activity. This definition of an endowment has been undermined historically by the tendency among Colleges in Oxford and Cambridge to transfer funds freely between endowment and reserves. Removal of tax incentives to increase or decrease the endowment will therefore help in curbing such transfers, which have proven to be detrimental to the long-term value of their endowment assets. The process of reform has begun; it is hoped that going forward such practices will be recognized as essentially inefficient in securing the long-term objectives of these institutions.

If Oxford and Cambridge wish to engage successfully in their stated aim to remain among the leading universities of the world, they will require significant sums of additional capital to underpin and sustain their operations. Endowment income will undoubtedly remain a significant means of securing this goal. As their financial and operational circumstances alter, the capital requirement of these institutions will also change. Colleges will have to make individual judgements about the prudence of spending endowment assets. Some, hopefully those that anticipate new endowment inflows, may feel able to spend from old endowments (if not permanent or specific) as long as substantial amounts are not extracted for other long-term purposes. Over the past several decades Colleges in Oxford and Cambridge have spent more than they could afford by dipping into reserves, which are periodically boosted by transfer of funds from the endowment. Such a strategy can only work as long as the long-term value of the endowment is preserved. If more is taken out of the endowment than it is able to accrue through its investment or fundraising activities, then depending on the rate of extraction the endowment is eventually bound to disappear.

If the endowments of top American universities have prospered, it is because these institutions have been successful in recouping their true cost in providing world-class education. It is not that Harvard and Yale manage without receiving funds from the federal government. They are not autonomous, self-financing operations. Their financial strength is bolstered by endowment support that is additional to, not a substitute for, federal funding. Government support has provided a valued source of stable income. A further source of stability is the operation of their endowments as independent entities, pursuing investment policies focused on preserving the long-term value of the fund while providing an acceptable level of support for current operations.

A significant factor that enhanced endowment accumulation among institutions, such as Harvard, Princeton, and Yale, is the scale of support they sought and received from non-federal, non-governmental sources. In the final analysis, it is the endowments of these universities that have long served as the financial cornerstone of their continued excellence in education and research, while active fund-raising and prudent investment helped secure the endowment in times of economic and stock market uncertainty. Endowment income distributed for operations is Harvard's and Yale's largest source of non-governmental income, constituting about a third of total income.

Though the percentage is similar in the case of Oxbridge Colleges, the problem lies in the actual amounts involved. Such a state of affairs may have arisen as a result of these institutions' inability to determine a fair value for their products and services following the British government's direct involvement in university financing since 1980. The Colleges were no longer independent entities free to run their affairs as they saw fit; no longer able to determine the rate at which they could charge for their services and products. Nor were endowment asset allocation policies considered to be independent of Colleges' overall financial and budgetary concerns. Such a concept remains alien among several institutions today.

It is worth noting that in terms of endowment assets per student, the comparison between universities with the largest endowments in the United States and UK brings into focus the striking contrast between approaches to funding higher education. Not all US universities with substantial endowments boast high endowment assets per FTE student; the range is revealing in terms of the disparity between public and independent institutions. Thus, average endowment assets per FTE students among independent institutions in the United States were some $101,000 compared with under $16,000 among public institutions. The overall average was just over $40,000.[30] Among independent institutions with endowments assets worth over $1 billion, endowment assets per FTE student rose to $363,000.[31] These numbers keep rising for educational institutions in the United States. Today, the financial strategies of state and private universities in America are converging as state budget deficits put additional pressure on state universities to increase student fees and build endowments from gifts from alumni and friends. At the same time, individuals and their families benefiting from that education are more willing to bear a larger share of the overall cost.

While Oxford and Cambridge feature among the top 10 university endowment assets per FTE student, the differential between Oxbridge and the very top US universities is worth emphasizing. The scale of the difference between input and output could be interpreted in favour of Oxbridge institutions' ability to function efficiently despite such constraints. It could be argued further that no action is necessary currently as these universities are doing a reasonably good job without the scale of support available to their US counterparts. In reality, however, there is little room for complacency, as this comparison fails to illustrate the extent to which endowment assets per FTE student have appreciated among the top independent institutions in the United States over the past decades while the value of such assets declined among institutions in Oxford and Cambridge. The net beneficiaries have, of course, been generations of Oxbridge students that have secured a high-quality education at very attractive rates.

Analysis of the rate of wealth creation among US universities compared to wealth destruction among UK universities is not available. It would be reasonable to suggest, however, that if nothing is done urgently to reverse the funding gap faced by institutions in Oxford and Cambridge—not to mention other highly rated centres of learning in the UK—they will struggle to retain their status among the top educational institutions in the world. Oxford and Cambridge have been able to withstand such pressures in the past because, apart from the private institutions in the United States, the rest of the world, including Europe, has not fared any better. In addition, there existed sufficient scope for efficiency gains within the Oxbridge system. Going forward, such options may not be available.

As James Tobin, the Nobel prize–winning Yale economist wrote in 1974: 'The trustees of an endowed institution are the guardians of the future against the claims of the present. Their task is to preserve equity among generations.... In formal terms, the trustees are supposed to have a zero subjective rate of time preference.... Consuming endowment income so defined means in principle that the existing endowment can continue to support the same set of activities that it is now supporting.'[32] Oxbridge institutions recognize that urgent action is required. In a world where there is severe competition for funds, these institutions need to develop policies that will help them build their endowments and secure resources from both public and private sectors.

Instead of being a source of strength, it is ironic that public funding appears to have left Oxford and Cambridge without the financial resources that would equip them to be truly world-class and successfully compete in the global arena. The complex structure of the Colleges and their relationship with the University is not a model that can easily be replicated. The collegiate University system may look messy, but it guarantees diversity and experiment. The real challenge, according to the dons at Oxford and fellows at Cambridge, is not fiddling with structures, but raising enough money to enable these institutions to exert greater freedom in managing their affairs.

Total financial freedom or freedom from state funding is not universally sought by Oxbridge academics, nor is it desirable. The best academic institutions in the United States depend greatly on government funding. But securing greater independence in managing their affairs, be it endowment asset allocation, fund-raising, issuing debt, determining the cost of their products and services, will equip these institutions to compete globally on a level playing field. Guarding the universities' autonomy is vital, but as Professor Alison Richard confirms, the idea of a break from the state would be self-defeating. According to her: 'At Cambridge, we must be explicit and clear about our societal obligations, and honour them even as we use our freedom to provide the quality of education and research that keeps us among the foremost universities in the world. Financially, we must broaden and deepen the range of our funding sources and avoid heavy dependence on any one source. Government should surely be amongst these sources, administering public funds on behalf of society collectively. But the terms of our relationship with Government must change, rapidly, for Cambridge to remain in the ranks of the very best.'[33]

Until a greater level of consensus emerges between society's expectations of universities and their need for financial support and greater academic freedom, some tension is inevitable; but creative tension is also transforming. For Alison Richard, 'managing this tension better depends first on developing a greater, shared understanding of the relationship between universities and society, and of the role of finance in mediating that relationship.' The top universities' worldwide aim to provide an outstanding education to high-calibre students, selected without regard to their background; these institutions also aim to pursue scholarship and research of the highest quality, and in a world more connected than ever before to share the results of that work for the benefit of humanity. Thus, how these institutions are nurtured is vital not only in determining the success of individuals and nations, but is also critical in shaping the future of mankind.

Oxford and Cambridge currently benefit from government funding; the government will continue to be the major source of funding for universities. This should be seen as an opportunity for these institutions in setting endowment asset allocation policies as well as in leveraging the stability of their diverse sources of funding. What Oxford and Cambridge need is not to forgo income from public sources, but to increase their private income substantially. To do so they must be able to demonstrate not just their pre-eminence as academic institutions but that the endowments under their management are performing efficiently. Donors like to be assured that their gifts are well spent—either in directly supporting academic purposes of the Colleges today or in the future. To remain in the international 'super-league', Oxbridge needs the financial strength to enable it to resource all of its activities to the highest standards.

Oxbridge institutions fully recognize the need for change that will enable them to deliver their stated objectives. Between 2003, when this study was initiated, and 2006, at the time of going to press, significant developments in endowment management in both Oxford and Cambridge have taken place. We have been privileged to record this process of transformation and to document the changes in attitude and thinking of key individuals in this context. The momentum of change can be variable, since some institutions are able to move faster than others. But when the collective university juggernauts move, which we reckon will be sooner than later, it will contribute to a revolution in endowment management practices in the UK as well as in Europe.

2

The Investment Committee

Introduction

Colleges in Oxford and Cambridge seek to follow best practice within the industry by appointing an Investment Committee responsible for overseeing the management of endowment assets and related investments. The main tasks of this Committee consist of determining strategic asset allocation, return and risk objectives, spending policy, selection of fund managers, and investment consultant; and in the case of the Universities, determining the dividend. Investment Committees are therefore the key drivers of investment policy; their decisions directly influence an institution's intergenerational equity. As primary fiduciaries of institutions, investment committees play an important role in this regard.

Among the committees included in the study, all bar one (Templeton College's investment matters are dealt with directly by its Governing Body) have a Committee charged specifically with the investment management of endowment assets. The name given to the committee charged with investment matters varies greatly though two-thirds of Colleges refer to it as the Investment or Investments Committee, as shown in Table 2.1.

In a third of Colleges (34 per cent), the committee reports to the Finance Committee or the Finance and General Purposes Committee, the Treasury Committee or the Board of Trustees. Thus, at All Soul's College, the Estates and Finance Committee, with assistance from its Investment and Property Subcommittee, oversee the management of the endowment and the finances of the College. For some Colleges (15 per cent), the Finance Committee serves as the Investment Committee. In others (17 per cent), the name of the Investment Committee ranges from the simple 'Bursarial Committee' to the stately 'Stocks and Share Advisory Committee and Estates Committee'.

While Oxford and Cambridge Colleges are independent and self-governing entities, the endowments are not. Oxbridge investment committees serve largely in an advisory capacity. The investment policy is recommended by the Investment Committee, either via the Finance Committee or directly

Table 2.1. Name of committee charged with investment management

Name of committee	Percentage of total
Investment/Investments Committee	68
Finance Committee	15
Endowment Committee	3
Bursarial Committee	2
Estates and Finance Committee	2
Finance and Estates Committee	2
Investment Advisory Body	2
Management Executive Team	2
Securities Committee	2
Stocks and Share Advisory Committee and Estates Committee	2

to the Governing Body of the College. The Investment Committee acts as an adviser to the Governing Body in determining appropriate policies for the management of the endowment assets. According to the 'Report of the Governing Body' of All Souls College in the *University of Oxford, Financial Statement of the Colleges, 2002–3*:

The Governing Body of the College comprises the Warden and Fellows. The Warden is the head of the College and superintends the government of the College and the management of its property, but may not act in important matters without the authority of a College meeting. The Bursar is responsible for overseeing the College's financial affairs and domestic arrangements, taking guidance from the relevant College Committees and Sub-Committees on most matters. The Governing Body is constituted and regulated in accordance with the College's Statutes. . . .

The Warden and Fellows, at the Stated General Meetings of the College held at least once each term, undertake overall responsibility for the ongoing strategic direction of the College, for its administration and for the management of its finances and assets. Advice is given to the Warden and Fellows by a range of committees including the Academic Purposes, Benefices, Domestic, Estates & Finance, General Purposes, Library and Visiting Fellowship Committees.[1]

The Governing Body of each College holds to itself the responsibilities for the ongoing strategic direction of the College, for its administration and for the management of its finances and assets, and is advised by a range of committees. The Governing Body or Council consists typically of the Head of the College and Fellows, excluding Emeritus, Supernumerary, Honorary, Foundation and other such Fellows. The Governing Body, constituted and regulated in accordance with the College's Statutes, undertakes overall responsibility for determining its key strategic decisions, including financial ones.

Similarly the investment committees of the two universities act in an advisory capacity. Cambridge University's newly established Investment Board, for example, will advise the University on all matters relating to its endowment and other investment assets, which currently amount to over £1 billion. While the investment committees' recommendations are usually implemented, the Governing Body of each College or the Council of the two universities are ultimately responsible for determining investment objectives and policy.

Management structure: Differences in approach

Harvard University directly oversees its investments, but the Harvard Management Company (HMC) is responsible for investing the Harvard endowment. Harvard Management Company, a wholly-owned subsidiary of Harvard University, was founded in 1974 to manage the University's endowment, pension assets, working capital, and deferred giving accounts. Harvard Management Company is governed by a Board of Directors appointed by the President and Fellows of the University. Harvard Management Company currently manages $31.4 billion, of which $29.4 billion is in the General Investment Account (GIA), a pooled fund that consists primarily of endowment assets.[2]

Similarly, the Yale Corporation Investment Committee has been responsible for oversight of the endowment since 1975. Yale's Investment Committee consists of at least three Fellows of the Corporation, including Yale University's President, and others with particular investment expertise, thereby incorporating senior-level investment experience into portfolio policy formulation. All of its members consist of alumni with requisite investment expertise. The Committee meets quarterly to review asset allocation policy, endowment performance, and strategies proposed by the Investments Office staff. The Committee approves guidelines for investment of the endowment portfolio, specifying investment objectives, spending policy, and approaches for the investment of each asset category. Eleven individuals currently sit on the Investment Committee. The Investments Office manages the endowment and other financial assets, and defines and implements the University's borrowing strategies. Headed by the CIO, David Swensen, the Yale Investment Office currently consists of 20 professionals, a rise from 16 over the last few years.[3]

There are some interesting differences between Harvard and Yale in their endowment management structure—differences that have been recognized in the strategic discussions held within the Universities of Cambridge and Oxford. While Harvard has relied to a considerable extent on an in-house asset management team, Yale's strategy has been based on hiring outside managers. Yale's superior returns have been attributed to a combination of asset allocation and superior manager selection. Harvard and the University of Texas System have traditionally emphasized the accomplishments of the internal managers. Like Yale, most universities outsource their endowment management to external fund management firms. The departure in October 2005 of Jack Meyer, HMC's president and chief executive officer since 1990, and the appointment of Mohamed El-Erian in 2006, may result in changes to HMC's approach.

A contributory factor in Meyer's departure is that Harvard's students, staff, and alumni protested about the salaries paid to HMC staff. In 2003, the top 6 people at HMC received compensation of over $100 million; similar compensation was paid out in 2004. As a separate entity, HMC had the autonomy to set compensation rates. Yale, however, maintains greater control over its investments office. Yale investment managers have their compensation rates approved by the University committees. Though Swensen's annual compensation is by no means paltry, it is widely acknowledged that he could be earning more on Wall Street.

Differences in management structures have consequences, not just in terms of compensation packages for managers but critically for the institutions as they benefit from superior long-term investment returns. Harvard's 10-year annual rate of return net of fees and expenses on its GIA was 16.1 per cent in 2005 compared with Yale's 17.4 per cent. The corresponding investment return for the Trust Universe Comparison Service (TUCS) Median, a universe of more than 100 funds with assets of over $1 billion in the United States, was 9.4 per cent. There is no TUCS median available for the foundation and endowment sector in the UK. The closest comparator was the average fund return for the WM Charity Fund Universe, which was 7.6 per cent per annum over the 10-year period to end-December 2005.[4]

Even a modest gap in annualized performance can have substantial impact over the long haul. The Yale Endowment's results over the past two decades reveal that sustained superior performance has translated into strong endowment growth, which has in turn provided higher income for the institution. Yale's investment returns of 16 per cent per annum produced a 2005 Endowment value of more than 10 times that of 1985. Over the past 10 years, for example, the Yale Endowment grew from $4.0 billion to $15.2 billion, and spending from the endowment rose from $149 million to $567 million. Taking into account the value of endowment assets for Oxbridge institutions in this study, of approximately $10 billion, an improvement of even 1 per cent in annual return will yield $100 million. Higher returns are potentially achievable by these institutions; they are truly long-term investors and are best equipped to achieve superior risk-adjusted returns.

Thus, governance and management structures matter, if they can improve asset allocation decisions that result in superior long-term performance. Institutions need to address such arrangements to ensure their investment management is organized efficiently. Oxbridge investment bursars can only dream of the independence and support, let alone the compensation packages, enjoyed by the chief investment officers of endowment companies at top American universities. If improved performance can be achieved by investment decisions that emanate from new ways of structuring the governance of such institutions, it is worth scrutiny and implementation. Harvard and Yale, along with other US institutions, reorganized their endowment management arrangements in the mid-1970s. They have served these institutions well. While Oxford and Cambridge support very different collegiate structures, both institutions are in the process of setting up independent endowment management offices.

Currently, the Investment Committee of a College is responsible for managing its endowment with the investment bursar serving as CIO. However, neither the Investment Committee nor the College Bursar has the authority to manage the endowment assets independently. Within the universities the structure is slightly different, with the Director of Finance being responsible, among other matters, for the Treasury department, whose head is secretary to the Investment Committee and responsible for all administrative arrangements. The Director of Finance is a member of the Investment Committee. And the head of the Investment Committee acts as a CIO.

An analysis of the institutional responses reveals that the Investment Committee takes responsibility for setting investment policy in over a third (38 per cent) of Colleges in Oxford compared to over half (52 per cent) in Cambridge. On a combined basis, about 44 per cent of Colleges indicated that the Investment Committee was entirely (100 per cent) responsible for investment policy. The scale of involvement of the Investment Committee in setting investment policy varied from 7 per cent of Colleges claiming no involvement in the process to 15 per cent considering the Investment Committee highly (75–99 per cent) responsible in determining investment policy.

The direct involvement of investment committees in strategic aspects of decision-making with reference to the endowment is significant. The Investment Committee plays a crucial role in the management of endowments. Among the richer Colleges, most committees assume full responsibility for setting and reviewing investment policy, compared to Colleges with lesser endowments where the strategic decision-making could be shared with the fund manager or other adviser. The majority of investment committees take full responsibility in defining strategic aspects of endowment policy such as setting and reviewing the investment policy as well as managing risk. They are also responsible for the selection and monitoring of consultants and fund managers. As far as asset allocation and rebalancing is concerned, some Colleges tend to share that responsibility with their asset managers and/or consultants. Significantly, it is in the area of performance measurement and attribution that the investment committees tend to delegate to or share more of the responsibility with the appointed fund manager or consultant.

Investment Committee membership

The Nominations Committee, appointed by the Governing Body or the College Council, usually makes recommendations on Investment Committee membership matters. Typically, there are three kinds of membership within each College's investment committee. First, there are the ex officio members of the College, such as the Master and the Bursar. Then, there are College members who are seconded to serve in the committee. The length of membership of this internal group tends to rotate more frequently than that of the ex officio members, whose appointment is made usually on a permanent basis. Finally, there are external members who are appointed mostly on the strength of their investment expertise.

Length of membership varies significantly for this external group of appointees; some tend to stay much longer than internal members. Length of membership also varies between Colleges, ranging from a third of the investment committee members rotating annually to no particular time limit being imposed on appointments. In some cases, the dynamics of the investment committee is such that once the current membership structure changes, the institution will find it impossible to replicate the arrangement, which appear to have served these Colleges well over the past decades.

Just under half (45 per cent) of the Colleges indicated that there was no particular term for investment committee members. Another 32 per cent suggest 3 years as a 'normal' length of membership, which is renewable; the remaining Colleges had investment committee members serving for varying periods: 5 years (2 per cent), 4 years (10 per cent), 3–4 years (2 per cent), 2–4 years (3 per cent), 2 years (2 per cent), and 1 year (5 per cent). Membership is usually renewable. The important criteria for external members are the suitability of the candidate—in terms of investment expertise—and the willingness to attend committee meetings regularly. Size of endowment appeared to have no bearing on length of investment committee membership. Educational endowments exhibit greater flexibility when appointing investment committee members, perhaps because the membership of the Governing Body is more stable compared to other institutions. Also, these institutions have considerable access to the goodwill and investment expertise of their alumni. While annual giving to one's university is not common practice in Europe, old members are very willing to express their gratitude by sharing their time and expertise.

More information is available from the *Commonfund Benchmarks Study: Foundations and Operating Charities Report* 2005, in which 317 independent, GIA, private and community foundations and charities in the United States participated, and whose total assets were worth around $167 billion. Of these participating institutions, roughly one-third (36 per cent in 2004, up from 34 per cent in 2003) reported having term limits in place for investment

Table 2.2. Who chairs the investment committee?

Chair	Oxford	Cambridge	Oxbridge
Head of College*	27	22	49 (80%)
Bursar**	4	2	6 (10%)
Internal member***	2	2	4 (7%)
External member	1	1	2 (3%)

* Including Master, Mistress, President, Principal, Provost, Rector, and Warden.
** Including Senior Bursar, Estates Bursar, or Emeritus Bursar.
*** Including Advisory Fellow or Ex-Vice Master.

committee members, with an average term length of 4.4 years (down from 4.9 years the previous year). In each of the most recent 2 years, at least 50 per cent of the largest institutions, with assets of over $1 billion, reported term limits and longer average term lengths (5.8 years in 2004, 8.2 years in 2003). Among smaller foundations (with assets between $50 million and $100 million), 45 per cent reported having term limits, a rise from 35 per cent the previous year; the average term length was 4.0 years, a slight fall from 4.4 years in 2003.[5]

The membership structure of Oxbridge investment committees, as shown in Table 2.2, indicates that 80 per cent of committees were chaired by the Head of the College—who is referred to variously as Master, Mistress, President, Principal, Provost, Rector, or Warden. The Bursar chairs the Investment Committee in 10 per cent of Colleges or sometimes an internal member does the job (7 per cent). In each university, in 1 College (3 per cent) an external member chairs its Investment Committee.

Investment Committee demographics

Membership numbers vary significantly within endowments and pension funds. As illustrated in Table 2.3, over half the Oxbridge Colleges appointed 8–10 members to their investment committees.

Thus, at the margins 12 per cent of Colleges had up to 5 members in their investment committees, while 3 per cent of Colleges reported

Table 2.3. Number of members in Oxbridge investment committees.

Institution	1–5	6–7	8–10	11–14	15–16
Oxford	5	7	17	4	0
Cambridge	2	6	14	3	2
Oxbridge total	**7**	**13**	**31**	**7**	**2**

NB: Templeton College in Oxford does not have an Investment Committee.

having 15 or more members in the investment committee. Under one-quarter (22 per cent) of Colleges had 6–7 members, and the remaining 12 per cent between 11 and 14 members. The average number of members on the Investment Committee in Oxford was 7, with a minimum of 4 members and maximum of 13. This compared with an average of 9 members in Cambridge, with a minimum of 4 and maximum of 16. The average membership for Oxbridge as a whole was 8 individuals per committee.

This compares with an average of 10 individuals sitting on investment management committees of institutional endowments in the United States. But there, the average range varied from committees with 3 members to ones with 50. While public educational institutions in the United States on average had the same number of individuals in their investment management committees (10 members), public institutions had a higher rate of dispersion in membership numbers (3–50) compared to independent institutions (3–23). Institutions with assets over $50 million but less than $100 million had an average of 11 members in the investment committee but reported a higher range in membership numbers (3–50) as well. While institutions with assets over $1 billion also had on average 11 individuals in their investment committee, the reported range was lower, at between 4 and 23 people on their investment management committees.[6] Table 2.4 reports the membership demographics in investment management committees in the United States, as reported by the NACUBO.

Compared with their US counterparts, Oxbridge institutions appear to have smaller investment committees. But, taking into account the size of assets under management and investment strategies employed, the number of individuals involved in the process is large. Some bursars indicated a desire for having smaller groups entirely focused on investment matters. The amount of assets under management and the lower spread of asset classes among Oxbridge endowments accounts for the lower membership numbers. With the rise in assets under management and increasing exposure to alternative

Table 2.4. Number of members in US investment committees

Endowment	Average number (and range)	
> $1,000 m	11	(4–23)
$500—1,000 m	10	(4–23)
$100—500 m	10	(3–31)
$50—100 m	11	(3–50)
$25—50 m	9	(3–25)
< $25 m	8	(3–23)
Public	10	(3–50)
Independent	10	(3–23)
All endowments	**10**	**(3–50)**

Source: 2004 NACUBO Study.

strategies, membership of investment committees within Oxbridge institutions may also rise to levels seen in American universities. It is clear from the US experience that, as institutions increased their use of alternative assets, the complexity of investment strategies and differences in legal structures, liquidity, risk analysis, and valuation techniques led institutions to appoint investment committee members with the necessary experience in these asset classes.

The Yale Corporation Investment Committee, for example, has been responsible for oversight of the Endowment, incorporating senior-level investment experience into portfolio policy formulation. The Investment Committee consists of at least three Fellows of the Corporation and other persons with specific investment expertise. The Committee meets quarterly, at which time members review asset allocation policies, performance of the endowment, and strategies proposed by Investments Office staff. The Committee also approves guidelines for investment of the endowment portfolio, specifying investment objectives, spending policy, and approaches for the investment of each asset category.

According to another study, the *Commonfund Benchmarks Study: Educational Endowment Report*, in which 707 institutions in the United States participated, and whose total assets were worth around $227 billion, committee size and investment expertise varied modestly by size and type of institution, but the role played by the investment committee was uniformly perceived to be crucial. In this study, institutions reported smaller investment committees, with an average membership of 8.2 in 2004 compared to an average of 8.6 members a year before. Larger institutions continued to report investment committees with more members than smaller institutions; membership ranged from an average of 10.5 members among institutions with assets over $1 billion to 6.1 members for institutions with assets under $10 million.[7] Within this sector, private foundations reported having at least one extra member above the average, namely an average of 9.2 members, while independent institutions had at least one member short of the average, namely 7.1 members.[8] Oxbridge Colleges' average investment committee membership of 8.0 is closer to the size of membership reported in the 2005 Benchmarks Study, though the size of Oxbridge endowments is smaller and the spread of asset classes narrower.

Levels of professional involvement: United States versus United Kingdom

In the United States, the investment committees of educational endowments reported that nearly half of their appointed membership (four members) consisted of investment professionals. Among top quartile performers, the size of the average investment committee was higher at 9 members, of whom an average of 4.5 members were investment professionals and an average of 3.1 had specific experience in alternative strategies. Among the top decile performers, average investment committee size was 8.9 members, of whom an average of 4.0 were investment professionals and an average 2.5 members had specific experience in alternative strategies.[9]

Over the last few years, the *Commonfund Benchmarks Study* has shown steady growth in the use of alternative strategies, hedge funds, real estate, and private capital. It is likely that this has helped to drive the average number of investment committee members who have specific experience in alternative strategies to 2.8. This average is higher at the largest institutions where alternative strategies allocations are considerable (an average 5.5 investment committee members with alternatives experience) than among the smallest institutions where greater reliance on funds-of-funds is the norm for their alternative asset allocations, and where fewer investment committee members (2.1 members) have such specialized experience.[10]

Analysis of investment committee demographics among US charities and foundations, as distinct from educational endowments, published by the Commonfund Institute, shows that these institutions reported an average of 6.6 members in 2004, up from an average of 6.3 members a year before and 6.1 in 2002. The smaller foundations ($50–100 million) had larger investment committees (an average of 6.9 members) than the largest foundations (over $1 billion) with an average of 6.1 members in 2004. By type of institution, operating charities and community foundations reported larger investment committees (with an average of 8.7 and 8.0 members, respectively) than independent or private foundations (with an average of 5.5 members).[11]

Growth in the size of investment committees reflects changes in asset allocation among these institutions. As the complexity and diversity of investment portfolios has increased, there has been an addition of investment professionals and members with specific skills and experience in alternative strategies. What is worth noting is that top decile performers reported larger investment committees (7.7 members on average), of which an average of 4.3 were investment professionals and an average 2.7 members had specific experience in alternative strategies. Top quartile performers similarly reported larger than average investment committees (6.9 members), of which an average of 3.4 members were investment professional and an average 2.5 had specific experience in alternative strategies. Of the total foundations group average of 6.6 members, an average 3.2 members were investment professionals and 2.4 had specific experience in alternative strategies.[12]

Wealthier foundations (with assets over $1 billion) had 3.1 members in the investment committee who were investment professionals, of whom 2.6 members had specific experience in alternative strategies. Foundations with assets worth between $101 million and $500 million reported having above average membership (3.4 members) in the investment committee, while the wealthier foundations had above average number of members with experience in alternative strategies.[13]

No discernible investment committee membership pattern exists among Oxbridge institutions. The richest among them (the Cambridge University Endowment) has the largest number of members in its Investment Committee (16 at the time of survey) while Colleges with smaller endowments also have large investment committees with 10–13 members. Inclusion of external members with requisite investment management skills in the overall composition of Oxbridge investment committees also depicts a high level of variation.

Among Colleges with no external members, who are generally appointed for their investment expertise rather than for other reasons such as their ability to raise funds for the institution, internal members' investment skills varied considerably. Table 2.5 shows that 35 per cent of Oxbridge Colleges did not have any external member in the Investment Committee; 20 per cent had under a quarter of its membership consisting of external candidates. Some 38 per cent of Colleges had between a quarter and a half of its membership from outside the College, while 7 per cent had more than half their investment committee comprising external members.

Of the 21 Colleges, with no external advisers in their respective investment committees, 95 per cent had internal members with varying levels of investment expertise. As shown in Table 2.6, 10 per cent of investment committees without an external member had internal members with very high levels of investment expertise—that is over 75 per cent of internal members were experts in investment management. About two-thirds of Colleges with no external members had internal members in the investment committee with

Table 2.5. Percentage of investment committee members who are external

Institution	None	<25%	25–50%	50–75%	All
Oxford	23	8	18	5	55
Cambridge	12	12	20	2	45
Oxbridge total	**35**	**20**	**38**	**7**	**100**

Table 2.6. Investment experience in committees with no external members

Institution	None	25–50%	50–75%	>75%	na	All
Oxford	19	19	19	5	5	67
Cambridge	—	14	14	5	—	33
Oxbridge total	**19**	**33**	**33**	**10**	**5**	**100**

varying levels of investment expertise; 51–75 per cent of members in one-third of committees without an external member had investment experience while 26–50 per cent of internal members in a further third of investment committees without external membership were competent in investment matters.

There were just four Colleges (19 per cent) with no external members in their investment committee (all, incidentally, in Oxford), where the Bursar was the sole finance specialist in the Committee. One of these Colleges had access to an investment consultant, but the consultant was 'used more for manager selection and for securing private equity exposure'. The same College was also considering appointing an external investment expert to its Investment Committee. Of the remaining three Colleges, one was in the process of appointing an investment consultant for access to private equity investments rather than for overall strategic consultation and the other two Colleges had no consultants advising them on their investment strategy, depending largely on their investment manager for such advice.

Over one-third (35 per cent) of Colleges relied on their externally appointed fund manager for asset allocation and other investment advice. With regard to the use of consultants, about a third (32 per cent) of Colleges reported using an investment consultant, though not for setting investment policy. Over 70 per cent of investment committees in Oxbridge do not hire consultants for investment advice; the figure is higher (89 per cent) for Cambridge. While these percentages are only indicative, they provide some insights on the limited role of investment consultants in setting investment policy within Oxbridge Colleges.

Table 2.7 shows that 9 per cent of institutions surveyed in Oxford and Cambridge had less than one-quarter of their membership with relevant background in investment matters, while 12 per cent of institutions had more than three-quarters of their members with specific investment expertise.

These figures fail to reflect the quality of the investment expertise in investment committees, which consisted typically of a diversified group of academics, scientists, economists, lawyers, barristers, ex-politicians, diplomats, leaders of industry, investment bankers, commercial bankers, and venture capitalists. With the steady influx of investment management professionals

Table 2.7. Percentage of investment committee members with professional experience

Institution	<25%	25–50%	50–75%	>75%	All
Oxford	9	15	27	5	55
Cambridge	—	18	20	7	45
Oxbridge total	**9**	**33**	**47**	**12**	**100**

joining the ranks of investment bursars and CIO positions in both Oxford and Cambridge, the average number of investment committee members that are investment professionals has risen significantly among these institutions over the past few years.

However, the differences in size of endowment assets and asset allocation strategies pursued among these institutions mean that the skill-set employed varied considerably. It bears noting that investment professionals now comprise roughly half the membership of investment committees in the United States, and members with experience in alternative strategies comprise, on average, a third of the committees, revealing the commitment to professional and informed oversight that boards in this sector are making. As allocation to alternative strategies within UK educational endowments has been low, the level of expertise within investment committees has also been low. Colleges with high level of exposure to property assets, for example, have the requisite expertise available within their committees or have direct access to such expertise build up over generations.

There is a discernible sense of change in approach as one generation of Oxbridge bursars retire and the newer bursars increasingly tend to have an established record in asset management, or are professionals within the financial sector. The appointment of a hedge fund manager as the Senior Bursar of Trinity College, Cambridge, is one example among many where recently appointed College Bursars in both Oxford and Cambridge have relevant expertise in asset management. Oxbridge investment committee meetings do not quite resemble that of Yale's where the quarterly Investment Committee meetings are like an advanced seminar in investment theory and practice, led by two Yale Ph.D.'s, viz. President Richard Levin and CIO David Swensen. However, the move towards managing Oxbridge endowment assets more professionally is steadily on the rise.

Other characteristics

The composition of Oxbridge Investment Committees reveals a national bias rather than an international one reflecting the composition of the faculty and staff members more than the student body. The composition of the Investment Committees of Ivy League Colleges in the United States exhibits a similar home bias. Practicalities of meeting as and when required for members who live in different locations worldwide is certainly an influencing factor, not to mention the fact that Colleges possess considerable access to a wide range of investment expertise within their own membership.

As far as the age of the investment committee membership is concerned, it can broadly be defined as 'mature' or 'experienced' though the study did not seek to collect relevant data on this subject specifically. According to one

Table 2.8. Number of investment committee meetings per year

Institution	2	3–6	6–7	8	9–12	All
Oxford (%)	12	30	10	2	2	55
Cambridge (%)	8	33	2	2	0	45
Oxbridge total (%)	**20**	**63**	**12**	**3**	**2**	**100**

Bursar, the interesting aspect of their Investment Committee 'was that the College appears to have received better value from the older members. The robust advice we hoped we might get from the younger external members has not quite materialised.'

Table 2.8 illustrates the number of meetings held for investment purposes.

It varied between two meetings annually among 20 per cent of Colleges to over 10 meetings by 2 per cent of Colleges. The majority (63 per cent) of institutions met between 3–6 times every year—that is once or twice a term—to review investment matters. These meetings formally lasted 2–3 hours each, sometimes followed by dinner where the discussions would be carried on, albeit on an informal basis. The number of meetings does not indicate time spent informally among internal College members via phone calls, emails, and discussions held on an ad hoc basis.

The additional time spent by investment committee members in the management of the endowment is, however, minimal in most cases. In some Colleges, the Investment Bursar worked closely with both external and internal members in developing investment strategy. In a third of Colleges the Bursar reported spending 10–15 hours annually on investment matters in addition to the time spent at investment committee meetings. These bursars reported receiving very little support in their overall role as College bursar, responsible not just for investments but general bursarial matters.

Practices in the United States varies among institutions, but according to the *Commonfund Benchmarks Study: Foundations and Operating Charities Report* 2005, investment committees generally meet a little more often than quarterly (4.3 times per year on average), and slightly fewer times in the past year than in the 2004 study (4.4 times per year). Size does not seem to be a factor in meeting frequency, but the investment committees of operating charities appear to meet more often on average (4.6 times per year) than other types of institutions.[14]

The Investment Bursar

The Investment Bursar is responsible for overseeing a College's financial affairs and domestic arrangements, taking guidance from the relevant committees and subcommittees on most matters. The role of the Investment Bursar is not uniformly defined, though one responsibility is clearly the management of the College's assets, including the endowment. The majority of bursars also endorse the view that the purpose of the College endowment is primarily to support the College in delivering its educational objective; preserving or growing the endowment for posterity is implicit in successfully fulfilling the main target.

The Investment Bursar is referred to variously as Bursar, Senior Bursar, Finance Bursar, Finance Officer, Treasurer, Estates Bursar, Finance & Estates Bursar, or simply Investment Bursar. In the majority of Colleges, the Investment Bursar appears to be charged with investment matters. At the other end of the spectrum, some Colleges have one part-time Bursar charged with both the management of domestic and financial matters, making it difficult for that person to do justice to investment matters. The Investment Bursar is typically a Fellow of the College.

The roles of the Investment Bursar and the Domestic Bursar are usually differentiated, though those of the Investment Bursar and the Property Bursar are not always clearly delineated. In some Colleges there are at least three bursars—for example, the Estates Bursar (responsible for property management), the Home or Domestic Bursar (responsible for the College's domestic affairs), and the Finance Officer (responsible for College accounts and general management of matters of a financial nature); or the Domestic Bursar, the Academic Bursar, and the Investment Bursar; or any combination of these. The Academic bursar is typically a member of Faculty who acts as bursar. To complicate matters further, sometimes the post of the Academic Bursar and that of the Investment Bursar is held by the same person; and that person can also be the Vice-Principal of the College and hold a professorial post in the University!

While most Bursars are recognized Fellows of their respective Colleges, in about a quarter of Colleges, an academic Fellow also holds the post of Investment Bursar—in one instance, the appointment lasted for an indefinite period; until the retirement of the Fellow. A quarter of bursars in Oxbridge today previously worked in the financial services sector, some in investment banking and asset management. That proportion as indicated earlier is steadily rising. Bursars in some Colleges inevitably wield more influence than others in managing their investment affairs. For the richest College, it is appropriate that 'the Finance Committee assists the Senior Bursar in the management of the College's assets'. It is also worth noting that the outgoing Senior Bursar of Trinity College, Cambridge, was from the investment banking sector and so is his replacement; both men had also worked at Barings albeit at different times and stages of their career.

In gender terms, Oxbridge prefers male investment bursars. Oxford has three female bursars among the 34 Colleges surveyed (9 per cent). Cambridge has four among the 27 Colleges (15 per cent), bringing the total to 11 per cent.

The figure is lower when all the Colleges and Permanent Private Halls are included. This preference applies mainly in the case of the investment bursars; the percentage of female domestic bursars is significantly higher.

In obtaining an insight into the complexities of managing an Oxbridge College endowment, we examined the extent to which the Investment Committee was supported by consultants, fund managers, and other advisers in the overall investment process. The Colleges depend on key advisers to formulate asset allocation policy and oversee manager selection and supervision; then there is a raft of administrative services including performance analysis and reporting that is also associated with the management process.

The responses reveal that many Colleges are managing these complex demands with limited professional staff, the Investment Bursar often being the only person responsible for a varied number of tasks. Sometimes a number of fund managers have to be monitored. In some instances, the active use of investment consultants means the process becomes administratively more complex. Large investment committees also makes the task of the Bursar demanding, as coordinating the various groups of people involved in the process and running the College's day-to-day affairs can result in lack of appropriate oversight. As most investment committees meet 3–6 times annually, the responsibility of managing the endowment portfolio on a daily basis rests largely on the Bursar. Sometimes, even the Bursar does not have sufficient time available for investment matters.

A comparison with the level of professional staffing among US educational institutions shows that as endowment portfolios have grown in size and become more complex in strategy, the need for focused, full-time professional investment management staff has grown. Despite increased demands, the *Commonfund Benchmarks Study: Educational Endowment Report, 2005* reveals 'institutions as a whole report an average of just 1.2 FTEs dedicated to investment management at their endowments.' However institutions with assets of $1 billion or more reported a substantially larger staff size—an average of 12.5 FTEs—compared to institutions under $10 million in assets, where staffing averages just 0.2 FTEs. The report also makes it clear that 'staffing levels have declined during the years we have conducted the Study. This raises critical questions about whether institutions are realistically assessing the demands of their investment activities and staffing accordingly.'[15]

The number of professional staff involved in investment management in Oxbridge institutions is estimated to be less than one; even the investment bursars of most Colleges perform a range of tasks, in addition to their endowment management responsibilities. There is no evidence to suggest there has been a decline in staffing within the investment office of Oxbridge institutions; there is no sign of any additions to staffing levels either. Managing the endowment consists of one of the responsibilities of Oxbridge bursars. Building important relationships with members of the Investment Committee,

Governing Body, and other related committees is also critical in the overall context of endowment management. While more Colleges are employing professionals as investment bursars, it appears many Colleges are managing the task with rather limited facilities. As the College Investment Office's CIO, unlike other professional CIOs, an Oxbridge Bursar typically lacks the resources and/or the freedom to manage the endowment.

Conclusion

A convergence of factors, such as the prolonged bear market of the early 2000s and changing economic conditions, led to the majority of Colleges reviewing their investment policy. This resulted in an increased level of activity within Oxbridge investment committees, particularly since the turn of the century, leading to substantial changes in investment strategy and the appointment of managers. As active managers underperformed during the preceding bull market, some Colleges switched to indexation. Others simply changed active managers to reflect their new investment policy.

The introduction of the Statement of Recommended Practice on Accounting in Further and Higher Education Institutions, commonly referred to as the SORP accounts, also generated a significantly higher level of activity as Colleges organized their financial affairs to comply with the new requirements. Changes in government funding and tax incentives also influenced general financial planning. Thus, investment committees have had to deal with a wide range of activity over the last five years. While the role and importance of the investment bursar is better appreciated among Oxbridge Colleges, the level of support they receive in executing their job is not always available.

A comparison with the situation in the United States reveals some interesting similarities and differences. Institutions in the 2004 *NACUBO Endowment Study* (NES) reported on average 10 members on their institutional investment committee, and one individual on staff whose primary responsibility was investment management. Institutions with assets greater than $1 billion had on average 11 members on the investment management committee and six staff members (a rise from five members in 2003), whose primary responsibility was asset management. Of more relevance to Oxbridge Colleges with mid-size endowments, US institutions with endowment assets between $100 million and $500 million had an average of 10 members on their investment committees and just one person on staff whose primary responsibility was investment management. These ratios are similar to those of Oxbridge Colleges where the investment committee had on average eight members with the bursar being primarily responsible for investment management. However, the average size of endowment assets among Oxbridge institutions remains lower and so are the types of asset classes and investment strategies used.

While public and independent institutions reported an average of one member of staff whose primary responsibility was investment management, the likely range of number of individuals on staff was between 0 and 35 in both categories. Even endowments with assets over $1 billion reported a range of 1–35 members on staff whose primary responsibility was investment management. The lowest reported range of members was among institutions with endowments between $50 million and $100 million. Institutions with assets worth $100 million to $500 million reported a range of 0–4.

Overall, 75.8 per cent of reporting institutions in the United States employed an outside consultant for investment guidance. The picture is reversed in Oxbridge where over 70 per cent of respondents did not use any external consultants for investment guidance. It is interesting that US institutions with assets worth over $1 billion were less likely to employ an outside investment consultant, with 53.3 per cent (a rise from 44.7 per cent in 2003) reporting that they did so. This is most likely because of the significant staff resources devoted to asset management by these institutions. At the other end of the spectrum, only 62.9 per cent of institutions with investment assets less than or equal to $25 million employed an outside consultant. This was probably due to financial constraints more than any other factor. The category of investors most likely to engage the services of an outside consultant (86.3 per cent of respondents) was institutions with assets between $100 million and $500 million.[16]

In Oxbridge, the use of consultants remains patchy. More institutions in Oxford employed external consultants compared to those in Cambridge. But, even in Oxford, several of these hires were for guidance on investments in private equity and absolute return strategies rather than for strategic asset allocation. Also within Oxford Colleges, there was little correlation between size of endowments and employment of consultants for investment guidance. Only a few institutions engaged a consultant for overall investment guidance; most did so for guidance regarding the hiring of asset managers. In general, Oxbridge Colleges appeared to be fairly pragmatic in their approach to hiring consultants, resorting to such measures only when necessary—as in gaining exposure to alternative asset classes.

One statistic worthy of note is the number of individuals involved in the overall management of Oxbridge endowment assets. The total number of investment committee members reported by the participating institutions was 477 (241 in Oxford and 236 in Cambridge). Taking into account the 224 fund managers employed (refer to Chapter 10 on *Manager Selection and Monitoring*) but not the analysts and other experts engaged by the external fund manager, over 700 individuals were involved in managing endowment assets worth less than £5 billion. Adding in investment consultants and other professionals, along with the investment committee members for the Colleges that did not take part in our research, the total number of individuals responsible for asset management was nearer 800. These numbers were expected to rise because several Colleges were in the process of implementing major changes in asset allocation and manager hires.

Oxford and Cambridge Colleges depend on key advisers to formulate asset allocation policy, oversee manager selection, and provide general oversight; many of these advisers consist of alumni and friends of the College. In addition, there is a raft of administrative services in which only the Bursar is involved. While there are an unusually large number of people in investment committees, the responses revealed that several Colleges are managing these demands with limited professional staff, the Bursar often being the only person responsible for a varied number of tasks. The challenge of managing the resources in support of the College's overall objectives cannot be emphasized enough.

As one bursar pointed out, 'some Colleges may have benefited from disinterested expert advice, and intermediation from old members and friends; others may have suffered from partial, self-serving and ignorant interventions from identical sources. Setting up a University wide advisory committee might be beneficial, even if the advice is not taken.' As a few Colleges in Oxford have set up a common investment fund, the Oxford Investment Partners, for efficient access to quality assets, developments are afoot in addressing some of these concerns. It is relevant that Colleges are debating the merits of pooling resources, intellectual assets as much as financial ones, as these institutions are prone to be highly competitive within the collegiate façade.

Though the structure of the Investment Committee in Oxford and Cambridge could benefit from injection of greater investment expertise, its role in determining and being responsible for overall prudent endowment management needs bolstering. Colleges without necessary expertise in their investment committees are committed to making the necessary changes. However, investment committees cannot bestow greater autonomy on themselves. Some committees appear to have as much autonomy as they desire, are not constrained in any way in their investment decision-making, and are able to operate relatively independently. In other cases, decisions detrimental to the long-term health of the endowment were made. As the role of the endowment in sustaining long-term institutional objective is being widely appreciated, Colleges are increasingly adopting 'good practice' in their endowment management.

3

Investment objective

Introduction

Endowments exist, usually in perpetuity, to provide income for institutions engaged in charitable activities. Unlike pension funds whose investment objectives may be construed as being similar, endowment purposes vary considerably. Endowment accumulation could be for any number of objectives. The high level of dispersion of objectives makes the investment analysis complex and challenging. Establishment of the endowed institution's specific objectives is therefore essential to defining its investment policy. Even then, institutions with similar objectives may interpret their mission differently, resulting in dissimilar asset allocations. A pension fund, on the other hand, has a specific need to match assets to liabilities.

Issues relating to intergenerational equity, a phrase coined by Yale economist James Tobin, also generate lively debate among endowed institutions. Intergenerational equity is achieved by developing and maintaining policies and practices that primarily seek to balance current spending from investment returns, gifts, etc. so that the institution can meet its current goals, while giving itself the best opportunity to realize its long-term goals in preserving the spending power of future generations. Each institution may also define intergenerational equity differently. Some endowments may not have such an obligation; others may opt to change their institutional mission. Educational institutions that have been around for centuries, such as Oxford and Cambridge, Harvard, and Yale, define their objective as remaining in the forefront of higher education, as the challenges they face intensify and their scope of operations become more global and perpetual in nature.

The challenge for the Wellcome Trust, the world's largest biomedical charity, for example, is how best to sustain the real value of its endowed assets and its grant-giving ability in perpetuity. This complex balancing act of maximizing spending today and spending tomorrow is a key concern among most endowments and foundations. One of the objectives identified by the Norwegian Petroleum Fund, which started accumulating assets from its oil revenues as recently as 1996, is to ensure that the benefits are enjoyed equitably by both current and future generations. The Fund has endowment-like characteristics and accompanying dilemmas in decision-making. Each step of the endowment asset management process can be fraught with potential conflicts of interest. A clearly defined objective on which investment policy is based therefore acquires eminence.

The wider not-for-profit sector makes a significant economic and social contribution to society. Fund managers in this sector aim to preserve the purchasing power of their assets. Taking into account the indeterminate nature of their liabilities, a successful investment policy that sustains flow of funds to the operating budget in real terms also assists to fulfil the goal of the endowment in perpetuity. The independence and stability that fosters excellence is ensured through implementation of efficient investment strategies. An inefficiently constructed portfolio can easily suffer a shortfall in annual return relative to an efficiently constructed portfolio with the same level of risk. This would result in a significant aggregate shortfall in current spending for the sector. Widespread improvements in asset allocation within the sector could release substantial funds for philanthropic purposes.

Similarly, an inappropriate risk profile can impose major costs on charities and their beneficiaries. For this reason, the revised Statement of Recommended Practice: Accounting and Reporting for charities (SORP) sets out to clarify the obligations of UK charity trustees; it requires trustees to define appropriate policies for selecting investment assets, to monitor investment performance, to consider the risks to which the charity is exposed, and to implement systems to mitigate those risks. To make the right decisions, it is important to be informed and guided by careful research. Yet trustees find impartial research is elusive because of the conflicting viewpoints of the different professionals and agencies involved in service provision: beneficiaries, volunteers, managers, trustees, advisers, consultants, regulators, and politicians.

In the world of endowment management, where the investment horizon may extend over centuries, investment decisions to support the objectives of endowed institutions pose a unique set of challenges. While the asset management industry provides an array of products, endowment fund managers find few investment opportunities that serve their long-term, fiduciary needs. Success, therefore, depends on a high level of discipline in implementing investment decisions reflecting the institutional objective. Investment policy statements therefore typically include definitions specifying issues relating to asset allocation and spending policies along with investment constraints, if any. The investment policy statement may also reflect the institutional philosophy in terms of management style and overall investment objectives.

Institutions address these issues formally or informally in their investment objectives, asset allocation strategy, performance benchmarks, and how returns relate to spending policy. We discuss these issues individually in later chapters; here we address issues surrounding the definition of the investment objective. Establishment of a benchmark or policy portfolio for some endowments is a way of defining the investment objective, with the benchmark asset allocation reflecting that objective. Thus, the benchmark allocation of assets is responsible for providing resources for current operations while preserving purchasing power of assets in the long term. The benchmark therefore reflects the institution's approach to various aspects of managing the endowment, including risk. The cornerstone for the management of the investments of the HMC, for example, is its policy portfolio, while the investment policy objective of the Yale Endowment is to exceed its internal benchmark.

While American institutions can be more quantitative in their approach, in Europe, many well-established institutions adopt a more qualitative approach. The Wellcome Trust, for example, defines its investment objective in the following words:

The Trust's overall investment objective is to seek total return in inflation-adjusted terms over the long term in order to provide for real increases in annual expenditure while preserving at least the Trust's capital base in real terms. This is to balance the needs of both current and future beneficiaries and the Trust's assets are therefore invested for long-term returns rather than to maximise short-term income. The Trustee considers at all times the need for liquidity, the risks involved and the good reputation of the Trust.[1]

According to the Charity Commission in the UK, the organization responsible for regulating the charitable sector, any investment policy statement should address the following considerations:

- the creation of sufficient financial return to enable the charity (together with its non-investment resources) to carry out its purposes effectively, and without interruption, where a charity sets out to provide services over a period;
- the maintenance and, if possible, enhancement of the value of the invested funds while they are retained;
- the management of risk; and
- the charity's stance on ethical investment (if any).[2]

Statements of Investment Principles (SIP) typically include such considerations. Not all institutions in Oxford and Cambridge, however, had formal SIP in place, though informal definitions of both investment policy and objectives were available.

In the case of educational endowments, such as Oxbridge Colleges, the overarching objective is defined as essentially existing to provide and promote undergraduate and graduate education within their respective universities, as well as to provide and promote scholarly research today and for generations in the future. Within these educational objectives, the Colleges also have various permanently endowed trust funds held for special purposes in connection with the development of College facilities and for scholarships, bursaries, prizes, and other educational purposes. The Governing Body of each College is responsible for determining the ongoing strategic direction of the College as well as its overall administration, which includes the management of its finances and assets. *Thus, the investment objective of these institutions is primarily to secure funds to underpin the educational objective.*

As stated in the *Annual Report and Accounts, 2003–4* of Gonville and Caius College, one of the largest in Cambridge, with approximately 500 undergraduates and 250 graduate students, over 110 fellows and 130 support staff, the financial objectives of the College is 'To ensure that the College's primary educational, research and religious functions are managed cost-effectively and supported by robust and well managed financial resources, which will sustain the enterprise in perpetuity.' The primary purpose of the College is not only the pursuit of education, research, and religion, but its 'overall objective is to rank amongst the highest achieving academic institutions in the world.'[3]

Such an objective cannot be achieved without financial independence, which for the Colleges is secured through a combination of measures such as enhancing returns from the endowment, increasing the scale of the endowment through fund-raising, enlarging revenues by reducing subsidies on fees, rents, and catering services that are not realistic while controlling costs efficiently. Oxford and Cambridge Colleges strongly recognize the contribution of the endowment in sustaining the objective of each College. The aims and objectives of Clare College, also in Cambridge, for example, state that the College has a strategic plan—

- to support a community of Fellows and students;
- to achieve excellence in education at both undergraduate and postgraduate levels;
- to promote academic research of the highest quality by the Fellows and postgraduate students;
- to maintain and enhance the endowments and benefactions, historic buildings, and grounds of the College for the benefit of future generations.

Remaining an independent foundation, forming part of a collegiate university, is fundamental to the College's long-term strategy.[4] As one bursar put it: 'The objective of the College is to produce academic output. We do not have a stated investment objective. However, the College depends largely on the endowment for what it does. We look at the long-term returns and the sort of income we can achieve from various asset classes; for example, the annual yield from our property portfolio is 6–7 per cent while that from our securities portfolio is just 2.3 per cent currently. We look at notional income, which is essentially permanent income, and we come to some conclusions on that basis.' Thus, in formulating investment policy, the Colleges broadly recognize that the primary investment purpose is to provide a sustainable maximum level of return consistent with a prudent level of risk.

In the words of another bursar:

The objective is to achieve an income flow to maintain the College's educational activity. Income for us is what the portfolio can generate on its dividend yield and fixed interest holdings, and the rent flow on the commercial and agricultural estate. We know what our expenditure is going to be in advance. We also know what level of income we will get from our property assets and fixed income investments. Therefore, the rest we need to get from the securities portfolio. We hold discussions with our fund managers to assess what they can generate; we may know of a legacy coming through or any other capital flows and we then agree on a return objective with our managers from our security portfolio.

As endowment support for College operations increases institutional autonomy, more Colleges are conscious of the need for defining investment objectives that clearly support institutional ones. While even the best universities benefit from incorporating wishes of their various constituencies such as students and faculty, donors, and governments, such influences can equally obstruct institutions from taking charge of their destiny. An institution with a larger share of stable income from its permanent endowment stands a better chance of fulfilling its desired objective. Endowment income therefore provides a level of operational stability that sustains long-term planning, assisting in achieving the institutional objective.

Defining the investment objective

Institutions within the endowment sector interpret their mission diversely. Even among institutions with similar objectives, such as academic ones, these objectives may be pursued in widely differing ways. As a consequence approaches to the management of the endowments can vary enormously, depending on a number of considerations such as the size of endowment, dependency on endowment for income, and related issues. While Oxbridge Colleges would all acknowledge the primacy of their educational and academic objective, their investment objectives in relation to their endowment were not defined similarly, even when the investment objective aimed broadly to acknowledge the need to preserve the real purchasing power of the endowment in perpetuity.

The investment objective of one College was described as 'maximising a sustainable spending target, or ensuring an adequate stream of funding for the College's (principally academic) activities, in perpetuity.' Not all bursars put an equal emphasis on preserving the endowment for future generations. According to one, the emphasis was clearly placed on the current generation: 'Though the College is far from being irresponsible in its treatment of the endowment, we view the endowment as a way of securing the College's present needs (in terms of its aim as an educational institution) rather than defer current spending in favour of future generations.' While many would view such an interpretation of objective as a clear breach of fiduciary responsibility, some consider issues in intergenerational equity as unnecessarily diminishing the clarity of a simple investment objective. According to another, 'the College manages its investments in securities and property to produce the highest return consistent with the preservation of capital value in the long term. A subsidiary aim is to enhance the value of the capital for future beneficiaries.'

In this instance, the bursar acknowledged the need to invest judiciously, which could be interpreted as being neutral to current versus future generations. The aspect of intergenerational equity raised in the second sentence—'A subsidiary aim . . . for future beneficiaries.'—may have more to do with spending policy than with defining investment objective, which in this instance is to secure the highest possible return within an acceptable level of risk. It could mean that the College invests for the long-term aiming to 'produce the highest return consistent with the preservation of capital value,' but when it comes to spending from the endowment to sustain the operations of the College, there is a preference for catering to the needs of current generation of College members.

As the investment objective typically exists to support the spending policy of these institutions, it is not surprising that several bursars refer to spending policy when defining the investment objective. Even among the small number (7 per cent) of Colleges in Oxford that reported not having any specific investment objective, there was evidence of very clearly defined views on spending. According to one bursar with a non-specific objective with endowment assets of around £45 million:

We have a spending policy that is 3 per cent of endowment. So, we aim to secure a commensurate return that can preserve the real value of the endowment. The assumptions we work on are that we will get around 8 per cent real return on our alternative assets, 5 per cent or so from equities, just under 5 per cent from property and 2.5 per cent from bonds. This translates to approximately 5 per cent total return in terms of our asset split. Whether this amounts to an investment objective, I do not know.

Our spending rate of 3 per cent is also not set in stone. The three-year downturn in equity markets makes it difficult for us to maintain the spending limit.

Table 3.1. Frequency distribution of alternative investment objectives

Investment objective	Proportion (%)
A: Maximize long-term total return at an acceptable level of risk	38
B: Long-term preservation of capital with a reasonable and predictable level of income	23
C: Maintain and enhance the real value of endowment and spending while minimizing risk	20
D: Preserve real value of endowment after spending 4.5%	3
E: Maximize a sustainable spending target	3
F: Aim to finance expenditure at a sustainable rate of 4%, allow the endowment to grow by more than wage inflation, and achieve all this at an acceptable rate of risk	3
G: Protect and grow the endowment on a long-term basis. Within that risk framework, aim to maximize return while ensuring a proactive SRI stance	3
ns: Investment objective not specified	7

We are exercising very stringent controls over our level of spending. Over a five-year period, we have an idea of what we have to cut in order to stay within our objective. We have projected forward our likely growth in income. If anything, we expect our income level to get worse. So, we are examining whether we need to cut certain expenditures or amalgamate with other colleges to curtail some costs. Also, the dilemma we face in setting our asset allocation is, taking into account our spending policy, whether our current allocation to bonds and cash is justified.

Table 3.1 provides a breakdown of definitions of investment objectives as enunciated by Oxbridge institutions. Some of the definitions reflect expected return from investments rather than investment objectives based on endowment purposes. While the definitions may have been expressed diversely, reflecting attention to detail rather than adopting generalized principles, they share broadly similar characteristics.

Over one-third (38 per cent) of respondents believed in maximizing long-term total return at an acceptable level of risk; and just under one-quarter (23 per cent) of respondents aimed for long-term capital preservation with a reasonable and predictable level of income. Twenty per cent of respondents wished to maintain and enhance the real value of endowment assets and spending while minimizing risk. These three investment objectives accounted for the bulk (81 per cent) of definitions. Of the remaining institutions, some wanted to preserve real value of endowment after spending 4.5 per cent of the endowment's value annually (3 per cent), others wished to maximize a sustainable spending target (3 per cent), and some aimed to finance expenditure at a sustainable rate while allowing the endowment to grow by more than wage inflation and achieve all this at an acceptable rate of risk (3 per cent). Just 3 per cent of Colleges included SRI considerations while defining their investment objective while 7 per cent indicated having no formally defined investment objective.

Some Colleges may not have formally defined investment objectives, but when asked about their investment aims, most bursars presented a clear rationale on which their investment decisions were based. In the words of one bursar: 'We have a three-fold aim of financing the College expenditure at a reasonable rate (a sustainable rate of 4 per cent), to allow the endowment capital to grow by more than the relevant rate of inflation [wage inflation rather than Retail Price Index (RPI)] and to achieve all this at a level of risk that the Governing Body can tolerate.' For another, the aim was to 'protect the real value of the capital while achieving gross annual income and a total return over a three-year rolling period in the upper half of the spread of the WM Charity Index.' Some objectives, expressed more succinctly, are a desire to 'grow the endowment' or simply to 'maximize sustainable income'.

Oxbridge investment objectives versus size of endowment

An analysis of the effect of endowment size on the definition of the Oxbridge Colleges' investment objectives is shown in Table 3.2.

Over twice as many Colleges with smaller endowments (26 per cent) reported the desire to maximize their long-term total return at an acceptable level of risk compared to richer institutions (11 per cent). Larger endowments (those with assets over £100 million) reported fairly similar investment objectives. For example, of the 13 per cent of Colleges in this category, stated investment objectives were split between maximizing long-term total return at an acceptable level of risk (7 per cent) and maintaining and enhancing the real value of endowment and spending while minimizing risk (5 per cent).

Table 3.2. Investment objectives (from Table 3.1) versus endowment size

Endowment size	A	B	C	D	E	F	G	ns	Total
£100–750 m	7	—	5	—	—	—	—	2	13
£50–100 m	5	7	2	—	2	3	—	2	20
Total > £50 m	**11**	**7**	**7**	**—**	**2**	**3**	**—**	**3**	**33**
£25–50 m	8	8	5	—	2	—	3	2	28
£10–25 m	10	7	7	2	—	—	—	—	25
< £10 m	8	2	2	2	—	—	—	2	15
Total < £50 m	**26**	**16**	**13**	**3**	**2**	**—**	**3**	**3**	**67**
Grand total	**38**	**23**	**20**	**3**	**3**	**3**	**3**	**7**	**100**

Objectives from Table 3.1. A = Maximize long-term total return at acceptable risk. B = Long-term capital preservation with predictable income. C = Maintain real value while minimizing risk. D = Preserve real value after drawing 4.5%. E = Maximize sustainable spending. F = Maintain sustainable spending at 4% plus real endowment growth. G = Grow the endowment, with an SRI stance. ns = Not specified.

The remaining Colleges with endowment assets worth above £100 million indicated not having a formal investment objective.

Among Colleges with smaller endowments or those with assets worth less than £50 million (over two-thirds, or 67 per cent, of respondents), About one-quarter (26 per cent) of all these institutions expressed the desire to maximize long-term total return at an acceptable level of risk; another 16 per cent, or over twice as many as among the richer Colleges, aimed for long-term preservation of capital with a reasonable and predictable level of income. A further 13 per cent of the less wealthy Colleges, but twice as many as Colleges with assets over £50 million, aimed for maintaining and enhancing the real value of endowment and spending while minimizing risk. While there appeared no strong correlation between reported investment objectives and endowment size, Colleges with smaller endowments were more interested in maximizing long-term investment returns.

Investment objective definition: Comparison with the United States

While most Oxbridge bursars defined their investment objective more qualitatively, the 2005 *Commonfund Benchmarks Study: Foundations and Operating Charities* suggests that investment objectives among US institutions were defined in more quantitative terms. For example, respondents most often indicated the objective was to outperform a specific benchmark, followed by a goal of exceeding a minimum rate of return; some indicated outperforming the peer group as the objective. Overall in 2004, 65 per cent of reporting institutions said their investment objective was to outperform a specific benchmark, up from 37 per cent in 2003. About 30 per cent reported their objective was to earn a minimum rate of return, a decline from 34 per cent the previous year. The average reported minimum rate of return was 7 per cent, down from 8 per cent in 2003.

About one-quarter (21 per cent) of US foundations reported their investment objective was to outperform a minimum 5 per cent rate of return; a fall from 24 per cent of respondents in 2003. Some respondents (16 per cent) wished to outperform a group of peer foundations. A striking feature of this data is the dramatic increase in those who sought to outperform a benchmark. Apparently, the focus of many managers during poor return environments is to make a minimum rate of return, while in better times the focus shifts to comparing returns to a benchmark or a peer group's return.

These findings also varied according to size of fund, with 38 per cent of the largest foundations (over $1 billion) reporting their objective was to earn a minimum 5 per cent rate of return, and a further 28 per cent reporting they aimed to earn a minimum rate of return with 5.7 per cent being the average reported minimum rate, down from 7.1 per cent a year ago. Interestingly, 34 per cent of smaller foundations ($50–100 million) reported their investment objective was to earn a minimum rate of return (similar to 38 per cent in 2003), with an average reported minimum of 7.8 per cent (also similar to the 7.9 per cent target reported in 2003). Another significant development was that more of the largest foundations reported their objective was to outperform a group of peer foundations (28 per cent), compared with the smaller foundation (10 per cent). In the previous year, the number of foundations with assets over $1 billion aiming to outperform a group of peer foundations as an investment objective was 0 per cent.

Among those foundations whose objective was to outperform a specific benchmark, the indexes cited varied, though over one-third (37 per cent) reported using a composite blend of benchmarks, while one-quarter (24 per cent) reported using 'various' indices as their benchmark. The specific benchmarks included a mix of the S&P, Russell, and Lehman Aggregate Bond Indexes, with a substantial proportion of respondents reporting 'Other' benchmarks. As portfolios become more diversified and complex, foundation managers have also turned to creating composite indexes to track their performance more accurately.[5]

Some of the more sophisticated examples among endowments whose investment objective is to outperform a specific benchmark include Harvard and Yale. In the case of HMC, the management of its GIA, a pooled fund that consists primarily of endowment assets, is the Policy Portfolio or the long-term asset mix that is most likely to meet the University's long-term return goals with the appropriate level of risk. It serves as the benchmark against which the performance of the actual portfolio is measured. Thus, the investment objective in the case of HMC is to outperform the Policy Portfolio benchmark, which is specific to Harvard.

Harvard Management Company's Policy Portfolio is a well-diversified portfolio with an attractive expected return-to-risk ratio. The Policy Portfolio for 2004, for example, included a higher allocation to foreign securities and commodity-based assets and a lower allocation to domestic fixed-income assets than the typical institutional fund in the United States. While performance is measured against the Policy Portfolio, the actual asset mix in the portfolio may differ from the Policy Portfolio for tactical reasons leading to HMC outperforming its benchmark. For instance, if domestic equities are perceived to be overvalued, the actual portfolio may hold less of it than the Policy Portfolio. The Policy Portfolio is regularly reviewed and modified in the light of experience and changing circumstances.[6] Thus, defining the investment objective as demonstrated in the case of HMC also involves defining related issues within the investment process.

Investment return target

Implicit in every asset allocation decision is an expected return target. Similarly, in defining the investment return target, institutions must first determine the appropriate asset allocation. Because investment management involves as much art as science, qualitative judgements play as important a role in portfolio decisions as purely quantitative ones. The definition of asset class, for example, can be subjective, requiring distinctions that may be difficult to quantify. Returns and correlations are difficult to forecast. Historical data on which a lot of quantitative analysis is based can only provide a guide, and need to be modified from time to time to recognize structural changes and adjust for anomalous periods. Quantitative measures may also find it difficult to incorporate factors such as market liquidity or the impact of low-probability but significant outcomes. Thus, the best asset allocation decisions often combine with quantitative process qualitative judgements.

According to the review of investment policy of the Yale Endowment in 2004, the target mix of assets produced 'an expected real (after inflation) long-term growth rate of 6.2 per cent with a risk (standard deviation of returns) of 11.7 per cent.' This is Yale's expected return target based on its investment policy, which consisted of a 26 per cent allocation to absolute return assets compared to a current target allocation of 25 per cent; 19 per cent to real assets compared to a target of 20 per cent, 14.5 per cent to private equity compared to a 17.5 per cent target; 15 per cent each to domestic and foreign equity, more or less in line with target; and 7.5 per cent to fixed-income assets, also in line with target. Primarily because of shortfalls relative to the target in private equity holdings, the actual allocation as indicated in the report was to produce a portfolio expected to grow at 5.8 per cent with a risk of 11.1 per cent.

Yale's measure of inflation is based on a basket of goods and services specific to higher education that tends to exceed the Consumer Price Index by approximately 1 per cent. The report also states: 'The need to provide resources for current operations as well as preserve purchasing power of assets dictates investing for high returns, causing the Endowment to be biased toward equity. In addition, the University's vulnerability to inflation further directs the Endowment away from fixed income and toward equity instruments. Hence, 92.5 per cent of the Endowment is targeted for investment in some form of equity, through holdings of domestic and international securities, real assets, and private equity.'[7]

Some institutions in Oxford and Cambridge define their expected investment return target concisely, though others remain imprecise. The answers elicited in response to: 'What sort of return the Colleges were aiming for?' ranged from non-specific, qualitative observations to more formally developed, quantitative ones. Not all institutions reveal their expected return target. The Annual Report of the HMC, for example, does not state its expected return target; only that the Policy Portfolio reflects its long-term return goals with the appropriate level of risk. The level of transparency that Oxbridge institutions wish to adopt varies among institutions. While the Colleges have been criticized for their lack of transparency in governance and management issues, this study benefited greatly from the openness with which our questions were addressed.

According to one institution, for example, with no specific return target: 'We do not have a specific return target nor do we have an income target. When you have 28.5 per cent of the endowment in property, you do not operate as you would when you have an equity oriented portfolio.' According to another bursar, also with a non-specific return target: 'We don't believe in setting return targets because you can't control both returns and risk, and we prefer to control risk.' While half the responses incorporate 'risk' when defining investment objectives, only one senior Cambridge bursar responded with a direct reference to risk when asked about return. Worth noting that both the Colleges cited above are among the wealthiest in Oxbridge and both have considerable property investments.

There appears to be a low correlation between size of endowment assets and investment return targets among Oxbridge institutions. Of the small (11 per cent) number of institutions with assets above £100 million, there was an equal distribution in defining investment return targets—ranging from those that were benchmark driven to others applying variable measures of inflation, from targets that did not refer to inflation at all to others concentrating on risk rather than return. Some 8 per cent of institutions with assets above £50 million aimed at an investment return target of 4–5 per cent in real terms.

Almost twice as many Colleges with smaller endowments also aimed at a similar rate of return—that is 4–5 per cent real annually. While none of the Colleges with larger endowments aimed at 3–4 per cent real return, 13 per cent of the smaller institutions did. Also, over twice as many Colleges with smaller endowments were not specific about their return targets compared with those with larger endowment funds. A small number (8 per cent) of Colleges aimed at an expected return target of above 5 per cent real; over half of these institutions had assets worth less than £50 million.

Oxbridge institutions with smaller-sized endowments reported greater willingness to seek higher rates of return at an 'acceptable' level of risk. If they are seeking higher returns, this might be accomplished without any increase in risk if they are better able to reduce risk through diversification, but smaller funds are unlikely to be in a position to diversify more effectively than their larger counterparts. If they aim to control costs better, this might also enhance returns, but again this is less plausible for small funds. It appears that the Colleges with smaller endowments are willing (or say they are willing) to take more risk than their larger counterparts, at least up to a point.

Table 3.3 shows the distribution of responses among the participants with reference to investment return targets.

Less than one-quarter of Colleges (23 per cent) aimed at an investment return target of 4–5 per cent in real terms. Among those expressing the return target in real terms, some measured inflation by the RPI, others by the Higher Education Pay and Prices Index (HEPPI). Some 20 per cent of respondents did not specify whether the returns they wanted were nominal or real.

In one Oxford College, where the Investment Bursar was responsible for managing the portfolio, the College secured 12.5 per cent annual compound growth over 40 years—that is since 1966, when the bursar took over the portfolio. 'I retire in a years' time,' said Mr Roger Van Noorden of Hertford College, Oxford: 'Whether we can sustain that level of return remains to be seen. Also, whether the sort of return we have seen from equities in the past will be available in the future is far from certain.' When asked about the real rate of return, Mr Van Noorden, thoughtfully added: 'Our long-term return net of dividend income is 7.75 per cent annually; we could have invested in the index and secured similar returns.' Not many investment professionals would have the humility to admit that active management does not always pay off.

The Colleges however are unanimous in their agreement that their expected return targets are to be achieved mainly through investment performance rather than fund-raising, for example, or via sale of assets not currently included in the endowment, such as operational assets, specifically property. Thus, the emphasis is on securing sustainable investment returns. One bursar pointed out that they examine 'alpha and beta exposure' in their portfolios. Alpha, in the terminology he was using, is the fund's relative-to-benchmark return, while beta is the underlying return achieved by the fund's benchmark. According to another bursar, sustainable income or the long-term yield of the portfolio was the key, while market volatility was not an issue:

The number we have come up with is something like 3 per cent. If you factor in inflation at 2 per cent (Oxford inflation is higher than Retail Price Index. So, for example, our salaries will rise by 2 per cent), we need a total return of 5 per cent. If you then look at long-term returns in various asset classes, we assume 5.5 per cent real return from equities, 4.5 per cent from property and 2 per cent from cash. As we have a high percentage in property, a return target of 3 per cent looks sustainable. We need to protect our endowment in the long term. We initially looked at the FTSE yield, which was 3.6 per cent in 1995, and so we thought we had a sustainable surplus. As the yields fell, we had a large deficit.

We were also not differentiating between property and equity. We have a more sophisticated model now, and we smooth our spending over five years. Currently we have a large deficit on the educational account of over £1 million, which includes all aspects of providing education at the College—including salary of

Table 3.3. Investment return targets and endowment size

Target	>£100 m	£75–100 m	£50–75 m	All > £50 m	£25–50 m	£10–25 m	<£10 m	All < £50 m	Total
Non-specific	—	2	2	3	2	3	2	7	10
Prefer to control risk	2	—	—	2	—	—	—	—	2
Income and growth	—	—	—	—	—	2	3	5	5
Benchmark driven	3	—	—	3	3	—	3	5	8
5.5–6.5% real	2	2	—	3	2	3	2	5	8
4–5% real	2	3	3	8	8	5	2	15	23
3–4% real	—	—	—	—	8	3	2	13	13
2% real	—	2	—	2	—	—	—	2	2
12% annual	—	—	—	—	2	—	—	2	2
7% nominal	—	—	2	2	—	2	2	3	5
6–7%	—	—	—	—	—	2	—	2	2
5–6%	2	—	2	5	—	3	2	3	5
3–4%	—	—	3	—	5	2	2	8	13
RPI + 2.5	—	—	—	—	—	—	2	2	2
HEPPI + 1	2	—	—	2	—	—	2	—	2
Total	**11**	**8**	**11**	**31**	**30**	**25**	**15**	**69**	**100**

RPI = Retail Price Index; HEPPI = Higher Education Pay and Prices Index.

tutors and student rent. The endowment currently plugs the educational deficit. Most Colleges have been hit by what we call a triple-whammy and have had to adjust to a loss of ACT (Advanced Corporation Tax), which in our case was substantial. We had the fee reduction, which cost us a further £100,000 and we also had an increase in the College's contribution to the University.

Taking into account the similarity of overall objectives among Oxbridge institutions, the level of dispersion in stated expected return target reveals that these institutions do not engage in decision-making that mimics the peer group. It is conceivable that their individual differences may dissipate within a few years due to an array of factors, such as Colleges merging their endowments to gain efficiencies, the greater influence of investment consultants in the decision-making process, and/or changes in the governance of these institutions' endowments. The scale of dispersion in asset allocation as seen among Oxbridge institutions is unlikely to be seen in the pension fund sector or even among larger and more established endowments and foundations that hold diversified portfolios. Looking forward, apparent inefficiencies among the Colleges are likely to decline over the next decade or so; at the same time, these institutions may also loose the diversity of approaches that is in essence the necessary ingredient of efficient and well-functioning markets.

Total return versus income

Until relatively recently, 'income-only' spending rules were mandatory in the UK. Consequently, Oxbridge institutions invested for income, which dictated asset allocation choices as well. Many foundations, endowments, and charities continue to invest for income. While funds constrained by asset mix are diminishing following the Trustee Act 2000, there exists a clear demarcation among institutions that prefer a discretionary (unconstrained) benchmark and those that opt for a distinct level of yield or monetary target. Clarification of spending rules pertaining to income and capital helped in adopting a 'total return' approach, where expenditure could be financed from the sale of assets without the need to secure it only through income. According to one Oxford bursar: 'An endowment management policy centred on the concept of a regular percentage rate of drawdown from the asset base removes the need for an income/capital gain distinction.'

When asked specifically whether the investment policy of the College endowment was geared towards total return or income, 70 per cent of institutions indicated a commitment to total return, although in some of these Colleges the policy was still to be implemented. By 2003–4, more institutions had adopted the new approach with 86 per cent of Colleges in Oxford reporting a total return policy in their annual reports and accounts compared with

83

52 per cent in Cambridge. As these institutions had, and still have, significant property assets, rental income continues to play a key role in investment strategy. The other factor driving investment policy was that dividend income was exempt from tax. The abolition of tax credits on dividends along with the Trustee Act 2000 accelerated the decline of funds constrained by asset mix.

The shift towards a total return approach frees asset allocation policy from income considerations. The ability to spend capital to meet annual funding requirement was critical for investors to focus on long-term asset allocation. Such an approach also made it possible to invest in overseas equity, private equity assets, or implement absolute return strategies, all of which typically yield no dividend. A total return approach facilitates long-term investors to focus on securing the highest returns available at any acceptable level of risk by diversifying the portfolio into a wider range of asset classes instead of having to investing strictly in high-yielding assets to deliver income.

It would be naive to suggest there is no connection between the spending decision and asset allocation strategy; in basic terms, one cannot plan to spend 5 per cent of assets annually and invest in a strategy with a return target of less than that. To spend 5 per cent without depletion of capital, one must invest to receive the required spending target adjusted for inflation. As returns vary from year to year, most institutions smooth their spending rate by spreading it over a few years—that is spend X per cent of assets equally weighted over Y number of years or some other weighting formula that helps in smoothing out fluctuations in the value of assets from year to year. To spend 5 per cent, assuming inflation rate of 2.5 per cent, a 7.5 per cent minimum annual nominal return is required if the endowment is to maintain its long-term value in real terms while providing a requisite flow of income. The major difference between a total return and income approach under such a scenario is that the fund's asset allocation is not limited to a single asset class such as high-yielding securities and bonds that deliver a minimum annual income of 7.5 per cent.

An investment approach where the institution depends on income from the endowment for its annual spending may distort asset allocation and long-term returns. While institutions in Oxford and Cambridge currently have a total return investment policy, it is a fairly recent development. Unlike endowments in the United States that invariably adopt a total return approach, many foundations and endowments in the UK invest for income. It is worth pointing out that while a total return approach plays a significant role in unshackling asset allocation from income constraints, it is not a substitute per se for efficient asset allocation or securing higher investment returns. Over the last 15 years, for example, funds in the WM Charity Fund Universe pursuing a 'high yield' strategy fared better than those with an 'unconstrained' one. Thus, understanding the nature of investment markets and trends in long-term returns is vital to appropriate asset allocation decisions.

As institutions in the United States and the UK operated in different investment environments, it is perhaps not unusual for differences in their approaches. One determining factor of US institutional returns has been its equity market, which has different characteristics and returns from the equity market in the UK. Over the last two decades, for example, US dividend growth has been less than might have been expected given the outstanding performance of its equity market. Part of the explanation for lower yields and dividend growth could be that companies have shifted away from paying dividends. The changing nature of US firms, caused by the explosion of IPOs by smaller, growth-oriented stocks that rarely pay dividends, may be partly attributed to tax considerations. While aggregate dividend payments do not seem to have fallen, US stock repurchases appear to complement dividend payouts, which have declined.[8] Such trends appear in the UK market but are less marked than in the United States. Recent tax changes in the UK may drive its equity market to resemble that of the United States.

While year-to-year market performance is driven by capital appreciation, long-term returns are heavily influenced by reinvested dividends. The difference in terminal wealth arising from reinvested income is large. Let us consider two benefactors, each of whom set up an identically managed equity trust fund at the start of the twentieth century with an initial investment of $1 each. One fund pays out all its income to beneficiaries, while the other reinvests its income. By the end of 2000, the latter would have appreciated to $16,797, representing an annualized nominal return of 10.1 or 6.7 per cent in real terms. Over the 101 years the accumulator would have amassed wealth 85 times larger than the spender, who would have ended up with assets worth $198, representing an annualized capital gain of 5.4 per cent. It is clear that total return from equities grows cumulatively larger than the capital appreciation. This effect is not specific to the United States but holds true for every market around the world. The longer the investment period, the more important is dividend income.[9]

Reflecting these differences in markets and constraints placed on investors, it is not surprising that philanthropic institutions in the UK, who are genuinely long-term investors, also opted for income-oriented strategies. The

Table 3.4. Frequency of citing total return versus income-oriented policy, in per cent

Institution	Total return	Income	All
Oxford	86	14	100
Cambridge	52	48	100
Oxbridge	**71**	**29**	**100**

move towards total return investing is a recent development, and some institutions remain sceptical about its advantages. Table 3.4 provides a breakdown of responses with regard to total return versus 'income' orientation among Oxbridge institutions. It shows, for example that 71 per cent of all institutions in Oxford and Cambridge reported using total return investment strategies in 2003–4. More Colleges in Oxford (86 per cent) reported such an approach compared with just over half (52 per cent) the Colleges in Cambridge. Data for Oxford Colleges are from the *University of Oxford, Financial Statement of the Colleges, 2003–4*. Data for Cambridge Colleges are from *Cambridge University Reporter, Accounts of the Colleges, 2003–4*.

While 86 per cent of Colleges in Oxford reported a total return policy in 2003–4, 73 per cent had done so in the previous year compared with about half during the course of our one-to-one meetings with bursars. A closer look at the published accounts of 2002–3 reveals that 58 per cent of Colleges in Oxford derived 50 per cent or more of their endowment revaluation gains from income while 42 per cent of Colleges disclosed more than half of the gains made in their endowment portfolios via capital appreciation. Taking into account the large property holdings in Oxbridge portfolios, a further analysis shows that 63 per cent of the gains were made through property revaluations compared with 37 per cent from securities. As security markets improved in 2003–4, gains from property revaluations declined, but still constituted 56 per cent of endowment appreciation for the year. Comparative data were not available for Cambridge Colleges.

Under a third of Oxbridge Colleges (29 per cent) continued to adopt an income driven investment policy; 14 per cent of Colleges in Oxford compared with almost half (48 per cent) the Colleges in Cambridge. A couple of Cambridge Colleges even reported switching from total return and/or 'growth' policy to one based on income. According to one bursar: 'It used to be a total return policy for the Corporate fund and income for the Trust fund. As the Statutes did not actually permit a total return policy for the Corporate assets, the College reverted to an income related policy for both the Corporate and Trust assets.' This College proposed to revert back to a total return policy once the College Statutes enabled it to do so. Another College was forced to move from a total return policy to an income-oriented one when half the endowment assets were diverted towards the development of the College buildings, making it difficult to sustain a total return policy.

At the initial stages of this study, several Colleges reported a move towards total return investing, though only a third of these institutions had clearly defined policies in place. The remaining Colleges were in the process of making the transition from income to total return; some by changing their College statutes first. It is worth noting that those Colleges better able to endorse a total return policy have relatively high proportion of their endowment assets invested in property. The steady income from property enables them to implement a total return policy with greater confidence than those without the cushion of a secure stream of income. 'We aim at long-term total returns from various asset classes, and ignore current income,' explained the bursar of one College whose endowment income as a proportion of total income is the highest in Oxbridge. The portfolio also has 45 per cent in property.

Although a significant number of Oxbridge institutions indicated a recent move towards implementing a total return approach to asset allocation (more institutions in Oxford than in Cambridge, perhaps due to the presence and influence of investment consultants such as Cambridge Associates), securing a sustainable level of income from the endowment was the paramount consideration from the Colleges' point of view. There was greater emphasis among Cambridge Colleges on securing income, but these institutions also attached greater importance to 'maximizing income', albeit at the conservative end of the risk spectrum. According to one Cambridge bursar:

The baseline objective is 'sustainable income.' Half of our endowment is in Trust funds, and most of the Trust funds have very specific needs. Hence, providing a sustainable level of income is what the funds are for. As a result, that is what we need to secure from our endowment and Trust funds. In nurturing the income, we have to take considerable account of the capital. Personally, I am not entirely persuaded that investing on a total return basis does fulfil that.

For another Oxford bursar: 'Our objective in managing the fund is not to achieve maximum total return, but to look at what we can do with our endowment to support the College's income requirement. Of course, we do not want investment objectives that destroy our long-term capital, but our primary objective is to service the College's income requirements.' Since the appointment of Vice-Chancellor, Professor Alison Richard, Cambridge University elected to move towards implementing a total return policy. While the transition from income to total return will take a few years to be embedded, Oxbridge institutions are in the midst of major changes. The momentum of change has accelerated greatly since we began our study; at the same time, these institutions remain highly cautious of change, particularly when it comes to greater sharing and public disclosure of information.

Role of endowment income

Analysis of the contribution of endowment income to total income among Colleges in Oxford and Cambridge indicates that the endowment plays a significant role in sustaining operations. The average ratio of annual income from the endowment to total income for Oxford Colleges, as disclosed in their Income and Expenditure Accounts, was 34 per cent in 2003–4 and 35 per cent in 2002–3. The ratio for Cambridge Colleges was similar, though the amount of investment income was higher for Cambridge Colleges at £82 million in 2003–4 compared with £72 million for Oxford Colleges.

As the Colleges have now moved to total return policy, the way in which they account for 'investment income' has also changed; total return includes income and capital gains. As the Colleges do not report uniformly, differentiating income and capital gains, simply adding reported capital gains to endowment income as reported in the income and expenditure accounts may result in double counting. As very few Colleges reported capital sales to realize income for their operations, in our analysis we have used the numbers for income from the endowment investments and total income as stated in the income and expenditure accounts of these institutions.

The role of endowment income in sustaining the operations of the two universities, on the other hand, remains insignificant. For the Colleges, the level of support received from the endowment is closer to what Yale and Harvard receive from their endowments. But the contribution of income from endowments to the total income of the universities of Oxford and Cambridge is less than 10 per cent. Recent changes in government funding along with volatile stock markets encouraged institutions in Oxford and Cambridge to build a more diverse income base. While other sources of income increased, contribution of endowment income also rose. Some 12 per cent of Colleges receive more than half their total annual income from the endowment, though the majority (62 per cent) of Oxbridge institutions still receive around 30 per cent of their total annual income from endowment assets.

According to the 2005 survey by the Commonfund Institute, the average percentage of operating budgets funded by endowment income declined in the United States among educational institutions, from 13 per cent in 2003 to 11 per cent in 2004. This was attributed to factors such as 'cuts to operating budgets during a year of improved returns and hefty increases in tuition income. The percentage funded grew at the largest institutions— from 13 per cent to 15 per cent—while shrinking significantly at smaller institutions—10 per cent to 7 per cent—and the smallest—10 per cent to 3 per cent.' The radical reduction in spending among schools with smallest endowments appeared to be a combination of a delayed reaction to the decline in the market value of their endowment during the bear market and their lower dependence on endowment income for their current operations. Overall, 17 per cent of institutions in the United States reported increases in the percentage of operating budget funded by endowment income, while 41 per cent reported a decline and 36 per cent reported no change.[10]

Independent educational institutions in the United States rely heavily on their endowments, drawing from them more than a quarter of their operating budgets. Thus, the Yale Endowment's contribution to the university's operating revenues grew from 28 per cent in the fiscal year 2002 to 31 per cent in

Table 3.5. Proportion of total income derived from endowment, in per cent

Proportion	Oxford	Cambridge	Oxbridge
<5%	3	6	4
5–10%	16	13	15
10–20%	24	23	24
20–30%	16	23	19
30–40%	11	19	15
40–50%	16	6	12
50–60%	3	6	4
60–70%	5	—	3
70–80%	—	—	—
80–90%	3	3	3
>90%	3	—	1
Total	**100**	**100**	**100**

Data for Oxford colleges are from the *University of Oxford, Financial Statement of the Colleges 2003–4*. Data for Cambridge Colleges are from *Cambridge University Reporter, Accounts of the Colleges*, 2003–4.

2004, and is expected to contribute 32 per cent of projected revenues in 2005. Endowment income distributed for operations is now Harvard's largest source of income, consisting almost a third (31 per cent) of total income. Just 10 years ago, in 1994, the Harvard Endowment supported 21 per cent of total income. In 1994, Yale endowment's contribution to the university's total revenues was 14 per cent compared to almost a third today.

The contribution of endowments in Oxford and Cambridge in sustaining institutional objectives has also grown considerably over the past several decades, but not as benignly as their counterparts in the United States. Oxbridge College endowments play a key role in supporting operations when compared with other higher educational institutions in the UK, whose endowment income contributed on average less than 2 per cent to total income and expenditure (1.47 per cent and 1.49 per cent, respectively).

Table 3.5 provides a breakdown of the proportion of income derived from the endowment by institutions in Oxford and Cambridge. Over one-third (38 per cent) of these institutions derive over 30 per cent of their overall income from the endowment. The two universities derive under 5 per cent of income from the endowment; a similar number of Colleges receive 80–90 per cent of their income from the endowment with All Souls deriving over 90 per cent of its income from its endowment. On average, Oxbridge Colleges derive about one-third of income from the endowment.

When compared with the contribution that endowments make to other higher educational institutions in the UK, those of the universities of Oxford and Cambridge rank among the top. As noted previously in Table 1.5, if the

Table 3.6. Endowment and interest income as percentage of total Income

Top 10 UK institutions	2004	2003
Royal Academy of Music	16.6	21.5
University of Wales	11.1	11.2
Royal College of Music	10.5	8.4
University of Oxford	8.1	7.0
University of Surrey	6.2	7.1
Royal College of Art	5.0	4.2
University of Cambridge	4.4	10.9
University of London	3.8	5.3
Royal Scottish Academy of Music and Drama	3.4	2.3
London School of Economics	3.0	1.5

Source: Higher Education Financial Yearbook 2003, 2005–6.

endowments of their constituent Colleges are included, they are the largest endowments in the country and make the highest contribution to the overall income of these institutions. Table 3.6 lists the top 10 higher educational institutions in the UK with the highest ratios of endowment income to total income.

It is worth noting that the level of support obtained from the endowment is low, ranging from 16.6 per cent (down from 21.5 per cent in 2003) for the Royal Academy of Music to just 3.0 per cent for the London School of Economics (up from 1.5 per cent). Even the two universities of Cambridge and Oxford depend considerably less on income from the endowment for their activities. Colleges in Oxford and Cambridge are therefore unique in receiving a significant level of support from the endowment. Such a high level of support for operations from internal resources and investments is rare in the UK or in Europe. There are a few secondary educational institutions in the UK such as Christ's Hospital, which depend on the endowment for significant support. Christ's Hospital, for example, derived 72 per cent of its income from the endowment in 2004–5.

When asked how important it was for the current level of contribution from endowment to sustain College activities, the responses uniformly emphasized the importance of the endowment to the Colleges' overall finances and operations. There was no correlation, for example, between the level of income received from the endowment and the perceived degree of its importance to the institution. Thus, a College deriving over 90 per cent of its income from the endowment gave the same response, 'Critical', as another receiving less than 10 per cent of income from endowment. Eighty-two per cent of respondents suggested endowment income as being Critical, 'Very Important', or 'Quite Important' in sustaining the current level of endowment income contribution towards the total income or being able to improve on that, regardless of their dependency on the endowment.

Table 3.7. Importance of endowment income, in per cent

Importance	Oxford	Cambridge	Oxbridge
Critical	18	7	25
Very important	20	25	44
Quite important	8	5	13
Relatively important	2	0	2
Building the endowment	8	5	13
Improve income	0	3	3
All	**56**	**44**	**100**

Institutions in Oxford and Cambridge are fully aware of the role that endowments play in sustaining their objectives and operations. Table 3.7 provides an account of the perceived importance of endowment income to Oxbridge Colleges.

Few (3 per cent) respondents, all in Cambridge, expressed a clear need to improve the level of endowment income. One bursar wishing to improve endowment income said: 'We need to be able to improve the level of contribution from the endowment to secure the College's long term viability.' That College derived 15 per cent of its income from the endowment. In another College, where the endowment provides over a quarter (27 per cent) of total income, the bursar pointed out:

The current income stream of 3.4 per cent of endowment assets enables us to bridge the gap between the College's annual expenditure and income derived from students and is used to fund teaching, bursaries, awards and prizes, the maintenance and upkeep and improvement of College buildings and facilities as well as for certain specific purposes designated by donors. As fee income continues to decline there will be need to increase expendable income from the investment portfolio by roughly 0.1 per cent per annum over the next 5 years.

Among Colleges in Oxford and Cambridge that stated they were in the process of building up their endowments, for one bursar endowment income was 'not critical to our current finances as we are cash generative from other operations, but it is critically important to our strategic aim of building the endowment for the future in order to preserve institutional freedom.' Another College, also building up its endowment to be admitted as a full College by the University, and currently not dependant on endowment income to support its operations, was in the advantageous position of running several successful business operations. Colleges appear to have in place a variety of strategies to fund their long-term objectives. Endowment accumulation served these institutions to secure a greater level of independence in both determining and fulfilling their objectives.

Table 3.8. Peterhouse College revenues and expenditures, as per cent of total income

Income or expense	Component	1970	2003
Endowment income	Property rents	23	54
	Dividends and interest	6	8
	Trust income	1	1
	Costs	(5)	(13)
	Subtotal	**25**	**50**
Endowment expenses	University tax	(2)	(2)
	Master and Fellows	(5)	(7)
	Surplus on endowment	**18**	**41**
Operating income	Teaching and support	26	17
	Accommodation and kitchen	32	18
Operating expenses	Teaching and support	(28)	(31)
	Accommodation and kitchen	(26)	(34)
	Building maintenance	(22)	(24)
	Surplus (deficit)	**(0)**	**(11)**

Source: Andrew Murison (2005).

Most bursars pointed out that with student fees failing to keep pace with the true cost of delivering teaching and support services such as accommodation and kitchen charges, the burden on the endowment in bridging that gap has increased substantially over the years. According to Andrew Murison, the role of endowment income in the management of the operations of Peterhouse, for example, increased significantly over the years, as revenue from other sources declined.

Table 3.8 compares the revenue and expenditure composition of Peterhouse in 1970 and 2003, expressed as a percentage of total income.

Despite the raised contribution from the endowment, Peterhouse had an operational deficit of £0.85 million in 2002–3. As Murison explained:

A comparison of the relative contributions of income and expenditure to the College's cash flow in 1970 and 2003 shows that the increased contribution from the endowment (an increase of 23 [percentage points] of total income, from 18 per cent to 41 per cent) has failed to stem the decline in the contribution from College tuition fees and charges, which have fallen by a similar amount (a decline of 23 per cent from 58 per cent to 35 per cent).

Regardless of the bibulous and sybaritic reputations of College Fellows beloved by novelists, their costs remain modest (7 per cent of income in 2003, compared to 5 per cent in 1970), mainly because of the below-average earnings that the intellectually most brilliant people in the country are supposed to live off these days. Despite the surplus of endowment income being used entirely to subsidise the student body, it is still not sufficient to prevent an overall deficit that has risen steadily from the 1980s to reach 11 per cent of total income. Thus, the burden on the endowment to perform, the pressure to reduce student subsidies and the drive to lower costs (and quality) has increased substantially over recent decades. The Peterhouse endowment has had to meet more than its share of the soaring cost burden in recent years not through new benefactions, unfortunately, but almost wholly as a result of capital appreciation and rising income.

Conclusion

It is worth noting that in the *University of Oxford, Financial Statement of the Colleges, 2002–3* and *2003–4*, most Colleges reported within a given format, including items such as Status, Objects, Governance, Scope of financial statements, Review of operations, Report of the Governing Body, Investment performance, Reserves, and Risk management. No specific reference was made to Investment objectives. Investment performance, for example, is typically described without reference to any stated investment objective or benchmark. Sometimes the broad asset allocation is given, but no information is available on 'investment objective' against which 'investment performance' is measured. Clarity in investment objective definition could assist in the overall investment process.

Though not stated explicitly, the Investment Committee of each entity sets performance targets and fund managers are reviewed periodically on such basis. Colleges provide some guidance on their investment strategy in the published accounts. Sample disclosures include:

- The College maintains an investment strategy committed to diversification, both in terms of asset classes and geographic spread, along with a relatively low risk profile, due to the importance it places on the preservation of capital. It seeks to achieve the highest total return in any asset class commensurate with the risk profile of such asset. (All Souls College)

Some definitions are open-ended:

- Endowment funds are invested in assets which fundamentally underpin and sustain the operations of the College at the desired level of activity in the long term. (Merton College)

Some disclosures relating to investment strategy serve as a proxy for 'stated investment objective' and are defined in terms of the spending rate:

- The investment strategy for endowment assets is to produce income equivalent to a spend rate of between 3.5 per cent and 4.5 per cent of asset value per annum while also preserving the real value of capital. (New College)

- In order to sustain the College's general level of activity into the future, the College has set itself the target of growing the endowment by 2 per cent in real terms per annum. (The Queen's College)
- The investment strategy for endowment assets is to allow expenditure of at least 3 per cent of the endowment per annum. (Trinity College)
- Investment Subcommittee pursues a total return policy for the investment of endowment and uses as its benchmark a long-term real return of 4.5 per cent. (St Catherine's College)
- The Investment Committee pursues a risk-averse investment policy, which is designed to preserve or increase the real value of the endowment over the long term while generating an income yield of 3 to 4 per cent. (Lady Margaret Hall)

The two Colleges with disclosures that include a stated investment objective are:

- The Investment Committee pursues a total investment return (from income and capital combined) objective of at least 4.2 per cent in real terms taking one year with another. The main portfolio of stocks and shares yielded a total investment return of 5.2 per cent in nominal and 2.1 per cent in real terms. (St Edmund Hall)

The other investment objectives as enunciated by University College states:

- Funding current spending at an appropriate drawing rate; our guideline rate is a maximum of 4 per cent of a rolling 3-year average of endowment and general reserves;
- Growing the capital sufficiently in the long term to keep pace with our own inflation rate; our guideline rate is Retail Price Inflation + 2 per cent p.a.;
- Seeking to earn additional returns to contribute to the cost of capital expenditure on functional assets.

Three Cambridge Colleges, as reported in the *Cambridge University Reporter: Accounts of the Colleges* for the year ended 30 June 2004, include a 'Statement of Investment Principles' (SIP). These definitions vary between Colleges. Churchill College, for example, lists 12 items under its SIP describing broadly what the College invests in, how the investment policy is determined, the composition of the Investment Advisory Committee, the benchmark for performance measurement, etc. The investment return target is not specified, but suggested as 'the Fund is invested to optimise total return.' The SIP also states: 'for the last five years, distributions [from the fund] have consisted wholly of income.'[11]

The SIP of Clare Hall sets out broad principles that govern its investment policy. The stated objectives of Clare Hall's Investment Fund are:

- Payment of an annual dividend which grows at a rate at least equal to the annual rate of rise in College costs, measured, inter alia, by reference to the HEPPI; and
- The maximum total return which is consistent with this objective and with an acceptable risk exposure.[12]

Downing College lists six items under its SIP, stating that the College 'manages its investments in securities and property to produce the highest return consistent with the preservation of capital value in real terms for the long term. A subsidiary aim is to enhance the value of the capital for future beneficiaries.' The SIP also includes information on the role of the Investment Committee in setting asset allocation while it delegates the management to Morgan Stanley Private Wealth Management, whose mandate 'is to achieve a real return of 4.5 per cent on a five year basis, using the long-term UK service sector wage inflation index to calculate inflation.'[13] Some SIPs include SRI policies; others do not. Even those institutions with a SRI stance state that the interests of the College are in general best served by seeking to obtain the best financial return from investment consistent with commercial prudence.

In the United States, institutional policy features typically include the investment objective of the institution, asset allocation strategy, how endowment earnings/returns relate to spending policy, investment performance benchmarks, the degree of risk in the investment pool, whether or how the investment portfolio should be rebalanced to maintain the asset allocation target, as well as considerations in hiring and retaining investment managers. However, such information is not uniformly supplied by US institutions; nor are they always defined quantitatively. Many definitions remain qualitative, providing some guidance.

The level of disclosure by educational endowments in the UK, in the form of annual reports or accounts, is lower as there is no requirement by them to do so. Nor is such information readily available for larger foundations and endowments, though some information on asset allocation is increasingly being made available. The Wellcome Trust, the largest foundation in the UK with a high level of transparency in its reports and accounts, provides information on asset allocation, investment objectives, spending policy, overall investment performance and lists its asset managers. But, there is no disclosure on the degree of risk in the investment pool, how the investment portfolio should be rebalanced, if at all, to maintain the asset allocation target, or considerations in hiring and retaining investment managers.

However, this level of voluntary disclosure is virtually unknown among US institutions such as Yale and Harvard, though nearly all (96.8 per cent) of US educational endowments formally address investment objectives in their investment policy, compared to 3 per cent that address those issues informally. Just 0.3 per cent of institutions participating in the 2004 *NACUBO Endowment Study* had no formal or informal policy in the way they defined investment objectives. Additionally, 96.1 per cent of endowments formally cover asset allocation strategy in their investment policy statements, compared to 3.5 per cent addressing these issues informally and 0.4 per cent with no formal or informal definitions. Among endowments with assets over $1 billion, 98 per cent defined their investment objectives formally while 93 per cent defined their asset allocation policy formally.

As far as covering how investment earnings or returns relate to spending policy, 85.8 per cent of institutions formally cover such issues in their investment policy statements compared to 8.6 per cent that address it informally and 5.6 per cent with no formal or informal coverage. Slightly more institutions (88.5 per cent) include investment performance benchmarks formally compared to 9.6 per cent informally; 1.9 per cent of institutions do not cover such issues formally or informally. These four aspects of investment policy—investment objectives, asset allocation strategy, performance benchmarks, and how investment returns relate to current spending policy—appear to be the core elements used to establish best practices for endowment management guidelines among educational institutions in the United States.

In an apparent shift in investment policy, only 54.5 per cent of institutions reported having a formal policy for the degree of risk in the investment pool in 2004, down from 82.3 per cent in 2003. Approximately one-third of respondents (32 per cent) reported no policy at all on risk in the investment pool. The cause of such a shift in policy was not available. Public institutions are more likely than independent institutions to have formal policies on these issues, while the latter are more likely to have an informal policy. Interestingly enough, the larger endowments with more than $1 billion in assets are more likely than smaller endowments to report having an informal policy for most policy features. Also, 40 per cent of larger endowments reported having no policy whatsoever for the degree of risk in the investment pool.[14]

Endowment income is critical in underpinning the activities of Oxbridge institutions; over two-thirds of Colleges acknowledge such contribution as being critical in sustaining the overall educational objective. Endowment income as a proportion of total income varies significantly among Colleges, from a high of 94 per cent (All Souls in Oxford) to a low of less than 5 per cent (Harris Manchester in Oxford and Wolfson in Cambridge). About half (46 per cent) of Oxbridge institutions derive 20–50 per cent of their overall income from endowment assets, while one quarter (24 per cent) receive 10–20 per cent of total income from the endowment. The average contribution of endowment income is higher in Oxford than in Cambridge.

Aiming to improve endowment performance even by 1 per cent would yield substantial returns for these institutions in aggregate.

Institutions with large, independent, well-managed endowments confirm that it remains the key to delivering objectives, which are supported by funds that are released within the spending rules. The main objective of educational endowments could be stated as providing adequate spending for current and future beneficiaries while not eroding the principal corpus of the endowment. Litvack, Malkiel, and Quandt (1974) suggest that endowed institutions should separate the investment management decisions from the spending decisions; that they should adopt a spending rule that protects the real value of the corpus of the endowment fund and aim to provide stable spendable endowment income for the institution.[15] The separation of the investment decision from the spending decision enables an institution to protect the real value of its endowment while providing a stable source of income.

Institutions in Oxford and Cambridge recognize the advantages of such a separation. The switch to total return policies from income-based ones will help in achieving such clarification in investment approach. Many Colleges have amended their statutes to reflect their new status as investors. The recently published accounts contain a lot of financial information about the Colleges, which is a major development in their governance. But information on endowment management is not readily available. These institutions could benefit from clearer enunciation of issues addressing how endowment returns relate to spending policies, investment performance benchmarks, the degree of risk in the investment pool, whether or how the investment portfolio should be rebalanced to maintain the asset allocation target, as well as considerations in hiring and retaining investment managers.

4

Spending policy

Introduction

Most endowments aim to preserve purchasing power in perpetuity while providing necessary support to the current operating budget. Trustees need to deal with these conflicting goals successfully. As Swensen points out, 'the high-risk, high-return investment policy best suited to serve asset preservation conflicts with the low-risk, low-return investment approach more likely to produce stable distributions to the operating budget. By specifying the trade-off between the desire for purchasing power preservation and the hope for stability of flows to fund operations, spending policies determine the degree to which endowments meet the needs of current and future generations.'[1] The concept of purchasing power preservation with provision of stable source of revenue to the operating budget is fundamental to establishing intergenerational equity, which essentially means that the endowment should be able to support the same set of activities it is supporting today indefinitely. Whether endowments are able to do so is the challenge that its managers and trustees face.

Surprisingly, a low proportion of trustees in the charitable sector in the UK made the connection between spending and investment performance. According to a survey conducted by Watson Wyatt, an investment consultancy services provider, in the UK around 45 per cent of the trustees of operating charities did not have a view on what the optimal rate of disbursement for a charity similar to theirs should be. In contrast to the United States, where foundations must pay out 5 per cent of their assets every year, the UK regulator of charities, The Charity Commission, provides little guidance on how, or even whether, charities should set a long-term expenditure target. Some 20 per cent of trustees of pure grant-making institutions were unfamiliar with the concept. And, among those who did have a view, it was not consistent, though most UK grants-making institutions tended to choose long-run targets in excess of 4 per cent.[2] Spending rates among top 500 registered charities in the UK ranges between 1 and 5.5 per cent of assets.

The concept of a spending policy, prevalent among major endowments and foundations in the United States, is relatively new among Oxbridge institutions. Until recently, they were able to spend only income; not unlike Yale and Harvard in the 1960s when those universities also limited their endowment's annual contribution to the operating budget to investment yield—the interest, dividend, and rental income. As stated by an experienced Chairman of a major Investment Committee:

Before I came to Oxford, I had never heard of spending rule or sustainable income as we call it here. It is a savings rule, if you think what it is all about. What most of us are trying to do is how best to allocate funds and how much to spend each year. While one knew about asset allocation, one did not know much about spending policy. Having spent some time now thinking about these matters, and with input from our Consultant, what we have now is a sort of a dividend rule, which says we should aim to increase our dividends each year by 3.5 per cent to continue to carry on our activities at more or less the same level.

One of the major challenges for endowed institutions is how best to maintain the level of spending in the long term, particularly during adverse market conditions. The risk for the institution lies not necessarily in the changes in the capital value of its endowment but ability of the endowment to provide the level of spending the institution is accustomed to. Therefore, spending rules minimizing the volatility of spending are favoured by institutions that depend on the endowment for sustaining their operational activities. Sensitivity of the institution to such a shortfall inevitably influences spending policy. A higher spending rate, for example, bears a greater shortfall risk. And a lower rate gives an institution greater flexibility to maintain spending during difficult conditions. These decisions also influence overall asset allocation. At the same time, a low rate of spending can be interpreted as benefiting future generations while too high a rate can be seen as favouring current beneficiaries. Thus, spending rules aim to maintain intergenerational equity.

Educational institutions consistently aim to maximize the stability of real spending over the long term as real value gets eroded during periods of low returns or high inflation; both factors lying beyond the control of endowments and foundations. As educational programmes or grants are ongoing and cannot be cut randomly, the need to maintain spending during bear markets and recessions is greater for such institutions. The challenge therefore lies in setting a spending policy that weathers unfavourable market and economic cycles. As these institutions also have a very long-term investment horizon, they have the flexibility of spending more of their endowment in difficult times. These institutions often adopt 'contrarian' spending policies to cushion the negative effects of market downturns.

An average 3.5–4 per cent spending rate among Oxbridge Colleges is a more conservative strategy than at corresponding US Colleges, which have spent on average 5 per cent over the past decade. Over the past 10 years, spending rates in the United States slowly but steadily increased from an average of 4.5 per cent in 1995 to 5.0 per cent in 2004 for all institutions participating in the 2004 NACUBO Endowment Study (NES).[3] A target spending rate serves as a guide in determining an endowment's ability to maintain intergenerational equity with higher rates indicating a bias towards the current generation of students and faculty and lower rates favouring future generations. While some foundations can opt to favour current beneficiaries, trustees of educational institutions have a fiduciary responsibility towards protecting the future as much as the present.

Today, the concept of a spending policy is widely understood among Oxbridge institutions though the methodology used in making withdrawals varies among institutions. The majority (92 per cent) of Oxbridge Colleges have a spending rule. Even those Colleges without a spending rule are in the process of formulating one. Only a minority suggested there was no need for such a policy. According to the bursar of one of Oxbridge's richest Colleges, 'the size of our endowment and the income from it does not constrain the College's expenditure. Also, our real return has not declined much. So, we do not have a spending policy.' This College's reported total annual income exceeded expenditure in the financial year ending 2001.

By 2003, however, its expenditure had risen considerably leaving the College with an operational deficit; total income had fallen to 93 per cent of total expenditure. During this period, endowment income as a portion of total income rose from 60 to 65 per cent. Though total income rose by 42 per cent, expenditure rose by 54 per cent. When such increases in expenditure occur within a relatively short space of time without matching rise in non-endowment income, some of that deficit is financed by higher contributions from reserves and/or the endowment. Lacking a well-defined spending rule, fluctuations in budgetary balance can be subject to manipulation though there is no suggestion that was the case in this instance. By 2004, the College's total income once again outstripped expenditure. As a wealthy College, it was able to regain a balance in its operations fairly swiftly. That may not always be an option for less wealthy institutions.

According to another College bursar, without a clearly defined spending rule, 'The College spends about £5 million annually. The total endowment is about £100 million, and it provides the bulk of the College's income and expenditure. If that income declines, then the College's activities also get curtailed. We do not have a spending policy.' This College spent between 4.5 and 5 per cent of its endowment assets over the last several years. When pressed further, the bursar added: 'We could assume a spending rate of 4 per cent of trailing 12-quarter average market value of the endowment.'

An approach where the operating budget is left open to fluctuations in income resulting in the curtailment of College activities is not ideal. It also

Table 4.1. Date when the current spending policy was established

Established	Oxford	Cambridge	Oxbridge
25 years ago	—	2	2
Several years ago	23	21	44
1994	—	2	2
1998	2	—	2
1999	3	3	7
2000	2	—	2
2001	3	3	7
2002	7	7	13
2003	8	3	11
Recent	—	3	3
Being set up	3	—	3
No spending policy	5	—	5
Total	**56**	**44**	**100**

reveals a greater willingness to sacrifice current activities rather than spend more of endowment income to bridge the deficit. At the same time, if an institution is willing to spend more than it can afford, even over a short period to sustain operations, it may be difficult for it to recover its equilibrium in terms of maintaining the real value of its long-term spending and capital.

Based on feedback from Oxbridge institutions, Table 4.1 illustrates the length of time current spending policies were reported to have been in place.

About 44 per cent of institutions suggested that current policy had been in existence for several years. However, a similar number said their spending policy was established more recently—that is post-1998. One Cambridge institution indicated its spending policy as being in place for at least a quarter of a century, if not longer. At the other extreme, two Colleges, both in Oxford, reported having no spending policy, nor did they indicate any plans to establish one within the foreseeable future.

Notwithstanding the positive returns reported by institutions during 2004, spending from the endowment remains the most controversial, challenging and discussed item on the agenda of investment committees. The bear market of 2000–3 focused institutional thinking on the Holy Grail of endowment management—how best to maintain the purchasing power of the endowment in perpetuity—causing institutions to seek better long-term solutions. Historically, Colleges in Oxford and Cambridge did not have formal spending policies; from time to time, special appropriations over and above the normal level of income were made to sustain operations. Even among US institutions with defined spending policies, exceeding the limit set by the institution 'is nothing new in the education business. Endowments have been viewed as a source of ready cash and emergency funds since their inception. However, the use of special appropriations to fund unplanned needs, if done on a regular and recurring basis, can have a corrosive effect on an institution's finances and undermine the discipline needed to maintain a long-term spending policy.'[4]

Spending and investment policies assist in supporting the purposes for which institutions have endowments. They help in determining issues in long-term asset allocation. Governing bodies of Colleges face the challenge in balancing the conflicting goals of supporting current operations and preserving endowment assets. Donors also expect their gifts to provide permanent support towards a specific activity, though Colleges usually prefer undesignated or general donations. New gifts add to the range of activities that Colleges are obliged to support in the long term, enlarging the size of the investment portfolio. Spending policies act as referees in the perpetual game between current and future players. A clearly defined spending policy also frees up the asset allocation decisions and enables the fund manager to focus on investment issues.

The spending rate

Traditionally, Colleges in Oxford and Cambridge targeted a certain level of annual expenditure adjusted for inflation rather than define an annual rate of drawdown from their endowment. As they were mandated to spend only income, their asset allocation was dictated by the needs of the annual operating budget. In the short term, a high yield, income-oriented policy delivers predictable distributions from the endowment. According to one bursar: 'We set budgets every year and in recent years have, because of the cash/spending requirements of the College, had to spend all the income we have earned. We cannot spend permanent capital, so deficits have been financed by a combination of spending expendable capital (of which we have a small amount) and "borrowing" capital from ourselves.'

A policy of providing fixed amounts to the operating budget annually can work reasonably well when market conditions are also stable. In times of abnormal, uncertain, volatile or hostile market conditions, such a policy can affect the long-term value of the endowment. Also, during periods of high inflation coupled with bear markets, spending at a level independent of the value of assets can result in permanent endowment depletion. By emphasizing budgetary stability, institutions express a clear preference for using the endowment as and when necessary to cushion the effects of changes in other sources of income for its operations.

The Yale endowment in the 1950s, for example, achieved a balance between growth and purchasing power preservation, even registering a 17 per cent surplus by 1959. After keeping pace through the 1960s, the endowment began to suffer with increases in inflationary pressures. During the 1970s, disastrous markets for financial assets and high inflation caused the endowment to end the decade 56 per cent below its target level. By 1982, the endowment reached a low point, with assets representing just 42 per cent of the targeted purchasing power goal. While the 1980s reversed the problems somewhat, it was not until 1994 that the endowment was at its 1950-targeted level, adjusted for inflation and gifts.[5] Though such analysis is not available for Oxbridge institutions, the Yale case illustrates the extent to which purchasing power can be eroded under harsh economic and market conditions, and how difficult it is to recover those losses through investment performance alone.

A spending policy assists in resolving such conflicting demands between competing goals of providing funds today and long-term endowment preservation. Institutions address these issues individually. Even Yale followed a practice of distributing for current expenditure its income generated in the form of interest, dividends, and rent. It was not until the mid-1960s that Yale began spending 'a prudent portion of the appreciation in market value', and noted two reasons for changing its policy:

First, it is only by coincidence that Yield will be a correct balance between the present and the future.... Second, when Yield is the sole measure of what can be spent for present needs, a situation of annually increasing needs, such as has been obtained for many years seems likely to continue for many more, forces investment policy to seek to improve current Yield. But this, in turn, under market conditions prevailing most of the time since World War II, could only be done at the loss of some potential Gain.[6]

In 1967, recognizing that simply spending yield could result in too high or too low a spending rate and could bias investment decisions towards securities with high-yield but low appreciation potential, Yale adopted a 'total return' spending policy. Under such a policy, the University supported operations with current yield plus a prudent portion of the appreciation of Endowment market value. Yale put in place a formal method, called the University Equation, to calculate the total amount that could responsibly be withdrawn from the Endowment annually. Under this method, spending in a given year was set by adjusting the previous year's spending by the difference between the University's long-term investment return and the current percentage of the Endowment being spent. Higher long-term returns would lead to higher annual spending, while lower long-term returns would lead to reduced spending. Unfortunately, this method based on the University's prior 20-year investment return, did not adjust rapidly enough to changes in the endowment's current market value. As a result, in the 1970s, when the rate of inflation increased and market returns dropped, the University spent an unusually high portion of its endowment to support current operations.

A decade later, in 1977, realizing that the rate of spending was eroding the real value of the Endowment, the Yale Corporation voted to cap spending at the existing level (adjusted for inflation) until the spending rate was brought in line with the expected real (after-inflation) return from the Endowment, which was taken to be 4.5 per cent in line with historical experience. In 1982, when the spending rate was at a more realistic level, the Corporation attempted to change the spending rule with a view to producing substantial income for current beneficiaries while preserving purchasing power parity for future generations. This new rule stipulated the Endowment spend the weighted average of 70 per cent of the previous year's spending, adjusted for inflation, plus 30 per cent of the targeted long-term spending rate of 4.5 per cent applied to the previous year's Endowment market value. The 70 per cent weight on prior year's spending promised budgetary stability, while the 30 per cent weight on current market value provided purchasing power sensitivity.

Since 1982, Yale's spending rule has been adjusted three times. In 1992, the Corporation authorized an increase in the long-term spending rate from 4.5 per cent to 4.75 per cent. In 1995, the target rate was raised to 5.0 per cent, and in 2004, it was increased again to 5.25 per cent; the smoothing rule was also altered from 70/30 to 80/20. The increase in the rate of spending resulted from improvement in Endowment portfolio characteristics. The change in weight assigned to budgetary stability stemmed from the recognition that higher budgetary dependence on Endowment income required stability in flows from Endowment to sustain operations.[7] Like any policy, spending rules need to be examined in light of altered circumstances and changed accordingly. Yale's history of spending illustrates the sort of challenges that institutions must face in arriving at individual solutions.

The most common spending rules can be broadly categorized under three definitions: spend all income, spend a fixed percentage of the moving average market value of the endowment, spend a constant amount each year that is adjusted for inflation. Each of these methods of determining the rate of spending influences asset allocation. Traditionally most Oxbridge institutions spent income as they were required to do so. The move towards embracing a total return investment policy, while simultaneously defining a spending policy, is a recent one; and at the time of this study was still being implemented by the Colleges. As Yale's spending history suggests, it may take some time to arrive at an optimal rule, though Oxbridge institutions, in addressing spending policy issues in the aftermath of a bear market coupled with the wealth of evidence from across the Atlantic, may have an advantage.

As shown in Table 4.2, many Oxbridge institutions were still in the process of moving away from income-only policies. When asked how spending policy relates to endowment income, 75 per cent of Oxbridge institutions said they spend only income derived from the endowment. A further 15 per cent indicated no correlation between spending policy and endowment income. There were four Colleges (7 per cent) that ignored income from the endowment in determining their spending and asset allocation decisions. They also ignored such income in planning their operating budgets. Among these Colleges, two

Table 4.2. Relationship between spending policy and endowment income

Policy	Oxford	Cambridge	Oxbridge
Ignore endowment income	3	3	7
Spend endowment income	39	36	75
No relationship	11	3	15
Aligned	2	2	3
Total	**56**	**44**	**100**

in Oxford have relatively large holdings in property in their endowment portfolio, from which they derive a stable source of income. The remaining two Colleges, both Cambridge, do not depend on endowment income for their operations; these Colleges reported they were building up their endowment assets.

As these institutions were traditionally obliged to spend only income (though they are no longer required to do so), many Colleges continued with such practice. Yet half (57 per cent) the participants reported no correlation between their asset allocation and spending decisions, while 43 per cent of respondents said spending policy influenced asset allocation. Among institutions that indicated the existence of some connection between spending and allocation of assets, there were both income-only investors as well as those adopting the total return approach. One bursar was of the view that their spending policy did not influence asset allocation, although he believed it should. 'The current asset allocation is something I inherited', he added. 'I have not yet made any major policy changes, although we are in the process of changing that.'

There were clearly some inconsistencies in the responses to this question, as Colleges with income-driven investment objectives claimed their spending policy did not affect their asset allocation, while some with total return investment policies claimed it did. One bursar with no formally defined spending policy suggested that it influenced their asset allocation. There were others more considered in their response, who as total return investors faced a dilemma in setting asset allocation: whether or not their 'current allocation to bonds and cash was justified, taking into account our spending policy?' In general, there existed an awareness of the need to address such issues. But, ways in which these issues were addressed appeared very distinctive, varying enormously among Colleges as they were at various stages of making the transition from income-only spending policy to a total return one.

It may take some time for these institutions to arrive at appropriate spending rules, but the ability to switch from spending 'only income' to both 'capital and income' has enabled Colleges to examine their overall approach to endowment management. In one case, the College adopted a new investment policy triggered by their ability to spend capital and not just income. It is difficult to judge whether this approach is the optimal one, but in the words of the College bursar:

We plan to spend 3 per cent of the value of the endowment on a rolling five-year average when it is necessary to do so. Historically, we have been spending our accounting income or the dividends and other such income we receive from our investments, which has typically been around 2 per cent of the endowment assets. We have been running deficits in our College budget and hence the decision to take more out of the endowment. Thus, the switch to spend not just income, but a percentage of the total value of the endowment is a recent one. During the course of last summer, we had a series of meetings and discussions about these matters, and that prompted a switch in our investment management strategy from active to passive.

It is not clear from the above statement whether the higher spending rate was arrived on the basis of long-term expected returns from UK equities adjusted for inflation. A spending rate of 2 per cent was significantly below the Oxbridge average, where two-thirds of institutions annually spend between 3 and 4 per cent. Further analysis reveals that the College did not depend on endowment income for its operations; endowment income was less than 10 per cent of total income in 2004. Smaller institutions are sometimes more flexible in their spending from the endowment, as they are less dependent on income from the endowment for their operations. They are also better able to restrain spending when faced with a difficult funding environment. The ability to adjust spending based on economic conditions and the needs of the institution fulfils one of the major purposes of endowments, that is to provide a level of support in times of economic uncertainty or volatility. Typically, spending as a percentage of the endowment tends to rise when endowment values decline due to fall in market valuations, and fall when endowment values recover with markets.

Spending rate and size of endowment

Unless there is a regulatory requirement to spend a certain percentage of endowed assets, spending rates can vary enormously, and the correlation between size of assets and rate of spending can be weak. In some instances, the size of the endowment can influence the spending rate as a lower rate of spending for a wealthy institution translates to a significantly higher absolute amount of spending for another institution with a higher spend rate but a much smaller endowment. At the same time, institutions with large endowments tend to depend more on the endowment for income compared to those with smaller endowments. Thus, the relationship between spending and

Table 4.3. Spending rate and endowment size

Endowment size	NP	2–3%	3%	3–4%	4%	4–5%	5%	5–6%	6–7%	Other	Total
>£100 m	2	—	—	3	2	3	—	—	—	2	11
£75–100 m	—	—	2	2		3	—	—	—	—	8
£50–75 m	2	—	—	5	3	2	—	—	—	—	11
All >£50 m	**3**	**—**	**2**	**10**	**7**	**8**	**—**	**—**	**—**	**2**	**31**
£25–50 m	2	2	3	15	8	—	—	—	—	—	30
£10–25 m	2	2	2	5	8	3	—	—	2	2	25
<£10 m	2	—	—	3	3	5	—	—	—	2	15
All <£50 m	**5**	**3**	**5**	**23**	**19**	**8**	**—**	**—**	**2**	**3**	**69**
Grand total	**8**	**3**	**7**	**33**	**26**	**16**	**—**	**—**	**2**	**5**	**100**

NP = No Policy.

endowment wealth is defined by the individual institution; it is also reviewed periodically to reflect the new set of circumstances.

Table 4.3 provides a breakdown of the reported rate of spending among Oxbridge institutions.

As rates of spending are not uniformly disclosed by Oxbridge institutions, either in the annual accounts or in any other document in the public domain, this analysis is based on information provided via the questionnaire. While it captures the relationship between size of endowment and rate of spending over a single year, the conclusions are no less valid. Table 4.3 illustrates that Colleges in Oxford and Cambridge with smaller endowments spent more of their endowment value in percentage terms. Over twice as many of the less well-endowed Colleges (23 per cent) spent 3–4 per cent of their endowment assets annually compared to their richer peer group (10 per cent). Similarly, 19 per cent of the less well off Colleges spent 4 per cent of endowment assets annually compared with 7 per cent of their richer peer group. Thus, twice as many Colleges with smaller endowments (29 per cent) spent 4 per cent or more compared with the richer ones (15 per cent). It is not surprising as Colleges with larger endowments are capable of providing substantial support for their operations by spending a smaller proportion of their endowment. As Colleges are not obliged to spend a fixed amount annually, the richer Colleges are able to provide substantial support for their operations without having to spend a larger portion of their endowment assets.

Results of the 2004 *NACUBO Endowment Study* show an average spending rate of 5.0 per cent with most institutions using a 3-year moving or rolling average market value approach and with larger endowments spending a smaller percentage of their assets than smaller endowments. Over the last decade, average annual spending rates rose steadily from 4.5 per cent in 1995 to 5 per cent in 2004. Public institutions reported lower spending rates compared to independent institutions for every year during that period. The year 2004 also marked the widest gap between reported spending rates among public (4.3 per cent) and independent (5.3 per cent) institutions. For public institutions, the 2004 spending rate was the lowest since 1997, while the rate for independent institutions was the highest over the past 10 years.[8]

According to the *Commonfund Benchmarks Study: Educational Endowment Report, 2005*, the average spending rate reported in the Study was 4.8 per cent, down from 5.1 per cent in 2002. The largest institutions spent at a higher rate than smaller ones: 5.1 per cent for those with assets over $1 billion compared with 3.5 per cent among those with assets under $10 million. 'The reason for this would appear to be the higher dependence on endowment income among larger institutions, a factor that can have negative effect in times of economic stress when other sources of revenue, such as government funding, are declining. Smaller institutions, on the other hand, are more often dependent upon gift flows and less dependent on endowment income, and can cut back on spending more quickly when faced with market declines or when they wish to rebuild their endowment after such a period of decline.'[9]

Fifty-two per cent of US educational foundations reported they made no changes to their spending rate in the past year; meaning that nearly half did. The Commonfund Study shows that over a 2- or 3-year period, a large proportion of institutions made 'changes to their spending rate. No doubt they are trying to adjust to changing economic and budget conditions at their institutions. Thirty-one per cent decreased their spending rate and 14 per cent increased their rate. The largest institutions report having increased their rate most often (31 per cent), while the smallest institutions report having increased it least often (9 per cent).'[10]

According to the *Commonfund Benchmarks Study: Foundations and Operating Charities Report*, 2005, which monitors community, private, and public foundations in the United States, the average spending rate in 2004 among the participating foundations was 5.8 per cent, down from 6.3 per cent in 2003 and 6.0 per cent in 2002. This may have been due to improving financial circumstances of grantees as charitable giving improved in most non-profit sectors. It may also signal recognition that consistent spending above 6 per cent annually will cause private/independent foundations to eventually go out of business in the absence of further additions to their funds.[11]

Community, private, and public foundations support different spending rules compared to educational institutions, which have different sources of income and wish to sustain their operations in perpetuity. Not all US endowments and foundations have to adhere to the IRS minimum 5 per cent spending rule. The 5 per cent spending rule for charitable institutions in the United States applies to private foundations defined by the IRS as institutions deriving the majority of their funding from a limited number of sources. Public foundations and university endowments are exempt from the 5 per cent rule. Just over one-third (35 per cent) of foundations in the

Commonfund Benchmarks Study, 2005, for example, report their spending rule as meeting the IRS minimum of 5 per cent. Smoothing the flow of spending is a challenge for private foundations, given the complexity of formulas and ratios legally required to calculate the rate of spending. Almost half (46 per cent) the institutions said they spend a percentage of a moving average each year.[12]

While the average 5 per cent spending rate among educational endowments in the United States exceeds the average spending at Oxbridge institutions, spending among Colleges is in line with other major endowments and charities in the UK. The Wellcome Trust, Britain's largest endowment and the largest biomedical charity in the world with an asset base of £10.6 billion in 2004, spends on average 3–4 per cent of its endowment assets annually. Spending as a proportion of the Trust's asset base over a 3-year rolling average (equally weighted) was 3.5 per cent over the past decade or so. Expenditure targets for the Trust may be over or under spent in any given year, reflecting the nature of its long-term commitments.

Not all educational institutions in the United States regularly spend over 5 per cent of their endowment assets annually. Harvard's spending rate, for example, was 4.5 per cent in 2004, 4.9 per cent in 2003, and 5.1 per cent in 2002, up from 4.8 per cent in 2001 and 3.3 per cent in 2000. Harvard University's distribution policies, like other established institutions committed to perpetuating their mission indefinitely, are designed to preserve the value of the endowment in real terms (after inflation) and to generate a predictable stream of spendable income. Endowment investments are managed to achieve the maximum long-term total. As a result of this emphasis on total return, the proportion of the annual income distribution funded by dividend and interest income or by capital gains may vary significantly from year to year. Amounts withdrawn from endowment capital gains to fund the fiscal year 2004 and 2003 distributions for Harvard totalled $644.9 million and $471.7 million respectively.

The portion of investment returns earned on endowment and distributed by Harvard each year is based on a rate that is annually approved by the Corporation. This rate is not set based on a specific formula, nor is it directly tied to current investment returns. Rather it reflects expectations about long-term returns and inflation rates and seeks to maintain the distribution rate at between 4.5 and 5.0 per cent of the market value of the endowment. The annual distribution rate does not mechanically follow annual total return, but is adjusted to reflect the endowment's distribution policies in terms of preserving its long-term value. In 2000, when the endowment's total return was 32.2 per cent, the amount distributed was 3.3 per cent; in 2001, total return declined by 2.7 per cent, while distribution rose to 4.8 per cent. Similarly in 2002, total return was down 0.5 per cent, while distribution from the endowment rose to 5.1 per cent. In 2003, total return picked up to

12.5 per cent and the distribution rate fell to 4.9 per cent; and in 2004, total return was 21.1 per cent while distribution rate was lower at 4.5 per cent. This flexibility to adjust the spending rate enables the University to maintain its long-term value in real terms.[13]

Smoothing mechanism applied in determining spending rate

Most institutions in Oxford and Cambridge have informal, if not formal, spending policies in place today. Those Colleges that do not have a spending policy expect to spend a notional level of income annually from the endowment. At the time of our initial interviews, 30 per cent of respondents had established spending rules which took into account the mechanism to be used in determining the annual rate of spending. Most of these Colleges opted for a specified rate of spending based on rolling, weighted averages of the asset base over a period. The University of Cambridge, in redefining its endowment management process recently, also adopted a Yale style spending rule.

More Oxford and Cambridge institutions have been defining and adopting some form of a spending policy since this study was initiated. There appear to be greater similarities of approaches adopted than differences. As one bursar, in the process of establishing a spending rule, explained: 'I think it will be defined as X per cent of the average valuation over the last N years, where N would probably be 3 and not 10 years. As things stand, we spend all income.' And so did the majority (56 per cent) of Colleges in 2002–3; they typically spent income and dipped into reserves as and when required. In the 2003–4 published accounts of Oxford and Cambridge Colleges, 86 per cent reported 'total return' policies in Oxford compared to 50 per cent of Colleges in Cambridge. As Cambridge institutions have recently moved towards total return investing, the latest 2004–5 accounts reflect comprehensive implementation of total return policies.

Table 4.4 gives a breakdown of the distribution of the rolling market value averages employed by Oxbridge institutions (26 per cent) that had a defined spending policy formula in place in 2002–3.

Most of these spending formulas were based on endowment market values, equally weighted, over a period. The smoothing formula adopted ranges from 1 year, for 22 per cent of respondents, to 6 years for half as many institutions (11 per cent); the majority (44 per cent) adopted a 3-year equally weighted moving average market value approach, which is widely used among US educational endowments. As Oxbridge Colleges were required to spend income until very recently, their spending was constrained by the level of income available from interest, dividends, and rents received from the endowment portfolio. As the data suggest, just a quarter of institutions, mostly in Oxford,

Table 4.4. Interval over which spending rate is smoothed, in per cent

Interval	Oxford	Cambridge	Oxbridge
1 year	11	11	22
2 years	—	—	—
3 years	17	28	44
4 years	6	—	6
5 years	17	—	17
6 years	6	6	11
All	**56**	**44**	**100**

had made the transition from income to total return. The majority of these institutions also conducted that process of change with guidance from their investment consultant. The low usage of investment consultants within the Oxbridge community, compared to the pension fund sector, was remarkable. While smaller charities in the UK were unlikely to employ an investment consultant, the larger ones typically do so.

Today, a larger proportion of Oxbridge institutions have adopted total return policies and employ relatively more sophisticated approaches to their spending and investment processes. One College described a distribution policy based on a smoothing formula spread over a 4-year period with decreasing weights attached, with a different mix of drawdown from its securities portfolio and its property assets. According to this bursar: 'We spend 3.6 per cent of the 4-year weighted (40, 30, 20, 10) average of the securities portfolio's value, and 4.5 per cent of a similar four-year average of the property portfolio's value.'

Other spending definitions were based on long-term asset returns. One bursar defined the College's spending rate in the following words: 'Assuming a long-term real investment return of 6 per cent, the annual amount taken from the endowment should not exceed 4 per cent of the average of the latest 5 years' year-end market valuations, subject to a floor and a ceiling.' For another: 'The College spends 4 per cent of the 6-year rolling average of its endowment assets. We are moving towards a total return investment policy. In calculating the 6-year average, we use full weight on the last 4 and half weight on the remaining two years.' On the whole, Colleges are putting in place what they consider are sustainable spending policies as they make the transition from income-only spending towards 'total return' policies.

In the United States, the large majority of educational institutions (82.6 per cent) reported using an annual spending rule that represented a pre-specified percentage of the moving average of endowment market values. Independent institutions were more likely (85.1 per cent) to employ such rules compared with public ones (77.0 per cent); also those with larger endowments, over $1 billion in assets, were less inclined to do so. Interestingly, the

Table 4.5. Frequency of spending rules within US educational institutions

Methodology	Proportion (%)
Spend pre-specified percentage of moving average of market values	82.6
Decide on an appropriate rate each year	7.6
Spend a pre-specified percentage of beginning market values	4.3
Increase prior year's spending by a pre-specified percentage	2.1
Spend a pre-specified percentage of current yield	1.5
Spend all current yield	1.4
Increase prior year's spending by the inflation rate	0.5

Source: 2004 NACUBO Study.

largest and the smallest asset size endowments were both less likely to use this spending rule (71.1 per cent in each case). Institutions with assets between $100 million and $500 million were most likely to spend a pre-specified percentage of moving average of market values (88.3 per cent) followed by those with assets between $25 million and 50 million (86.2 per cent) and those between $500 million and $1.0 billion (84.6 per cent).

The largest and the smallest asset size endowments in the United States also shared another characteristic; both reported they prefer to decide on an appropriate rate to spend each year, 15.8 and 14.0 per cent respectively. Only 5.0 per cent of independent institutions reported such a policy, while the average for all the institutions in this category was 7.6 per cent. Institutions with more than $1.0 billion in endowment assets were also more likely to increase prior year's spending by a pre-specified percentage (10.5 per cent). Only 2.6 per cent of the largest endowments increased prior year's spending by the rate of inflation. Less than 2 per cent of institutions spend all current yield.[14]

Table 4.5 summarizes the methodology employed by US institutions in determining the annual spending rule. The table is ranked by the frequency with which each rule is followed.

Institutions across all endowment categories in the United States are far more likely to base their spending policy on a pre-specified percentage of the moving average of market values than on any alternative strategy. According to the *Commonfund Benchmarks Study: Educational Endowment Report, 2005*, 63 per cent of institutions in the US report 'they employ either a three-year or 12-quarter moving average of market value as a smoothing mechanism in their spending formula; 38 per cent use the three-year and 25 per cent use a 12-quarter moving average. It is more common among the largest institutions to use a longer time period (five years) for their moving average, or to report some other spending policy entirely. It is worthy of note that overall 8 per cent decide on an appropriate rate each year, a practice reported by 22 per cent of the smallest institutions. Also, 29 per cent of participants reported changing their spending policy in the past year.'[15]

The recent bear market caused many institutional administrators and boards of trustees to re-evaluate their endowment spending policies. Strategies under consideration in 2003 were: expanding the traditional 3-year-moving-average to a 5-year average; the creation of income stabilization reserves; increasing the prior year's distribution by a fixed percentage each year; and setting minimum and maximum distribution ranges. Severe multi-year bear markets are once-in-a lifetime events. Therefore, institutions should consider the full range of factors influencing investments rather than using the rare event of a bear market as the sole basis for a decision to change their spending practices.[16]

Traditionally, Colleges in Oxford and Cambridge distributed their endowment income to support operations, supplementing other sources of income such as fees and other charges. The aim was to balance the budget over the medium term. When Colleges ran a deficit, they reduced spending; if that was not viable they dipped into College reserves or borrowed from the endowment at zero rate of interest. 'I suppose the way we would argue', explained one bursar 'is that we have built up reserves over the past years. So, there is a certain amount of our capital, which is not endowment capital. Essentially we eat into that or add to it depending on the overall state of our finances. In the late 1990s, we added to it; now we are taking money from it to tide us over.'

As Colleges in Oxford and Cambridge have only recently started developing total return spending policies, they have had the advantage of a bear market cycle in addition to a low inflationary environment as a base to build on. Determining spending rates at the peak of a bull market, for example, or in an inflationary environment imposes a different set of challenges. Some Colleges have minimum and maximum distribution ranges in place as well as stabilization reserves. Though the typical spending rate is around 4 per cent of assets, these ratios appear to be defined individually among institutions. Many spending rates continue to be linked to the yield of the UK stock market rather than to long-term total return target based on a globally diversified portfolio of assets. As institutional investments are spread widely across assets and markets, the bias towards determining spending rates based on the dividend yield of the home market also needs to be addressed.

As one bursar explained the home yield bias: 'As the running yield for the [inflation] index-linked gilt-edged stock 2009 is 2.48 per cent, if it is then accepted that the College can spend 2.48 per cent of its capital with the aim of still protecting its capital against inflation, then the advised spending should not be more than 2.48 per cent—including capital spending and spending directly from endowment income.' Another bursar had a similar view: 'What we spend is close to the FTSE All Share yield. We try to avoid deficits in the College's spending. Thus, if we had no endowment, one would spend 20 per cent less (as that is the income derived from the endowment), or find another source of income. Our investment take from the endowment has been reduced to 3.5 per cent on a three-year moving average.' These observations convey a reasonable level of analysis of the status quo, as well as a high level of prudence; but they are consistent with income-only spending practices. As institutions such as Harvard and Yale currently invest in a significantly wider range of assets, they no longer think in terms of the yield on their investment, but determine their spending rate based on expected long-term return of their portfolio.

It will take some time for institutions in Oxford and Cambridge to make that strategic shift towards total return thinking. A number of Colleges in Cambridge, for example, reported they were 'not allowed' to spend capital as opposed to choosing to spend income. The number of Colleges with total return investment objectives in Cambridge were significantly less than at Oxford at the time of this study. However, Cambridge made a formal transition towards adopting total return policies, and Colleges are in the process of implementing new spending rules. As one bursar explained, referring to their spending policy: 'We take 4 per cent from our endowment assets. We smooth it by adjusting the deficit or the surplus in our budget each year. We are running a deficit at the moment and aim to adjust our budget downwards over the next few years to bring it into balance.' Many Colleges were in a similar position, running operational deficits for the last several years, with the deficits financed from reserves and the endowment. The recovery in market values since 2003 enabled most of these institutions to recover from operating such deficits, particularly in 2004–5.

Spending rate and inflation

In determining the spending rate, institutions typically take into account their internal rate of inflation to achieve their twin goals of providing a consistent flow of revenue to the operating budget while preserving the purchasing power of future generations. Lowering their exposure to volatile changes in market value of their endowment is a dominant concern, as is the need to ensure a stable source of inflation-adjusted income. Two-thirds of Oxbridge spending policies are linked to the institution's internal rate of inflation, which was defined as Retail Price Index (RPI) plus 1 per cent or more. As salary costs comprise the bulk of academic institutional costs, most bursars indicated their internal inflation rate as being higher than RPI (by 0.5 to 2 per cent), depending on the average rate at which academic salaries appreciated.

Table 4.6 shows how respondents defined spending rate with reference to inflation.

Over one-third (36 per cent) of respondents did not refer to inflation when defining the spending rate, though a widespread recognition of higher

Table 4.6. Linkage between spending rate and inflation, in per cent

Link to inflation	Oxford	Cambridge	Oxbridge
Did not refer to inflation	20	16	36
No more than RPI	7	5	11
HEPPI	3	2	5
Oxford inflation	7	8	15
Inflation above RPI	20	13	33
Total	**56**	**44**	**100**

RPI = Retail Price Index; HEPPI = Higher Education Pay and Prices Index.

inflationary pressures within the educational sector was greatly in evidence among the rest of the respondents. Costs for higher education were expected to continue to rise at a rate higher than general inflation. Educational endowments aim to work their assets harder to be able to retain their long-term spending power. Preserving the long-term purchasing power of the endowment requires that assets must grow above the rate of inflation assumed by the institution. According to one Oxford bursar:

The spending policy has been defined in an informal way since I was here and before, but it was formally established a month ago. The 4 per cent figure has been circulating among various Oxford Colleges. Some Estates Bursars get together from time to time, and there are some who advocate 4.5 per cent and others advocate a lower figure. It has always seemed to me that 4 per cent is a reasonable target to aim at, partly of course because one hopes that the total return will be higher than that, but on the other hand many of our costs are salary costs which rise faster than RPI. So you need a growing endowment to cope with salary cost rises. So, if we take 4 per cent, and the endowment actually goes up by 5 per cent in real terms then at least we are safeguarding the future to some extent.

Another Oxford bursar pointed out that as the College 'income was growing slightly lower than Oxford inflation', going forward 'the College faced a problem, as certain expenditures cannot be curtailed'. Roger Van Noorden of Hertford College in Oxford runs what is informally known as the Van Noorden index, based on inflation data collected from among the Oxford Colleges. Most Colleges use the Higher Education Pay and Prices index (HEPPI) in determining expected rates of investment return and spending. In the words of one bursar: 'The way we factor in inflation is reflected in our biggest expenditure, which is of course, salary. Then we also have maintenance costs. For the past few years, our inflation rate has been 3.2–3.5 per cent. We do look at the Van Noorden index, but we may not always agree with its assumptions. So, currently the way the endowment is managed, there is not much room for growing it, or even sustaining it in real terms.'

115

According to another Oxford bursar, defining the College's spending policy with specific reference to inflation, the assumptions were surprisingly different:

The rate of expenditure from endowment is about 3.5 per cent, which comprises almost 60 per cent of the College's total expenditure. Over 50 per cent of expenditure is payroll related (which is rising no more than at the rate of RPI as many of our staff are low-paid and work also on a temporary basis), and repairs, amortisation, cleaning and property-related running costs account for a further 30 per cent. The rate of pay increase is related to pay scales rather than the absolute level of pay. Academic pay tends to increase at a slower rate than non-academic pay, because older academics are retiring and younger ones are being appointed at lower scale points, and because there is no discretion with regard to academic pay which is subject to national 'negotiation'.

The endowment is sufficiently robust to sustain current levels of expenditure for the foreseeable future, but could not withstand significant capital expenditures, or additional ongoing revenue projects. The College is heavily dependent upon endowment, rather than operating revenues, for its survival, and the rate of capital appreciation in endowment is constrained. The College must continue to cultivate other sources of funding. Around 55–60 per cent of the College's annual revenue expenditure has been met from endowment. In order to sustain this level of expenditure, endowment return should be not less than 3.5 per cent.

This bursar was the only Oxbridge bursar to suggest that their College's rate of inflation was lower than RPI. It is widely accepted that educational institutions face different challenges in restraining their expenditures. Cuts in operating budgets were made across the sector as a result of the 2000–3 bear market. While certain inefficiencies have been addressed, it is clear that Colleges do not have significant scope for further reductions in their expenditure without compromising on the quality of their services. Most Colleges seek to enhance returns on their endowments to be able to secure a higher level of support from the endowment.

As one bursar, whose spending rate was relatively high (4.5 per cent) in the Oxbridge context, pointed out: 'In order to spend more, we need to invest aggressively. Holding on to a lot of property, cash and fixed interest does not deliver a 5.8 per cent spending, which the College had been spending historically. So, we had to cut back our spending while altering our asset allocation as well. When the College was rich, it got used to spending at that rate. But, when times changed, that was no longer viable. Portfolios that generate higher returns do not also offer high yields. Hence, changing the asset allocation of the College has been necessary for the long-term viability of the College.' If Colleges are more open to exploring new asset allocation policies that could yield higher long-term returns, it could well support higher spending rates.

In the United States, 14 per cent of participants in the Commonfund Benchmark Study indicated using the Higher Education Price index (HEPI), with 40 per cent of the largest institutions and 6 per cent of the smallest institutions indicating they did so. Very few (5 per cent) independent schools use the index at present, while 18 per cent of private and public institutions reported using HEPI. Among those who use the index, more than half indicated applying it to their budget process, with the smallest institutions most frequently reporting this use (83 per cent) and the largest institutions more often citing other uses, such as determining purchasing power, analysis or comparison, or to explain or rationalize tuition or fee increases. One-third of private foundations indicated they used HEPI in setting spending rates, while all other types of institutions more often used the index in their budget process.[17]

Conclusion

Analysis of endowment income distribution (among the 36 Colleges in Oxford and 25 in Cambridge that published 2003–4 accounts in the SORP format, but excluding the two universities) as a percentage of the market value of the endowment at the end of the previous financial year revealed that endowment spending among Oxford and Cambridge Colleges ranged from a low of 1.7 per cent to a high of 13.0 per cent. All Souls College, for example, distributed £4.4 million in 2003–4; this represented 3.1 per cent of the market value of its endowment at the end of financial year 2002–3. One exception was Templeton College, which reported distributing 29 per cent of its endowment value compared to 67 per cent the previous year.

The average distribution from the endowment was fairly similar—4.1 per cent for Oxford compared to 4.3 per cent for Cambridge. Table 4.7 illustrates how the Colleges in Oxford and Cambridge distributed income from the endowment.

Data for Cambridge Colleges serve as a guide only as the aggregate numbers exclude the contribution of six Colleges with significant endowments; they include Trinity, St John's, Queens', Christ's, and Emmanuel. Overall. 39 per cent of Oxbridge Colleges spent 4–5 per cent of endowment assets; 26 per cent spent over 5 per cent, 23 per cent spent 3–4 per cent, 8 per cent averaged 2–3 per cent while 5 per cent spent less than 2 per cent of assets.

More Colleges in Oxford distributed 4–5 per cent of endowment assets annually compared with Cambridge where the distribution was more evenly spread between Colleges that spend 4–5 per cent and others that distributed 3–4 per cent annually. On average, Cambridge Colleges spent more from the endowment than Oxford Colleges; 92 per cent of Colleges in Cambridge distributed more than 3 per cent of the endowment compared with 83 per cent

117

Table 4.7. Distribution of spending rates, in per cent

Rate	Oxford	Cambridge	Oxbridge
>5%	22.2	24.0	23.1
4–5%	41.7	36.0	38.8
3–4%	19.4	32.0	25.7
2–3%	11.1	4.0	7.6
<2%	5.6	4.0	4.8
Average	**4.1%**	**4.3%**	**4.2%**

Data for Oxford colleges are from the *University of Oxford, Financial Statement of the Colleges, 2003–4.* Data for Cambridge Colleges are from *Cambridge University Reporter, Accounts of the Colleges, 2003–4.*

in Oxford. As the average size of endowments among Cambridge Colleges is also higher, Cambridge institutions tend to spend more in absolute terms as well compared with Colleges in Oxford.

In 2002–3, distribution rates were marginally higher, as market values of endowments were lower in 2002. Stock markets recovered during 2003–4, and with it the equity-oriented portfolios of these institutions, enabling Colleges to distribute less from the endowment to sustain operations. In 2002–3, for example, spending rates among Colleges in Oxford ranged from a low of 2.2 per cent to a high of 11 per cent; the average was 4.2 per cent. In 2002–3, one-quarter of Colleges in Oxford distributed 5 per cent or more of the market value of their endowment during the previous year. About a third (30.6 per cent) of institutions spent 4–5 per cent of the endowment, while a similar number spent 3–4 per cent. About 14 per cent of Colleges spent less (2–3 per cent). Comparative data were not available for Cambridge Colleges. Anecdotal evidence suggests that on average Colleges have been spending 4–5 per cent of income from the endowment over the past several years; thanks to their income-only spending policy in the past. Some Colleges spent significantly more, but such excesses are relatively rare today.

Comparison of spending policy and investment return target for Oxford and Cambridge institutions suggests that distribution rates and expected total return from endowment assets did not have a correlation. More Colleges suggested an average spending rate that was higher than their internal targeted rate of return from the endowment; it was not clear in some instances if the higher rate of inflation among these institutions was accounted for. The numbers reported could be misleading as the majority (75 per cent) reported spending only income without spending any capital.

There are not enough long-term data in the public domain to analyse the extent to which the purchasing power of Oxbridge College endowments have been eroded over, let us say, the last half-century. Such data inevitably exist in the Colleges; hopefully, such information can be accessed and analysed in the future to shed light on the investment and spending practices of these institutions over the past century, if not earlier. In the recent past, there is no evidence to suggest that endowment capital was annually augmented by the combined rate of distribution and inflation. On the contrary, there is evidence that Colleges regularly borrowed from the endowment at preferential rates, typically zero rates of interest. Thus, spending income can be no more prudent than implementing a spending policy that is not linked to investment returns and inflation.

Among institutions participating in the 2004 NES survey in the United States, the spending rate varied from nil to 18.4 per cent of assets with one institution reporting 100 per cent payout. The full-sample average spending rate for 2004 was 5.0 per cent. Over the last decade average annual spending rates increased from 4.5 per cent in 1995 to 5.0 per cent in 2004.[18] The same cannot be said of educational institutions in the UK, where spending was based on income received from the endowment. US institutions also appear to attach greater importance to intergenerational equity issues. Thus, over half (54 per cent) of respondents in the Commonfund Study 2005 reported the principle underlying their spending policy was to maximize the likelihood of achieving intergenerational equity. Thirty-seven per cent reported their aim was to provide a consistent and growing stream of income to the operating budget, while 32 per cent reported spending policy principle was to simply provide a consistent stream of income.[19]

In determining spending policy among educational institutions, it is important to consider not only the needs of current beneficiaries but also that of future generations. The percentage of annual drawdown from the endowment is as important as the need to maximize investment returns at any given level of risk. The methodology used in making such withdrawals is therefore critical as is evident from Yale's experience. Using an annual withdrawal formula simply transmits the market volatility into the operating budget assumptions. Most US institutions use, for example, a rolling 3-year average market value approach resulting in the spending of 5 per cent of the endowment value. There is no hard and fast rule for setting spending policies. As the 2003 *NACUBO Endowment Study* states:

An institution should compare its practices with peer institutions, taking into consideration a number of factors such as endowment size, endowment payout as a percentage of total operating budget, need for income stability, portfolio risk, enrolment growth, and relationship between unrestricted and restricted endowment funds. While the moving market value approach has worked reasonably well, the increased volatility in the capital markets are causing many institutions to consider other distribution approaches that may provide additional stability to their operating budgets. One approach involves the creation of income stabilization reserves; another relies on an automatic increase to the amount distributed during the prior year.

One other important measure relates to endowment per student. A reporting institution's total may include the endowment of its medical school, with a relatively small student population, making the endowment-per-student number much higher than it would be were only the undergraduate programs included. Also enrolment growth should be taken into consideration as sharply rising annual enrolment can quickly reduce the endowment-per-student numbers. Using a carefully selected group of peer institutions, about which one holds certain critical information, makes comparison data much more useful.[20]

Determining a sustainable spending rate is among the key decisions that the Governing Body of a College is responsible for. If an institution places emphasis on its current academic operations alone, then distributions from the endowment may not be adjusted for fluctuations in the market value of investments. At the other extreme, focusing on endowment preservation may mean that funds over and above the rate of inflation alone would be made available for current spending. Setting a sustainable spending rule assists in greater fiscal discipline. The move towards adopting total return policies among institutions in Oxford and Cambridge is a welcome development as Colleges implement asset allocation strategies that focus on long-term returns rather than providing only income. Total return strategies offer opportunities as well as challenges; inappropriate allocation of assets can prove equally detrimental to preserving real value of endowment while providing a stable source of income.

5

Asset allocation

Introduction

Maximizing spending today while preserving the purchasing power of the endowment for posterity is one of the most fascinating challenges for truly long-term investors. Even among institutions with very similar objectives, such as Colleges in Oxford and Cambridge, not to mention the world of foundations, endowments, and charities in general, seemingly minor differences in character result in amazingly diverse purposes and objectives. Investment objectives therefore serve as the framework within which appropriate portfolios are generated. Investors examine combinations of portfolio asset allocations and spending policies to generate a portfolio that best reflects long-term institutional goals.

Most foundations and endowments use a strategic asset allocation approach in arriving at their policy portfolio. They commonly use a quantitative model, which factors in risk, return, and correlation assumptions, leading to an average annual return projection over a market cycle. Several issues influence the overall investment strategy, portfolio management and long-term planning goals. Factors such as the size of an institution's endowment, the spending rate, the mix of restricted and unrestricted funds in the endowment all impact on long-term asset allocation and investment performance. The best investment committees take a long-term view, and ensure that buoyant markets do not mask flawed investment and spending policymaking.

Institutional investors generally consider asset allocation to be critical to investment returns though market timing and security selection also play a role. Studies suggest that more than 90 per cent of variability of institutional portfolio performance is derived from asset allocation; market timing and security selection make at best marginal, often negative, contribution to overall returns.[1] Given the difficulties associated with selecting portfolios of outperforming securities, not to mention getting market timing right, most long-term investors hold broadly diversified portfolios and in general do not engage in highly active trading strategies, though they might include such strategies in their risk allocation. Institutional investor behaviour is therefore responsible for the importance of asset allocation in determining investment returns.

By placing asset allocation at the centre of the investment process, institutions define the essence of their investment policy. In selecting the assets they choose to buy, institutions similarly extend that definition. Assets are chosen with a view to meeting fundamental investment objectives. There is historical evidence to support the view that equities provide higher returns than bonds.[2] While these returns vary from country to country, equities generally yielded a higher return to compensate for their higher risk characteristics. Investors seeking to maximize long-term expected returns gravitate towards higher allocations to assets that generate equity-like returns, including investments in alternative strategies. A diversified portfolio thus fulfils the fiduciary obligations of trustees by securing higher long-term returns at a selected risk level.

Achieving higher returns is one way of resolving the conflict that endowments face in providing for operations today while preserving future purchasing power. Managers of endowments believe that maximizing long-term investment return is critical in meeting the challenge of maximizing spending today and tomorrow. For example, about half (47 per cent) the institutions in Oxford and Cambridge emphasize maximizing returns as their investment objective. The ability to pursue asset allocation policies that enhance the scope for maximizing investment return within acceptable risk parameters enables institutions to meet their twin objectives.

In principle, institutions in Oxford and Cambridge are not constrained in their choice of investments. Though the size of individual endowments and the historical asset mix can influence asset allocation; for example, the inability to access investments in alternative strategies, such as private equity or hedge funds, due to the small size of individual College endowments. The need to secure a certain level of income annually also appears to impact allocation decisions. While Colleges have been innovative in finding solutions by setting up collective investment vehicles for hedge funds and private equity, not all Oxbridge institutions have invested in such diversification strategies. Also, there are Colleges with substantial direct exposure to property assets with considerable development potential.

The lack of a developed market in real estate investment trusts (REITs) in UK/Europe coupled with direct ownership of prime property assets in the UK appears to have affected asset allocation. Colleges with significant allocation to property argue: 'Endowment management revolves around determining the future spending rate of the College and locating matching assets of impeccable earnings power to meet the needs of current and future generations.' According to Peterhouse's Murison: 'Some scepticism at Peterhouse regarding equities and indeed all assets other than property is clearly illustrated since the College's endowment is 85 per cent invested in real estate. It is certainly out of line with the popular convention to diversify across asset classes. But by eschewing the cult of equity, the College has, over the last 30 years, exceeded the real return on the FTSE All-Share index by an average of just over 25 per cent annually. That might be described as a useful result of sceptical pragmatism.' As REITs and private equity tend to be more correlated with listed equities, investment bursars at Oxbridge consider their direct investment in property as a better diversifier.

Asset allocation can be defined as among the key responsibilities of fiduciaries. Success of long-term institutional goals depends on making appropriate allocation decisions. The level of involvement of investment committees in determining asset allocation varied among institutions in Oxford and Cambridge. A significant proportion (89 per cent) of investment committees reported being involved in the asset allocation process, but only 28 per cent considered themselves wholly responsible in making such decisions. A small number (11 per cent) of Colleges suggested their investment committees played no role in this critical process. The investment manager made a significant contribution in determining asset allocation for these institutions; over half the Colleges (54 per cent) reported using the manager in this capacity. Twenty per cent of Colleges (a slightly higher percentage in Cambridge than in Oxford) assigned a substantial portion (25–50 per cent) of the allocation process to their fund manager with 10 per cent of Colleges relying fully on the manager.

Asset allocation: Oxford institutions

The distribution of asset categories, provided by participating institutions in Oxford for which data are available for the financial year ending, July 2002, is shown in Table 5.1.

Data supplied by two Colleges were for calendar year-end 2002. Where data were not available, it is indicated as such. The last line is the equally weighted average allocation for each asset class. As Colleges are not required to disclose their endowment asset allocation in the published annual accounts, this study has benefited enormously from the information supplied to us by the participating institutions. Most Colleges provide a breakdown of assets between property and non-property investments in their published accounts, but there is no information on the distribution of assets within these broad asset categories.

The endowment portfolios of Oxford Colleges have significant exposure to equity; the highest total equity allocation represented 80 per cent of total assets, the lowest was 10 per cent, and the average allocation was 55 per cent. The highest exposure to UK equities was 62 per cent; the lowest (excluding

Table 5.1. Asset allocation of Oxford colleges, in per cent

College	Equity			Fixed income	Alternatives			Property	Cash	Total
	UK	OS	Total		PE	HF	Total			
1	60	20	80	5	1	—	1	—	14	100
2	54	26	80	6	5	9	14	—	—	100
3	60	19	79	19	—	—	—	—	2	100
4	na	na	79	—	—	—	—	—	21	100
5	56	19	75	16	—	—	—	7	2	100
6	45	30	75	24	—	—	—	—	1	100
7	54	18	71	28	—	—	—	—	1	100
8	48	24	71	26	—	—	—	—	3	100
9	na	na	71	—	—	—	—	29	—	100
10	54	14	68	13	na	na	5	6	7	100
11	62	6	67	10	—	1	1	16	6	100
12	49	17	66	18	1	—	1	5	10	100
13	47	19	66	11	1	—	1	8	15	100
14	43	13	56	17	2	1	3	—	25	100
15	37	18	55	10	—	—	—	33	1	100
16	21	33	54	5	—	9	9	26	6	100
17	36	18	53	18	na	na	3	23	4	100
18	36	13	49	11	2	—	2	20	19	100
19	36	12	48	8	1	—	1	8	35	100
20	22	22	44	—	na	na	2	46	8	100
21	19	26	44	19	—	2	2	7	28	100
22	39	3	42	26	—	—	—	3	29	100
23	na	na	40	5	—	—	—	40	15	100
24	22	17	39	9	4	3	7	44	1	100
25	21	18	38	9	1	—	1	48	6	100
26	16	21	37	16	2	1	3	42	2	100
27	24	13	36	3	4	1	6	55	1	100
28	26	6	33	—	—	1	1	49	17	100
29	26	6	32	—	1	1	2	64	2	100
30	20	10	30	32	—	5	5	30	2	100
31	na	na	10	12	—	—	—	75	3	100
Average	**38**	**17**	**55**	**12**	**1**	**1**	**2**	**22**	**9**	**100**

OS = Overseas; PE = Private equity; HF = Hedge Funds.

the only College with 10 per cent in equities, which did not provide its UK proportion) was 16 per cent. The average holding, at 38 per cent, was more than twice the average exposure to overseas equities (17 per cent), in which asset category the highest allocation was 33 per cent and the lowest 3 per cent.

As far as investment in other asset classes was concerned, five (16 per cent) Colleges in Oxford had no exposure to fixed income, though the overall average allocation was 12 per cent. Four of the five Colleges with no fixed income assets also held significant property assets, ranging from 29 to 64 per cent of their endowment portfolios. Only one College reported having no property or fixed income assets in its portfolio; instead, it had 79 per cent invested in equities, and the rest was in cash. The stable income-yielding virtue of property was valued as a reliable substitute for fixed income assets by most Oxford bursars.

Over one-third (35 per cent) of Colleges in Oxford had no investments in alternative strategies. Over half the Colleges (52 per cent) had no investments in private equity, and a similar number (55 per cent) had no exposure to hedge funds. The equally weighted average allocation of 2 per cent to alternative strategies among Oxford Colleges rose to 3.4 per cent if one excluded the Colleges with no exposure to such investments. Only 19 per cent of institutions had 5 per cent or more invested in alternative strategies. While some investment strategists believe that less than 10 per cent allocation to any asset class is not meaningful, for investors new to alternative strategies, a gradual increase in such allocation is the prudent approach. The cost of switching in and out of such strategies can be punitive. So, building up a portfolio to match the policy target over a period is recommended.

It is interesting that over one-quarter (26 per cent) of Colleges in Oxford reported no property holdings in their endowment portfolios though some of these Colleges own substantial operating property assets. If these Colleges were required to report on a total asset basis, regardless of whether the assets were classified as operational or endowment, then the asset distribution would appear significantly different. Among Colleges reporting an allocation to property in the endowment, the highest allocation was 75 per cent and the lowest was 3 per cent.

Asset allocation: Cambridge institutions

The distribution of assets as disclosed by 26 Cambridge institutions for financial year ending, June 2002, is given in Table 5.2. The asset mix supplied by six Colleges was at financial year-end June 2003; and two Colleges reported their allocations at calendar year-end 2002. Some Cambridge Colleges also did not give a full breakdown of their asset allocations. Where data were not available, it is indicated as such. The last line shows the equally weighted average allocation for each asset class.

Cambridge Colleges also reported significant allocations to equity assets in their endowment portfolios; the highest being 90 per cent, the lowest 10 per cent, and the average exposure was 52 per cent. The highest reported allocation to UK equities was 76 per cent (compared with 62 per cent for Oxford Colleges) and the lowest was 5 per cent (compared with 16 per cent for Oxford); the average for UK equity was 38.7 per cent in Cambridge (similar to Oxford's 38.2 per cent), which in Cambridge was closer to thrice the average holding in overseas equities at 14 per cent. It can be argued that individual institutions in Cambridge were more willing to take investment decisions that diverged from the norm.

Table 5.2. Asset allocation of Cambridge colleges, in per cent

College	Equity			Fixed income	Alternatives			Property	Cash	Total
	UK	OS	Total		PE	HF	Total			
1	66	24	90	10	—	—	—	—	—	100
2	76	12	88	10	—	—	—	—	3	100
3	63	20	83	16	—	—	—	—	2	100
4	58	22	81	7	—	—	—	6	6	100
5	45	28	72	14	—	—	—	11	3	100
6	53	19	72	14	—	—	—	13	1	100
7	63	9	71	23	—	—	—	—	6	100
8	42	27	70	29	—	—	—	—	2	100
9	60	7	67	27	—	—	—	—	6	100
10	42	21	63	14	—	—	—	16	7	100
11	48	14	62	6	1	—	1	13	19	100
12	na	na	58	5	—	—	—	33	3	100
13	45	5	50	4	—	1	1	37	8	100
14	na	na	43	—	1	—	1	43	14	100
15	27	16	43	46	—	—	—	6	5	100
16	32	8	40	19	—	—	—	41	—	100
17	19	17	37	7	—	—	—	50	7	100
18	18	15	34	6	na	na	6	53	2	100
19	14	19	33	6	na	na	5	42	14	100
20	25	8	33	28	3	—	3	30	6	100
21	na	na	32	—	1	—	1	66	1	100
22	23	9	32	7	—	2	2	58	1	100
23	28	2	30	10	—	—	—	48	13	100
24	19	10	29	5	—	—	—	66	—	100
25	20	8	28	7	—	—	—	62	3	100
26	5	5	10	—	—	—	—	90	—	100
Average	**39**	**14**	**52**	**12**	**0**	**0**	**1**	**30**	**5**	**100**

OS = Overseas; PE = Private equity; HF = Hedge funds.

Three (12 per cent) Cambridge Colleges had no fixed income investments, though the average allocation for the asset class was 12 per cent, exactly the same as in Oxford. Of the three Colleges with no fixed income assets, all had high exposure to property, ranging from 43 to 90 per cent of total endowment assets. The average holding in property for the three Cambridge Colleges with no fixed income investment was two-thirds (66 per cent) of their overall endowment portfolio. Like their counterparts in Oxford, about one-quarter (23 per cent) of Cambridge Colleges also had no property assets in their endowment portfolios, though some of these Colleges owned significant property assets albeit outside the endowment portfolio. The highest allocation to property within a Cambridge College (90 per cent) was substantially higher, compared with Oxford Colleges; and the lowest allocation in Cambridge of 6 per cent was twice the lowest allocation in Oxford.

Almost twice (69 per cent in Cambridge vs. 35 per cent in Oxford) as many Colleges in Cambridge had no investments in alternative strategies. A significant number (77 per cent) of Cambridge Colleges had no private equity assets, and an even greater number of Colleges (85 per cent) had no exposure to hedge funds. The aggregate average allocation of just 0.7 per cent to alternative strategies rose to an average of 2 per cent if Colleges without any exposure to such assets were excluded. Less than 10 per cent of Cambridge institutions had 5 per cent or more invested in alternative strategies.

Asset allocation: Oxford versus Cambridge

Like other institutional investors, the investment committees of endowments in Oxford and Cambridge apply a traditional approach to asset allocation whereby risk, return, and correlation assumptions are factored into an optimization model resulting in average annual return forecasts for the portfolios over an investment cycle. By combining quantitative analysis with a sound qualitative approach to strategic asset allocation, these committees generally arrive at their preferred portfolio.

Mean variance optimization models are useful in identifying efficient portfolios, though Oxbridge institutions have been reluctant users of highly quantitative modelling tools, as they typically fail to meet the very specific needs of these institutions. The high allocation to direct property in many endowment portfolios within Oxford and Cambridge limits the usefulness of quantitative analytical tools that are unable to include meaningful inputs on a third of their investments. The optimization framework, in failing to consider attributes such as liquidity and marketability of various assets, also limits its applications. Such models also assume annual rebalancing of portfolio allocations, which is difficult to achieve in a cost efficient manner for less marketable assets such as direct property holdings.

As a group of institutions with similar investment objectives, Colleges in Oxford and Cambridge exhibit a high level of individualism in their investment decisions. As far as endowment asset management is concerned, there is little evidence of herding or following the latest investment fad. Colleges have an idea of what the peer group in the University is doing in investment terms, but there is little evidence of following the leader, as it were. If anything, these institutions are conservative and can best be described as adopting a 'contrarian' investment approach. As a result, it is fascinating to compare their aggregate allocation to traditional investments such as UK equities, where both Oxford and Cambridge have very similar allocations.

The average allocation in the endowment portfolios for the Colleges at the end of the 2002 financial year is shown in Table 5.3.

The average investment in UK equities (38–39 per cent) was remarkably similar for both universities; so was their exposure to fixed income assets

Table 5.3. Comparison of average Oxford and Cambridge allocations, in per cent

Institution	Equity			Fixed income	Alternatives			Property	Cash
	UK	OS	Total		PE	HF	Total		
Oxford	38.2	17.0	54.5	12.1	0.9	1.2	2.2	22.0	9.2
Cambridge	38.7	14.1	51.8	12.3	0.2	0.1	0.7	30.1	5.0
Average	**38.4**	**15.5**	**53.2**	**12.2**	**0.5**	**0.7**	**1.5**	**26.1**	**7.1**

OS = Overseas; PE = Private equity; HF = Hedge funds.

at 12 per cent. The differences were mainly in allocations to foreign equity, property, cash, and alternative assets. Oxford Colleges had 2.2 per cent in alternative assets compared with less than 1 per cent (0.7 per cent) for Cambridge institutions, who also had significantly higher investments in property (30 per cent) while Oxford Colleges held more cash. Colleges in Oxford also had more foreign equities. On average, their asset mix was consistent with Oxford funds being somewhat better diversified portfolios than their peer group in Cambridge.

Analysis of the highest and lowest allocation to each asset category among Oxbridge institutions suggests that asset allocation was more a residue of stock selection. Portfolios reflect the specific circumstances of these institutions today though such allocations may have originally been the result of historical developments. Thus, if Peterhouse had 85 per cent of its endowment in property in 2003–4, it was as much the result of historical circumstances that enabled Cambridge's oldest College to accumulate property in the past as much as the College's current thinking on investments. With the retirement of Andrew Murison in 2003, and the appointment of a new senior bursar, Mr R. S. G. Grigson, investment allocation may change. At end of financial year 2005, allocation to total property investment remained at 85 per cent.

What individual portfolios never suggest is the use of peer group benchmarking, as Colleges appear willing to invest in assets of their choice without reference to the peer group. While average exposure to some assets appears remarkably similar in Oxford and Cambridge, such as the exposure to UK equities and bonds, the divergence from what could be presented as an Oxbridge benchmark, as represented in Table 5.3, conveys an equally powerful story. Unlike pension funds in the 1980s and early 1990s, when balanced mandates based on peer group benchmarks were the norm, Oxbridge institutions remain refreshingly original in their investment approach. Such conviction investing may disappear for a host of reasons, including the rise of 'professional' investment bursars and greater involvement of investment consultants in strategic decision-making.

Table 5.4. Comparison of highest and lowest allocations to each asset, in per cent

Allocation	Institution	Equity			Fixed income	Alternatives			Property	Cash
		UK	OS	Total		PE	HF	Total		
Highest	Oxford	61.6	33.0	79.7	32.1	5.1	9.0	14.1	75.0	35.2
	Cambridge	75.7	27.5	89.7	46.0	2.6	2.0	6.0	90.0	19.0
	Average	**68.6**	**30.3**	**84.7**	**39.0**	**3.9**	**5.5**	**10.0**	**82.5**	**27.1**
Lowest	Oxford	16.0	3.0	10.0	2.6	0.5	0.7	0.5	3.0	0.7
	Cambridge	5.0	4.5	10.0	3.9	0.5	1.3	0.5	6.3	1.3
	Average	**10.5**	**3.8**	**10.0**	**3.2**	**0.5**	**1.0**	**0.5**	**4.7**	**1.0**

Table 5.4 illustrates the highest and lowest asset allocations in each asset category for institutions in Oxford and Cambridge.

The highest exposure to UK equity investments in Oxford was 61.6 per cent and the lowest was 16.0 per cent. The divergence was greater in Cambridge where the highest exposure to UK equity was 75.7 per cent and the lowest 5.0 per cent. While the highest average total exposure to equity assets was 10 per cent higher in Cambridge, at 89.7 per cent, the lowest average total equity exposure for both collegiate universities was the same at 10 per cent.

The average highest allocation to equity assets among all Oxbridge institutions was 84.7 per cent compared with an overall equity average of 53.2 per cent and an average lowest equity allocation of 10 per cent. The spread in allocation to property was larger, with the highest average being 82.5 per cent, the overall average 26.1 per cent, and the lowest average 4.7 per cent. The average highest allocation to UK equity at 68.6 per cent was more than twice the average highest for non-UK equity investments at 30.3 per cent. The average highest allocation to fixed income investments (39 per cent) was over three times the overall average (12.2 per cent).

The greatest disparity in allocations appears in alternatives where the average highest allocation was 10.0 per cent and the average lowest allocation was 0.5 per cent with the overall average being 1.5 per cent. Taking into account the differential allocations in various asset classes among institutions in Oxford and Cambridge, it can be inferred that asset allocation decisions were arrived at quite independently.

There exists a high level of sharing of information among the Colleges, inevitably; but there is no evidence to suggest that institutions shared asset allocation data with a view to establishing an aggregate policy portfolio or benchmark. Colleges cooperated, for example, in creating an internal inflation index in Oxford. Not all Colleges used the Van Noorden inflation index, but the fact that it existed and was consulted by some Colleges is relevant. These institutions never felt the need to refer to any external peer group asset allocation benchmark or establish one internally.

Table 5.5. Comparison of asset allocations with WM and NACUBO, in per cent

Asset class	Oxford	Cambridge	Oxbridge	WM charity	NACUBO
Equity	54.5	51.8	53.2	76.1	57.4
Fixed income	12.1	12.3	12.2	16.6	26.9
Alternative strategies	2.2	0.7	1.5	0.0	7.1
Of which					
Hedge funds					5.1
Private equity					0.9
Venture capital					1.1
Real estate	22.0	30.1	26.1	3.4	2.7
Cash	9.2	5.0	7.1	3.8	3.9
Natural resources	0.0	0.0	0.0	0.0	0.4
Other	0.0	0.0	0.0	0.0	1.6

Source: NACUBO data for the United States, and WM Company for the UK (based on universe for charities unconstrained by income).

Comparing asset distribution in Oxford and Cambridge with allocations made by higher education institutions in the United States reveals that in 2002 (the year for which Oxbridge data are available) the equally weighted average allocations though different for all asset classes had broadly similar average equity allocations.[3] Table 5.5 illustrates different approaches to asset allocation distribution, based on studies by the National Association of College and University Business Officers (NACUBO) in the United States, and the WM Company in the UK.

As there are no comparable asset allocation data for educational institutions in the UK, comparing asset allocation breakdown of the not-for-profit sector (as represented by the WM Unconstrained Charity Universe in the UK at the end of 2002) with that of Oxbridge and NACUBO revealed some interesting differences. The allocation to equity, for example, among US educational institutions, at 57.4 per cent, was higher than the average allocation in Oxbridge (53.2 per cent). But charitable institutions in the UK were hugely overweight in equities. There was a considerable home-bias in their allocation; ownership of UK equities was 57 per cent of total assets.

Allocation to fixed income securities was also interesting as US institutions at 27 per cent held more than twice as much as Oxbridge institutions (12 per cent). The charitable sector in the UK at almost 17 per cent was still considerably underweight than institutions in the United States. Similarly, US institutions were significantly weighted in alternative strategies (7 per cent) compared with the meagre exposure to such investments in Oxbridge (1.5 per cent). Charities in the UK had no exposure to the asset class in 2002.

The salient feature of Oxbridge endowment portfolios is their allocation to property, which at an average of 26 per cent was vastly overweight compared to the 2.7 per cent invested in real estate assets by US institutions or the

3.4 per cent by the not-for-profit sector in the UK. Oxbridge's property allocation was similar to ownership of fixed income assets among US institutions.
The fixed income like characteristics of property was cited as a determining
factor among Oxbridge institutions as their rationale for investing in the asset
class. Oxford and Cambridge institutions also held more cash (7 per cent)
compared with US institutions (4 per cent) or UK charities (3.8 per cent).

Asset allocation and size of endowment

Results of the 2003 NACUBO Endowment Study (NES) show that the most
significant variable that influenced differences in institutional endowment
performance in the United States was asset mix or allocation, particularly
in alternative strategies. For example, institutions with assets greater than
$1 billion had 19.9 per cent in hedge funds compared to 8.3 per cent for
colleges with endowments in the $100 million to $500 million range.[4] As
total institutional assets rose, the exposure to alternative assets rose with
it. Thus, US higher education institutions with larger endowments also had
more exposure than smaller endowments to private equity. Institutions with
endowments valued at more than $1 billion allocated 5.2 per cent to private
equity compared with 4.2 per cent for institutions in the $501 million to
$1 billion and 2.2 per cent for colleges and universities in the $101 million
to $500 million category. Institutions with endowments worth less than $51
million on average allocated less than 1 per cent to private equity. In general,
the 2003 NES shows that size of endowment dictated the use of alternative
investments. Institutions with the largest endowments were more likely to
allocate a greater proportion for investments in real estate, venture capital,
and natural resources than those commanding lesser endowment assets.[5]

As a group, US higher educational institutions with larger endowments had
smaller allocations to equities and fixed income with offsetting differences
invested in alternative assets. It is important that on average all institutions
allocated more than 54 per cent of their assets to equity investments—with
the exception of the greater than $1 billion group of endowments, which
allocated 44.8 per cent on average to equities in their portfolios.[6] Analysis of
asset allocation in Oxford and Cambridge, based on endowment size, revealed
that larger endowments (over £45 million worth of assets) had a different asset
mix compared to allocations made by institutions with smaller endowments
(less than £45 million). As endowment assets rose, allocations to alternative
assets increased while those to traditional assets declined. Table 5.6 illustrates
the variations in asset mix and size of endowment among Colleges in Oxford
and Cambridge.

The wealthier Colleges invested less (17 per cent less) in UK equity though
the differential in overseas equities was lower (2.4 per cent). Overall, richer

Table 5.6. Asset allocation and endowment size, in per cent

Endowment	Institution	Equity			Fixed income	Alternatives			Property	Cash	Total
		UK	OS	Total		PE	HF	Total			
Over £45 m	Oxford	28.4	14.8	43.2	10.5	1.1	1.3	2.8	38.6	4.8	100
	Cambridge	17.9	9.5	36.4	9.1	0.4	0.2	1.6	49.5	3.5	100
	Average	**23.2**	**12.2**	**39.8**	**9.8**	**0.8**	**0.8**	**2.2**	**44.1**	**4.2**	**100**
Under £45 m	Oxford	35.5	14.8	59.8	12.8	0.6	1.0	1.9	14.1	11.3	100
	Cambridge	44.5	14.3	61.5	14.3	0.1	0.1	0.2	18.0	6.0	100
	Average	**40.0**	**14.6**	**60.7**	**13.6**	**0.4**	**0.6**	**1.1**	**16.1**	**8.7**	**100**

OS = Overseas; PE = Private equity; HF = Hedge funds.

Colleges held substantially less of equity (21 per cent less), cash (4.5 per cent less), and fixed income (3.8 per cent less) assets. The richer Colleges were also significantly overweight in their allocation to property; they had 28 per cent more in property than Colleges with lesser endowments. Wealthier Cambridge Colleges had almost a third (31.5 per cent) more in property compared with Colleges in Cambridge with smaller endowments. Less well-endowed Colleges in Cambridge also invested more (26.6 per cent more) in UK equity assets compared with the better off Colleges in the same university. The divergence in asset allocation strategy appears clearly when one compares the three sets of aggregate averages.

Table 5.7 shows, for example, that richer Colleges in Oxford and Cambridge (with assets above £45 million in 2002) allocated 15 per cent less to UK equity compared with the average allocation of its peer group; they also had 3 per cent less in overseas equity and 13 per cent less of equity in total compared with the overall average.

Table 5.7. Oxbridge asset allocation by size of endowment, in per cent

Endowment size	Equity			Fixed income	Alternatives			Property	Cash	Total
	UK	OS	Total		PE	HF	Total			
Over £45 m	23.2	12.2	39.8	9.8	0.8	0.8	2.2	44.1	4.2	100
Under £45 m	40.0	14.6	60.7	13.6	0.4	0.6	1.1	16.1	8.7	100
Oxbridge Average	**38.4**	**15.5**	**53.2**	**12.2**	**0.5**	**0.7**	**1.5**	**26.1**	**7.1**	**100**

OS = Overseas; PE = Private equity; HF = Hedge funds.

The highest discrepancy in asset allocation among these institutions appeared in property. Richer Colleges invested 18 per cent more in property compared with the average holding of Oxbridge Colleges, which stood at 26 per cent. Of course, in declaring a larger allocation to real estate, these wealthier Colleges are in many cases simply reporting the holdings of the very assets that made them wealthy. Institutions with endowment assets valued under £45 million had 10 per cent less in property investments compared with the overall average. As well as holding more property, wealthier Colleges invested more in alternative strategies and less in UK equity, fixed income and cash. Colleges with smaller endowments were less resourceful or less able to access investments in alternative strategies.

It is interesting to compare Oxford and Cambridge College allocations with that of educational endowments in the United States, where the shift towards investments in alternative assets is more clearly established. As the size of investment assets under management get larger, institutions on average are more likely to cut their allocation to traditional assets, such as equity and bonds, and are more willing to take on incremental risk by investing in alternative opportunities. Also, independent institutions tend to allocate a larger proportion to alternative strategies compared to public ones.

Table 5.8 gives a breakdown of allocations to various asset classes by US educational institutions participating in the 2003 NES study.

Comparing these average sector allocations to those made by the endowments of Harvard and Yale illustrates the extent to which allocations varied, even among larger endowments in the United States. Harvard and Yale, for example, had an asset mix that differed from that of other educational endowments in the United States with assets over $1 billion. Also, the largest university endowments pursued asset allocation policies that were significantly different from those of institutions with smaller endowments. Table 5.9 shows the breakdown of the Policy Portfolio of Harvard Management Company and the actual allocation of the Yale Endowment for fiscal year-end 2002.

As Harvard does not disclose its actual holdings, for the sake of comparison, its policy allocation to high-yield securities (5 per cent) is included in absolute return assets; allocation to domestic bonds (11 per cent), foreign bonds (5 per cent), and inflation-indexed bonds (6 per cent) are aggregated into fixed income, while the allocation to commodities (13 per cent) is included in real assets. In 2002, both Harvard and Yale made very similar allocations to domestic equity; allocation to foreign equity was also broadly similar. Harvard invested more than twice as much in fixed income assets (22 per cent) compared to Yale (10 per cent). And Yale's allocation to absolute return strategies (26.5 per cent) was significantly higher than Harvard's (17 per cent), though allocation to private equity assets was similar.

Average equity allocation among educational endowments with assets over $1 billion in the United States, at 45 per cent of total assets, was 50 per cent higher compared to allocations made by Harvard and Yale. Institutions with lesser endowments invested at least twice as much (60.2 per cent) in equity assets compared to allocations made by Harvard and Yale (at 30 and 28.2 per cent respectively). Total allocation to alternative assets and strategies, which can broadly be defined to include absolute return, private equity, and real assets, by Harvard and Yale far exceeded the average for institutional

Table 5.8. Asset allocation: institutional groups in the United States, 2003, in per cent

Asset class	>$1 b	$0.5–1 b	$0.1–.5 b	$50–100 m	$25–50 m	<$25 m	Public	Independent	Average
Equity	44.8	54.4	56.5	58.7	60.2	57.0	58.1	56.7	57.1
Fixed income	18.6	18.2	23.5	27.2	27.7	29.8	27.9	24.9	25.9
Real estate	4.2	4.2	2.9	2.8	2.6	2.2	2.1	3.1	2.8
Cash	1.8	1.4	2.7	4.9	3.5	6.6	4.0	4.0	4.0
Hedge funds	19.9	13.4	8.3	4.3	4.2	1.6	4.3	6.9	6.1
Private equity	5.2	4.2	2.2	0.6	0.2	0.2	0.9	1.5	1.3
Venture capital	3.0	2.7	1.3	0.3	0.2	0.1	0.5	0.9	0.8
Natural resources	1.9	1.1	0.8	0.1	0.1	0.0	0.4	0.4	0.4
Other	0.7	0.4	1.8	1.1	1.4	2.5	1.6	1.6	1.6
Total	**100**	**100**	**100**	**100**	**100**	**100**	**100**	**100**	**100**

Source: 2003 NACUBO Endowment Study.

Table 5.9. Comparison of Harvard and Yale asset allocations, 2002, in per cent

Asset class	Harvard	Yale
Domestic equity	15.0	15.4
Foreign equity	15.0	12.8
Fixed income	22.0	10.0
Absolute return	17.0	26.5
Private equity	13.0	14.4
Real assets	23.0	20.5
Cash	(5.0)	0.3

Source: Harvard College Financial Report, 2002; Yale Annual Report 2002.[7]

Table 5.10. Harvard, Yale, and large US educational endowments, 2004, in per cent

Asset class	Harvard	Yale	Endowments >$1 b
Domestic equity	15.0	14.8	31.9
Foreign equity	15.0	14.8	14.4
Fixed income	22.0	7.4	15.2
Absolute return	17.0	26.1	20.2
Private equity	13.0	14.5	8.4
Real assets	23.0	18.8	6.6
Cash	(5.0)	3.5	2.7
Other	0.0	0.0	0.7

Source: Harvard College Financial Report, 2004; Yale Annual Report, 2004; 2004 NES.

endowments with assets above $1 billion. In the case of Harvard, more than half (53 per cent) the endowment was invested in such assets; in the case of Yale, the amount invested in absolute return, private equity, and real assets stood at 61.4 per cent of the overall portfolio. Endowments with assets over $1 billion in the United States also invested over one-third (34 per cent) of their portfolios in alternatives, but these allocations were significantly lower compared with Harvard and Yale.

2004 allocations for the Policy Portfolio of the HMC remained unchanged while the Yale Endowment's actual allocation, at June 2004, had not altered in any strategic way. Yale reduced its fixed income holdings further while increasing its investments in foreign equity. Allocation to real assets fell as cash positions were built up. Table 5.10 shows the 2004 Policy Portfolio and actual allocations by the endowments of Harvard and Yale along with the allocations reported by the larger endowments (with assets over $1 billion) in the United States.

Asset allocation data reported by US educational endowments reveal that the percentage of assets invested in hedge funds increased for all investment pool asset categories during 2003–4. The tendency of larger endowments to invest heavily in the asset class was reflected in the total dollar-weighted averages, which was 14.7 per cent compared to 7.3 per cent for the equally weighted average for all participating institutions. Also, institutions with assets above $1 billion may have reached the upper limit of their exposure to this asset category.[8] The allocation for various asset categories among US educational endowments for the fiscal year 2004 is given in Table 5.11.

When compared to allocations in 2003, the percentage of assets invested in equities increased for all investment pool asset size categories in 2004. As equity markets also performed well during this period, it is possible that this increase was partly attributable to market performance; also investors were more comfortable with higher equity allocations. The greatest proportional increase in equities occurred within institutions with assets less than $25 million—an increase of 8.3 per cent in 2004. Conversely, the percentage of fixed income assets within the investment pool decreased in all categories with the largest declines seen among endowments with assets greater than $50 million but less than $100 million.

Asset allocations, as reported by educational endowments participating in the *Commonfund Benchmarks Study*, for fiscal year-end 2004, differed significantly from those reported by the 2004 NES. The average allocation reported in the Commonfund Study was 34 per cent to alternative strategies, 31 per cent to domestic equities, 16 per cent to international equities, 15 per cent to fixed income, and 4 per cent to cash and other short-term securities.[9] As the Commonfund Study allocations are dollar-weighted, we compared it with the dollar-weighted allocations reported by the 2004 NES. Table 5.12 compares the asset allocation for 2004 as reported by participating institutions in the NACUBO Endowment Study and the Commonfund Institute's Benchmark Study for educational endowments. The reported allocations varied in all asset classes except in 'venture capital' and 'other' asset categories.

Both the 2004 *NACUBO Endowment Study* and the 2005 *Commonfund Benchmarks Study* confirm that the most significant development in asset allocation over the last few years among US educational endowments, across all institutions, was higher allocation to alternative assets including natural resources. Allocations to equity assets also rose but these institutions have traditionally been equity oriented. Thus, a return to a 59.9 per cent, equally weighted, allocation to equity in 2004 was lower than levels invested in 2000 (62.1 per cent). Allocation to fixed income assets fell in 2004 as expected returns from such investments did not compare favourably with returns expected from equities and alternative assets. These developments not only reflect a recovery

Table 5.11. Asset allocation of various sized US institutions, 2004, in per cent

Asset Class	>$1 b	$0.5–1 b	$0.1–0.5 b	$50–100 m	$25–50 m	<$25 m	Public	Independent	Average
Equity	46.3	56.9	59.1	62.5	61.5	61.7	61.3	59.2	59.9
Fixed income	15.2	15.7	19.5	22.1	24.6	27.2	23.7	21.3	22.1
Real estate	4.0	2.9	3.1	2.7	3.3	1.3	2.1	3.1	2.8
Cash	2.7	1.9	2.5	4.6	1.8	5.0	3.6	3.7	3.7
Hedge funds	20.2	14.4	10.0	5.6	4.6	1.8	5.6	8.1	7.3
Private equity	4.9	4.5	2.0	0.5	0.3	0.2	1.1	1.5	1.3
Venture capital	3.5	2.1	1.2	0.4	0.2	0.0	0.6	0.9	0.8
Natural resources	2.6	1.2	0.9	0.2	0.2	0.0	0.6	0.6	0.6
Other	0.7	0.4	1.7	1.5	1.4	2.6	1.4	1.7	1.6
Total	**100**	**100**	**100**	**100**	**100**	**100**	**100**	**100**	**100**

Source: 2004 NACUBO Endowment Study.

Table 5.12. US educational endowment asset allocation percentages, dollar weighted

Asset class	Commonfund	NES
Domestic equity	31.0	48.9
Foreign equity	16.0	11.0
Total equity	47.0	50.8
Fixed income	15.0	17.2
Hedge funds	16.3	14.7
Private equity	4.8	3.5
Venture capital	3.1	3.1
Real estate	5.1	4.0
Natural resources	3.7	3.0
Cash	4.0	2.6
Other	1.0	1.1
Total	**100**	**100**

Source: Commonfund Benchmarks Study: Educational Endowment Report 05; 2004 NES.

in equity market performance, but also a fundamental shift in asset allocation whereby investors sought alternative assets and strategies for diversification and risk control.

Equity allocation

Foundations and endowments constantly struggle to sustain the real value of their assets and spending in perpetuity. The challenge in asset allocation for such institutions is to reconcile these two apparently conflicting objectives, which is best achieved by investing in assets that provide the highest return over the long term. As Gary Steinberg, chief investment officer of the Wellcome Trust, 2000–5, pointed out: 'The Trust's asset allocation is based on the belief that equities are most likely to deliver the best returns over time. As a result, the Trust runs an equity-based portfolio aiming for growth over the long term. There is historical evidence to support the view that equities have delivered 5–6 per cent real returns per year.' While these returns may differ from country to country, the Trust's strategy was and still is based on the belief that such returns are achievable in the long term. Thus, 85 per cent of the Wellcome Trust's assets remain invested in public and private equity investments. While the Trust currently has a new CIO, and the overall approach to investments may alter, allocation to equity-like assets has not changed; if anything, the appetite for the equity risk premium has increased.

The need to provide resources for current operations as well as to preserve the purchasing power of assets dictates investing for high returns, causing many endowments to be biased towards equity assets. In addition, educational institutions' vulnerability to inflation further directs endowments and foundations away from fixed income towards equity. The Yale endowment, for example, targets over 90 per cent of its assets towards some form of equity investments, through holdings of public and private equities in the United States and in international markets, along with real assets and absolute return strategies.[10] The Harvard endowment has invested 20–25 per cent of its assets in fixed income, but the overall bias is towards equity.

The equity culture also prevails in Oxford and Cambridge. Like other institutional investors in the UK, as in the United States, investing in equity has been rewarding, particularly over the last two decades of the twentieth century. However, Oxbridge institutions, by holding on to their high allocation to property, challenged the status quo revealing a healthy individualism, even scepticism, in their approach. Only one College, Balliol in Oxford, decided to sell its endowment property assets some two decades ago. Most Colleges in holding on to property took a more contrarian view; no other group of institutional investors anywhere in the world own as much property in their endowments as Oxbridge institutions. The average allocation to equity, public and private, for these institutions was 55 per cent, compared with 80–90 per cent allocation among other major endowments and foundations.

Like other long-term investors in the foundation and endowment universe, Oxford and Cambridge Colleges typically invested to maximize returns within an acceptable level of risk. Over two-thirds (69 per cent) of Colleges had more than 40 per cent of the endowment invested in equity. A quarter of Colleges allocated one-third (30–9 per cent) of their endowment portfolio to equity assets, and a further 23 per cent invested 70–80 per cent in the asset class with almost twice as many Colleges in Oxford (29 per cent) reporting such an allocation compared with Cambridge Colleges (15 per cent). Seven per cent of Colleges, all in Cambridge, invested over 80 per cent of their endowment in equity. At the other end of the investment spectrum, 8 per cent of Colleges, mostly in Cambridge, had less than 30 per cent in equity. Cambridge Colleges reported a higher range of dispersion in their endowment asset allocation, though no Oxbridge College reported holding less than 10 per cent of its total portfolio in equity assets. Table 5.13 provides a breakdown of the range of total allocation to listed equity investment in Oxford and Cambridge endowment portfolios.

A breakdown of the equity allocation into domestic (UK) and international (non-UK) revealed that 43 per cent of responding institutions held 40 per cent or more of their assets in domestic equity, while only 2 per cent (one College in Cambridge) had less than 10 per cent invested in domestic equity. Just under one-quarter (23 per cent) of Oxford and Cambridge institutions allocated 20–30 per cent of their portfolios to domestic equity, with more Oxford Colleges reporting such allocations; 26 per cent of Oxford Colleges compared with 19 per cent of Cambridge Colleges.

Table 5.13. Total allocation to listed equity investments, in per cent

% in Equities	Oxford	Cambridge	Oxbridge
>80	—	15	7
70–80	29	15	23
60–70	13	12	12
50–60	13	8	11
40–50	19	12	16
30–40	23	27	25
20–30	—	8	4
10–20	3	4	4
<10	—	—	—
Total	**100**	**100**	**100**

Table 5.14. Allocation to domestic equities, in per cent

% in UK Equities	Oxford	Cambridge	Oxbridge
70–80	—	4	2
60–70	10	15	12
50–60	13	8	11
40–50	16	19	18
30–40	16	4	11
20–30	26	19	23
10–20	6	15	11
<10	—	4	2
na	13	12	12
Total	**100**	**100**	**100**

As with total equity allocation, there was greater dispersion in UK equity allocation among Cambridge institutions, with one College investing less than 10 per cent and another over 70 per cent in the asset class. Four times as many Colleges in Oxford invested about one-third (30–40 per cent) in UK equity, representing 11 per cent of total responses received. While 12 per cent of total respondents did not provide a breakdown between domestic and overseas equity holdings, allocations to domestic equity dominated most endowment portfolios; averaging 38 per cent for Oxford and Cambridge institutions compared with 48 per cent for educational endowments in the United States. Table 5.14 provides a breakdown of UK equity allocation in endowment portfolios of institutions in Oxford and Cambridge.

On average, Colleges in Oxford and Cambridge invested twice as much in domestic equity as in overseas equity. Though a highly diversified international portfolio is recommended, as the larger UK companies invest overseas and derive an increasingly bigger portion of their revenues from abroad, asset allocation analysis based on the geographical listing of a company may fail to show diversification of the sources of income of underlying investments. Thus, if a portfolio is invested mainly in small- and mid-cap companies, the need for diversification may be interpreted as being greater than a portfolio invested in a broader base of companies in the UK or in the FTSE All Share, for example.

Asset allocation also reflects an underlying set of expected return assumptions within certain risk parameters. The equal weighting in domestic and foreign equity policy allocations by Harvard and Yale cannot be simply interpreted as reflecting equal return expectations. Oxford and Cambridge institutions also invested 15 per cent of their assets in overseas equity. But the definition of 'overseas' for a UK institution includes United States, Europe, Japan, and Emerging Markets, or a larger share of global economic output compared with a US-based one. Also, for a US-based investor, diversification into foreign equities over an economic cycle when the dollar was in the process of major downwards adjustment, thanks to a high current account deficit in the world's largest economy, was probably a sound investment strategy compared to a UK-based investor's rationale for diversification. While diversification can be achieved in a portfolio invested in fifty stocks, the argument for diversifying risk plays a critical role in determining the asset mix.

Table 5.15 gives a breakdown of the international (non-UK) equity allocation among Oxford and Cambridge endowment portfolios. Around 40 per cent of Colleges reported investing 10–20 per cent in overseas equity, while 21 per cent invested 20–30 per cent of their portfolios in international equity. Only 4 per cent of Colleges (both in Oxford) held around one-third (30–40 per cent) of their endowment assets in non-UK equity investments. About a quarter (23 per cent) of Oxbridge institutions allocated less than 10 per cent to foreign equity assets; in Cambridge the number of institutions allocating less than 10 per cent to overseas equity investments rose to over one-third of Colleges.

Table 5.15. Allocation to overseas (OS) equities, in per cent

% in OS equities	Oxford	Cambridge	Oxbridge
>40	—	—	—
30–40	6	—	4
20–30	19	23	21
10–20	48	31	40
<10	13	35	23
na	13	12	12
Total	**100**	**100**	**100**

Oxford and Cambridge invested more in overseas equity assets than educational endowments in the United States, where the average allocation was 11 per cent in the fiscal year 2004, compared with an Oxbridge average of 15.5 per cent at the time of our survey. As institutions in Oxford and Cambridge do not report their detailed asset allocation annually in their published accounts, it has not been possible to analyse long-term trends in asset allocation among these institutions. The average allocation of the top-10 performing educational endowments in the United States was 14.5 per cent to publicly traded international equities in the fiscal year 2004.[11] Independent institutions invested more in overseas equities (11.2 per cent) compared to public institutions, which held less (10.7 per cent) of the asset class. While larger endowments, with assets over $1 billion, invested 14.4 per cent of their assets in foreign equity, smaller endowments, with assets less than $25 million, invested only 6.9 per cent in the asset class.

In the fiscal year 2004, the endowments of Harvard and Yale both reported allocations of 15 per cent to international equity, which was slightly above the average for the top performing US educational endowments. While these institutions made similar allocations to domestic equity (15 per cent) assets, the average equally weighted allocation to US equity among educational endowments stood at 48.9 per cent revealing the strong home-bias among US investors. Public institutions held more in US equities (50.6 per cent) compared to independent ones (48.2 per cent). Also, the larger endowments, with assets over $1 billion, invested less (31.9 per cent) of their assets in US equity while the smaller endowments, with assets less than $25 million, reported investing 54.8 per cent of their endowment in US equity.[12] Richer Colleges in Oxford and Cambridge also allocated less to UK equity compared to the average allocation; they also owned less overseas equity and invested less in equities in total.

Asset allocations, as reported by participating institutions in the 2005 *Commonfund Study*, show that average allocations were significantly different—with 31 per cent in domestic equities and 16 per cent in international equities. This compared with an overall financial year 2003 allocation of 32 per cent to domestic equities and 14 per cent to international equities. The modest increases in these assets were largely at the expense of fixed income investments, an adjustment that allowed many institutions to capture the stronger returns in these asset classes.[13]

As equity markets recovered after the bear market of 2000–3, fuelled by stronger than anticipated growth in corporate earnings and macroeconomic surprises on deflation, institutions with high allocations to publicly traded equities prospered. For the 12-month period ending 30 June 2004, equities performed well; the Russell 3000 Index (representing approximately 98 per cent of the US equity market) returned 20.5 per cent while the small-cap stocks and international equities posted stellar returns of 33.4 per cent (Russell

2000 Index) and 32.4 per cent (MSCI EAFE Index) respectively. Between 2000 and 2004, overall changes in asset allocation—reductions in fixed income and increases in equities and alternative strategies—became evident across institutions.

According to the 2003 NES, the allocation to non-US listed equities by educational endowments in the United States was less than 10 per cent. The overall equity allocation, at 53 per cent for institutions in Oxford and Cambridge, was lower than the 57 per cent allocated by US educational endowments. On average, Oxbridge institutions invested more in overseas equity assets; 15.5 per cent for Oxbridge compared with 9.5 per cent for US educational endowments in 2003; they also held 47.7 per cent in US equity[14] compared to 38.4 per cent in UK equity among Oxford and Cambridge Colleges.

Historically, the strong tradition of international investing in the UK helped it secure such an eminent position in the industry globally. The sheer size and diversity of the US economy traditionally discouraged US fund managers from investing overseas. Today, globalization and market liberalization has enabled more and more investors, particularly US institutional investors, to increase their share of the global capital market, particularly in the UK, European, and Emerging Markets.

Allocation to alternative assets

The largest growth within the fund management industry over the past decade or so has been in the alternative assets market. Alternative strategies, primarily designed to generate abnormal performance, or alpha, by hedging the stock market and the interest rate risk that drive returns in more traditional, long-only strategies, have little correlation with traditional asset classes, largely due to the dynamic trading strategies they use in exploiting inefficiencies in global capital markets. Truly long-term institutional investors, such as endowments, under increasing pressure to maintain their eroding returns, took the lead in investing in absolute return strategies. Major university endowments in the United States actively pursued higher return strategies. Table 5.16 shows allocation to various asset classes over the past 5 years among US educational endowments.

Educational institutions, with a diversified income base, are better placed to allocate risk more efficiently compared to other investors such as pension funds, which clearly defined liabilities and sometimes with no other sources of cash flow. Across all endowment sizes in the United States, institutional allocation to hedge fund investments continued to rise as did allocations to real estate, private equity, and natural resources.

Compared with US educational endowments where the average allocation to alternative assets was 7.1 per cent in 2002, institutions in Oxford and

143

Table 5.16. Five-year comparison of US asset allocation percentages

Asset class	2004	2003	2002	2001	2000
Equity	59.9	57.1	57.4	59.4	62.1
Fixed income	22.1	25.9	26.9	24.9	23.3
Real estate	2.8	2.8	2.7	2.4	2.0
Hedge funds	7.3	6.1	5.1	4.2	3.0
Private equity	1.3	1.3	0.9	0.9	1.0
Venture capital	0.8	0.8	1.1	1.5	2.4
Natural resources	0.6	0.4	0.4	0.4	0.4
Cash	3.7	4.0	3.9	4.1	4.1
Other	1.6	1.6	1.6	2.2	1.7
Total	**100**	**100**	**100**	**100**	**100**

Source: 2004 NES.

Cambridge had significantly less exposure to the asset class. The average allocation to alternative strategies among Oxbridge Colleges was 1.5 per cent in 2002. Average allocation to hedge funds, venture capital, and private equity assets among US educational endowments rose to 8.2 per cent in 2003 and 9.4 per cent in 2004. Anecdotal evidence suggests that allocation to alternative assets is steadily rising in Oxford and Cambridge, but on average such investments remain low compared to their peer group in the United States.

Though the average allocation to private equity investments in Oxbridge, at 0.5 per cent, was closer to the average US allocation of 0.9 per cent, they seem to have arrived at such a point from opposite ends of the investment spectrum. While US educational endowments have been reducing exposure to private equity, Oxbridge endowments have been building up their exposure to the asset class, albeit from a negligibly low base. The average highest allocation to alternative strategies among institutions in Oxford and Cambridge was 10 per cent while the average lowest was 0.5 per cent. Richer Colleges with assets over £45 million had 2.2 per cent invested in alternative strategies while Colleges with smaller endowments had 1.1 per cent exposure to the asset class.

The low rates of return associated with traditional asset classes during the recent bear market caused most institutions to take a closer look at alternative strategies when assessing new investment directions, regardless of the size of the endowment. Thus, Colleges in Oxford and Cambridge with the highest allocation to alternative assets are not necessarily among the wealthiest. The College with the largest allocation to alternative assets, for example, is not even among the top 20 in terms of endowment wealth. This College also has no property assets in its endowment portfolio, though the second and the third largest investors in alternative strategies had 26 and 44 per cent respectively in property. The largest holder of alternative assets was also the largest investor in publicly traded equity, with over 50 per cent in UK equity and about half that in international equity. This College, however, has a low dependency on endowment income (less than 10 per cent) to sustain its operations.

Over half of Oxford and Cambridge institutions (59 per cent in Cambridge compared with 44 per cent in Oxford) did not have any exposure to alternative strategies in 2002–3. There emerges no discernible pattern in their decision not to adopt such approaches to endowment management. While Colleges with smaller endowments suggested that size was an inhibiting factor, others indicated a desire to make an allocation or to increase current exposure as and when such an opportunity arose. Over one-third (38 per cent) of Colleges pointed out that they were willing to increase their exposure to alternative strategies, provided they were able to find suitable managers and/or investment vehicles to do so. Table 5.17 illustrates that institutions with highest allocations to alternative assets were not the wealthiest in Oxbridge; only 4 of these Colleges appeared among the 10 richest.

Colleges have been innovative in employing Cambridge Associates and Fauchier Partners in creating common investment funds in private equity and absolute return strategies respectively for easier access to these investments. Oxford Colleges took the lead in this direction; though some Colleges, such as All Souls, with larger endowments have better access to direct partnerships within private equity and hedge fund sectors. Cambridge Colleges were slower in diversifying into such investments, though since our interviews were conducted two Colleges, Gonville and Caius and Christ's, have made significant investments in hedge funds and some nine Colleges are committed to private equity investments. A small number of institutions (11 per cent) said they

Table 5.17. Oxbridge endowment size verses allocation to alternative assets*

College	Endowment £ m**	Alternatives (%)
1	31.9	14.1
2	27.4	9.0
3	116.9	7.0
4	49.2	6.0
5	81.7	5.7
6	187.7	5.2
7	20.2	5.0
8	77.2	4.6
9	89.3	3.0
10	54.1	2.6

* Alternative assets as a percentage of endowment, as reported by the Colleges.

** Endowment assets are at financial year-end 2002. Based on the *University of Oxford: Financial Statements of the Colleges, 2002–3*.

had no plans to invest in alternative strategies; these institutions may also have changed their preferences by now.

Among Colleges without any exposure to alternative assets, the main concerns related to potential risks associated with such investments, and the small size of endowment that limited such risk-taking. According to one bursar, not invested in the asset class, 'both hedge funds and private equity funds are risky and illiquid. Hedge funds by definition have a problem. They always end up operating outside their remit. And, private equity is illiquid.' Another bursar pointed out: 'The view we have taken is that under current market conditions, there is better value in going long only rather than going short or using any of the investment styles that alternative strategies use. We may change our decision in due course. Also, we do not feel we have the size of assets that allow us the kind of diversification that alternative strategies offer.' 'We feel we are low in property and would like to add to that asset class,' was an alternative point of view.

In the words of one Oxbridge investment committee member, where the endowment portfolio had no specific allocation to alternative strategies:

Existing private equity investments are included in the relevant geographic asset class and are monitored by the fund manager. The Fund has a small investment in private equity currently. Any new investment in alternatives would require the approval of the Investment Sub-Committee.

Though members of the investment committee referred to were fairly knowledgeable and experienced investors, it had not been possible to make any major changes to asset allocation in the area of alternative assets in the management of the endowment. Since our meeting, such changes have indeed been implemented, leading us to believe that investments into alternative investment strategies will follow. As several institutions were instituting reform, we expect institutions in Oxford and Cambridge to increase their allocation to hedge funds and private equity assets, particularly in Cambridge where David Swensen's influence appears to have made an impact, as he is on the University of Cambridge's recently reconstituted Investment Board.

Oxford and Cambridge Colleges are not averse to holding assets in alternative strategies, though finding an appropriate manager or a fund-of-funds manager was frequently cited as a major deterrent to investing in such assets. One of the major obstacles in identifying successful hedge funds is that these partnerships tend to perform better when they are small and young, without an established track record, outside the radar of investment consultants and advisers. The difference in investment return between younger hedge funds (under 2–3 years, for example) and their older counterparts can be high. The gap is significant even after taking into account the failure rate of start-ups, namely survivor bias in addition to incubation bias.[15] The picture is similar in the private equity sector. Thus, the risk of getting the manager selection wrong in hedge funds and private equity partnerships is higher than in ordinary active equity managers.

Many of the existing relationships between Oxbridge Colleges and their fund managers go back a long way, sometimes over decades. Colleges prefer to appoint asset managers they know. As there are not many successful absolute return fund managers with acceptably long performance histories, it poses a challenge for many institutions, not just Oxbridge ones. In Oxford the investment consultant, Cambridge Associates, with a long history of advising educational endowments in the United States, made an early impact in altering investor behaviour, though the same consultant has not had a similar level of influence in Cambridge.

'Cambridge Associates have been essential to our entry into hedge funds/private equity investments,' commented one Oxford bursar. The consulting firm has been successful in setting up a private equity fund-of-funds for Oxbridge institutions. Along with Cambridge Associates, Fauchier Partners have also been instrumental in creating a fund of hedge funds for these institutions. 'We already have 5 per cent of our intended allocation of 10 per cent to hedge funds with our fund manager,' commented another bursar. 'We've got some of our investments with Patrick Fauchier (disappointing performance though) and some with Liontrust Asset Management, their long/short strategy,' added a third Oxford bursar. It is worth noting that the latter's investment with Liontrust came about as a result of a personal introduction. A member of the College's investment committee introduced the manager to the College. Another bursar hit the nail on the head when he said: 'We like to back individuals we know and that seems to have worked.' Knowing the fund manager or the adviser is a critical factor in the due diligence process.

However, over one-third (38 per cent) of Colleges did not like investing in alternative strategies, particularly hedge funds, and perceived it as being too risky. Among those open to investing in such strategies, one-quarter (equally balanced in both Oxford and Cambridge) indicated a preference for private equity assets. Only 16 per cent of institutions preferred hedge funds; interestingly enough, more Cambridge Colleges indicated a preference for hedge funds compared to private equity. And 18 per cent of Colleges in both universities said they liked both private equity and hedge funds, and would be willing to increase their exposure to both categories of investments, provided they found suitable managers. Two Oxford Colleges said they preferred property to alternative assets, and planned to increase their property allocation. Apart from a distinct preference for property, it appears that these institutions would like to increase their exposure to hedge funds and private equity assets, at least to the initial 5 per cent level.

Among bursars with no taste for private equity or hedge funds, lack of knowledge and internal expertise in the asset class were cited as major contributing factors. As one bursar pointed out, 'We need more information on the subject to have a preference.' Another said: 'Currently, I get more information on hedge funds and very little on private equity investment opportunities. Need more information to compare the two asset classes.' The lack of an income stream was also cited as a hindrance for a small number of Colleges. If the size of endowment assets increased, these bursars would also be more willing to consider investing in alternative strategies. According to them, size of the endowment was the limiting factor, though other Colleges did not perceive size to be a necessary constraint for diversifying into alternative assets.

More Colleges were exploring the possibility of investing in hedge funds, but some thought the timing was inappropriate considering the strong flow of funds into the sector. Capacity constraint was a real concern, although Oxbridge bursars were far from major investors in such strategies. According to one bursar, 'We prefer hedge funds to private equity—due to its absolute return characteristics.' Also, the College has an internal expert in the field. Most Colleges with a preference for hedge funds refer to its total return characteristics as being the incentive for investing in such strategies. According to one bursar, 'hedge funds in their non-directional investment strategies are less risky and hence more suitable than a highly economy-dependent, directional investment in private equity.' Equally, there were others who found hedge funds difficult to understand and monitor, and/or found it difficult to identify good fund managers in the sector. For one bursar, investing in a 'fund of funds in the hedge fund sector' was a possibility. 'But, it is difficult to find good fund of funds hedge-fund managers.'

Some investment committees preferred private equity assets. According to one bursar with a preference for private equity investments, 'We feel we are a bit small to be accepted by hedge fund managers. Also, the Fellows of the College may not quite agree to its investment style. We might have a fiduciary problem as well in that area.' 'We need to understand the asset class better, for a start. We would like to increase our private equity allocation; we have already made a start there. Also, we need to be a larger size to enable us to take greater risk with our investment,' explained another. For others, 'in the long term, we see private equity as a larger holding than hedge funds.' And according to another bursar: 'We have a target allocation to private equity, but we are not convinced about the actual (as opposed to the theoretical) advantages attributed to hedge funds.' A senior bursar made his preference very clear: 'We are currently invested in some 24 private equity funds. And, we are going to invest in the fund being set up by Cambridge Associates. We aim to invest 5 per cent of our financial portfolio in private equity. This College has a clear preference for private equity assets.'

Not all College bursars have such a clear preference in the matter of investing in hedge funds and/or private equity: 'Our current target is 5 per cent, but that is split equally between the two. No clear preference; keeping an open mind on the subject,' commented one bursar. Some bursars view alternative assets as a diversifier. Hence, the question of preference elicited the response—'Silly question'—from one bursar. 'They are there to provide diversification.' Overall diversification of assets was acknowledged as a good thing, regardless of whether the Colleges were invested in alternative assets or not.

A few Colleges prefer property to either private equity or hedge funds. According to one such bursar, 'We view property as our quintessential invest-ment for the long term. It provides us with the bulk (75 per cent of endow-ment income) of our income and we like it as a long-term investment.' The same College also planned to increase its existing high exposure to property; diversification was not a great concern for this institution. It is among the oldest Colleges in Oxbridge, and thus has centuries of experience of investing in property. It has also benefited from such allocation.

When asked: 'If you are not invested in private equity or hedge funds, under what circumstances would you consider making an allocation to these assets?' most of the respondents said when they have a 'larger endowment.' Size of endowment was the key to greater diversification into alternative strategies. A lesser endowment of say £10–15 million was perceived as a constraint in tak-ing the sort of risks that were perceived to be associated with alternative assets, such as liquidity constraints, the lack of transparency, lack of resources to monitor these investments, and so on. 'Our portfolio is too small to consider such assets. We would find it difficult to explain it to the Governing Body,' said one bursar. 'It is extremely unlikely for us to consider investing in such assets,' explained another. 'We would need to have enough assets to be able to consider a wider diversification than current. If we had at least twice the size of funds we have currently, then we may consider some of these alternative asset classes. Taking into account the size of our funds and the College, such an issue does not figure in our discussions. We have discussed it in the past and come to these conclusions for what it is worth.' The same College had 75 per cent of its endowment assets in indexed public equity funds.

According to another College with investments in public equity indexed strategies and a high exposure to property, which provided 60 per cent of its endowment income, 'It is a personal preference. If somebody in the Invest-ment Committee pointed out that we were missing out in our policy by not being in private equity, for example, we might reconsider our allocation. As far as hedge funds are concerned, it will also depend on the Committee. Last time we had a look, we were not persuaded.' For a larger endowment that currently has all of its assets with one fund manager with a 'value' orientation, allocation strategies would most likely only be reviewed 'when the Investment Sub-Committee takes a view that its investment strategy needs to be altered involving a change of fund manager.'

Ideally, many institutions in Oxford and Cambridge would like greater exposure to alternative strategies. The main issue for these institutions, compared with more established endowments such as Harvard or Yale, is how best to achieve such exposure as capacity is a serious constraint. Some of these institutions were also concerned about the merits of absolute return strategies; the major issue being who is going to deliver those returns? The vast majority of investment managers have failed to deliver superior relative returns. There are a few smart people in the sector; but the vast bulk of absolute return managers are increasingly becoming asset-gatherers. Many Colleges were unsure of the credibility of the new breed of hedge fund managers. They were also expected to work under various constraints; so it was difficult to see where the performance would come from.

The greatest challenge for Colleges with smaller endowments was not only how to identify in advance those managers who could add incremental returns to their portfolios, but how to persuade these super-managers to include them in their closed partnerships. This challenge, common to all investors, is magnified in the alternative assets area where the performance differential between the below-median manager and the top-quartile one is significant. The ability to gain exposure to the best fund managers is the main concern for investors in any asset class. It is particularly noticeable in the alternative strategies arena where the skill of the individual manager makes all the difference. Unlike traditional investment assets such as fixed income and equity, the poor choice of manager in alternative strategies can result in substantial underperformance, thereby increasing the cost of such a decision.

Allocation to property

Compared with educational endowments in the United States where the average allocation to real estate was just 2.7 per cent in 2002, rising to 2.8 in 2004, institutions in Oxford and Cambridge invested significantly more in property. The average allocation for all Oxbridge Colleges was 26 per cent, almost 10 times the US average for educational endowments in 2002. The average highest allocation to property in Oxford and Cambridge was 83 per cent while the lowest was 5 per cent, almost twice as much as the average US allocation. Richer Colleges in Oxford and Cambridge, with assets over £45 million, had on average invested 44 per cent of their endowment assets in property. Even Colleges with endowments worth less than £45 million had 16 per cent in property. The income-generating capacity of property was valued highly among these institutions along with the asset's potential as a strategic diversifier.

Colleges with the highest allocation to property were not among the richest in Oxbridge, suggesting that size of endowment was not the driving factor in determining such allocation. Three of the top ten investors in property

Table 5.18. Oxbridge endowment size versus
allocation to property*

College	Endowment £ m**	Property (%)
1	75.0	90
2	28.2	75
3	196.8	66
4	491.4	66
5	27.3	64
6	22.3	62
7	62.5	58
8	81.7	55
9	49.2	53
10	29.4	50

* Property assets as a percentage of endowment, as
reported by the Colleges.
** Endowment assets are at financial year-end 2002.
Oxford data are based on the *University of Oxford: Financial Statements of the Colleges, 2002–3.*

were Oxford Colleges, but only one of the three was among the ten richest
Colleges in Oxford. Of the remaining seven Colleges in Cambridge, just two
were among its wealthiest. While the smaller size of the endowment was put
forward as a reason for not investing in alternative assets, the size of the
endowment did not pose a barrier when investing in property. In 2002, for
example, a College with endowment assets worth £22 million had almost
as much property in its endowment as a College with assets worth £491
million. Table 5.18 illustrates the ten highest allocations to property among
all institutions in Oxford and Cambridge in 2002.

For the financial year ending 2004, the list of Colleges with the highest allocations to property had altered; so had the property holdings as a percentage
of the overall endowment. As reported in the 2003–4 annual accounts, the
top 10 property investors in Oxbridge were equally divided among the two
universities. This was due to the fact that property assets had performed well
since the market recovery in 2003. As a result, more Colleges in Oxford and
Cambridge either increased their allocation to property or superior market
returns resulted in larger allocation to the asset class.

Table 5.19 shows the 10 highest property investors in Oxford and Cambridge in 2003–4. Among these, Trinity, Peterhouse, Jesus, and Pembroke in
Cambridge are among the 10 wealthiest, while in Oxford only Jesus and University are among the 10 richest in terms of endowment wealth. Endowment
wealth appears to have greater impact on asset allocation in favour of property
among Cambridge Colleges.

While endowment wealth is not a clear indicator of size of property investments of institutions in Oxford or Cambridge, the age of some of the Colleges
may have been an influencing factor. The oldest Colleges do not all have high

Table 5.19. Allocation to property versus size of endowment, 2004

College	University	% in Property	Endowment £ m
Peterhouse	Cambridge	83.8	75.5
Oriel	Oxford	79.2	50.3
Trinity	Cambridge	68.0	649.9
Jesus	Oxford	57.6	99.5
Lincoln	Oxford	55.0	37.7
Jesus	Cambridge	53.8	77.8
Corpus Christi	Cambridge	52.5	52.8
Pembroke	Cambridge	51.6	59.6
Corpus Christi	Oxford	49.7	41.5
University	Oxford	48.7	67.5

Source: University of Oxford, Financial Statements of the Colleges, 2003–4; Cambridge University Reporter: Accounts of the Colleges, 2003–4.

allocation to property, but their average holding is the highest within their peer group. Not all the oldest Colleges held on to their historical property assets. Several Colleges got rid of some of their less attractive holdings; others were more pioneering in their approach by diversifying into science parks and other schemes with development potential. In Oxford, Balliol College, for example, decided to sell its direct property holdings about 20 years ago. Whatever property exposure it has currently is via a recently acquired property unit trust. Thus, Balliol's asset allocation decision today is driven purely by financial considerations.

Balliol used to have about half its property portfolio in real estate and direct holdings. A decision was made over 20 years ago that the stock market was going to provide better returns, and so a 20-year programme was initiated to divest the College of its direct property investments. The nature of stock markets since 2000 and long-term expected returns from investments in traditional equity assets to some extent reduced the advantage of this wholesale move out of property. By the time the College had achieved its target set two decades ago, it was time to reinvest in the asset class. By 2002–3, the College endowment was invested 10 per cent in the Charity Property Fund, in which other Colleges were also invested. The College had successfully moved out of its direct, illiquid investments in property to more liquid assets, enabling it to determine its asset allocation with greater flexibility.

Table 5.20 shows that the average property holding of the 10 oldest Colleges in Oxford and Cambridge was higher than the average for Oxbridge Colleges in general at 26 per cent (see Table 5.3); it was also higher than the average property holding among the wealthiest Oxbridge Colleges at 44 per cent (see Table 5.6).

The average property holding of the 10 oldest Colleges in Oxford in the fiscal year 2003–4 was 42 per cent; in Cambridge it was higher at 49 per cent.

Table 5.20. Date of foundation versus property allocation in 2004

Oxford	Founded	Property (%)	Cambridge*	Founded	Property (%)
University	1249	49	Peterhouse	1284	84
Balliol	1263	8	Clare	1326	31
Merton	1264	48	Pembroke	1347	52
Exeter	1314	15	Gonville & Caius	1348	46
Oriel	1326	79	Trinity Hall	1350	13
The Queen's	1341	47	Corpus Christi	1352	53
Christ Church**	1363	41	Magdalene	1428	46
New College	1379	35	St Catharine's	1473	44
Lincoln	1427	55	Jesus	1497	54
All Souls	1438	45	St John's	1511	66
Average		**42**	**Average**		**49**

* Excludes King's, Queens', and Christ's.

** The Cathedral was founded in the 8th century, Canterbury College in 1363 and Christ Church College in 1546.

These averages were higher in 2002 at 44 and 50 per cent for Oxford and Cambridge respectively. The overall average property exposure at 45.5 per cent in 2004 (47.4 per cent in 2002) was significantly higher than the averages for any other group within Oxbridge.

It can safely be concluded that Oxbridge endowments value property as an asset class. As they have owned some of the choicest property assets in the UK for periods longer than other financial assets such as equities and fixed income assets, for example, such a stance appears rational. A detailed breakdown of property assets, such as holdings in commercial, residential or agricultural, held by the Colleges is not currently available. Many Colleges are in the process of creating more diversified endowment portfolios while aiming to hold a more balanced mix of property assets.

At the same time, there are Colleges that strongly believe concentration in quality assets is the key to investment success, be it in equity or property. As Peterhouse's Murison pointed out:

The College will not diversify into anything it does not understand. The College will continue to favour concentration in assets which it understands. The Governing Body agrees with John Maynard Keynes, the First Bursar of King's College in 1930s, who was of the view 'that the right method in investments is to put fairly large sums into enterprises which one thinks one knows something about and in management in which one thoroughly believes. It is a mistake to think that one limits one's risk by spreading too much between enterprises about which one knows too little and has no reason for special confidence.'

Regardless of the individual approach, long-term historical experience of property as an investment is a distinctive characteristic of Oxbridge endowment portfolios. Not all Colleges, nor the universities, have such a predilection for the asset class; but the majority of Colleges are content to hold a third of their assets in property. Some of these institutions planned to reduce their exposure to a lower level, around 20–5 per cent, but were in no great rush to get there.

Cash allocation

Contrary to the US experience, where there has been a steady decline in monies allocated to cash investments over the past decade, from 6.5 per cent of endowment assets in 1995 to 3.7 per cent in 2004, with the current allocation being the lowest over the decade, Oxford and Cambridge institutions held substantially more cash. US institutions have been reducing cash holdings, possibly with a view to being fully invested so as to boost their overall rate of return. Oxbridge institutions appear to have increased their cash, at least during the bear market, also with a view to boosting their return in a falling market. In 2000, US institutions had 4.1 per cent in cash, less than the 6.5 per cent reported in 1995.

Cash in Oxbridge endowment portfolios played a significant role as several Colleges reported holding substantial amounts of it. One-quarter of institutions in Oxford and Cambridge reported holding 10 per cent or more in cash. It would be misleading to read too much into 1 year's asset allocation, in the middle of a bear market. However, it can be assumed that the relatively high allocation to cash among these institutions indicated a general scepticism of returns expected from financial markets in 2002; though 2003 and 2004 offered decent equity returns. The average cash holding among Colleges in Oxford was 9.2 per cent compared to 5 per cent for Cambridge. The average for Oxbridge, at 7.1 per cent, was almost twice as much as the 3.9 per cent held by educational endowments in the United States in 2002.

Less wealthy Oxbridge Colleges held over twice (8.7 per cent) as much cash as the richer ones (4.2 per cent). The average cash allocation among Colleges with endowments valued at less than £45 million was 11.3 per cent compared to 6.0 per cent for Cambridge Colleges. The richer Colleges in Oxford also had more cash (4.8 per cent) compared to their peer group in Cambridge (3.5 per cent). Less well-endowed Colleges in the United States also held more cash (6.6 per cent) compared to institutions with endowments over $1 billion (1.8 per cent). When compared to the allocations made to cash by Yale and Harvard, it becomes clear how institutional investment thinking varied; the Yale Endowment had no cash while Harvard's endowment was geared (5 per cent) in 2002.

The highest allocation to cash in an endowment portfolio in Oxford and Cambridge was 35 per cent and the lowest was 0.7 per cent—both incidentally in Oxford. The College with the highest cash allocation also invested half its assets in equity. According to the Investment Bursar of this College, 'Most of our cash is held in the University Deposit Pool, which provides us with an excellent return. The facility with which one can add or withdraw cash makes it an easy and attractive vehicle for us.' Over one-third (38 per cent) of Colleges in Oxford were invested in the Oxford University Cash Deposit fund invested in fixed-term money market deposits, which proved to be an attractive vehicle for Colleges in managing their cash as it provided relatively good rates of return along with easy access. According to one bursar:

The University cash account is easy to get in and out of. In a falling interest rate environment, the University cash fund—partly invested in bonds—has offered a very competitive rate of return. The way it works is that the rate of distribution is based on the long-term rate of return of these bonds. So, to some extent this policy favours those who enter at the margin because at the end of each quarter they take the total return and share it out among the current investors. As a result, the return is higher than available elsewhere.

Some 41 per cent of Colleges reported 'in-house' management of their cash; over half the Colleges in Cambridge (56 per cent) managed cash in-house compared with less than one-third (29 per cent) in Oxford. In-house cash management meant that the College bursar and the bursarial team were responsible for deciding where the cash was to be deposited. One-quarter (25 per cent) of Colleges invested in the University Deposit Pool (38 per cent in Oxford compared with 7 per cent in Cambridge) and about a third (34 per cent) deposited it with external managers.

About one-quarter of Colleges had cash holdings above the 10 per cent level, and the top 5 allocations to cash, ranging from 21 to 35 per cent, were reported by Oxford Colleges. Overall, one-quarter of Colleges with cash levels at or above 10 per cent were in Cambridge. Of the 11 Oxford Colleges with more than 10 per cent in cash, about one-third invested in the University Deposit Pool. None of the four Cambridge Colleges with high cash allocations invested in an equivalent cash fund managed by the University. One College in Oxford left the cash management to its accountant; the three remaining Colleges deposited their cash with various investment banks; no clear reason existed for such a choice except that the College had a relationship with the bank concerned.

Regardless of their actual high cash holdings, in their strategic asset allocation Oxbridge institutions had a fully invested policy for their external managers. Thus, the residual cash in the securities portfolio was typically left to the discretion of the fund manager or broker. The working capital (for the daily needs of the College) was managed by the bursar and invested in Bank deposits and/or with Building Societies. Cash management was ultimately the responsibility of the investment bursar and his team, which in some cases included the College accountant. Some Colleges reported high cash holdings as a result of planned internal expenditures, which in some instances were substantial.

Conclusion

Institutional portfolios with long-term investment horizons, such as endowments, are best invested in assets capable of generating equity-like returns, including private equity and absolute return strategies. To mitigate equity risks, portfolios also include fixed income, real estate, and other assets such as commodities or natural resources. Compared to larger US educational endowments, institutions in Oxford and Cambridge had less exposure to alternative assets and strategies. However, they invested significantly more in direct property assets, and for the Colleges it often appeared that their real estate was a counterpart to US holdings of fixed interest securities. (Many US institutions regard their real estate holdings as an alternative asset.) The Oxbridge allocation to absolute return strategies remained low; over half the Colleges did not have any investment in hedge funds, which were considered riskier than more traditional assets such as equity or property. The size of some of the endowments was perceived as a constraint in taking the sort of risks associated with alternative strategies, such as liquidity risk, lack of transparency, due diligence, and fiduciary risk.

While there was a general sense of scepticism about the merits of investing in hedge funds, overall attitudes towards alternative strategies appeared to be shifting; more Colleges expressed a willingness to consider investing in a wider range of assets than they were traditionally accustomed to. At least, half the Colleges indicated a clear intent to increase allocation to alternative strategies; there was some preference for private equity compared with hedge funds. Oxbridge College endowments had undergone a high level of restructuring over the recent past, moving from income-only policies towards total return ones; they were thus in the process of creating more efficient, better diversified portfolios. Taking into account the role of property in their endowment portfolios, their overall performance was protected from the recent market volatility, particularly during the bear market of 2000–3.

Asset allocation remains one of the greatest concerns among investment committees as Colleges aim to secure future income and preserve long-term purchasing power. Considerable uncertainty was expressed with regard to expectations of long-term returns from financial assets and its impact on spending policy. The changed economic and financial landscape of the past decade has been challenging even for experts in the field. It has been even more demanding for trustees of foundations and endowments, sometimes without adequate access to necessary expertise within their governing bodies to address the complexities of allocating assets in an altered financial environment. Evaluating and predicting outcomes of various investment strategies and management decisions was perceived as being more difficult in the current environment for all investors.

As educational institutions, Oxford and Cambridge will benefit from government funding. The level of income from public sources is unlikely to be affected dramatically though the sources of future income may need to change. An effort has been made by the Government to enable educational institutions to build up their endowments. Most Colleges rely on endowment income to secure their operations. Simultaneously, their diversified income base provides them with a level of stability, empowering them to pursue higher risk, higher return strategies. To what extent institutions in Oxford and Cambridge have embraced opportunities inherent in such a funding environment is not clear. Taking into account that until very recently, these institutions were obliged to follow income-only investment strategies, it is not surprising that they implemented policies that best matched their particular needs.

Endowment management practices as reported within Oxbridge offer significant opportunities for change. It would be incorrect to suggest that investment bursars lack an overall level of professionalism. It can be argued that certain practices persisted as a result of historical circumstances, resulting in a lack of 'sophistication' in the overall approach to endowment asset management. Investment objective though subject to the overarching educational objective should not deter these world-class institutions from holding efficient portfolios. In the final analysis, asset allocation is appropriate allocation of risk. While bursars acknowledged that risk management remains an area of concern, and the definition of risk associated with individual Colleges varies, there exists no clear methodology of examining such issues formally. Investment consultants too share some responsibility as a large number of bursars indicated their inability to find an adviser with the appropriate scale of experience in asset management for endowments with asset allocation strategies skewed in favour of property. Colleges without any property in their endowment also did not benefit from such specialist advice. None of the Colleges in Oxford or Cambridge with nil allocation to property had an investment consultant.

However, these institutions have collectively embraced major changes over the last few years though some Colleges have always been innovative in their policymaking. In the words of one newly appointed Treasurer:

Until 2003 the endowment and reserves of the College were entirely invested (excluding only a little private equity) in the pooled fund products of one fund manager, who had a broad discretionary mandate to switch between own funds including new products. The College Investment Committee played a passive role, receiving quarterly reports from the manager. With the benefit of two additional external members, alumni with distinguished careers in fund management, the same committee now undertakes all strategic and tactical asset allocation and fund selection decisions and invests in a much broader portfolio of products. This is feasible through an execution-only agreement with our manager. We have a consultant providing performance measurement. These changes have had an impact on returns and the investment process itself.

The transition process often takes several years to become visibly embedded. Over the past few years, for example, institutions in Oxford and Cambridge have implemented total return investment strategies, moving away from purely income-oriented ones. They also made the shift from policies that encouraged income-generating investment assets towards establishing sensible spending rules that freed up asset allocation decisions. They have accepted the concept of a Policy Portfolio based on long-term analysis of institutional objectives while introducing alternative assets into their portfolios. At the same time, they have had to deal with real cuts in higher education funding, not to mention cope with charges of being elitist (Harvard, Yale, and other 'Ivy League' institutions in the United States take pride in being so), and for not being more open about their investment policies just when they opted to be more transparent in all aspects of their operations.

At the time of going to press, Colleges in Oxford and Cambridge published their accounts for financial year ending 2005; the third year of accounts for Colleges in Oxford in the new format, and second for Cambridge Colleges. It is worth comparing how asset allocation has evolved since our interviews were conducted in 2003. Those institutions that had made progress in defining investment objectives, adopting total return investment policies and implementing appropriate asset allocation strategies, such as All Souls College in Oxford, have not altered their asset allocation substantially over this period. All Souls had very similar allocations to listed equity, domestic and international, in 2002 and 2005. The only differences were in allocations made to alternative assets such as hedge funds and private equity (which have gone up to 9 per cent from 7 per cent in total) and property (which has also risen from 44 to 47 per cent); these increases have been offset against fixed income and cash (down from 10 per cent of portfolio in 2002 to 5 per cent today).

There were other institutions, such as Cambridge University, which were in the middle of major restructuring; the asset allocation in the annual account for 2004–5 does not illustrate the extent and nature of changes to come. The full impact of the newly established Investment Office will become evident a few years after the appointment of the Chief Investment Officer. It took the University of Oxford almost a decade to get to its current asset allocation since the decision was initially made to move to total return investing in 1997.

Somewhere in between are Colleges that are more nimble, achieving major shifts in asset allocation over a shorter period; these include Colleges such as Gonville and Caius in Cambridge. Barry Hedley, the Senior Bursar, joined in October 2000. In 2003, the College had 42 per cent of its endowment assets in property, 33 per cent in listed equities, 5 per cent in alternatives, and 20 per cent in liquid assets such as cash and fixed income. By 2005, the asset allocation of the endowment had moved to 47 per cent in property, 31 per cent in listed equity, 12 per cent in alternatives (private equity and hedge funds), 5 per cent in commodities, and 5 per cent in liquid assets such as cash and fixed income. The College has since reduced its property exposure and plans to raise its allocation to hedge funds.

From data that are available, allocation to property has risen across the Colleges, largely as a result of market appreciation. But, in the case of hedge funds and private equity, higher allocations reflect a mix of market appreciation and new investments. Oxford Colleges' aggregate allocation to property in 2005 was 45 per cent compared with 31 per cent in 2003. The aggregate exposure to alternative strategies is not available, but there is evidence to suggest it has increased over this period. The increasing professionalism evident in investment approaches by way of superior diversification strategies embracing assets, investment styles (leading to a rise in the appointment of specialist managers) illustrates what can be achieved within a relatively short time frame given the requisite framework for decision-making.

6

Investing in property

Introduction

Like absolute return strategies, property or real estate assets serve not only as a powerful diversifier, they protect the portfolio by generating returns that are not typically correlated with other traditional assets such as publicly traded equities. Private equity, for example, depends on many of the factors that influence the return of public equity assets. Unlike commodities or natural resources that do not have a stream of income attached, high quality property assets typically yield above average income, and have the potential of decent capital gains in the long term. Property thus contributes to diversification and extension of the efficient frontier.

Colleges in Oxford and Cambridge historically owned significant property assets in their endowment portfolios. Their decision to maintain relatively high allocation to property assets today is driven by the desire to diversify risk as well as to secure a steady source of income. Top US educational endowments have been pioneering investors in asset classes where greater inefficiencies were likely to exist, such as in private equity. They also invest in strategies better equipped to exploit market inefficiencies such as with hedge funds. In both types of investing, greater risk-taking is involved. Harvard and Yale never considered themselves taking irrational risks because they understood the nature of their risk-taking. Similarly, Oxbridge Colleges have been investing in what they know best, as they have owned property as a strategic asset over centuries. In the majority of cases the benefactions received historically were in the form of land. Some of the Colleges know more about investing in property than any comparable group of investors.

Property generally acts as a secure hedge against unexpected changes in inflation, and these institutions recognize that attribute. 'If there was no property in the portfolio, we would have other inflation hedging assets,' said one College bursar. The inflation-hedging characteristic of property works efficiently when the market is in a reasonable state of equilibrium. If there is a huge oversupply or surge in demand, prices inevitably adjust even if inflation is relatively controlled. As institutions in Oxford and Cambridge own some of the prime properties in the UK, the value of their assets have been protected— both when equity markets corrected during 2000–3 and when the property market declined during the 1990s. For some Colleges, the risk is not from the quality of assets held, but from the concentration of these assets, sometimes in one location—that is in Cambridge, Oxford, or London, as a percentage of the overall endowment. In the case of Peterhouse, for example, 39 per cent of total endowment assets were represented by a single property, Albany, which consists of elegant apartments off Piccadilly, in the heart of London.

Though such a degree of concentration in any single asset defies modern portfolio theory, in this instance it has served the College's investment purpose over the very long term, not just during the recent bear market. As unanticipated inflation generally tends to benefit property assets and damages bonds, and unexpected deflation helps bonds and harms property, Colleges in Oxford and Cambridge appear to have done well by holding on to their property investments. Also, if economic conditions remain buoyant, then even in a non-inflationary environment property prices rise when other financial assets fail to deliver, as was the case in the UK and some other overseas markets, post-March 2000. Interest rates declined as stock markets failed to deliver and there was fear of deflation. Demand for property remained strong as businesses in the UK flourished and government relaxed its immigration policy. The enlargement of the EU meant more people from Europe made their way into the UK looking for a financially better way of life. House prices soared, particularly in areas of greater economic activity such as in London; almost doubling over a five-year period.

As institutions in Oxford and Cambridge are truly long-term investors, short-term considerations do not affect their strategic asset allocation, though they may result in more tactical allocation. Thus, some Colleges let their property assets rise as a percentage of their actual portfolio compared to their policy benchmark. Conventional wisdom states that optimal portfolios are typically diversified ones, but the extent and nature of diversification is determined by the objectives of the individual investor. Many bursars expressed a desire to identify the optimal asset allocation for educational endowments such as theirs against which they could benchmark their individual allocation. The asset allocation strategies employed by Harvard and Yale did not reflect their needs due to a host of reasons that included the Oxbridge Colleges' lack of access to quality managers in private equity or the hedge fund sector. In addition, their existing exposure to property acted as a substitute for investments in alternative assets. 'The College treats its property holdings as integral to a diversified portfolio,' was one bursar's explanation. Property is regarded as a core asset by a significant proportion of institutions in Oxford and Cambridge.

Property investments span a range of assets from equity to debt as well as assets combining debt and equity-like characteristics. Property can also be privately owned with infrequent valuations or be publicly quoted as any other marketable security, thus providing the diversifying attributes that justify its status as a separate asset class. According to one experienced Cambridge bursar: 'Some property behave like bonds; others like equity. We have a 99-year ground rent on a car park in Harley Street, London, with a rent review in 30 years, which is like a bond. We also have investment in a Garden Centre where we have a sort of venture capital type investment in the company as well. And, we have standard investments in property that are like equity with similar returns. As a result, it depends on which type of property one is talking about.' For this institution, income from property was estimated at one-quarter (25 per cent) of total endowment income.

Some Oxford and Cambridge institutions view their core property assets as a substitute for bonds. 'A large exposure to property means that our exposure to bonds is low; so property is seen as a substitute for bonds,' remarked one bursar. 'We see our property holdings as a substitute for gilts, and thus a source of income, in addition to being a diversifier. Agricultural holdings are also a source of one off capital sums,' conveyed another. Property holdings therefore serve an array of institutional needs, influencing overall asset allocation even when the asset class does not feature in the endowment portfolio. According to yet another bursar, 'commercial property associated with the College's inalienable operational buildings resulted in a rather high proportion of property in the portfolio. Hence, we tolerate a lower proportion of fixed interest securities than would otherwise be the case.'

At the same time, there are Colleges such as Balliol that took a strategic decision over two decades ago to sell their property assets, though Balliol has recently been building up its investments in the sector by buying into property funds. The introduction of REITs to the UK market is likely to change investment behaviour, as institutions seek to hold more diversified portfolios. Some Oxford and Cambridge Colleges are considering consolidating their property assets, though property remains a sensitive and contentious issue. As the correlation of REITs to equities is higher, direct property assets act as superior diversifiers; but, the existence of a new asset class in a more liquid form will influence investor behaviour.

Institutions in Oxford have already set up collective funds for alternative asset classes, such as hedge funds and private equity. Oxford Investment Partners was created specifically to provide asset management services across all asset classes to institutions in the philanthropic sector. Today Cambridge Colleges also invest in the private equity and hedge fund sectors via pooled funds. While there is no plan to launch an Oxford or Cambridge REIT, there is no reason why Colleges may not opt to do so in the future. Colleges could turn out to be more imaginative in their approaches to managing property; they could leverage their expertise in the sector by launching such products. The trust deeds of the Colleges, going back several hundred years, may make pooling difficult though not impossible. While such transition will take time and consideration, the Colleges are in a unique position to map their future.

Over the past half-century or so, Colleges reduced their original estates and now hold portfolios that include equities, fixed interest securities, alternative assets, and property. Not all Colleges hold property in their endowment portfolio. There are Colleges with significant property holdings that are not part of the endowment assets. One quarter (23 per cent) of Colleges reported having no property assets in their endowment; some of these Colleges owned large estates, which are 'operational' assets and whose value is not disclosed in the annual reports and accounts. Thus, institutions in Oxford and Cambridge own significant property assets, but not all such assets are included in the endowment. There are about 10 Colleges in Oxford and 4 in Cambridge with no property investments in their endowment funds, including Colleges like St Hugh's and Keble in Oxford with sizeable operational properties. It is not possible to indicate the development value of these assets though the potential exists for the securitization of such assets in the future.

Many Colleges have subsidiary trading companies, which often include property.[1] Some property holdings may not appear in the endowment, but Colleges that presented consolidated accounts include such investments in their financial statements. Trading activities undertaken by All Souls College's subsidiary company, Chichele Property Company Limited, for example, is liable to corporation tax like any other trading company. Profits made by the company are donated to the College, which in turn distributes them to other charities and worthy causes as determined by All Souls College's General Purposes Committee. Similarly, Churchill College in Cambridge has three wholly-owned operating subsidiaries which exist to provide additional revenue to the College and to optimize the use of the College infrastructure. These three companies are all registered and their accounts filed at Companies House annually. There were also some Colleges that did not present consolidated accounts, opting out under the exemptions provided for medium sized groups by the Companies Act 1985.

Allocation to property

The range of allocation to property assets within the endowment portfolios of Oxbridge institutions is summarized in Table 6.1. Just under

Table 6.1. Range of allocation to property within the endowment, in per cent.

Property	Oxford	Cambridge	Oxbridge
75–100%	—	4	2
50–75%	9	19	13
25–50%	29	30	30
10–25%	9	15	11
<10%	21	7	15
No property*	24	22	23
No response	9	4	7
Total	**100**	**100**	**100**

* No property assets in the endowment.

one-third of Colleges (30 per cent) invested over one-quarter to a half of their endowment assets in property; 13 per cent of Colleges invested a half to three-quarters in property, while 1 College held 87 per cent of its endowment in property. About 15 per cent of Colleges owned less than 10 per cent in property, and 11 per cent owned 10–25 per cent of the asset class in their endowment portfolios. It is significant that about one-quarter (23 per cent) of institutions currently do not own any property in their endowment.

As noted above, 1 college is at the extreme end of the asset allocation spectrum. The endowment portfolio of Peterhouse College, Cambridge, in 2002–3, consisted of 87 per cent in property, with the remaining 13 per cent invested in equity. The College historically invested heavily in property, but increased it allocation further during the second half of 1990s. Thus, between 1963 and 1993, the College invested 22 per cent of its endowment in equity and the rest in property. The 2003 equity allocation, at 13 per cent, was at a historic low. Also, the concentration of its property assets was significant; just one investment, Albany in Piccadilly, London, accounted for 39 per cent of the endowment. An additional 23 per cent was represented by houses and flats in and around a single market, Cambridge; and a further 21 per cent was in commercial property, spread over Cambridge, London, and the provinces.

Table 6.2 illustrates the changing asset allocation within Peterhouse's endowment portfolio since the 1960s.

According to Andrew Murison, such concentration on the certainty of future income streams is the essence of successful investing. Citing an example of the College's philosophy of 'sceptical pragmatism', he explained:

Rational speculation is fine so long as the investment is fundamentally under-pinned by secure income. The College added to its farmland holdings in the early 1990s, when prices were depressed, in carefully selected areas of potential planning gain—mainly within the curtilage of villages which might attract building

Table 6.2. Peterhouse College endowment asset allocation, in per cent

Asset	1963	1993	2003
Property %			
Albany	38	22	39
Cantab Residential	19	28	23
Commercial	9	22	21
Land	12	7	4
Equities %	22	22	13
Total (£ m)	**1.3**	**34.5**	**74.8**

Source: Andrew Murison.

permission. Amongst other parcels dotted around the country, the College bought 86 acres north of Cambridge for £1,500 an acre, down from £2,000 an acre a couple of years before. The College let it for £65 an acre which produced a running yield that was well covered by the market rate and met the College's 4 per cent annual income test. So, the College could afford to wait for 50 or 100 years while development pressure compounded capital value. Nearby acreage recently zoned for development was valued at £365,000 an acre.

Relative success with an asset is inevitably the mother of concentration, since the asset accounts for a higher proportion of the portfolio. More importantly, concentration—when soundly based on relative economic value—is inevitably the mother of success. By contrast, a policy of automatic portfolio re-balancing, regardless of economic values, will, in the College's view, merely serve to cut the flowers and feed the weeds. It may be a safe policy for those who, for whatever reason, cannot restrict their activities to the relatively few opportunities that stand out at any one time, reliably promising a rising income to meet future liabilities. But if an endowment can confidently make these judgements (that is, really understand the dynamics of the asset), it should.

The investment style of the College has involved managing risk on an asset-by-asset basis, rather than on a portfolio approach. This stance has been as true of its equity assets as its property investments. In the equity portion of the endowment, individual stocks were bought solely according to the solidity of the underlying earnings power and its predictability into the future. 'The equity portfolio's asset allocation is a residual of stock selection, although after the event an assessment is made of the extent to which specific risks are mutually offsetting. Our equity portfolio was limited to 15 holdings and, since the systemic risk of randomly selected equities is 95 per cent diversified away at that level, the specific risks usually were offsetting. But our equities were most certainly not picked at random, so this has to be carefully checked. The essential ingredients we looked for in a company were the extent of the predictable cash return on incremental equity and the reinvestment rate—in other words, the potential for compounding cash earnings over time,' added Murison.

Concentration is considered to be risky if the sources of income in the underlying assets are insecure, as they often are with equities. Thus, one considers the question: 'how should success and risk for an endowment fund be defined'? According to Murison:

The answer lies in the fact that capital gains should not feature over-significantly in the criteria for success. This may seem strange, as *ex post facto* they have been vital to keeping the College afloat. But capital gains *per se* are not the purpose of the endowment. Income to meet cash liabilities (including those of a capital nature) as they fall due is the key. By contrast, absence of *realised* capital losses (which reduce future income) must be at the very top of the list of goals. Let us not confuse *realised* capital losses with volatility in book value, which merely mirrors change in fickle opinion rather than the permanent creation or destruction of earnings power. Anything other than investing with great confidence for the long term in predictably sustainable earnings power is risky speculation—the triumph of hope over relative certainty. Management of the endowment revolves around determining the income required by the College's present and future liabilities, and then locating matching assets of impeccable earnings power to meet the estimated needs of current and future generations. Impeccable earnings power is defined as 'the greatest certainty of sustaining necessary yield in real terms into the future.'

By this definition, equities over the very long term qualify as an impeccable investment class. However, as 'the College itself lacks the ability to identify with confidence businesses that can be relied upon to maintain their earnings power over the long-term, it tends to eschews equities,' added Murison. Understandably, with an investment policy based on experience and conviction, Peterhouse has favoured concentration of investments in assets it understands. Superior knowledge of individual investments remains the key to success when investors essentially take on risks that can be diversified.

Considering that the average allocation to property in the endowment portfolios of institutions in Oxford and Cambridge was 26 per cent (22 per cent in Oxford and 30 per cent in Cambridge), it is worth examining the asset distribution among institutions that did not have any exposure to the asset class. About one quarter (23 per cent) of respondents reported having no property assets in their endowment fund (24 per cent in Oxford and 22 per cent in Cambridge). All these Colleges also had smaller endowments, assets under management varying between a low of £5 million to a high of £36 million; the average endowment size was £14 million. Table 6.3 shows how these institutions allocated their funds among different asset classes and strategies.

Interesting differences appear in asset distributions between Oxford and Cambridge. Among Colleges with no exposure to property, those in Cambridge had no exposure to alternative strategies though they had more in UK equity and fixed-income assets, and held significantly less cash. Oxford

Table 6.3. Asset allocation: Colleges with no property assets, in per cent

Institution	Equity			Fixed income	Alternatives			Cash	Total	AUM
	UK	OS	Total		PE	HF	Total			
Oxford	52.0	21.3	74.0	15.6	1.0	1.2	2.2	8.3	100	(17.8)
Cambridge	61.4	16.6	78.0	19.1	0.0	0.0	0.0	2.9	100	(10.3)
Average	**56.7**	**18.9**	**76.0**	**17.3**	**0.5**	**0.6**	**1.1**	**5.6**	**100**	**(14.0)**

OS = Overseas; PE = Private equity; HF = Hedge funds; AUM = Average assets under management in £ millions.

Colleges held more non-UK equity, alternative assets and cash. The average holding in alternative assets for institutions in Oxford was distorted by 1 College's high (14 per cent) exposure to the asset class. A third of Colleges in Oxford with no property investments in their endowment also had no exposure to alternative strategies. What is striking is how average allocation among Colleges with no investments in property compared with the overall average asset allocation. The average allocation to property was 26 per cent, and among Colleges that did not hold any property, that allocation was made to UK equities.

Historical benefactions of land may have biased Oxbridge Colleges towards property. These assets have served the Colleges well in generating income and in increasing their long-term capital value while being a strong diversifier. It is a perfect investment for these institutions. In the words of one Oxford College bursar with significant experience in the asset management industry:

There is no clear investment case at present for reducing property exposure—in fact, the opposite is probably true, with property currently one of the highest-yielding asset classes. Property is illiquid as an investment: even if we were to time a sale perfectly at the top of the market, it is likely that we would be unable to re-acquire property assets at the low point in the cycle. This is not to preclude decisions to sell individual properties, each taken on their individual merits, and in light of re-investment opportunities. But, it would be hard to argue for the wholesale shift out of property on the basis of a (somewhat theoretical) risk/return study.

The target policy portfolio of the Harvard Management Company (HMC) exemplifies many of the best practices in investment—in particular the portfolio is sufficiently diversified to avoid exposure to the catastrophic event scenario. The asset allocation split is very different from most Oxbridge Colleges. The HMC portfolio is roughly 60 per cent equities, 20 per cent bonds and 20 per cent non-core investments. The property component, included in the 20 per cent non-core, is around 7 per cent. This sort of split is not uncommon among other larger US endowed institutions. Smaller ones tend to have a smaller component in non-core assets. Given a blank sheet of paper, the Harvard model is one, which this College might like to consider as a target portfolio. Asset/liability studies identify the risk/return characteristics of this sort of asset mix as appropriate for endowed funds, with their long-term investment horizon combined with a need to diversify. That said, I would not propose this as a target to be adopted in anything like the near future. First, we do not have a blank sheet of paper.

There is a stronger case for adopting a Harvard-style target portfolio for the financial investments in the College's endowment, by themselves. However, again I would not propose doing anything quickly. To shift to a 60:20:20 portfolio from a 100 per cent equities portfolio would seem imprudent at this stage in the equity market cycle, with equities weak (having arguably suffered the 'catastrophic event' scenario), and interest rates and bond yields low. The time for diversification away from equities was when the equity market was strong, and will be so again. The risks associated with our very concentrated asset allocation are discomforting, but are less so than when equity markets were 25 per cent higher. There are good lessons in the Harvard-style portfolio, and it would be good to bear these in mind in future asset allocation decisions for our endowment portfolio. In particular, I would have it in mind when relative values are more favourable to be reducing the equity portion in the financial assets portfolio in favour of bonds.

Among Oxbridge bursars as among other institutional investors familiar with the dilemmas of managing endowments for the long term, one of the major issues in asset allocation is that you do not start from a blank page. Turning around a portfolio with one-third in direct property assets is not an easy proposition, particularly when the asset provides income and diversification. As was the case with Balliol, the decision to sell their property holdings took the College a couple of decades. By the time they reached their target asset allocation, a decision that was made several years ago, the changes in the global economic environment necessitated a new asset allocation; it was time to buy back the asset class. While financial investments are easier to trade, property and private equity assets pose a challenge. Thus, asset allocation decisions based on philosophical principles on which endowments are founded serve as a guide in creating desirable investment portfolios.

Endowment income derived from property

As property plays a significant role in endowment asset management, it is scarcely surprising that the level of income derived from property investments among institutions in Oxford and Cambridge is a key factor in that decision. But the level of contribution from property assets to the total income derived from the endowment varied considerably, ranging from 75 per cent of total to nil. On average, a significant proportion (60 per cent) of institutions derived over 10 per cent of their endowment income from property.

Table 6.4. Proportion of endowment income from property, in per cent

% of income	Oxford	Cambridge	Oxbridge
None*	26	19	23
<10%	15	7	11
10–25%	9	15	11
25–50%	18	19	18
50–75%	21	22	21
>75%	3	15	8
No response	9	4	7
Total	**100**	**100**	**100**

* No property assets held in the endowment.

About one-quarter (23 per cent) of Colleges reported no property assets in their endowment; these institutions derived no income from such a source. One-fifth (21 per cent) of Colleges reported receiving a half to three-quarters of their endowment income from property, while a further 18 per cent received a quarter to half (25–50 per cent) of their income from property. Almost a third (29 per cent) of Colleges derived over half their endowment income from property investments. Eleven per cent of participants derived less than 10 per cent, and a similar number of Colleges received 10–25 per cent of endowment income from property. Table 6.4 illustrates the distribution of income received from property investments by the participating institutions in Oxford and Cambridge.

Among Colleges with no property assets in the endowment portfolio, one bursar explained that the College regarded all its property holdings as 'operational assets' though income received from such assets amounted to '45 per cent or so of total income if you include operational property assets that generate revenue but are not part of the endowment. If you add all those assets to the endowment, property will consist of 48–50 per cent of overall assets.' In some cases, half the College income was derived from rentals. But as such assets were considered to be operational, they did not appear in the endowment account; nor was the income derived from such assets reported as endowment income.

According to another bursar, 'Apart from the £1.25 million income from investment properties, the College also receives some £70–80,000 annually from the Charities Property Fund (CPF). The total income from property is about 60 per cent of the endowment income. Other property assets are not included in endowment assets but are held as operational assets. The CPF contributes less than 10 per cent of endowment income. But, if one were to include all the property assets in the endowment, they would comprise of at least half the total assets—if not more.' Typically, Colleges do not account for

169

residential income from members or income derived from conferences and other such functions as part of endowment income.

The recently introduced Statement of Recommended Practice on Accounting in Further and Higher Education Institutions (SORP) does not influence the way in which Colleges are required to account for their property assets. Apart from consolidating the accounts of the College and its subsidiary undertakings, the only difference appears to be in the provisioning that some Colleges used to make for the maintenance of their property assets. According to All Soul's College in its 'Review of operations and finance' in the *University of Oxford, Financial Statement of the Colleges, 2002–3*:

The majority of the College's buildings are Grade I listed buildings dating from the 15th and 18th Centuries. The Warden and Fellows take their collective responsibility for the preservation and sensitive maintenance of these buildings extremely seriously. In past years, the College, in addition to insuring its buildings, has deemed it prudent to build and maintain reserves equal to at least 5 per cent (approximately £2.2 million) of the insured value of its buildings. Under the new form of accounts introduced this year, such provisioning is no longer possible.

The insured value of All Soul's operational property assets is around £44 million, which is not part of the College's endowment. In the case of this College, property holdings within the endowment amounted to £56.4 million in 2003 (40.5 per cent of its total endowment value) and £70 million in 2004 (45 per cent of total endowment value). It is not clear from endowment valuations today of the Colleges what amounts have been withdrawn annually from the endowment to finance buildings and estates over the years along with the loans that have been made internally at nil rates of interest to support operational activities.

Related issues in property management

As a result of the nature of the benefactions, Colleges that historically received land as gifts, and currently have the highest endowment allocation to property, have retained direct ownership of these assets, notwithstanding the relatively high cost of management. A significant proportion of Oxford and Cambridge institutions (41 per cent) have direct property investments; more Colleges (44 per cent) in Oxford reported such holdings compared with Cambridge (37 per cent). Only 13 per cent of Colleges were invested in property indirectly or via a pooled fund, such as the Charity Property Fund. A further 16 per cent of institutions were invested both directly and indirectly; more Colleges in Cambridge (30 per cent) reporting such a combination of investments. Only 6 per cent of Colleges in Oxford opted for direct and indirect investment in property. Among Colleges reporting no allocation to property,

Table 6.5. Nature of property holdings in the endowment, in per cent

Property holding	Oxford	Cambridge	Oxbridge
Direct property holdings only	44	37	41
Invested in property funds	15	11	13
Invested in funds plus directly	6	30	16
No property*	26	19	23
No response	9	4	7
Total	**100**	**100**	**100**

* Property not included among endowment assets.

more Colleges in Oxford (26 per cent) did not own any property in their endowment.

Table 6.5 sets out the nature of property ownership in Oxford and Cambridge.

Like equity, property assets are differentiated between various categories such as commercial, agricultural, residential. Unlike equity, the cost of managing property varies considerably between asset types, as well as from one particular investment to another. When asked how the property portfolio was managed, about a third (31 per cent) of respondents indicated hiring land agents and external managers for such purposes. As the characteristic of each property can be different from the other, Colleges tend to employ advisers with specific knowledge of the asset involved. Therefore, such relationships can exist over long periods. One of the main requirements of College investment committees in the selection and appointment of investment advisers, particularly in asset allocation, was the knowledge and experience of the adviser on property issues. Investment consultants with little knowledge of investments in property failed to make their mark as the average allocation to property in Oxford and Cambridge was about a third of their assets.

Almost one-quarter (21 per cent) of Colleges that reported managing their property assets internally also indicated using the services of land agents and property advisers. Only 18 per cent of Colleges reported investing in property via pooled funds that were managed professionally, thereby delegating the management of such assets to the external fund manager. But over half (52 per cent) the respondents indicated that the management of property was the overall responsibility of the College bursar or the property bursar, if such a position existed, with the assistance of land agents and external managers. Taking into account their long-term investment in such assets, several College bursars tend to have considerable expertise in the sector.

Table 6.6 summarizes the responses of investment bursars in Oxford and Cambridge with regard to the management of their property assets. Twice as many bursars in Cambridge manage the College's property investments

Table 6.6. Use of external managers in property management, in per cent

Property manager	Oxford	Cambridge	Oxbridge
Managed by College bursar	15	30	21
External managers/land agents	29	33	31
Invested in property funds	21	15	18
No property*	26	19	23
No response	9	4	7
Total	**100**	**100**	**100**

* Property not included among endowment assets.

compared with Oxford Colleges. Similarly, about a third of Cambridge Colleges employ the services of external managers and/or land agents in the management process. More Colleges in Oxford (21 per cent) invested in property funds that are managed externally.

Some of the responses with reference to the management of property are recorded as follows:

- 'The entire portfolio is managed by the property bursar with the help of external managing agents and in consultation with other members of the investment committee.'

- 'This College is unusual in that we manage all of our own direct property in-house. We have a member of staff who is a Fellow of the College responsible for just that. The Land Agent is in fact the member of staff who is also a Fellow.'

- 'We have a domestic bursar who looks after the College's residential properties. But, we employ professional managers to look after our commercial investments.'

- 'We employ land agents and solicitors to assist us in the property management. We employ three management agents—two for our commercial property and one for our agricultural property. We have a mixed property portfolio, which includes a large exposure to commercial properties (42.8 per cent) and some agricultural property; the remaining holdings are spread between a West End Leisure Centre and a Hotel site, also in the West End of London. We do not have a lot of residential sites, they are high maintenance; but we do have about a 100 such sites and the rent collection is done by us, which helps in reducing costs. The overall management is left to the management agent.'

Colleges with substantial interests in direct property holdings employ land agents who fulfil a valuable role. The land agent 'essentially manages the property, but key decisions are referred to the Bursar and the Finance Committee for their approval,' explained one bursar. Like a securities broker, the land agent is closer to the property market and has a better concept of the pricing, management, and related issues that matter. The land agent is also responsible for 'visiting the properties at least once a year, sometimes more often,' added the same bursar. The land agent also prepares a valuation of the College's property portfolio. While a more formal valuation is undertaken over a period, such as three or five years, land agents provide informal valuations on a 'desk top' basis annually.

One of the limitations of such a process of valuation is that the volatility of the asset is often understated by the appraisal-based methods that are employed by investors to value such assets. According to Swensen: 'Lacking a ready market for pricing assets, investors hire appraisers to assess market values, using discounted cash flows, comparable sales, and replacement cost as valuation metrics. Conducted infrequently, often by the same firm year after year, the appraisal process smooths the observed series of prices, understating true volatility.'[2] Such a method of pricing contrasts with the behaviour of publicly quoted, stock market traded REITs. While Swensen is correct in his interpretation of how the pricing process can understate volatility, he is not referring to the specific set of properties held by Oxbridge institutions. His observations apply equally to private equity investments.

As the publicly quoted real estate market in the UK is not developed, Colleges in Oxford and Cambridge appear to have benefited from prevailing inefficiencies in the real estate market as these institutions hold quality assets in prime locations. When the REIT market matures in the UK, the Colleges stand to benefit from such development. Though it appears unlikely and improbable at the moment, as collectivization of property is a highly sensitive issue, it is worth considering the prospect of an Oxbridge property investment trust or bond issue, and the value that might be attached to such a REIT based on the combined property assets of these institutions? A publicly traded security structured on the income-generating property assets owned by these institutions would secure a premium in the property sector.

Apart from the Charity Property Fund in which some 17 Colleges invested, there were at least 19 property managers or land agents additionally engaged in the management of Oxbridge College property assets. Table 6.7 illustrates the number of mandates held by the external managers/agents.

Thus, 11 different managers held a single mandate each, while 17 Colleges invested in a single fund, the Charity Property Fund, managed by Carr Sheppards Crosthwaite Savills Fund Management. Only three property managers/agents or advisers had five or more mandates each. Due to the specific location and type of the property ownership, consolidation in the appointment of managers may not be an option for Oxbridge institutions. The use of 20 managers is significantly more focused than the number of fund managers employed to invest the financial assets of these institutions, where there is greater evidence of inefficiencies in manager diversification.

Table 6.7. Distribution of mandates among external property managers

No. of mandates	No. of managers
1	11
2	2
3	1
4	2
5	1
6	1
8	1
17	1

Due to the historic nature of the acquisition of property assets, Colleges have in place relationships with their advisers that can be traced back over decades. There exists a clear rationale for the appointment of a larger number of managers or advisers in direct property investments as these assets are also very individualistic in character.

Real estate assets lack a wide selection of properties that define an investible benchmark for investors. Typically, benchmarks serve as a guide rather than a usable measure of performance. As far as the use of benchmarks is concerned in property management, most bursars do not find it terribly relevant to compare their very individual holdings and performance with that of an external benchmark, such as the Investment Property Database (IPD) index, which does not include the bulk of assets the Colleges are invested in. College investment committees review the overall performance of the IPD index, but more for the sake of comparison.

Though there is a reasonable amount of information sharing among the Colleges, they have not felt the need to develop an internally customized property benchmark. As these institutions have held the assets over centuries, and most of the property has been in the form of gifts and benefactions, it raises problems relating to the method of valuing such assets. The majority of the buildings, for example, are Grade I listed buildings, some dating back to thirteenth or fourteenth centuries. As these assets were often the result of historic circumstances, it would be virtually impossible to acquire them today. While bursars keep themselves apprised of developments in the marketplace via their various advisers, in reality there is little scope for them to reallocate their property holdings in the short term in any meaningful way.

As one bursar commented, 'We look at the IPD and the Combined Actuarial Pension Service (CAPS) data, but there is no appropriate benchmark for the particular mix of property and other assets in our ownership. Though we do not have a relevant benchmark, we do assign a market value to the property assets every quarter. Currently, we have the bulk (52 per cent) of our property holdings in commercial assets such as shops and offices, 33 per cent in industrial holdings, 13 per cent in residential and the rest in agricultural land. We have some other domestic property assets, such as the Fellows Housing Scheme and other College housing.' The bursars and finance officers of Colleges regularly compare notes with each other to keep track of costs and returns. But, as there is no adequate index that matches the mix of their property assets, comparing their performance vis-à-vis any other benchmark would be misleading. 'We monitor rentals in Cambridge very closely, but do not measure our performance against any property benchmark as we do not think it relevant,' was another response.

About one-third (31 per cent) of institutions indicated no formal use of any particular index in managing and measuring their property portfolio, while less than one-quarter (21 per cent) referred to the IPD index. Those Colleges (18 per cent) invested in real estate funds, such as the Charity Property Fund, used the IPD index provided by the fund manager as a benchmark. Some Colleges used internally established benchmarks in their overall assessment and evaluation process. According to one Cambridge College bursar:

The College uses the IPD benchmark in its property management; the total return on property investments should not be less than IPD (All Property) Total Return Index over a three-year period. Income from property should be at least 1 per cent more than the Gross Redemption Yield on 10-year gilts. The College holds a mix of retail, commercial, industrial and domestic properties either held individually or through property unit trusts. Investment in overseas property is not excluded. But, the College does not plan to invest further in agricultural property.

According to another bursar: 'The investment objectives for our direct property portfolio are as follows:

(a) To aim for future growth in net rental income at least equal to the rise in University costs as measured by the Higher Education Pay and Prices Index (HEPPI)

(b) To secure the maximum current income that is consistent with the objective above, whilst maintaining real capital value and acceptable risk exposure.

(c) To achieve the 25th to 33rd percentile of the IPD monthly index over a 3 year rolling period.'

The relatively higher allocation to property assets in endowment portfolios over the centuries means that the Colleges themselves have a much better notion of the long-term returns attached to their particular investments than any other group of investors. While capital values have risen substantially, the higher yield from property has also enhanced the attractiveness of such assets. As Colleges move towards a total return investment approach and as more real estate funds become available, average property holdings are most likely to decline over the long term. But in the short to medium term, as a proportion of total assets, property will continue to attract a higher allocation among these institutions.

The higher volatility of REITs along with a higher correlation to small-capitalization stocks causes many investors to conclude that REITs behave more like equities than bonds. Regardless of the behaviour of private and public holdings of real estate, both assets offer opportunity for diversification. Pricing differences in such markets also offer opportunities for investors to create their unique property portfolios, though such opportunities are admittedly more to be found in marketable securities. At the same time, inefficiencies in the pricing and opportunities in locating property assets demand active management. Like all active strategies, it involves higher cost; as long as the manager possesses a higher level of skill, the potential to maximize returns is also enhanced.

Impact of property on asset allocation

The role of property in endowment asset allocation and contribution to income earned from such assets owned by Colleges in Oxford and Cambridge cannot be emphasized enough. For institutions deriving a higher percentage of endowment income from property, the impact of such holdings on the balance between other assets in the endowment portfolio can be significant. As property assets are among the largest in an Oxbridge College's overall portfolio of assets, regardless of whether they are classified as operational or endowment, they are seen as core holdings.

Therefore, it was ironic that some Colleges in reporting asset allocation, excluded property holdings. Apart from Colleges without any property assets in the endowment portfolio, it is worth noting that one-third of Oxbridge institutions reported their existing property holdings as having no significant influence on overall endowment asset allocation. As summarized by one bursar: 'The property portfolio is historical. It does not impact on our overall asset allocation.' Taking into account the average allocation of 26 per cent to property assets among Colleges, such a response contradicted itself.

It is also worth noting that Colleges with above average exposure to property had a similar response compared to those with below average allocations. According to another Oxford bursar for whom the property assets yielded about two-thirds of the total annual endowment income of the College: 'We have half of our endowment investments in property. This has been an attractive asset compared to others more volatile in recent years. Also, we have held it for centuries. So, we are used to holding such a large portion of our endowment in property. We need to review that in a strategic way. We need to talk to experts, to people who know a lot about the sector before we can determine our future course of action. *Currently, it does not influence our asset allocation in any significant way.'*

'It does not affect our investment decision-making per se within the securities portfolio. As far as the overall asset allocation goes, I suppose it has been about half property and half securities, more due to market forces,' commented another investment bursar. But by adding: 'We plan to be more opportunistic in selling our property assets,' we were given a clue as to how that College might respond if an opportunity arose to reduce its exposure to property. This willingness to be opportunistic is the key to successful management in the sector as most of these assets are held and operate within what is essentially a private property market, or at best an illiquid one.

Many bursars thought of their endowment assets as being split into two portfolios—property and securities. Taking an overview of all the investments within the endowment appears to be a more recent development, perhaps a result of embracing a 'total return' approach. The traditional approach to endowment management was dominated by income considerations. Thus, property was valued for its income-generating capacity; also knowing how much they could expect from property assets via rentals and sales enabled Colleges to instruct their fund manager how much income was needed from the securities portfolio.

Colleges with lower-than-Oxbridge-average exposure to property also believed that property had no impact on asset allocation. 'It does not influence the overall asset allocation as the exposure to property is low,' commented one bursar. 'We have only £0.5 m in new direct residential property holdings. It is too small to change our overall policy. We would not sell our property holdings. We think we are underweight in the sector.' According to another bursar with no property investments in the endowment fund, 'If we were to invest in property we would always prefer to do it through a professionally managed and liquid pooled vehicle, especially one that could not be hammered by a discount. We look forward to REITs in the UK.' As every experienced investor knows, REITs, like other closed-end funds, rise or fall out of favour, thereby either commanding a premium or deserving a discount relative to the value of its holdings.

Some investment bursars displayed a more pragmatic approach in their property investments. According to one such bursar, 'the College only invests directly in property held for strategic purposes. In the case of commercial property, the investment analysis must demonstrate an acceptable commercial yield. For any investment in residential property, for use by the College's students, the net yield must be positive, with the prospect of an appropriate capital gain. Such purchases must also take account of the College's overall liquidity and income requirements.'

There were some responses indicating that Colleges treated property as any other financial asset, and invested in it for financial advantage. For one bursar,

Table 6.8. Impact of property on asset allocation

Impact	Oxford	Cambridge	Oxbridge
No impact	32	33	33
Substitute for bonds	12	15	13
Helps in total return	12	11	11
Helps in diversification	9	11	10
No property*	26	19	23
No response	9	11	10
Total	**100**	**100**	**100**

* Property not included among endowment assets.

property influences overall asset allocation 'only to the extent that we look at property as an asset class as any other, and look at comparative returns when making our investment decision. We invested in the Charities Property Fund in 2000 as equities looked expensive at that time.' 'We treat property as an asset class and our investment view is based on our return expectation from alternative competitive asset classes,' reported another. 'Property is treated as an asset class and its weighting vis-à-vis the total portfolio is agreed and rebalanced as required,' explained a third.

Table 6.8 illustrates the range of responses elicited to the question: How does property impact overall asset allocation?

Only 13 per cent of respondents said that existing property holdings acted as a substitute for bonds, and a further 10 per cent identified diversification as a major consideration in asset allocation. Also, 11 per cent of respondents suggested property assets assisting in the transitioning to total return—that is the steady stream of income from property investments cushioned the College's overall income and provided greater flexibility to invest in alternative assets such as private equity and hedge funds that typically do not generate any income. 'We treat our property assets as our "core" investments,' explained one bursar; property assets accounted for 80 per cent of the endowment income of this institution. 'Our equity assets are for greater risk taking,' clarified another bursar. 'Our property assets provide us with a steady stream of income enabling us to invest without having to look for income from our financial assets,' commented a third Oxbridge bursar whose College derived about two-thirds (66 per cent) of endowment income from its property holdings.

'Given that we are talking about total return,' explained one bursar, 'we treat property as an asset class with a steady income stream. We have been selling property of late and our total income is therefore lower than usual. The allocation between property and equities shifts according to our expectations of the respective markets.' High property holdings also assist in implementing a more tax efficient investment strategy. 'Our income from property has been high,' said another bursar. 'Hence the total return policy saves us some tax.

In 2002, for example, income from property was 50 per cent of total income, up from 43 per cent in 2000. We recognize the need to pay our way and our property portfolio has provided us with a steady stream of income. In embracing a total return approach, we wanted better access to our capital. In the past, as you are aware, we were not able to do so. As we hold so much property, the income stream from property has been paying the way. However, as we sell property and increase our securities portfolio, we need to ensure that we can sell some of it to bridge our deficits as and when required.' Property assets clearly assisted many Colleges in employing a total return strategy for the endowment portfolio.

For those Colleges not dependent on income from their financial portfolio, as a result of income from the property portfolio, implementing a total return investment strategy was easier without being exposed to liquidity risk. According to one bursar, 'the income from our property holdings currently amounts to 6–7 per cent compared to 2.8 per cent for the non-property portfolio. The entire endowment of £98.5 million is expected to provide an annual yield of around £4.26 million. The property portfolio has cushioned the effects of the downturn in markets and the low yields available from the non-property holdings. While we remain long term, total return investors, the steady decline in income from the non-property portfolio remains a concern. While we are considering increasing our exposure to other asset classes such as private equity, we are likely to be more opportunistic in our property transactions.'

Most Colleges viewed the bulk of their property holdings as a core asset that yields high income. For one College deriving half its endowment income from property, 'a specific element of the College's asset allocation is property. This is managed to be 35 per cent of the portfolio at present and it is re-valued annually. If it grows out of proportion, there are sales to rebalance the allocation.' At the same time, many bursars are unsure whether they should retain such a high exposure to property in their endowment asset allocation. In the words of one bursar: 'We used to have a high proportion in property; it was something like 60 per cent of the portfolio. We felt that the asset distribution should be the reverse—i.e. we should have 60 per cent in securities.'

Another Oxford College bursar currently engaged in a phased divestment programme aimed to reduce its property holdings in the endowment from 26 to 10 per cent. According to this bursar, 'Historically, the College ended up with a lot of land for different reasons. As things stand today, we think land as an asset generates income; it also provides the necessary diversification for our portfolio. Whether we need as much of it as we have today, we do not think so. Hence, our overall investment strategy for the long term is to switch from some of our land into other assets that will provide us with the total return we are seeking.'

One response that covered many aspects of property investing for a typical Oxbridge College was summarized by one bursar in the following words:

The College owns a large amount of valuable direct property that would be difficult to sell. Ideally we would wish to diversify the investment profile and perhaps halve the weighting to property. Our total endowment income from property is over 50 per cent. When I started doing this job in the early 1990's, about two-thirds of the College endowment was in direct property holdings and 40 per cent of that was in agricultural estates. So, what I've been trying to do since then was to try to switch out of property to secure a better diversification of investments. However, property does provide a large income stream and thus helps us greatly in meeting our income requirements. As there is a strong rental stream, we can effectively ignore income constraints in other areas of endowment asset management. However, the imbalance of property gives rise to liquidity constraints.

Among those respondents (13 per cent) who considered property to be a substitute for bonds, one of the bursars commented: 'It does impact our overall allocation—we do not have any bonds for example at the moment. That is mainly due to our high income from property. Property is also regarded as the Colleges' historic endowment. So, there is a lot of passion associated with the asset class. Any major divestment of the property holdings would generate a lot of debate. Also, any notion of pooling together of the Colleges' property assets would not be popular. The disparities of wealth among Oxford Colleges make it more difficult to be cohesive than the Cambridge Colleges, as Trinity dominates Cambridge. The structure of Oxford Colleges is such that they tend to guard their independence more closely.'

There were a few (8 per cent) Colleges with a very high (over 75 per cent) dependence on property assets as a major source of income. Property remains a core holding for these Colleges, and they indicated no scepticism of their position. According to this bursar, 'Although we receive a large (82 per cent) proportion of our income from property, we do not constrain our fund managers in any way—in terms of obtaining our investment objectives. We have only been invested in equities since the 1950s. Land has been our major asset for historical reasons over centuries. As we have never found an optimal asset allocation policy that we could adhere to, we do not know how our land holdings should or may be affecting our investment policy.'

The impact of property investments on overall asset allocation does not concern institutions where these assets do not appear in the endowment portfolio: 'We have not changed the mix of our endowment assets as a result of our income coming in from the property holdings,' explained the bursar. Almost half (45 per cent) of this College's income is from its operational property holdings. As property is considered an operational asset, the contribution of income from this asset class to endowment income is nil. If all property assets are deemed operational assets, then it has no impact on the asset allocation decision of the endowment portfolio.

'We do not include the commercial rents we receive from property as part of our endowment income,' explained another bursar. The issues that arise as a result of such accounting have already been commented upon. The level of subsidy that Colleges provide their students is also an issue. The Colleges, particularly the ones that are less well off, would like to charge more competitive rates for housing to their students. In the words of one bursar: 'We like to achieve a market rent, as the student rents are non-competitive; also some of our other properties have sitting tenants in them.' In a more competitive world, uneconomic assets are a drain on resources. More and more Colleges have opted to charge economic rents to students, thereby reducing the level of subsidy to the future generation of students.

Conclusion

Colleges in Oxford and Cambridge have significantly high ownership of real estate assets. At the same time, Colleges with smaller-sized endowments were the least likely to hold property assets in their endowments. About one-quarter of Colleges reported not owning any property assets in the endowment. Some Colleges with no property investment in the endowment were considering building up such exposure. In Oxford, for example, 28 per cent of Colleges did not own any property in the endowment. Among the remaining Colleges, the ratio of property to endowment assets rose from 31 per cent in 2003 to 33 per cent in 2004. Three Colleges reported a decline in their property valuations over this period: Christ Church reduced its property assets from £81 million to £74 million, bringing it down from 47 per cent of the endowment to 41 per cent in 2004; Jesus reduced it from 60 per cent of the endowment to 57.6 per cent, while Oriel reduced its property investments from 89 per cent of the endowment portfolio to 79 per cent. Comparable data were not available for Cambridge Colleges.

Regardless of the high allocation to property in the endowment and their ownership of some of the best-maintained listed buildings in the country, assumptions of the fabulous wealth of Oxbridge Colleges are also misleading. In the words of Murison:

Mindful of the assumption by undergraduates and journalists that Oxbridge Colleges are rich beyond the dreams of avarice, I did some research when I became Bursar. I discovered that in 1871, the peak year of Oxbridge holdings of agricultural land, in which they were overwhelmingly invested, the acreage owned by all the Oxbridge Colleges combined was 319,000 acres. The British peerage at the same date owned 42 million acres—120 times as much. Between the introduction of income tax in 1898 and outbreak of the Kaiser's War, the aristocracy sold 14 million acres—over 40 times as much land as the Colleges had owned at their peak. So much, then, for that twaddle that in the old days it was impossible to ride between Oxford and Cambridge without leaving College-owned land. Or that even today the Bursar of Trinity College, Cambridge, can inspect the College's acres all the way from Cambridge to Dover.

It is true that College endowments have increased in value over the centuries, both through benefactions and capital appreciation. In the overwhelming majority of cases the benefactions were in the form of land. Significantly, following the government's involvement in university financing, benefactions to Colleges declined. Offsetting the benefactions to the Colleges over the centuries have been great expenditures on the College buildings and estates, and on providing bursaries and scholarships to poor students. The withdrawal of such expenditures from the endowment has also made it difficult to calculate the true return on property investments for these institutions. In an increasingly competitive environment, there has been greater pressure on Colleges to work their investments harder. Compared to the wealth of Ivy League Colleges in the United States, built up essentially since the 1970s, the wealth or the lack of it of Oxbridge Colleges is indeed surprising.

If one were looking for an overall Oxbridge consensus with regard to property investments, it can be suggested that the Colleges (not the Universities) regard property as a core asset. Some Colleges were considering reducing their large property holdings with a view to creating more diversified portfolios. At the same time, there were others planning to increase their allocation, precisely for the same reason. Among Colleges with substantial exposure (over 40 per cent) to property and considering reducing such exposure indicated that holding between a quarter and a third of the endowment in property was desirable.

Colleges were, however, moving away from agricultural assets towards commercial investments, but even such reallocation was far from straightforward as agricultural properties that have development potential get transformed into residential properties and thus appreciate rapidly in value. Magdalen College's joint venture with the Prudential Assurance Company Ltd. in 1991 to set up the Oxford Science Park is one such example; Magdalen's investment was worth £16.3 million in 2004 (£18.6 million in 2003). Oxbridge Colleges generally consider investing in property to be a good thing. Some Colleges responded to the recent bear market by increasing their property holdings by taking out long-term fixed interest bank loans at attractive rates. The market environment was dominated by uncertain returns from marketable securities and low rates of interest, the lowest in several decades, coupled with enlargement of the EU and higher than expected economic growth in the UK. This resulted in increased demand for property assets in areas of strong economic growth in the country, and investing in property could be compared with active strategies in the hedge fund sector.

Oriel College's 'Review of operations and finance', for the financial year ended 31 July 2003 in the *University of Oxford, Financial Statement of the Colleges, 2002–3*, stated: 'The endowment assets of the College were substantially increased in 2002–2003 by purchases of investment properties financed by cash and long term fixed interest bank loans.' There has been a corresponding increase in income from these assets and expenditure from servicing the loans. 'College liquidity is good,' confirmed the report, 'and will improve next financial year when some underperforming properties are realised.' In 2004, the College raised £5.6 million from its land and property investments, realizing £1.2 million of revaluation gains from the sale. The £19.4 million of secured endowment assets bank loans were subject to fixed interest between 5.04 per cent and 5.81 per cent.

Jesus College also financed its commercial property purchases in January 2002 with bank loans; the income on these properties was largely offset by the interest payments on the sum borrowed to enable the purchase. The College's 2003 endowment assets were worth £96.8 million of which £24.4 million were in the form of long-term loans. Interest on the loan was payable at a fixed rate of 6 per cent over a period of 25 years. By financial year-end 2004, the loan outstanding was £23.9 million while the value of property assets stood at £57.5 million, down from £58.1 million the previous year. In 2004, the College raised £2.2 million from its land and property investments, realizing £1.4 million of revaluation gains in the process. As a long-term investment, the acquisition of 13–21 Cornmarket Street at the heart of Oxford would count as a strategic asset for any Oxford College.

While American educational institutions have been leveraging their endowment assets in multiple ways, securing cheap bank loans backed by endowment assets is a recent development in the UK. Hopefully, such practice will contribute towards preserving the long-term purchasing power of endowments as Colleges follow best practice by not borrowing from the endowment at highly preferential rates. Historically, Colleges borrowed at nil rate of return to the endowment. Such practices caused substantial damage to the net wealth of the endowment. College officers in Oxford and Cambridge are no less astute in their overall management as their peer group in the United States, but they have not always had the freedom to focus on the long-term preservation of the endowment, having been under constant financial pressure as a result of declining student fees and lack of any other means of financial support.

Universities need to borrow to fund a range of activities such as estate refurbishment, expansion of academic, library, research and sports facilities, as well as develop revenue-earning activities such as accommodation and development of industrial parks. The way these activities were funded remains controversial. It is an issue that needs addressing; transactions involving the endowment should be transparent. Borrowing is necessary and it can be made cheaply, as evident from what Colleges like Oriel in Oxford are already doing.

If the Colleges recognize their collective bargaining power, they could, for example, borrow against the endowment, making use of structured products thereby unlocking the value in assets that currently generate uneconomic rents, and transfer the risks to third-party purchaser of the rent. But first the Colleges and the Universities need to be more open to innovations in financial markets, and conduct their affairs in the most efficient way so as to fulfil their stated long-term objectives.

Oxbridge institutions may not have been pioneering by investing in private equity or hedge funds, but they have been innovative in their approaches to investing in property, albeit without a conscious strategy in doing so. While such approaches to asset management may have evolved from the constraints imposed on them historically, the Colleges have evolved into niche players in the property market by virtue of their long-term ownership of prime property assets. There are few other groups of investors that have such a long track record of investing in property. As the endowments were never managed as independent entities and no records kept of their performance, the Colleges cannot summon a stellar record of endowment management in their defence. Endowments existed historically to support the educational and related objectives of these institutions. The notion of an independent endowment with defined objectives, spending rates and policy portfolio is a modern construct. Undoubtedly such clarification will help in preserving intergenerational equity. Such awareness is increasing among endowments and foundations in the UK, but these are also concepts with which trustees and members of the investment committees of such institutions are coming to terms.

7

Issues in portfolio management

Introduction

In an uncertain world, investing for the truly long term is a continual challenge. In determining which assets are held, and in what proportions, asset allocation becomes the centre of the management process. As institutions also have diverse objectives, sometimes with no clearly defined liabilities, asset allocation offers immense possibilities. In the past, Colleges in Oxford and Cambridge invested in property, bonds, equity-like assets including private equity; they also own original works of art, rare books, vintage wine, and other such assets that would typically have been bequeathed to them. The range of assets may not have been significantly enlarged, but financial innovation has created more options whereby traditional assets can be accessed in a more efficient manner.

Philanthropic institutions, particularly in the UK and Europe, continue to invest in traditional assets they best understand. The investment universe has been greatly enriched over the past few decades reflecting the progress made in the application of financial analysis and innovation. Use of computers and global communication technology has translated into an increased use of quantitative techniques in the management of assets. The increasingly abstract nature of investing, the rise in the use of derivatives, futures, options, insurance contracts, indexation, programme trading strategies as well as absolute return strategies are all part of this development. While the application of 'derivative instruments' within endowment asset management has been limited, going forward attitudes to risk management may well change.

In addition to the question of risk and return, there are a number of philosophical questions that are relevant to the selection of the policy portfolio. The Colleges weathered a three-year stock market downturn between March 2000 and March 2003. Financial markets recovered over the next three years, but the issues that confront long-term investors today are relatively more complex. The Colleges are also in the process of implementing massive changes in the way they manage their portfolios, as they move towards 'total return' strategies, define their investment objectives, and construct portfolios that lie on the efficient frontier. In addition, intergenerational equity issues make asset allocation more challenging. Is the long-term preservation of capital in real terms the right path, or is there a case for spending more currently? 'Is there an optimal asset allocation for genuinely long-term investors such as educational endowments?' was a question we were frequently asked as these were the kinds of issues that investment committee members faced.

The aim of this study is not prescriptive, particularly with regard to issues surrounding individual asset allocation and implementation. Like medical practitioners, investment advisers need to spend considerable time with the patient, have access to comprehensive information on individual case histories; conduct a wide range of diagnostic tests before arriving at any conclusion. Also, the available solutions may vary according to individual profiles—as some patients with hypertension for instance might need beta-blockers instead of more exercise, sleep and possibly a mild sedative while others need calcium channel blockers. We aim to explore the rationale for the decisions taken by these individual institutions in their endowment management. We also aim to provide an analysis in the context of developments in the sector comparing such practice with international ones wherever available.

Some Oxbridge Colleges have been investing in portfolios generated after discussions with their investment consultants and other advisers. The bursars of these institutions are the ones most likely to be worried about issues in optimal asset allocation. Investment consultants often end up offering generic asset allocation solutions to investors with similar profiles though investment objectives may vary among these institutions that appear disarmingly similar. Thus, some Colleges with more concentrated portfolios, for example in property, have a level of conviction in their investment strategy that defies modern theories of portfolio management. These are not the sort of institutions in search of the Holy Grail of optimal asset allocation. Their scepticism protects them from both modern theories of investment and investment consultants, making them invest in assets that have worked for them over the long term.

Academic research does not aim to denigrate any of the work that is being done among investment consultants specializing in the sector. On the contrary, it is hoped that by holding up an analytical mirror, institutions in Oxford and Cambridge among other endowments and foundations, can benefit from an objective view of current endowment asset management practice conducted by a select group of truly long-term investors with considerable knowledge of the subject. It is not as if Oxbridge institutions are unaware of major developments in the United States, nor is it they lack influence in bringing about change. A significantly high number of Prime Ministers, Cabinet Ministers, and senior civil servants in the UK went to Oxford or Cambridge. Yet until very recently, most charitable institutions were required to invest for income. Government and regulators may appear to have been slow in leading the way, but apart from the United States where endowments have been examining their practices for almost half a century, there existed no alternative model. Even today, investment thinking in the endowment universe is dominated by US institutions as these institutions have been pioneering in their approaches to issues that arise in asset management.

In this chapter, we examine issues that relate to the overall asset allocation decision, primarily because it is effectively the decision that shapes the individual portfolio. In order to hold diversified portfolios, investors examine not only expected return and associated risk parameters, but they need to consider geographical, manager, and style diversification. Thus, strategic allocation includes tactical issues such as rebalancing in addition to decisions relating to indexation versus active management. The ability to choose managers is perhaps as important as getting the overall asset allocation right. Harvard and Yale, for example, follow completely different strategies as Harvard has historically managed the bulk of its endowment assets in-house while Yale has been more successful in identifying external asset managers with the ability to deliver higher than average rates of return in various asset categories. If institutions believe they are better at selecting managers, then opting for an active strategy makes sense. For others, indexation may be the right path, though in a majority of cases, investors opt for a combination of active–passive strategies.

Role of indexation

As most investors wish to outperform the market, active managers face serious obstacles taking into account costs and market impact. Markets with inefficiently priced assets offer active managers greater scope to outperform than markets that are relatively efficient, such as the developed equity and bond markets. With no direct measures of market efficiency, the behaviour of active managers provides an indication of the available opportunities or inefficiencies in a market. Active managers in reasonably efficient markets often end up as closet indexers, while active managers in less efficient markets tend to hold more diverse portfolios with a higher level of dispersion in the rate of returns. Thus, savvy investors treat all active strategies with a healthy dose of scepticism.

For one Oxbridge bursar who preferred to control his risk allocation, 'as active managers were no longer taking the sort of risks they were being paid for, but were behaving more like closet indexers,' indexation was the key to managing overall portfolio risk. 'We do not favour active fund management,' he added explaining the move away from active management towards indexation, 'thus making our own risk assessment. Large direct property investments help in the diversification of risk, as returns from property are not correlated with that of other asset classes. Portfolio managers are no longer willing to take risk; they demand very clear instructions from their client in such matters. As asset allocation is clearly more important than stock picking, we focus on determining that. What we aim to do with regard to risk is widen the asset base so that returns from the various asset classes in our portfolio remain highly uncorrelated.' Indexing is typically used as an investment strategy where return and risk reflect that of the selected index.

One of the advantages of indexing, apart from reducing diversifiable risk, is avoiding the risk of poor manager selection. The last decade witnessed an unprecedented rise in the use of indexed strategies among UK pension fund managers. The asset management industry became more global in the 1990s. Since then, particularly during the second half of the decade, the asset management industry in the UK has been in the throes of restructuring. Manager volatility was high with takeovers and mergers. The situation was compounded by increased volatility in markets. The rising exposure to indexed strategies in the UK was also the result of below-average performance of 'balanced' managers in the pension fund sector where poor portfolio construction resulted in higher levels of risk and inefficient use of information in return forecasts.

Thus, investors were more likely to opt for a lower-cost core (indexed equity/bonds) with a performance-related satellite. Many investors tend to interpret the core-satellite approach as one where an indexed equity portfolio is applied along side an active one. Indexation offers an attractive option when used as a component of a mix of techniques ranging from a core-indexed portfolio to market neutral strategies, absolute return strategies along with exposure to private equity, commodities and other assets such as property. While the rate of growth in indexation declined as global markets experienced the long-awaited correction, the rise in quantitative, absolute return techniques spurred the growth of the hedge fund sector and other exotic fixed-income products.

The convergence of rising markets until March 2000, the inability of active managers to beat the market, the creation of new products, and the ease of cheaply distributing such products contributed to the ascendance of passive management strategies. Cheaper indexed options were themselves a contributing factor in the rising market. By opting for passive strategies within assets that are efficiently priced, investors also save on costs. Today, some asset managers specializing in passive strategies are willing to pay their institutional clients for managing their assets. Thus, several factors conspired in the indexation revolution. Skilful quantitative active management, utilizing derivatives, helped combine active management with the benefits of passive management, thereby offering investors the advantage of security selection (alpha) while retaining the performance from underlying asset classes (beta).

188

Increased use of derivatives in the management of risk introduced a dimension to the investment process as never before. Investment strategies that use derivative products with a view to generating higher-than-market returns access the best financial tools available to fund managers in managing risk and return. Beta, in the form of indexation, is cheaply acquired. William F. Sharpe established conclusively decades ago that it is mathematically impossible for the average active manager to beat the market over a relatively long period. The record of the median performance of active managers over the long term shows no evidence that active managers of equity portfolios outperform the index. Collectively, active managers have not been able to sell at the top nor invest back at the bottom of markets.

While some Colleges in Oxford and Cambridge switched to passive strategies over the past decade, the majority (64 per cent) of these institutions endorse active management. Taking into account the view that most bursars are ultimately seeking to derive a steady source of income from their assets, the range of asset allocation choices made by the Colleges is fascinating. Table 7.1 provides a breakdown of percentage of assets that were invested in indexed strategies.

Only 10 per cent of Colleges had more than 50 per cent of their portfolio invested in indexed products, and many of these had embraced passive investment strategies fairly recently. Though two-thirds (64 per cent) of Colleges were not invested in indexed strategies, the active management strategies employed by them did not embrace absolute return strategies. Less than 5 per cent of Colleges managed 70–90 per cent of their endowment portfolio passively, all of it invested in equity. As shown in Table 7.1, 8 per cent of institutions had less than 10 per cent of their endowment portfolio indexed; 9 per cent had invested between 10 and 30 per cent of the endowment in

Table 7.1. Percentage of portfolio indexed

% Indexed	Oxford	Cambridge	Oxbridge
0%	53	78	64
1–10%	12	4	8
10–20%	0	4	2
20–30%	12	0	7
30–40%	9	7	8
40–50%	3	0	2
50–60%	3	4	3
60–70%	6	0	3
70–80%	3	0	2
80–90%	0	4	2
90–100%	0	0	0
Total	**100**	**100**	**100**

indexed products; a further 8 per cent between 30 and 40 per cent and another 8 per cent between 40 and 70 per cent.

It is worth noting that the majority (78 per cent) of Colleges in Cambridge did not employ indexation as an investment strategy. At the same time, Cambridge Colleges were the least exposed to absolute return strategies in their portfolios and on average held more property. Thus, property may provide a clue to the asset allocation distribution. If indexation is the lowest risk strategy when investing in equities (not all bursars would agree with such a premise), and equities are more risky compared to Treasury bonds/gilts though not necessarily more risky than some high yielding Emerging Market bonds, and hedge funds and private equity are perceived as highly risky, then property is seen as a relatively low-risk asset among institutions that have owned such assets for centuries. From the standpoint of some Colleges, even indexed equity investments are not as secure as property in yielding the desirable level of income. The concentration of a narrow band of stocks and sectors within the UK equity market, the FTSE indices, also acted as a deterrent in adopting a passive approach.

More Colleges in Oxford implemented indexation as an investment strategy along with absolute return ones, such as hedge funds and private equity. 'We expect to use more passive instruments in future. The passive/active distribution shifts with perception of market risk,' commented one bursar. A few Colleges in Oxford managed their entire public equity allocation passively, while making small allocations to more 'risky' strategies such as private equity and hedge funds. Many of these Colleges also reported a higher than average allocation to property which provided them with a steady annual income, thus facilitating implementation of a more efficient asset allocation strategy. Not all Colleges following passive strategies had exposure to property. Hence, it is not possible to arrive at any hard conclusions about the investment strategies of institutions in Oxford and Cambridge based on such limited evidence. One thing was clear; Colleges sought a certain level of income from their endowments. Generating efficient portfolios was not the primary focus. For Colleges with a reasonable contribution of income from property assets, it was relatively easier to generate more efficient portfolios.

Endowment size appears to have little influence on risk allocation. Comparison of the top allocations made to alternative investment strategies within Oxford and Cambridge College endowments with those made to indexed-strategies and property assets by the same institutions does not reveal any clear pattern of risk budgeting. Thus, a College with over half (57 per cent) its assets invested passively, one-quarter (26 per cent) invested in property and less than 10 per cent in alternative strategies had a small-sized endowment (£24 million) compared with a College that had a sizeable endowment (£180 million) but had no passive investments, along with a low (5 per cent) exposure to active alternative strategies and an above-average allocation

Table 7.2. Allocation to various strategies by Colleges that hold alternatives assets*

College	Alternatives	Passive	Property	Endowment £ m
1	14	<5	—	36
2	9	57	26	24
3	7	39	44	120
4	6	40	53	49
5	6	25	55	81
6	5	—	30	180
7	5	—	6	16
8	5	14	42	77
9	3	37	42	88
10	3	33	30	54
11	3	—	—	27
12	3	—	23	45
13	2	66	46	162
14	2	—	58	63
15	1	—	37	39

* As a percentage of the endowment portfolio.

(30 per cent) to property. It can argued, for example, that institutions with smaller assets under management and lesser resources to spend on the investment management process are better off implementing passive strategies. But that was not always the case.

There were more institutions with smaller-sized endowments that pursued active strategies suggesting that these institutions were more willing to take risk. Some of these Colleges did not have a high level of dependency on the endowment income for sustaining their operations. One cannot therefore infer that Oxbridge institutions with small endowments opted for cheaper indexed strategies, or that institutions with larger endowments were more willing to invest in alternative strategies.

Table 7.2 shows the 15 highest allocations made to alternative strategies within Oxford and Cambridge endowments and compares them with allocations made to indexed-strategies and property assets by the same institutions.

Colleges with smaller endowments also pointed out that they were more willing to add to their current allocation to alternative assets, if they had more funds under management. However, the College with the highest allocation to hedge funds and private equity among institutions in Oxford and Cambridge had a medium-sized endowment, worth £36 million in 2002–3. It had less than 5 per cent invested in indexed strategies and had no exposure to property in its endowment portfolio. At the other end of the spectrum, Colleges with low exposure to alternative strategies, say less than 5 per cent, did not exhibit any discernible pattern of investing in passive strategies or in property.

Table 7.3. Allocation to various strategies by Colleges with large index holdings*

College	Indexation	Alternatives	Property
1	88	—	6
2	75	—	—
3	70	1	—
4	66	1	16
5	57	9	26
6	52	—	33
7	47	1	5
8	40	6	53
9	40	1	49
10	39	7	44
11	37	3	42
12	33	3	30
13	29	2	46
14	25	1	48
15	25	2	7
16	25	6	55

* As a percentage of the endowment portfolio.

Table 7.3 shows how Colleges with the highest allocation to indexed strategies invested in alternative assets and property. The top three allocations to indexation, for example, had low or no allocation to alternative strategies or property. It is worth pointing out that among the top three highest indexers in Oxbridge, one College owned considerable operating property assets that did not appear in its endowment.

There was no evidence of an active risk allocation process in overall asset allocation among institutions in Oxford and Cambridge. There exists great diversity in the distribution of risk among Oxford and Cambridge College endowments. The distribution appears to have been more artistic in nature; not very scientific or quantitative. A number of these institutions may have ended up taking inappropriate, ill-informed risk, but have not been appropriately compensated for that risk. There is no evidence to suggest that they have evaluated investment opportunities consistently by taking into account relevant data, which are widely available. It is possible that the level of inadvertent or unintended risks inherent in active portfolios could drown out the source of alpha (superior performance), thereby reversing the intended outcome—that is leaving the endowment with a higher than intended level of risk and a negative alpha. Risk-adjusted performance is not something that is widely measured among Oxbridge Colleges. Bursars are deeply conscious of such a deficit and wish to address the problem; the question that engages them most is how best to do so.

Compared to just over a third (36 per cent) of Colleges in Oxford and Cambridge investing a portion of their assets passively, in the United States more than half (51 per cent) the institutions responding to the 2004 NES reported

Table 7.4. Percentage of assets managed passively by US educational endowments

Endowment	0–5%	5–10%	10–15%	15–25%	25–35%	35–50%	50–75%	>75%	NR	Total
>$1,000 m	11.1	8.9	11.1	15.6	2.2	2.2	2.2	—	46.7	100
$500–1,000 m	17.3	15.4	11.5	7.7	5.8	3.8	5.8	—	32.7	100
$100–500 m	7.0	9.3	10.6	10.6	8.4	7.5	2.2	2.6	41.0	100
$50–100 m	8.8	4.0	5.6	5.6	7.2	4.8	8.8	1.6	53.6	100
$25–50 m	5.7	7.6	4.4	9.5	2.5	6.3	2.5	5.7	55.7	100
<$25 m	7.9	4.3	2.9	2.9	3.6	5.0	3.6	14.3	55.7	100
Public	6.4	5.6	6.4	8.6	9.4	6.9	5.6	6.4	44.6	100
Independent	8.9	8.4	7.4	8.0	3.7	5.3	3.1	4.3	51.0	100
Average	**8.2**	**7.5**	**7.1**	**8.2**	**5.5**	**5.8**	**3.9**	**5.0**	**49.0**	**100**

NR = No response.
Source: 2004 NES.

that a portion of their assets were passively invested. Respondents indicated an inverse relationship between investment pool size and the percentage of assets that were passively managed—institutions with large investment pool assets tending to index a smaller portion of their asset bases compared to those with smaller investment pools. Among the larger educational endowments in the United States, with assets over $1 billion, only 6.6 per cent invested more than 25 per cent of their assets passively. This percentage rose to 26.5 per cent for institutions with investment assets less than or equal to $25 million; and further to 28.3 per cent for public institutions. Just 16.4 per cent of independent institutions managed more than 25 per cent of their assets passively. On average 20 per cent of institutions indexed more than one-quarter of their assets.

Table 7.4 shows what percentage of investment assets were managed passively among endowments in the 2004 NES.

Rebalancing

The objective of portfolio management lies in the determination and implementation of long-term policy targets. If investors deviate consistently and substantially from these targets, then the resulting portfolio fails to reflect the risk-return preferences expressed through the allocation process. Rebalancing ensures that portfolios maintain assets at their target levels, thereby exposing the fund to the desired return and risk characteristics. Market performance causes the fund's actual allocations to drift away from its target. Rebalancing involves necessary action to ensure that the actual portfolio is close to the targeted one. Such action involves a high level of contrarian investment behaviour.

When markets change dramatically, the issue is not simply a question of mechanical rebalancing, but do investors have the courage of their convictions? As Swensen reminds us, 'Rebalancing represents supremely rational behaviour. Maintaining portfolio targets in the face of market moves dictates sale of strong relative performers and purchase of poor relative performers. Stated differently, disciplined rebalancers sell what's hot and buy what's not. Under normal circumstances, rebalancing asks for modest degrees of fortitude. When markets make extreme moves, rebalancing requires substantial amounts of courage.'[1]

Regardless of the importance of maintaining target asset allocations, few investors follow such a disciplined approach. In the real world of fund management slippages occur consistently as investments in illiquid assets result in actual holdings deviating from target levels. Even when actual allocations match desired targets, performance can deviate from index returns as a result of management techniques. This does not take into account the use of leverage in portfolio management, which by magnifying outcomes fundamentally alters the underlying attributes of the portfolio. Thus, deviations from the target allocation occur more frequently than anticipated and for a diverse set of reasons.

After establishing the ideal asset mix, risk control requires regular rebalancing to policy targets. Some funds rebalance monthly, others quarterly or annually, and some when the actual allocation deviates widely from the targeted range of allocation. While a level of gradualism is highly recommended in rebalancing in the alternative assets sector, as far as marketable securities are concerned, most disciplined investors rebalance their portfolios regularly. The frequency of rebalancing differs reflecting the reason for rebalancing to some extent. According to Swensen, the 'pursuit of continuous rebalancing provides greater risk control with potentially lower costs than either the calendar or trading range approaches'[2] offer. As the target allocation essentially captures the risk-return profile of the portfolio, allowing the portfolio to drift away from its long-term policy target exposes the institution to avoidable risks.

The fundamental role of rebalancing is risk control, not enhancing return. Trend following or market-timing strategies are not desirable strategies for long-term investors. As Burton Malkiel writes in *Managing Risk in an Uncertain Era*:

We are particularly averse to the suggestions that a university try to move in and out of the stock market according to its capacity to forecast market trends. Investors who wish to play this timing game must possess an unusual degree of prescience about the course of the general economy, corporate profits, interest rates, and indeed the entire set of international, economic, political, and social developments that affect the securities market. The existence of such omniscience, to say the least, is hard to document.[3]

In the world of professional investing, risk lies squarely with the owners of assets rather than with the appointed asset managers. What is relevant

Table 7.5. Proportion of US educational institutions with a rebalancing policy

Endowment	Formal	Informal	No policy
>$1,000 m	64.4	28.9	6.7
$500–1,000 m	78.8	17.3	3.9
$100–500 m	79.5	16.7	3.7
$50–100 m	88.0	7.6	4.4
$25–50 m	82.0	14.9	3.2
<$25 m	75.4	20.4	4.3
Public	82.0	15.0	3.0
Independent	78.7	16.8	4.5
Average	**79.7**	**16.3**	**4.0**

Source: 2004 NACUBO Study.

among institutional managers today is the recognition of the importance of the policy portfolio, and whether or how the investment portfolio should be rebalanced back to the benchmark. Among US educational endowments, for example, the investment policy features typically include formal, if not informal, definitions of such process. Table 7.5 shows the percentages and categories of reporting institutions with rebalancing policies, as reported by the NACUBO.

Thus, 80 per cent of endowments in the United States have formal rebalancing policies, 16 per cent informal ones, while 4 per cent of institutions reported not having any such policy. Smaller endowments (between $50 million and $100 million) are most likely (88 per cent) to have formal rebalancing policies, while two-thirds (64 per cent) of the largest endowment assets reported having such policies.

The concept of a benchmark or policy portfolio and whether or how the actual portfolio is rebalanced to maintain the target asset allocation is relatively new among endowments and foundations in Europe. The Wellcome Trust, the largest biomedical charity and among the largest endowments in the world, did not employ a policy portfolio until recently. In the final quarter of 1998, the Trust undertook a comprehensive review of its investment management arrangements. An asset liability study was commissioned to help determine the optimal mix of investments to ensure a sustainable level of expenditure by the Trust.

The Trust had not previously employed the concept of a policy portfolio. The creation of a policy portfolio based on long-term risk return assumptions reflected recognition of the Trust's liability and risk profile, as well as the acceptance of the policy portfolio as being critical to the Trust's asset management policy. As a result of this exercise and based on the underlying strategic asset allocation, a number of significant changes were made to the Trust portfolio's asset allocation and to its external management arrangements.

With the appointment of a new CIO in 2005, the Trust is reported to be moving away from such a concept.

The function of the customized benchmark or policy portfolio is not only to assess how a manager has performed relative to the index; the selection of the benchmark itself is the critical investment decision as it defines the risk-return characteristics of the portfolio. Choosing the policy portfolio or the target asset mix is the single most important investment decision made by investment committees. Whether customized or peer group oriented, it is a matter of judgement based on analysis. That judgement like any other can be flawed. The risk is that the benchmark does not deliver the pot of money that the institution needs to honour its liabilities.

Thus, investment committees choose an asset allocation policy because they believe, on available evidence, that a particular allocation will best enable them to meet their liabilities, not because other funds have a similar allocation. Oxbridge College investment committees exhibit a refreshing level of independence and self-determination in their asset allocation process. Pension fund trustees typically resort to using an asset-liability model and then appointing one or more fund managers to manage these assets according to the specified benchmark. Trustees of endowed assets, without always having a clearly defined liability profile, also use quantitative analysis in determining their mix of assets to deliver the highest level of return commensurate with the desirable level of risk. The manager is typically responsible for stock selection and perhaps for any tactical asset allocation, leaving the strategic allocation to the investment committee.

It is true that creating a customized benchmark is indeed an extremely complex process and some members of investment committees may simply not be equipped to address such matters for a variety of reasons. A large number of investment consultants use what is commonly referred to as the stochastic asset-liability model when choosing a benchmark. As is often the case with any model, the outcome is determined largely by the data that are fed into the model. Asset-liability modelling is particularly challenging as there is a wide array of assumptions about long-term interest rates and other economic indicators such as inflation and growth as well as asset classes all of which require long historic, time-series data.

One of the major handicaps for Colleges in Oxford and Cambridge in resorting to quantitative risk analysis is the lack of long-term data on the property assets under management. The large property content of Oxbridge institutions may well account for the relatively low usage of investment consultants whose expertise does not extend to the very specific property holdings of the Colleges. The other major factor in such decision-making is that, by definition, the process excludes any asset-class that is new and does not have historic time-series data; or precisely those areas of economic activity in the marketplace where inefficiencies occur and where chances of capturing alpha may also exist, if the skill is available.

While institutions in Oxford and Cambridge are increasingly examining the merits of absolute return strategies, the major problem for them is who is going to deliver the absolute returns? The asset allocation model, for example, may suggest 10–20 per cent in uncorrelated strategies such as hedge funds and private equity. The problem for the Colleges like other investors is how best to acquire such exposure. The creation of collective vehicles for the Colleges by Fauchier Partners in hedge funds, for example, has not been a particularly rewarding experience. The private equity fund-of-funds set up by Cambridge Associates has not been in place long enough for investors to gauge overall performance. Thus, these institutions are sceptical of asset allocation models that cannot be realistically implemented.

The responsibility for defining the policy portfolio as well as the rebalancing policy among Oxbridge institutions rests largely (in 84 per cent of cases) with the respective investment committee. Under half (46 per cent) the Colleges considered their investment committee as being fully responsible for rebalancing. Only 16 per cent or 10 Colleges (5 each in Oxford and Cambridge) said the investment committee was not involved in the rebalancing process. Consultants were generally not used in determining such policy, though 12 per cent of Oxford Colleges said they involved the investment consultant in the process. However, the level of contribution of the consultant was not significant. Only one College in Cambridge said the consultant was responsible for 25–50 per cent of the rebalancing decision. About two-thirds (67 per cent) of Cambridge Colleges expected their investment manager to rebalance the securities portfolio as and when required: 19 per cent of Colleges left it entirely to the asset manager compared with 15 per cent of institutions in Oxford. Over half (52 per cent) the respondents did not consider it the responsibility of the manager.

Use of target asset allocation or a policy portfolio may not be entirely new among institutions in Oxford and Cambridge, but due to the nature of their asset mix, less than one-quarter (23 per cent) of them reported having a rebalancing policy or a policy portfolio to rebalance to. Some Colleges have wide bands of asset allocations, such as 60 per cent in financial assets and 40 per cent in property or something similar, which result in infrequent rebalancing. Also property assets are rarely sold, unless there is a very good reason for doing so, but rebalancing is not one of them.

Two-thirds (64 per cent) of Colleges reported rebalancing informally, or taking a more tactically flexible approach, while 13 per cent of Colleges indicated not having any policy, formal or informal. Among Colleges reporting informal rebalancing, not all the Colleges reported having accompanying policy portfolios to rebalance to. Flexibility in rebalancing can be advantageous if the

Table 7.6. Adoption of portfolio rebalancing policies within Oxbridge

Policy	Oxford	Cambridge	Oxbridge
Formal policy	26	19	23
Informal policy	59	70	64
No policy	15	11	13
Total	**100**	**100**	**100**

institutions have the capability of exploiting short-term market movements. The largest endowments in the United States, for example, are most likely to have tactically flexible rebalancing policies.

Table 7.6 summarizes the responses provided by Colleges in Oxford and Cambridge as to whether the institutional investment principles included rebalancing.

According to the 2005 *Commonfund Benchmarks Study: Educational Endowment Report*, overall 90 per cent of institutions reported having target/policy portfolios, with 89 per cent reporting that they followed their policy. Virtually all (97 per cent) the larger institutions reported having target/policy portfolios and following them. A lower percentage (78 per cent) of the smallest institutions reported having these portfolios and most (77 per cent) followed them. Also, 78 per cent of respondents had rebalanced their portfolios in the past year, an increase from 75 per cent in FY 2003 and 62 per cent in FY 2002.[4]

The most commonly reported method of rebalancing portfolios was via fixed mechanism of rebalancing to target/percentage; 55 per cent of institutions that rebalanced in the past year employed such an approach. Forty per cent reported their rebalancing strategy as being tactically flexible. The largest institutions were most likely to employ a flexible approach (63 per cent), while the smallest more often used a fixed mechanism (58 per cent), which may be due to human resource limitations at the smaller institutions. Among institutions that rebalanced their portfolios in the past year, about one-third (36 per cent) reported doing so quarterly, while one-quarter (27 per cent) of institutions did so annually. As the largest institutions predominantly rebalance tactically, it is not surprising that 40 per cent of this group rebalanced its portfolios 'as needed'. In comparison, 20 per cent of the smallest institutions rebalanced semi-annually.[5]

Reasons for rebalancing

The major purpose of rebalancing is to reflect the intended risk-return profile of the portfolio. Changes in equity markets and return expectations, changes in internal investment objectives resulting in different risk-return profiles are typically responsible for changes in strategic asset allocation. And rebalancing assists in maintaining that asset allocation. The decision to retain some flexibility instead of rebalancing mechanically can be described as a policy too. Thus, strategic asset allocation is a completely different process compared to the rebalancing one.

As Swensen pointed out, 'rebalancing ensures that investors face the risk profile embodied in the policy portfolio. Institutions that follow no particular rebalancing policy engage in a peculiar form of market timing. By allowing portfolio allocations to drift with the whims of the market, portfolio risk and return characteristics change unpredictably, introducing more noise into an already highly uncertain process. In fact, over long periods of time, without rebalancing, portfolio allocations move toward the highest return asset, increasing the overall risk level of the portfolio. Ultimately disciplined rebalancing provides risk control, increasing the likelihood that investors achieve investment goals.'[6]

Analysis of institutional approaches to rebalancing in Oxford and Cambridge revealed that almost all the Colleges had made significant changes to their portfolios over the past couple of years, and many were in the middle of major reconstructions. Most of these institutions had moved to implementing total return policies in the recent past as well. Such alterations to portfolios were not as a result of 'rebalancing' though some Colleges had established target or policy portfolios and employed tactical flexibility in rebalancing. Like other aspects of endowment management in Oxbridge, the diversity of considerations implicit in such considerations is worthy of emphasis.

Some Colleges reported having strategic long-term plans to alter asset allocation, such as reducing the property portfolio over decades. According to one bursar:

If we look at the total endowment, then a significant re-balancing is in process because we have an overall objective to reduce the property exposure to 25 per cent over a ten-year period. So, we have a major re-balancing exercise going on, which is largely dependant on the ability to realise the underlying value of the property assets we hold. Our aim to hold a portfolio with 75 per cent securities and 25 per cent property is also based on the assumption of 6 per cent long-term real return on equity. The approach we have at the moment has not been going long enough for us to consider extensive re-balancing on the securities side of the portfolio.

While such a definition does not strictly adhere to what is traditionally referred to as rebalancing, many Colleges described all changes made to their portfolios as a kind of rebalancing. One College for example with an income-oriented investment strategy reduced its overseas equity holding in 2003 due to lack of dividend income from such assets. According to the treasurer of this College: 'At one point the fund manager was urging the College to be more exposed to overseas equities, but the College's view was that it was already highly geared to overseas economies via its student composition; 80 per cent of our students are from abroad. There are students from 57 different countries; so the College is massively exposed to the fortunes of the countries where the students come from. The low dollar, for example, is hurting the students from America. This year we need to be careful about our review of room rents, otherwise we will end up with unsecured debts. All our costs are in sterling, but our sources of income are not hedged against that.' The need to secure income was a significant determinant of investment policy. The greatest investment risk was the failure to receive the desired rate of income.

There were several such examples of rebalancing, which would normally be referred to as strategic changes in asset allocation policy. According to another College bursar for whom endowment income was not a major concern in managing the budget:

There is a case for rebalancing—for example, for a long-term investor to say this is our asset allocation and we must re-balance our portfolio every quarter because we believe markets are efficient. We take the view that that may be true of highly liquid developed markets (excluding e.g. developed equity and bond markets), but we are not efficient market theorists, and we believe there are people skilled enough to identify and arbitrage fat tails. So we are prepared to shift our asset allocation tactically when we think we have identified very large anomalies but we are cautious about the process of convincing ourselves.

Some decisions are clearly market timed; others are determined by the specific requirements of the College. The need to manage the endowment efficiently is widely recognized; the differences lie mainly in the ways in which efficiency is defined and achieved. About 10 per cent of Colleges were in the process of formulating and implementing such policies, mostly with a view to creating more efficient portfolios. 'We are altering the structure of our portfolio,' explained one, 'because we were told we did not hold an "optimal" portfolio or that we were not placed on the efficient frontier; so the assumption is that we could improve our return for the same level of risk.' The issue of internal efficiencies and savings is also being considered in the overall management of this College; the overall mood being for making efficiency gains wherever possible.

Though only 10 per cent of Colleges indicated a benchmark orientation, and from time to time rebalanced their portfolios back to the policy target, there was a general awareness of long-term targets. Many Colleges delegated such responsibility to the investment manager. Others with clearly formulated benchmarks suggested a great degree of flexibility in their rebalancing, taking a more tactical approach that enabled them to benefit from short-term market movements; for example, allowing property as a portion of the portfolio to grow during the period of the stock market downturn. As one bursar commented, 'In January 2002, we agreed to allow property to continue to grow as a percentage of the total endowment, rather than re-balance.' Many bursars had taken such a stance with regard to their property holdings.

A similar tactical approach was reported, particularly among larger US endowments, with assets over $1 billion, among whom 63 per cent of institutions reported tactically flexible rebalancing policies. Fifty-nine per cent of endowments worth between $500 million and $1 billion also rebalanced tactically, while 46 per cent of endowment valued between $100 million and 500 million did so. Among the smallest endowments (worth under $10 million), one-quarter adopted such an approach, and among endowments worth $10–50 million, about one-third (32 per cent) did so. Among medium-sized endowments ($50–100 million), 38 per cent employed flexible policies. Overall, 40 per cent of institutions reported tactically flexible rebalancing policies. Tactical rebalancing as reported among US endowments indicated a shift in their approach to rebalancing. The need to be tactically flexible was driven by increased market volatility. Only a third (33 per cent) of the largest institutions employed a fixed rebalancing mechanism compared to over half (55 per cent) the institutions reporting so.[7]

Most responses relating to rebalancing among institutions in Oxford and Cambridge had more to do with changes in investment policy decisions rather than rebalancing per se. For example, 7 per cent of Colleges switched from active to passive management in response to active managers' poor performance; they were also concerned about changes in ownership of asset managers and the increased focus on asset gathering within the industry. Others made changes in investment policy due to internal reasons. One College went from having a growth-oriented, total return investment policy to an income-oriented one due to the collapse in the value of its endowment portfolio as a result of a sizeable internal borrowing from the endowment. Another 5 per cent of bursars gave no specific response to the question; rebalancing was simply not a relevant issue. The range of responses is illustrated in Table 7.7.

It is worth noting that about a third (30 per cent) of the rebalancing within Oxbridge College endowment portfolios was triggered by issues relating to property. One-quarter (24 per cent) of Colleges in Oxford and over a third (37 per cent) in Cambridge rebalanced their portfolios due to decisions that emanated from their property investments. Taking into account the high property content of these institutional portfolios, such a state of affairs is perhaps not revelatory. What is interesting though is the diversity of investment views expressed on the management of the property portfolio. For one bursar: 'The equity portfolio is more a residue of our main decisions relating to property. The capital value of the portfolio is not a major consideration.' For another: 'We nearly rebalanced in July 2003. The property band is 10–20 per cent. Currently, we hold 16 per cent in property. We decided

Table 7.7. Examples of rebalancing cited by Oxbridge Colleges

Reasons	Oxford	Cambridge	Oxbridge
Allowed property to grow	5	3	8
Plan to reduce property long term	5	—	5
Investing in property currently	2	2	3
Switch from direct property to funds	2	2	3
Rebalancing within property portfolio	—	5	5
Switch from property to equity	—	2	2
Switch from equity to property	—	2	2
Switch from gilts to property	—	2	2
Switch from active to passive	3	3	7
Switch from growth to income	—	2	2
Increase allocation to equities	5	—	5
Increase allocation to Japan	2	—	2
Increase allocation to UK	2	—	2
Increase allocation to European equity	2	—	2
Reduce overseas equities	—	2	2
Switch from equity to bonds	3	2	5
Switch from bonds to equity	—	2	2
Invest in private equity	2	2	3
Reduced fixed income	3	2	5
Increased cash during market downturn	5	—	5
Switched managers	3	—	3
Left to fund manager	2	—	2
Benchmark orientation	3	7	10
Tactical rebalancing	—	2	2
In the process of formulation/implementation	8	2	10
No response available	—	5	5
Total	**56**	**44**	**100**

Table 7.8. Relative importance of motives for changes in asset allocation

Reason	100	50–100	25–50	0–25	0	NR	Total
Investment policy review	16	26	16	9	18	15	100
Change in risk profile	2	12	22	10	39	15	100
Market forces	3	14	16	13	39	15	100
Other	8	3	3	5	66	15	100

NR = No response.

that the property team could purchase additional property up to their limit of 20 per cent, if they wanted to. So, we had to find some cash to enable them to do so. That money was taken from long-dated gilts, which was an investment policy review.'

The bulk of portfolio changes reported among Oxbridge institutions were the result of investment policy reviews, changes in the risk profile of the fund, changes in the market environment, or similar factors. The extent to which changes in overall allocations were driven by these considerations is illustrated in Table 7.8.

For 16 per cent of institutions, investment policy review was entirely responsible for changes in portfolio allocations, and for over one-quarter (26 per cent) of Colleges such a factor was largely (50–100 per cent) responsible for triggering alterations in allocations. Changes in risk profile, for example, had no impact on 39 per cent of respondents. Only one College thought a change in risk profile impacted its decision to change the fund profile. Just 2 Colleges (3 per cent) indicated that rebalancing the portfolio was totally responsive to movements in markets, 14 per cent indicated market movements had a significant (50–100 per cent) impact, while 39 per cent of institutions suggested that market forces had no impact. Thus, for a significant number of institutions the concept of rebalancing is at best new and not fully in place.

Two-thirds of respondents (66 per cent) did not cite any 'other' factors influencing their policy in maintaining asset allocation or changing such allocations. For those that acknowledged other factors, the reasons offered were unique to the Colleges concerned. Eight per cent of Colleges expressed a need to secure income as an overwhelming factor in rebalancing the endowment. For one bursar, the inability to 'manage College fellows' was partly responsible (20 per cent) for such a move. 'Poor performance of managers' and the need to service the College buildings were also cited as reasons contributing (50 per cent) to changes in asset allocation by two bursars, both in Oxford.

In one instance, asset allocation changes were driven by the need to provide student housing; in another case, it was 'the need to avoid investments in Emerging Markets.' In the latter, the fund manager had invested in Japan, which action the College did not approve, and so the investment had to be sold. The portfolio was invested in several pooled funds of the investment manager, which meant that from time to time investment actions by the manager were 'politically insensitive' from the College's point of view. This College aimed to invest in well-known companies in Europe and the United States, not in Emerging Markets. 'So, when the fund manager recommends risky investments such as hedge funds or investing in Japan, which is not what we have in mind for our portfolio, we instruct them to adhere to our guidelines. So, while this might reflect an investment policy decision, in reality it represents a combination of issues for the College,' explained the bursar; the manager's style drift and lack of adherence to the management agreement being relevant issues for this College.

Use of derivatives

Investment committee members of institutions in Oxford and Cambridge define themselves as being essentially risk averse; they perceive themselves as being conservative in their overall approach to endowment management. Investing a third of the endowment directly in property is not considered overtly risky as they have done so over centuries. The Governing Body members may be experts in their chosen fields, but they are not all conversant with markets, particularly with recent developments in financial innovation. It has therefore not occurred to them that their property assets could be collectively securitized; it is only recently that some of the Colleges opted for indexation as a means of securing cheap exposure to an asset. While investment decisions are generally left to investment committee members, the ultimate responsibility for managing the endowment lies with the Governing Body. Unless an investment strategy has the endorsement of both the Investment Committee and the Governing Body, it is unlikely to succeed. It is not surprising therefore that, in managing the endowment portfolio, the use of derivative instruments was limited to currency hedging.

The majority (66 per cent) of institutions did not use derivative instruments in their asset management, though one-quarter (25 per cent) of bursars in Oxford and Cambridge indicated their willingness to use financial instruments. Only a third of bursars reported their inability or unwillingness to do so. Interestingly, twice as many bursars in Cambridge reported the use of derivative instruments, 33 per cent in Cambridge compared with 18 per cent in Oxford. Overall, 10 per cent of Oxbridge bursars reported using financial instruments in managing their endowments. But, among these institutions, such use was confined to traded options or currency hedging, which in the words of one Oxford bursar could not be regarded as making use of complex derivative instruments: 'One cannot regard taking out a foreign exchange contract for hedging purposes as making use of a derivative instrument.' As this bursar has considerable experience as a fund manager, such a remark was not surprising. As more bursars are appointed with relevant industry experience, overall approaches to asset management are set to change.

Though most bursars did not use derivative instruments in managing their endowment assets, they allowed their fund managers to do so, albeit within certain constraints. One College, for example, authorized its fund manager 'to effect Written Calls (covered) and Written Puts (covered). No more than five positions may be open at anyone time. And each position is limited to £500,000.' Respondents using derivatives also limited its use by the fund manager to currency hedging alone. Some bursars who did not use derivatives pointed out that they could do so, if they wished to take such action. They were free to use derivatives, but chose not to do so. Two-thirds of bursars reported that they did not use derivative instruments in managing their portfolios, but they recognized their fund managers' need to do so, particularly hedge fund managers.

Conclusion

Like pension funds and insurance companies, endowments and foundations are driven by asset allocation being determined primarily by appointed members of the investment committee with help from investment advisers and managers. However, unlike pension funds and insurance companies, investors in the philanthropic sector have increasingly recognized their edge as truly long-term investors. As a sector, they have emerged as the true risk takers. While most pension funds think long-term investing refers to a few decades, for academic institutions it typically refers to centuries if not in perpetuity.

The Ivy League College endowments in the United States as a group have invested differently when compared with investors in the pension fund or retail sector. The same cannot be said of investment policies followed by endowments, foundations, and charitable institutions in other parts of the developed world or even among institutions in Oxford and Cambridge. Most charities in the UK were obliged to invest for income; on average they also distributed less of the value of their endowment assets compared with their counterparts in the United States. While some spent less than 5 per cent of their assets, the overall requirement to do so in the United States resulted in greater risk-taking, including the freedom to invest in unconventional assets. The pioneering strategies adopted by major US endowments are now widely recognized.

As a group, institutions in Oxford and Cambridge exhibit a refreshing lack of standardization in their approach to asset allocation, which plagued the pension fund sector in the UK through most of the 1980s and 1990s. The absence of investment consultants in the strategic asset allocation process may have contributed to this development in Oxford and Cambridge, as well as the accompanying diversity of approaches to investing prevalent among endowments and foundations in Europe. With greater awareness of peer group activity and the rise of a new breed of professional philanthropic investors, it is conceivable that the current level of individualism manifested in the endowment sector may disappear.

Historically, investment committee members in Oxford and Cambridge have not actively determined asset allocation, or established policy portfolios. Thus, strategic asset allocation was often the result of individual investment decisions rather than the point from where portfolio construction began. It is surprising that indexation as an investment strategy for the publicly traded securities in the portfolio is not more widespread among these institutions, as overcoming the cost of active management is itself a huge challenge. In the words of Swensen: 'In the context of an extraordinarily complex, difficult investing environment, fiduciaries tend to be surprisingly accepting of active manager pitches.'[8] Serious investors should consider low-cost passive strategies before pursuing high-cost active management strategies, where the returns are at best uncertain.

The concept of risk among Oxbridge institutions is also interesting. A theoretical definition of risk is often of little use to these individuals; what they are more comfortable with is the residual outcome. For example, many investors within this sector believe that market volatility is of little consequence to the portfolio as long as income is not affected. The major risk for them is the failure to secure the required income from the endowment. Only a few seek absolute returns from all their investments—that is never wish to lose any of the invested capital. In an ideal world, these investors would like a sustainable source of income, inflation-hedged, and not have to worry about how exactly to secure that. Such a way of conceptualizing risk is also the reason why these investors like property as an asset class. It can be argued that Colleges manifest a higher level of diversity in their overall approach to asset allocation in their endowment portfolios mainly due to their property holdings. Such policies may not be based on quantitative analytical models, but deriving income from property over centuries has provided some of these institutions with an insight into the importance of income diversification.

While over half of US institutions used a fixed mechanism to rebalance to their target range, such an approach was never employed among Oxbridge institutions. Many Colleges in Oxford and Cambridge were in the process of moving their portfolios towards the efficient frontier—that is towards the policy portfolio or the portfolio they should be holding, if they did not have any investment constraints and had a clean sheet to start from. As the Colleges have long experience of investing in property, they are sceptical of asset allocation models that do not include the asset class. Currently, as a group, the Colleges' investment policy features do not formally cover issues such as rebalancing, though many bursars expressed the need to identify an 'ideal asset allocation policy for long-term educational institutions' such as their own Colleges. This question was indicative of a need to do the right thing, while acknowledging their inability to determine what that might be in investment terms.

These institutions are not afraid of adopting asset allocation policies that challenge basic investment concepts such as diversification; for example, by holding over 60 per cent of the endowment portfolio in property. The most frequently cited approach to rebalancing was 'tactical', employed by the majority of Colleges. This translated sometimes to allowing property assets to overshoot even their acceptably high allocations. While such a response appeared responsible during the first three years of the market downturn, from March 2000–3, the recovery of equity markets since March 2003 favoured investors who rebalanced their assets back into equity.

The importance of tactical asset allocation as opposed to a mechanical rebalancing approach was cited as a reason for not following the advice given by investment consultants. In the words of one bursar: 'Cambridge Associates is our investment consultant. The College has used them for over three years. Consultants have their limitations in relying too much on historically based statistical models. They also believe that you should set a long-term investment policy and rebalance the portfolio automatically in response to market movements, which seems tactically inefficient.'

The significance of property in the endowment portfolios of institutions in Oxford and Cambridge cannot be emphasized enough. It influences institutional approaches to related issues in asset allocation. Rebalancing, for example, is not as straightforward if you have 30–40 per cent of your portfolio directly invested in property, not via REITs. The Colleges do not have a blank sheet of paper to start with; it took Balliol a couple of decades to sell their property assets. By the time they had done so, it was time to buy back some of the asset class, which they did in the form of property funds rather than direct holdings. There are of course Colleges with smaller endowments without any property assets in their portfolios. While these institutions have as it were a clean slate, and could own efficient portfolios that best match their long-term investment objectives, there is no evidence that this is indeed always the case. Endowment asset management among these institutions may appear too individualistic, but such practice is not significantly different from their larger counterparts in the United States.

8

Portfolio risk

Introduction

Experienced investors recognize that understanding the risk profile of the overall portfolio lies at the heart of any assessment of investment alternatives. At the same time, risk is defined individually by every investor, and thus more difficult to generalize, except in absolute terms. As individual perception of risk varies, diversification improves the risk-return profile of a portfolio by enabling investors to achieve higher returns for any given level of risk or lower risk for any given level of return. Developing a set of inputs for portfolio optimization is often based on qualitative notions, and not clearly defined quantitative ones. Thus, adjusting assumptions to reflect the appropriate risk-return balance is critical to risk control.

According to the guidance provided by the Charity Commission in the UK, the regulatory body for charities, there are essentially two aspects to the consideration of risk: counterparty risk and investment risk. Counterparty risk refers to the risk that one of the firms with which a charitable corporation does investment business—such as banks, stockbrokers, investment managers—defaults on its contractual obligations. The risk of loss is perhaps low in a climate where financial services are regulated, and where compensation schemes are in place; but this does not, by any means, cover the whole investment universe. Investment committee members and trustees may be more or less concerned with this issue, depending on the nature and extent of the investments which they make. They should not lose sight of the possibility of counterparty default, and of the need to assess and manage the risk in the context of their particular investment strategy. Investment risk on the other hand is the risk which is inherent in any investment. At one level, the risk may be seen as lying in the failure or underperformance of a particular investment, but this risk can be mitigated to some extent by having a suitably diversified portfolio.[1]

An attempt to identify the risks to College endowment portfolios (on a scale of 1 to 5 with 1 being not very important and 5 very important), with reference to various aspects of portfolio risk (such as market risk, risk relative to benchmark, liquidity risk, fiduciary risk, and 'other' risk factors) provided clues to the risk framework within which Colleges in Oxford and Cambridge invest. It is worth noting that a majority (85 per cent) of Colleges consider their investment committees as being responsible for risk management of endowment assets, with about half the Colleges reporting that the job is done internally without the assistance of any expert external guidance. The involvement of investment consultants in managing portfolio risk, as with most other aspects of the investment process, is minimal; 90 per cent of respondents did not use a consultant in the risk assessment process. Even in Oxford, where more institutions reported using the services of investment consultants, only 15 per cent of Colleges used a consultant in risk management.

The input of the investment manager appears to be significantly higher, with 43 per cent of Colleges relying on their manager for such assessment and follow-up action. Some Colleges reported the Finance Committee typically undertaking risk assessment as part of their overall responsibility in managing the finances of the College. In Cambridge, almost half the Colleges delegated risk management to their investment manager, with 22 per cent depending entirely on the manager for such assessment. In Oxford, more than one third of Colleges involved the investment manager in risk management, and about one quarter attributed significant (25–50 per cent) contribution of the external manager to the overall process.

The importance of risk management is acknowledged in the *University of Oxford, Financial Statement of the Colleges, 2002–2003*; most Colleges make a disclosure under 'Risk management' though there appears to be no established best practice. Most Colleges state something to the effect that 'the major risks to which the College is exposed, as identified by the Governing Body, have been reviewed and systems have been established to mitigate these risks;' occasionally adding that the major risks are 'considered to be those that would prevent the College from carrying out its charitable objects permanently.'

All Souls College, Oxford, one of the institutions providing relatively more information on the subject, stated in its published annual reports and accounts the following risk statement:

The College is engaged in risk assessment on an ongoing basis. When it is not able to address risk issues using its own resources, the College takes advice from outside experts with specialist knowledge. Policies and procedures within the College are reviewed by the relevant College committee. Risk involving general strategy, compliance and operations are reviewed by the General Purposes Committee, chaired by the Warden. Financial and investment risks are assessed and monitored by the Estates & Finance Committee, with input from its Investment and Property Sub-Committees. The latter two, in turn, deal with a number of external professional advisers regarding the risk profile and performance monitoring of various assets held in the College's endowment. The College also appoints two of its Fellows to act as Financial Delegates for alternating two-year stints. They meet with the auditors each year to review financial controls, accounting systems and the report of the College's financial position. The Domestic Committee oversees employment and health and safety issues. Outside advisors are consulted when necessary to assist in risk assessment in these areas and the College maintains an annual retainer with a specialist advisory firm for these purposes. In addition, the Bursar, Manciple and domestic staff departmental heads meet once a term to review health and safety issues. Training courses and other forms of career development are regularly offered to, and undertaken by, members of the College staff to enhance their skills and awareness in risk related areas.

The *Cambridge University Reporter, Accounts of the Colleges, 2004*, contained no separate disclosure under Risk management though the section under 'Responsibilities of the Governing Body' referred to 'internal financial control' rather than any established risk management criteria for the endowment fund. The disclosures vary among the Colleges, though many contain references to the Governing Body's responsibility to take reasonable steps in ensuring that there are appropriate financial and management controls in place to safeguard the assets of the College. Most Colleges report the existence of appropriate financial and management controls to safeguard the assets of the College, as well as to prevent and detect fraud, in addition to securing the economical, efficient and effective management of the College's resources and expenditure. There is also the recognition that any system of internal financial control can only provide reasonable, not absolute, assurance against material misstatement or loss.

As far as risks to the endowment portfolio are concerned, the view is that it is an essential aspect of the overall management process. Institutions in Oxford and Cambridge perceive themselves as being essentially conservative and risk averse. Traditionally risk was not actively nor quantitatively managed, but approached more qualitatively by investing in a more diversified portfolio. Though some Colleges did not consider holding over 50 per cent of their endowment in a single asset class such as property or domestic equity as being unduly risky. While higher returns come with the price of higher expected volatility, diversification particularly among uncorrelated assets and strategies provides investors with a mechanism to control risk. Some of the larger endowments also take into account manager and style diversification. The recent restructuring of most endowment portfolios in Oxford and Cambridge helped in the implementation of an investment policy that actively sought total return over the long term, as well as an appropriate balance between capital growth and income, to provide for real increases in annual expenditure. But formal investment policy statements on risk management were not a priority for these institutions.

Table 8.1 shows to what extent risk features were reported in the investment policy statements of US educational endowments.

Table 8.1. Degree of risk in institutional investment pool

Endowment	Formal	Informal	No policy
>$1,000 m	44.4	15.6	40.0
$500–1,000 m	42.3	21.2	36.5
$100–500 m	53.3	15.9	30.8
$50–100 m	60.8	11.2	28.0
$25-50 m	58.2	12.0	29.8
<$25 m	54.3	10.0	35.7
Public	60.5	14.1	25.3
Independent	51.8	13.2	35.0
Average	**54.5**	**13.5**	**32.0**

Source: 2004 NACUBO Study.

A comparison with US educational institutions and their approach to risk management shows that over half (54.5 per cent) formally defined the degree of risk in the investment pool, with medium-sized endowments (assets between $50 million and $100 million) along with public institutions more likely to do so than any other group. Also, about one-third of institutions (32 per cent) had no policy on the degree of risk inherent in the endowment investment pool, with independent institutions more likely to adopt such a stance.[2]

Market risk

Long-term investors with disciplined investment practices ignore market timing, not market valuations. Disciplined investors stick to their investment philosophy through market cycles. Predicting market changes is difficult due to the challenges involved not only in identifying the multitude of factors that influence markets, but also in accurately forecasting the timing of such events occurring. However, all investors take a view about markets and adjust their asset allocation accordingly. Investors taking a negative view, for example, of equities may decide to reduce their exposure to the asset class while increasing allocation to other assets such as bonds, property, or alternative assets. Even when passive strategies are employed, investors are implicitly expressing their view of the market. As predicting market changes is not the same as investing for the long term, seasoned investors prefer to remain fully invested.

It is worth noting therefore that over half (59 per cent) the institutions in Oxford and Cambridge reported market risk as being very important; almost one-third (65 per cent) of Oxford bursars thought that to be the case compared with over half the bursars in Cambridge (52 per cent). At the same time, equity allocations made by these institutions averaged 55 per cent for Oxford and 52 per cent for Cambridge, with exposure to domestic equities at around the

Table 8.2. Oxbridge perceptions of market risk

Risk scale	Oxford	Cambridge	Oxbridge
5 Very important	65	52	59
4 Fairly important	18	19	18
3 Middling	6	22	13
2 Fairly unimportant	6	7	7
1 Unimportant	—	—	—
0	—	—	—
No response	6	—	3
Total	**100**	**100**	**100**

38–9 per cent level. The averages mask the discrepancies in the relationship between reported perception of market risk and the equity allocation strategies followed by these institutions. Investment in fixed income averaged at 12 per cent, while exposure to absolute return strategies was virtually non-existent, though property accounted for over one-quarter (26 per cent) of endowment assets. Property also accounts for their more tactical approach to publicly tradable assets, as direct property holdings are more difficult to sell.

Table 8.2 provides a breakdown of the responses to the Colleges' perception of market risk. For the sake of convenience, scores have been rounded upwards. In two instances, respondents gave scores that were not in the survey, for example 4.5 is shown as 5 in Table 8.2 and 2.5 as 3 in Table 8.3.

About a third (31 per cent) of respondents rated market risk as being fairly important, rating it 3–4 in the risk scale. Considerably more institutions in Cambridge (22 per cent) indicated market risk as being of average concern (risk scale 3) compared with Oxford, where just 6 per cent of Colleges thought that to be the case. Thus, 83 per cent of Oxford institutions considered market risk as being a concern, rating it at the higher end of the risk parameter (4–5 in the risk scale) compared with 71 per cent of Cambridge institutions. Only a few (7 per cent) of Oxbridge institutions did not consider it to be a major risk to their portfolio; a very small number of Colleges (3 per cent) did not respond and/or did not have a view on the subject.

While major conclusions based on such analysis can be misleading, it does suggest that over half the participants were concerned about the stock market being a major source of risk during 2003–4, when the interviews were conducted. Most Colleges expected markets to fall further, not rise or recover. The overall allocation to equities, long-only strategies, at over 50 per cent of assets does not reflect such a perception of the equity market. As many Colleges also engage in tactical asset allocation, such a degree of market pessimism would have translated to lower exposure to equities. It is therefore not clear whether these high-equity allocations were the result of active management policies or reflected their bias as investors.

According to Swensen, 'Finance theory and common sense support three long-term asset allocation principles—the importance of equity ownership, the efficacy of portfolio diversification, and the significance of tax sensitivity.'[3] If these institutions are assessed on these criteria, they score well; they recognize the importance of equity ownership, investment in property adds a measure of diversification and income generation that many institutional investors would envy; and the Colleges are highly sensitive to tax-related issues although as charitable institutions they are mostly exempt from tax.

Colleges in Oxford and Cambridge were relatively cushioned from the overall market impact via their property allocations, particularly during the bear market of 2000–3. As long-term investors, it made sense for these institutions to continue to hold at least half their assets in equity. The allocations to property, bonds, and cash consisted of the remaining assets, as access to alternative strategies was severely limited. In rising markets, long-only indexed equity strategies are the cheapest way of investing in beta. As both the FTSE All Share and the MSCI World indices recovered strongly after the bear market of 2000–3, it can be interpreted as a smart tactical move.

US endowments responded to changes in the market environment by investing in absolute return strategies; the larger endowments investing aggressively. However, the highest levels of concern over hedge fund investments were reported around risk controls (with an average of 4.1 on a scale of 1 through 5, with 5 representing a high level of concern) and oversight/due diligence (with an average score of 4.0). Individual manager risk, operational or business risk came close at 3.7 and 3.5 respectively followed by transparency (3.2) and fees (3.1). The largest institutions reported generally higher levels of concern across the board, while the smallest institutions rated only oversight and due diligence higher than 3.0. This may reflect the fact that many smaller institutions rely on their fund-of-funds manager to focus on risk management in the hedge fund area, while larger endowments had greater exposure to such strategies.[4]

Risk relative to benchmark

In contrast to market risk, none of the respondents thought of risk relative to the benchmark as being important to their overall risk profile. In other words, most bursars considered the stock market was more likely to disappoint than the ability of their investment managers, or any other source of risk that might be a contributing factor in influencing the performance of their portfolios. Whether one can conclude from such observations that institutions in Oxford and Cambridge considered themselves as having superior manager selection skills, or that they thought their investment advisers

Table 8.3. Oxbridge perceptions of risk relative to benchmark

Risk scale	Oxford	Cambridge	Oxbridge
5 Very important	—	—	—
4 Fairly important	15	7	11
3 Middling	29	19	25
2 Fairly unimportant	29	63	44
1 Unimportant	21	7	15
0	—	4	2
No response	6	—	3
Total	**100**	**100**	**100**

had such skills, compared to their ability to predict market returns is not conclusive.

Table 8.3 provides a breakdown of responses with regard to risk relative to benchmark.

When questioned further, some of the participants admitted to not being sure what 'risk relative to benchmark' meant. When explained that it referred to the portfolio's potential to underperform its chosen benchmark and thereby fail to achieve its return target and investment objective, only 11 per cent classified such risk on a 1–5 scale at 4, and a further 25 per cent identified it as being reasonably important, at 3. A large proportion of responses suggested that greater risk was associated with the manager's failure to deliver income rather than total return target implicit in the benchmark. For 44 per cent of institutions, risk relative to benchmark was gauged at 2. The Colleges exhibited a healthy sense of scepticism as far as active managers were concerned. Taking such level of scepticism into account, it is surprising that more institutions did not invest passively. One Cambridge College bursar indicated that its risk relative to benchmark was zero. With the bulk of its assets managed passively, such risk can indeed be low though not nil; for example, the fund manager could be exposed to risks that are unknown as was the case with Barings in 1995.

Few suggested that risk was inherent in the benchmark itself, that is the policy portfolio was not optimal and thus a source of risk—as was the case with the pension fund sector with the prevalence of peer group benchmarking during the 1980s and 1990s. Though some herding is inevitable, Colleges in Oxford and Cambridge remain highly individualistic in several key aspects of their endowment management. As a result, the benchmarks used are typically customized, sometimes having evolved over decades reflecting the special characteristic of each institution. However, there was not enough evidence to suggest that such a state of affairs had evolved out of a conscious design; nor was it clear that existing portfolios had been tested empirically as being the most efficient. Many bursars, for example, commented on their high exposure to property and how such allocation constrained their long-term return expectations. Some Colleges had started the long process of rebalancing the endowment portfolio, away from the heavy allocation to property.

The search for an ideal asset allocation for educational endowments such as theirs remained a shared concern. Simulating the American educational endowment model, with high allocations to alternative strategies employed by Harvard, Yale, Princeton, or Stanford, was not seen as a realistic solution for institutions with relatively high ownership of prime property assets. The key to understanding the asset management dilemmas faced by these institutions is their long exposure to property—an asset class they have considerable experience of managing, and which delivers two key requirements of providing income and diversification. The pension fund world, on the other hand being restricted by its size, does not have the sort of choices that are open to endowments.

In one instance the chairman of a large Oxbridge endowment admitted that their investment consultant was of the view that they held a suboptimal portfolio. As he put it, 'we were not placed on the efficient frontier; so the assumption is that we could improve our return for the same level of risk.' Endowment portfolios of several institutions in Oxford and Cambridge could benefit from such optimization analysis. While most bursars expressed a desire to find out more about the efficacy of a policy portfolio, they were not sure that existing investment research took sufficient cognizance of their particular asset mix. Much of the research on endowment asset allocation by investment consultants has failed to take into account property. While consultants such as Cambridge Associates have conducted extensive research on endowments and foundations in the United States, their coverage of educational endowments in the UK remains limited. In Oxford, Cambridge Associates appears to have made some impact though many bursars remain sceptical of the value of the research they receive.

Only a handful of institutions indicated they were perhaps not invested in an efficient portfolio, but were in the process of addressing that issue. According to one bursar: 'We will end up with Cambridge Associates as our consultant as part of their package for investing in their private equity fund of funds. We would not normally have appointed them as our consultant. But, we would like some exposure in private equity and the fund they are specifically creating for Oxford Colleges seems like a good thing.' The same bursar also explained: 'Apart from monitoring the performance of the private equity fund for which they will be hired, we would also expect them to give us positive input in asset allocation, risk instruction, and establishing the benchmark. We are not sure whether we have an appropriate benchmark—at least, the one created by our investment manager.' The investment manager is currently responsible for the benchmark and hence the need to address the issue with regard to risk, as the benchmark risk is perceived to be high.

Liquidity risk

One of the main concerns of endowments is securing adequate funding for their operations. Thanks to the diverse sources of income available to educational institutions, dependence on endowment income varies among such entities. While a total return approach enables investors to focus on asset allocation with a view to growing capital and income in real terms in perpetuity, liquidity remains an important concern. With Oxbridge institutions holding an average of 7 per cent in cash (9 per cent for Oxford Colleges and 5 per cent for Cambridge Colleges) liquidity was not perceived as a significant risk. Over half (56 per cent) the responding institutions rated it low, at 1; over one-third of Colleges (68 per cent) in Oxford reported liquidity risk as not being very important compared to 41 per cent of institutions in Cambridge.

Access to adequate resources from the endowment on an annual basis was rated as a major factor in influencing asset allocation; as these institutions were only recently investing for income, such considerations were only natural. However, Colleges with low dependence on the endowment for their overall income did not think that liquidity influenced asset allocation. Table 8.4 shows how institutions in Oxford and Cambridge rated liquidity as a source of risk to their portfolios.

With allocations to property and cash, at 26 and 7 per cent on average for both Oxford and Cambridge, comprising about a third of endowment portfolios, institutions in Oxford and Cambridge did not view liquidity risk as being relevant. Two Colleges (3 per cent), one each in Oxford and Cambridge, thought it posed no risk at all; both Colleges held very high levels of cash in their portfolio—one had 21 per cent and the other 14 per cent in addition to their property assets. Neither of these Colleges considered their high-cash allocation as being a source of risk—that is not being fully invested in the market.

One College in Cambridge identified liquidity risk as being very important, reflecting the College's high allocation to property in its endowment (90 per cent). No other College had such a significant exposure to property.

Table 8.4. Oxbridge perceptions of liquidity risk

Risk scale	Oxford	Cambridge	Oxbridge
5 Very important	—	4	2
4 Fairly important	—	11	5
3 Middling	12	7	10
2 Fairly unimportant	12	33	21
1 Unimportant	68	41	56
0	3	4	3
No response	6	—	3
Total	**100**	**100**	**100**

The next highest allocation to property was 75 per cent, and for that College (in Oxford), liquidity risk was thought to be at a level on the 1–5 scale of 2, as the College had sufficient cash flow. Both Colleges with high-property holdings were among the ones also with an absolute return approach to their equity investments; that is, they were intolerant of any loss in the capital value of their equity portfolios.

Eleven per cent of institutions in Cambridge considered liquidity risk to be fairly important, though they were not among the Colleges with the lowest cash holdings. One of these Colleges held 2 per cent cash, the remaining 7–8 per cent cash; yet they considered liquidity risk to be high at 4, or at 80 per cent on the risk scale. One-third of Cambridge institutions rated liquidity risk at 2. Fewer Colleges (74 per cent) in Cambridge, compared with 80 per cent of Colleges in Oxford, did not consider liquidity risk as a significant source of portfolio risk. On average, Colleges felt comfortable with the cash flows they were able to drawdown from the endowment in the form of income from property as well as their relatively high-cash positions.

Very few Colleges indicated an imminent shift in their asset allocation though several of these institutions were in the middle of major restructuring to their endowment portfolios, and would have changed their cash allocations at least over the next few years. Thus, allocations today would most likely indicate lower cash positions; perhaps even lower allocation to property. Anecdotal evidence suggests some of this would have been invested in alternative strategies. Barry Hedley, for example, joined Gonville and Caius College in Cambridge as Bursar the month after the FT All Share peaked in 2000. He recalled wryly that he had been appointed on the expectation that he would reshape the College's endowment more aggressively towards equities, in place of its former orientation towards property and gilts!

He helped the College establish an overall financial objective for the first time, and how it was linked formally to consistent spending rules and investment policies, including the essential transition to 'total return' accounting, the latter requiring Privy Council's approval for changing the College Statutes. The tactical difficulties involved in transforming the endowment from its starting position to its strategic target allocation, given the volatility and downward trend in equities prevailing in the capital markets in the early 2000's along with the need to achieve consensus among the College Fellows on the actions to be taken, were monumental indeed! Nevertheless, by mid-2006, the changes were almost complete, with an almost 100 per cent reshaping of the College's endowment portfolio into a broadly diversified structure including significant allocations to hedge funds and private equity, major reductions in bulk equities as well as gilts and cash, and considerable (and gently continuing) reductions in its commitment to property.

Apart from investments in property that tend to be illiquid, institutions in Oxford and Cambridge were invested in marketable securities and not heavily exposed to hedge funds or private equity assets, which tend to be less liquid in times of greater market volatility. Therefore, these institutions did not consider liquidity risk as being a relevant source of portfolio risk. As illiquidity can also be a source of abnormal performance, or alpha, it is a characteristic that long-term investors are more willing to accommodate. The lack of information relating to illiquid assets creates the investment opportunity. Highly liquid, large capitalization securities receive a lot of analyst attention. In competitive markets, it is difficult to capture alpha over a period. The lack of available information among private companies thus creates the challenge and the opportunity. Also, investors realize the value of their investments when the private equity companies acquire a stock market listing.

A similar advantage exists in the very specific property assets owned by institutions in Oxford and Cambridge. These assets are illiquid and realizing their intrinsic value may take longer than private equity investments. Most Colleges do not seek to realize the potential of such investments; property is typically considered a core asset. Operational property consists of the inalienable assets of the College. Only property assets held within the endowment can be sold, based on financial sometimes on other considerations. The sale of property can be a complicated and lengthy process. Unlike marketable securities, property assets are illiquid; thus Colleges with higher allocations to property also carry a higher liquidity risk. As Oxbridge Colleges have a truly long-term investment horizon, they are better placed to manage such risks. More importantly, rental values attached to property provide a secure and acceptable level of income for these institutions.

Fiduciary risk

The definition of fiduciary risk is very broad. It is effectively anything that can occur leading to an unpleasant outcome—be it financial, compliance, operational, etc. Thus, investment committees in charge of risk management have broad mandates, and take their charge seriously. As Table 8.5 illustrates,

Table 8.5. Oxbridge perceptions of fiduciary risk

Risk scale	Oxford	Cambridge	Oxbridge
5 Very important	—	—	—
4 Fairly important	9	—	5
3 Middling	—	11	5
2 Fairly unimportant	24	26	25
1 Unimportant	59	63	61
0	3	—	2
No response	6	—	3
Total	**100**	**100**	**100**

none of the institutions in Oxford or Cambridge considered fiduciary risk as being relatively high on their list of concerns.

The fiduciary responsibilities of trustees in the UK are not dissimilar to those defined in the United States; the concept of 'prudence' is almost universally recognized. It includes the management of intergenerational equity, present and anticipated financial needs, price-level trends, in addition to understanding the outcome of current and anticipated global economic conditions. Managers of endowments are particularly sensitive to downside risk as that might reflect on their fiduciary responsibility to balance today's spending and future growth of the endowment fund as they are required to generate sufficient return to cover both spending today, which takes into account inflation.

About one-quarter (25 per cent) of institutions in Oxford and Cambridge placed fiduciary risk at a risk level of 2, or 40 per cent on the scale of 1–5. Only 10 per cent of respondents put it higher, at 3–4 on the risk scale. A fairly high number (61 per cent) of Oxbridge Colleges thought there was inevitably some risk in the business of managing the College endowment, but assessed it as being rather low. One bursar (in Oxford) even suggested their fiduciary risk was nil. The confidence placed on their investment managers as well as on their own ability to judge such outcomes appeared both naive and misplaced, particularly within a sector riddled with scams, collapses, regulatory breaches, and takeovers.

Other risk factors

Apart from risks associated with financial markets, the benchmark, liquidity and fiduciary matters, the majority (79 per cent) of institutions in Oxford and Cambridge did not identify any other risk factors as being terribly important in their overall endowment asset management; an overwhelming 94 per cent of institutions in Oxford reporting no other risk factors compared with 59 per cent in Cambridge. Table 8.6 summarizes these responses.

Table 8.6. Oxbridge perceptions of other risk factors

Risk scale	Oxford	Cambridge	Oxbridge
5 Very important	—	30	13
4 Fairly important	6	4	5
3 Middling	—	—	—
2 Fairly unimportant	—	—	—
1 Unimportant	—	7	3
0	—	—	—
No other factor	94	59	79
Total	**100**	**100**	**100**

About one-third (30 per cent) of Colleges in Cambridge raised other risk factors as being 'very important' risks factors to their portfolios, but none of the Colleges in Oxford identified any. The other risk factors identified by these Colleges included:

- Single name exposures. Of the nine Colleges in Cambridge reporting other risk factors to their portfolio, two reported high 'single name expo-sures' or relatively high stock specific risk exposure. In one College, the legacy of a single stock comprised of a significant allocation (30 per cent) of the endowment's total exposure to UK equities, which itself was high at 65 per cent of the portfolio. While such exposure can be hedged at relatively low cost, the College had not considered doing so.

- Failure of College-owned businesses from delivering income. For one Col-lege, highly dependent on its thriving businesses for operational income, the risk inevitably lay in the businesses failing to deliver the desired level of income in the future. It is more difficult for this College to hedge itself against such potential losses. It currently does not use any income from its endowment and thus has a buffer to fall back on. However, the College is also building up its endowment to secure its educational objective; fall of desired income from its non-core business activities may ultimately jeopardize its overall objective.

- Failure of the fund manager to deliver income. The ability of the fund manager to deliver the agreed level of income was a major concern for six (22 per cent) Cambridge institutions whose dependency on endowment income varied between a high of 62 per cent of total income to a low of 12 per cent (other endowment income/total income ratios were 50, 42, 27, and 19 per cent). As one bursar pointed out: 'The greatest risk for us is the competence of the fund manager—will the manager perform?' However, the risk is not significant enough for the College to change its fund manager.

- A highly concentrated property portfolio was also of concern to another Cambridge College bursar, as the portfolio was not diversified enough and a downturn in property values and yields would inevitably impact on income from the endowment.

The majority (94 per cent) of Oxford Colleges did not identify any 'other risk' factors as influencing the outcome of their endowment portfolios. There were two Colleges with some other concerns with regard to risk; in both cases they were related to possible manager failure to deliver income; in one instance the endowment income was 12 per cent of total income and for the other it was 21 per cent. The concern was not rated high enough to elicit a change of manager.

The high cost of changing managers was cited as a disincentive. As there can be no guarantees that the new manager's performance would be superior over the long-term, enough to pay for the overall cost of such action, investors in general are better off sticking with their appointed manager over an investment cycle. Uninformed investors are easily drawn to managers with the best short-term performance record, and thus end up getting the fund manager performance cycle wrong. Like stock selection, where it pays to think contrarily, manager selection also benefits from such an approach. This is assuming that investors have conducted their due diligence and manager research. Market timing in manager selection is as difficult as in stock selection, the chances of getting such decisions wrong being significantly higher.

Risk instructions given to investment manager

Most Colleges in Oxford and Cambridge recognize they have yet to address the issue of risk management comprehensively. As relationships with asset managers dated back to several decades in some cases, investment management agreements (IMAs) were either not in place and if they were, it was not clear if they were reviewed regularly. A written IMA between the asset manager and the client is a regulatory requirement in the pension fund sector in the UK. Among foundations and endowments, it is a matter of good practice, though recent changes in the regulation of charities imposed a greater degree of formalization of such requirements for institutions in the philanthropic sector.

According to the guidance issued by the Charity Commission, trustees cannot appoint an investment manager unless they have prepared a statement which gives guidance to the investment manager as to how the investment functions should be executed. When preparing such a policy statement the trustees must formulate it in such a way that it is clear and ensures the manager will carry out his responsibilities in the best interests of the institution. The policy statement must, like the IMA, be in writing. The agreement must include a provision requiring the manager to comply with the policy statement (and any revision or replacement of it).

The preparation of the policy statement is the responsibility of the trustees or the investment committee members of the institution concerned; and the statutory duty of care in the Trustee Act applies to its preparation. The preparation of the policy statement cannot be delegated to the investment manager, but trustees are entitled to take independent expert advice on the preparation of the policy statement, and may well find it helpful to do so. In any event, the Charity Commission recommends that the trustees should prepare the policy statement in consultation with the proposed investment manager. As indicated above, the manager is obliged to comply with the policy statement, and may, therefore, be in difficulty if he finds impracticable a policy statement which the trustees have prepared without such consultation.

It is considered that a policy statement is required whenever discretionary investment management is delegated on or after 1 February 2001, whether the power of delegation relied on is the statutory power, or a power in the charity's governing document, or an authority from the regulatory body itself. However, where the discretionary management agreement was properly entered into before 1 February 2001, then the statutory requirement for a policy statement does not apply unless or until the agreement between the charity or its trustees and the investment manager is replaced with a fresh agreement. As many of the Colleges had investment managers appointed a long time ago, such agreements had not been reviewed recently. In those cases, where a new manager was appointed, new agreements were in place.

A charity's policy statement is intended to give guidance to the manager to whom investment management has been delegated. It clarifies the responsibilities and the extent of the authority of the investment manager appointed by the trustees. A charity's policy statement provides a written framework for a charity's investment strategy and contains the principles that will govern the detail of the investment decisions taken by the investment manager. These decisions must be taken within the parameters set out in the policy statement.

As endowments, foundations and charities have different investment objectives, it is likely that the content and complexity of each investment policy statement will reflect that difference. The Trustee Act does not dictate the content of a policy statement. However, the Act states that trustees must formulate any guidance given in the policy statement with a view to ensuring that the functions of the trustees which will be delegated to their investment manager will be carried out in the best interests of the charitable institution.

As a general guide provided by the Commission, a charity's investment policy statement might well contain information and guidance in the following areas:

- the charity's aim in investing its funds, including the charity's position on risk;
- an indication of the trustees' asset allocation strategy;
- the benchmarks and targets by which the performance of the manager will be judged;
- the charity's stance on ethical investment;
- the balance between capital growth and income generation which is sought by the charity (or, as the case may be, the nature of the charity's total return policy); and
- the scope of the investment powers.[5]

A very large proportion of institutions in Oxford and Cambridge had a formal IMA with their external fund managers (later in this chapter we discuss their agreements further). With the introduction of total return investment policies coinciding with changes in market and economic conditions since 2000, several Colleges took the opportunity to examine their investment policy statements leading to substantial changes in both asset allocation and manager appointments. Where new investment management relationships were set up, an up-to-date IMA existed. According to the Chairman of the University Investment Committee of Oxford, for instance, 'As part of the overall portfolio rebalancing, the University is in the process of agreeing new contracts with a number of fund managers. Specialist lawyers have been appointed to cover (*inter alia*) some of the guidelines referred to in the policy. Specific areas such as tracking risk and performance targets are set at the outset by our advisers, Cambridge Associates.'

Thanks to their investment consultants, Cambridge Associates, and the expertise available in the membership of its investment committee, the Oxford University Endowment reported reviewing its IMA regularly. As Cambridge University was in the unusual position of having a single fund manager in charge of its endowment, reviewing the IMA was not so much an issue as the efficacy of such an arrangement. The endowment was clearly exposed to the risk associated with the manager—in terms of asset allocation, performance, and fiduciary risks relating to manager takeover among other considerations. Cambridge University's relationship with Foreign & Colonial, the oldest investment trust manager in the UK, dated back over half a century or more. Diversification in manager appointments along with other strategic policy changes is imminent in the overall management of Cambridge University's endowment; the point is that it was not done earlier.

Several Colleges were in the process of reviewing their IMA without changing managers. In some cases, reviews were conducted as part of an overall restructuring of the endowment portfolio. As reviews of management agreements had not taken place recently for some institutions, investment management charges had also not been reviewed for decades. Managers value the prestige attached to having an Oxbridge institution as a client, and individuals responsible for these relationships also valued such connection. Some Colleges reported upward revision in fees for no real improvements in service from their managers as a result of such reviews. About a third (30 per cent) of respondents indicated their IMA did not include any specific instruction to their fund manager with respect to risk; one-third of Colleges in Cambridge reported such a gap in the instruction they gave their managers compared with one quarter of Colleges in Oxford.

In the words of one bursar: 'We used to have someone on the Investment Committee who used to discuss betas etc. with our fund manager, but we don't currently as it did not get us anywhere.' According to another bursar, 'by choosing the manager we are implicitly choosing a low-risk strategy, e.g. an aversion to high beta stocks.' A third stated simply: 'We instruct our fund managers to take a low risk approach to investing.' Another bursar said he reviewed risk with the fund manager 'eight times a year', though he did not clarify what the risk review process involved. According to another bursar, 'The fund manager offered us a certain risk profile and we thought that was acceptable.'

Eight respondents said they delegated risk management to the investment manager, with some managers providing 'a quarterly BARRA risk analysis' of endowment portfolios. 'We believe it better not to set out a benchmark criterion for our manager, but leave the risk decision to them,' commented the senior bursar of a Cambridge College. A further 5 per cent of institutions managed their endowment assets directly and so were fully responsible for their own risk management. One bursar pointed out: 'We do not have external fund managers. We take a very long-term view of our investments and do not worry overtly about market risk, only stock specific risk.' One College indicated using a consultant to monitor portfolio risk by screening manager risk. The remaining (55 per cent) Colleges provided a wide array of risk instructions to their fund managers.

Some Colleges employed a combination of strategies; examples of instructions given to fund managers included:

- The sector portfolios should be invested in such a manner as to limit the deviation from the benchmark within the range of −1 per cent to 3+ per cent. Dispersion between asset classes should also be such as to limit the performance within the range of −1 per cent to 3+ per cent against the composite benchmark. Within each sector portfolio no individual holding should exceed 10 per cent of total portfolio value.

- Fund managers have got the benchmark and targets and what the expected outperformance should be. That is most likely to create their investment strategy and risk parameters. We also impose limits on holdings in individual stocks (5 per cent).

- We invest for the long term, spread risk and do not leave the fund heavily exposed in any one direction. We talk about currency risk and various other risks from time to time.

- As most of our investments are indexed, the risk instructions are mostly restricted to tracking error, standard deviation, etc. We also try to monitor whether performance is impacted by stock lending. On the property side, the risk of any particular investment would be discussed in some detail before any action is taken.

Table 8.7 illustrates the sort of instructions Colleges in Oxford and Cambridge provide their fund managers, with regards to risk. The responses were broken

Table 8.7. Instructions to Investment Manager regarding risk

Guidelines	Oxford	Cambridge	Oxbridge
Stock limits and exclusions	9	11	10
Tracking error	3	7	5
Target income	6	7	7
Invest in collective funds	3	4	3
Hold a diversified portfolio	12	7	10
Policy portfolio or benchmark	24	11	18
Absolute return strategy	3	4	3
Consultant monitors risk	3	0	2
Left to investment manager	9	7	8
Not specified	26	33	30
Assets managed in-house	3	7	5
Total	**100**	**100**	**100**

down into various categories such as the use of a benchmark (18 per cent), implementation of diversification strategies (10 per cent), use of stock limits and exclusions (10 per cent), income targets (7 per cent), tracking error (5 per cent), investment in collective funds (3 per cent), and use of absolute return strategies (3 per cent).

Some of the benchmarks used for risk management also employed return targets for the fund manager. According to one bursar, 'the risk constraint is implied in the return target—i.e. the FTSE All Share with an income yield of 3.5 per cent. Diversification within the main sectors of the economy is considered to be a way of spreading risk.' As explained by another bursar: 'Our main instructions have more to do with return rather than risk. An example is one of our hedge fund managers where the return target was set at 12 per cent. What we tend to set are benchmarks.' According to a third bursar: 'We use risk management in our property investments. As far as our securities portfolio is concerned, we tend to be very risk averse—i.e. we never wish to lose any money.'

Another bursar offered a different perspective on the matter: 'We tell our managers that we do not accept volatility as a true definition of risk at all. What risk means to us is permanent capital loss. We manage risk on that basis by focussing on high quality assets only and holding them for the long term. We do not diversify risk by investing in poor quality assets. We believe that share-values do reflect intrinsic economic value, and prices reflect fundamentals over the long term. We want our managers to take risk and back what they believe in. We also take a reasonably contrarian investment view.' He went on to add: 'We wanted to take more risk with our equity investments and appointed our managers on that basis. They have an absolute return objective, no capital loss with 4 per cent real return over 3–5 year investment horizon.'

Some institutions in Oxford and Cambridge manage risk at the macro level. As one bursar explained, 'Each manager is asked to manage his portfolio in a normal way consistent with a benchmark, if any. Our portfolio construction then comes into play to increase or decrease risk, which is not something each manager needs to worry about although each is aware of the bigger picture and where he fits in.' According to another bursar, the risk instructions they give to their managers 'depends on the mandate, but we only hire managers having satisfied ourselves that they genuinely operate best risk management practice, since we regard managing the risk budget as a necessary condition of successful long term investment. We are also discussing ways of improving the investment committee's ability to monitor the risk profile of the entire composite portfolio, but there are difficulties associated with hedge funds or short selling where the information only becomes available retrospectively.'

Characteristics of the Investment Management Agreement

The Investment Management Agreement is an important document as it formalizes the relationship between the sponsoring institution and the appointed manager who also acts as an adviser. In the words of Swensen: 'The fundamental goal in establishing contractual arrangements consists of aligning interest to encourage investment advisory agents to behave as institutional fiduciary principals. Slippage between what the investor wishes and what the adviser does imposes substantial costs on institutions, reducing the likelihood of meeting basic goals and objectives.'[6] Aligning the interest of the sponsor and the fund manager, though hard to achieve, is not insurmountable.

Overall, 82 per cent of participants had an IMA with their manager. A further 10 per cent were either in the process of reviewing the matter internally (5 per cent) or simply did not see the need to have a written agreement with their broker (5 per cent) as the broker had been associated with the College for a considerably long period, and typically acted according to the express wishes of the bursar. In the unlikely event that the broker wished to do something different, he was expected to seek the permission of the bursar first. Typically the bursar was the point of contact for the broker or fund manager concerned. As one bursar confirmed it, 'My impression is we do not have proper investment guidelines; having said that, they (the broker/manager) would have a clear idea of our requirements. We are currently drafting a Statement of Investment Principles.' The remaining 8 per cent of Colleges that invested in collective funds did not have separate IMA with their appointed managers.

An analysis of the extent to which the IMA reflects the interests of the sponsoring institutions, defining clearly issues such as accountability, investment

Table 8.8. Extent to which IMA defines accountability and authority

Response	Oxford	Cambridge	Oxbridge
Defines accountability	76	78	77
Managed in-house	3	7	5
Collective funds	12	4	8
Not specific	6	4	5
No/under review	3	7	5
Total	**100**	**100**	**100**

Table 8.9. Extent to which IMA identifies permissible investments and limits

Response	Oxford	Cambridge	Oxbridge
Identifies limits	74	59	67
Managed in-house	3	7	5
Collective funds	12	4	8
Not specific	3	15	8
No/under review	9	15	11
Total	**100**	**100**	**100**

goals and objectives, identification of permissible and non-permissible invest-ments and limits, and guidelines regarding the use of derivatives and tracking error, reveals that there exists scope for improvement. The tables that follow (Tables 8.8 to 8.14) provide an overview of the characteristics of the IMA as reported by participating institutions in Oxford and Cambridge.

Table 8.8 shows to what extent the IMA defines accountability and author-ity, that is the IMA defines what the manager is responsible for and the extent of its authority in implementing agreed policy.

As reported, in a majority (77 per cent) of cases in Oxford and Cambridge the IMA reflects issues such as accountability and authority. A small number of Colleges (5 per cent) were not sure whether the IMA defined accountability and authority. A similar number of Colleges were in the process of reviewing the terms of agreement. And 8 per cent of Colleges invested in collective funds and did not have an IMA.

In terms of identifying permissible and non-permissible investments and limits, over two-thirds (67 per cent) of Colleges reported the existence of IMA that did so; significantly more (74 per cent) institutions in Oxford reported such agreements compared with Colleges in Cambridge (59 per cent). Table 8.9 provides a breakdown of responses to the question of whether the IMA identified permissible and non-permissible investments and limits.

Those Colleges (8 per cent) with endowment assets invested in externally managed pooled funds were obliged to accept the investment restrictions that applied to the fund. Sometimes, institutional investment objectives were not aligned with that of the fund. As the endowment funds were small, it was considered appropriate by the College, perhaps on the advice of their manager, to invest in the pooled funds managed by their chosen asset managers, rather than invest in indexed products.

About 19 per cent of respondents reported not identifying investment limits in their IMA with the manager; more than twice (30 per cent) as many Colleges in Cambridge reported not having such instructions in the IMA compared with 12 per cent in Oxford. Among the 19 per cent of respondents with such an agreement, 11 per cent did not define permissible and non-permissible investments and limits, and 8 per cent of Colleges were not sure whether such limits were indeed set out in the IMA. Though more Cambridge institutions reported not being clear about the existence of investment limits in the IMA, one of the more detailed instructions on accountability and authority was also provided by one Cambridge institution where the IMA contained the following stipulations:

- Every investment should be held at a portfolio weight within 5 per cent (either side) of its weight in the benchmark index. The limit does not apply if exceeded due to a scheme merger; issue of new shares or debentures by way of capitalization of profits, reserves, or rights; the amalgamation of two or more companies, whether through the acquisition of the share capital of one by the other or through a holding company or otherwise; and market fluctuations. Where the limits are exceeded due to any circumstances above, the investment manager will resolve this position as soon as reasonably practicable.

- The Investment Manager may invest up to 10 per cent of the total market value of the portfolio in regulated or unregulated collective investment schemes managed by the investment manager or its Associates.

- The portfolio may not hold more than 5 per cent of the issued capital of any one company.

- The portfolio is invested only in UK equities; no direct investments in property.

- No investments in unlisted securities or overseas equities.

- No more than 5 per cent of the portfolio to be held in cash.

The majority (80 per cent) of respondents reported the inclusion of guidelines that applied to the use of derivatives in their IMA. Table 8.10 summarizes these responses.

Those Colleges that invested their endowment assets in pooled funds (8 per cent) were bound by the fund's guidelines that applied to the manager's discretion vis-à-vis the use derivative instruments. Most pooled funds define

Table 8.10. Extent to which IMA includes guide-lines on use of derivatives

Response	Oxford	Cambridge	Oxbridge
Provides guidelines	79	81	80
Managed in-house	3	7	5
Collective funds	12	4	8
Not specific	3	4	3
No/under review	3	4	3
Total	**100**	**100**	**100**

Table 8.11. Extent to which IMA specifies tracking error and downside risk

Response	Oxford	Cambridge	Oxbridge
States risk levels	15	7	11
Managed in-house	3	7	5
Collective funds	12	4	8
Not specific	3	7	5
No/under review	68	74	70
Total	**100**	**100**	**100**

whether derivatives are allowed in the management process, and if they can be used what their specific function was likely to be. Some 6 per cent of Colleges either did not have such a guideline in their IMA (3 per cent) or did not have an IMA (3 per cent).

Three-quarters (75 per cent) of institutions in Oxford and Cambridge did not specify tracking error or downside risk in their IMA. Just 11 per cent of bursars said they did so, over twice as many in Oxford than in Cambridge. Though a larger proportion of bursars with a 'professional' background (i.e. fund management or investment banking) were from Oxford, there was no evidence that these bursars were better able to secure agreements with their managers on various aspects of investment matters.

As a large number of Colleges did not formally have a policy portfolio, tracking error was not a significant issue. In the days of income-only spending, asset managers were required to deliver a certain level of income. Hence tracking error and downside risk would not have been included in the IMA; the risk would have been not to deliver the required level of income. Since the switch to total return policies, many Colleges use benchmarks to which performance is linked. But it was not clear that they specified tracking error and downside risk in their new IMA. Interestingly, those institutions with absolute return strategies also did not specify downside risk in their IMA.

Table 8.11 identifies the responses of the College bursars to the question whether the IMA specifies tracking error and/or downside risk.

When asked whether the IMA sets out performance targets and explains specific actions to be taken in case of performance not meeting the target, over half the respondents (54 per cent) indicated that performance targets were clearly set, but the IMA did not stipulate what actions were to be taken when performance failed to match target. As summarized by one bursar: 'Generally, the College specifies quite closely the issues relating to accountability, investment limits, etc. Weaknesses would relate mainly to tracking error, downside risk or in setting out performance targets or explaining what specific actions are to be taken in case of policy not meeting the target, where it is hard to be clear about what will result in termination—i.e. what's the equivalent of "Three strikes and you're out".'

The majority of institutions in Oxford and Cambridge have mutually agreed performance benchmarks set with their managers, such as '1 per cent per annum after fees over rolling 5-year period index return' but no agreement, formal or informal, exists on the course of action to be taken if the performance falls short of benchmark or for that matter if performance was consistently above benchmark. As performance analysis is not conducted externally, the lack of a rigorous performance attribution process, for example, does not exist. Colleges receive information on performance from their asset managers, but they are not fully equipped to make use of such analysis.

Table 8.12 shows that just two Colleges in Oxford (3 per cent of total participants) set out performance targets in their IMA which also defined specific actions to be taken in case of performance not meeting the target. About one-third (30 per cent) of Colleges either did not do so or were not specific enough in their response.

When asked if the investment management policy guidelines were applied consistently to all fund managers, almost half the respondents (48 per cent) indicated the existence of a single manager, and most of these consisted of balanced mandates. Table 8.13 summarizes the responses.

Table 8.12. Defined performance targets and required actions if target is missed

Response	Oxford	Cambridge	Oxbridge
Targets defined	6	0	3
Managed in-house	3	7	5
Collective funds	12	4	8
Not specific	3	7	5
No	18	33	25
Yes and No*	59	48	54
Total	**100**	**100**	**100**

* Yes, the IMA sets out performance targets but does not explain what actions are to be taken when performance does not meet the target.

Table 8.13. Consistency of application of investment management guidelines

Response	Oxford	Cambridge	Oxbridge
Applies to all managers	6	19	11
Managed in-house	3	7	5
Collective funds	12	4	8
Not specific	3	7	5
Employ one manager	44	52	48
No	32	11	23
Total	**100**	**100**	**100**

Table 8.14. Extent to which investment management guidelines were agreed in writing

Response	Oxford	Cambridge	Oxbridge
Yes	79	74	77
Managed in-house	3	7	5
Collective funds	12	4	8
Not specific	3	11	7
No	3	4	3
Total	**100**	**100**	**100**

In the case of hedge funds or private equity partnership agreements, practices varied widely. About one-quarter (23 per cent) of Colleges reported having different agreements with their private equity and hedge fund managers as the individual partnerships did not cover many of the issues that applied to traditional segregated equity and/or balanced mandates. Only 11 per cent of respondents indicated that their IMA was the same for all their external managers, but most of these institutions had fewer than five investment managers and the endowments had no allocation to alternative strategies.

All investment management policy guidelines between the Colleges and their external fund managers were agreed in writing; 77 per cent of institutions reported they had an IMA in writing, marginally more Colleges (79 per cent) in Oxford reported the existence of an IMA compared with Cambridge institutions (74 per cent). Eight per cent of Colleges had their endowment assets invested in pooled or collective funds, and thus did not have individual IMAs with their managers. A small number (10 per cent) of institutions were either not specific enough in their response (7 per cent) or did not have an IMA (3 per cent); and a further 5 per cent of Colleges managed their assets internally. Table 8.14 summarizes these responses.

Conclusion

If differences in asset allocation, based on assessment of individual objectives, are interpreted as being more efficient, then these institutions in behaving independently appear to be on the right path. From defining investment policy to risk management, there is little herding among these institutions, though they agree broadly on investment issues, and there appears to be a minimum level of sharing of information among them. Their considerable individualism can best be described as the Galapagos Islands of the investment world, and it may be in great risk of disappearing with a need to inject economies of scale, not to mention greater centralization in decision-making.

As the major risk to the Colleges are those that would prevent them from carrying out their charitable objects permanently, sustaining (if not increasing) the contribution of the endowment to the Colleges' total operating budget is critical. Focusing on endowment asset management should therefore be a major objective of the Colleges in their overall risk management. None of the institutions formally cover issues relating to the degree of risk in their investment pool. At best, risk is managed through diversification—in terms of asset classes, though not always through investment strategies and fund managers. It is perhaps the least expensive way for institutions with relatively small-sized endowments to manage portfolio risk. But there is no evidence to conclude it is the most efficient or the least efficient way of managing portfolio risk.

In general, Colleges report monitoring various aspects of endowment asset management relating to manager accountability, investment limits, etc. Weaknesses relate mainly to tracking error, downside risk, setting out clear performance targets and in explaining what specific actions were to be taken in case of performance not meeting the target, particularly where it is hard to be clear about what would result in manager termination. Most manager appointments tend to last over a long period, over several investment cycles in most cases. In those instances where the fund manager has been appointed recently, Colleges appear to have an IMA in place with several of the relevant management issues included in the agreement. The weaknesses arise in cases where manager appointments have not been reviewed formally over the past several years.

9

Consultant selection and monitoring

Introduction

Compared to the pension fund sector where trustees regularly use external investment consultants in the asset management process, the use of external investment advisers among institutions in Oxford and Cambridge is low. This may be due to the high level of professional expertise available internally, including alumni and others within the investment committee who are willing to offer their independent advice. Lack of any regulatory requirement for external expert advice and the historical asset mix of the endowment may have also contributed to the lack of professional employment of investment consultants in managing the endowment.

About two-thirds of surveyed Colleges in Oxford and Cambridge, for example, did not use any external investment consultants in the management of their endowment portfolios. And among those Colleges that did, several registered dissatisfaction with the consultant's ability to deliver a value-added service. Less than 10 per cent of bursars reported plans to appoint a consultant for the sake of strategic asset allocation or risk assessment. Most institutions suggested using the consultant either for gaining access to investments in alternative strategies or for manager selection and monitoring.

The large property content of these endowments may account for the relatively low penetration of investment consultants whose expertise does not typically extend to the very specific property holdings of Oxbridge institutions. In the words of one bursar: 'Yes, we use Cambridge Associates; they are helpful in some ways, but not so in other areas such as in dealing with our sort of portfolios with large property holdings. They appear not to know very much about property. Also, their research is more US-oriented.' For another bursar: 'Their (Cambridge Associates) asset allocation does not take property into account, which we find a bit worrying. So, we are not entirely happy with their advice.' According to a third bursar, 'we use Cambridge Associates, but more for manager selection and, when necessary, for retrieving information on asset returns, but largely in our private equity investments. As we have a high property content in our overall portfolio, we do not see Cambridge Associates as having sufficient experience in the sector to be able to advise us in our asset allocation and other strategic investment decision making.'

In addition to the consultant's lack of expertise in property matters, which made it difficult for Colleges with larger property holdings to employ their services, Colleges with smaller endowments or those Colleges that were not major property owners or investors also considered the investment consultant as offering limited value to their investment process. According to one bursar, whose College endowment was worth £16 million: 'Cambridge Associates were appointed primarily for manager selection in the summer of 2000. The appointment was for a year only as the College did not think it got much value from its consultant in investment policy or asset allocation. This view is shared by several Oxford Colleges whose portfolios were not large enough to invest in private equity and hedge funds.' As a result, the use of external consultants in managing the traded securities portfolio of the endowments in Oxford and Cambridge is low when compared with such usage in the pension fund sector, where investment consultants appear to play a major role not only in manager selection but equally in determining asset allocation.

The practice of not using investment advice of external consultants is not confined to Colleges in Oxford and Cambridge. It is widespread across the philanthropic sector in the UK. Only the larger foundations and endowments employ the services of investment consultants in their decision-making. It can be argued that the smaller organizations do not have sufficient assets to justify the expense of hiring investment consultants. Consultants too have no exposure to the sector, and thus remain unfamiliar with the issues that concern these institutions.

Such practice contrasts with that in the United States where on average 75.8 per cent of educational endowments employed an outside consultant for investment management guidance. However, institutions with more than $1 billion in endowment assets were less likely to employ an external investment consultant, with just over half (53 per cent in 2004 compared with 45 per cent in 2003) of these institutions reporting such use. This was most likely because of the significant staff resources devoted to investment management. Smaller endowments, or those with assets less than $25 million, were also less likely to appoint an external investment consultant; 63 per cent of such institutions reported doing so in 2004 compared with 59 per cent in 2003. This was probably due to financial constraints more than any other reason. Also, public educational endowments were more likely to appoint an external adviser (74 per cent in 2004 compared with 76 per cent in 2003) while independent institutions reported a slightly higher usage (77 per cent in 2004 compared with 74 per cent in 2003). Over 86 per cent of endowments with assets between $100 million and $500 million employed an outside consultant while 79 per cent of endowments with assets over \$500 million and less than \$1 billion did so.[1]

According to the 2005 *Commonfund Benchmarks Study: Foundations and Operating Charities Report*, the use of external investment consultants rose to 79 per cent from 70 per cent in the previous year. Unlike educational endowments, the largest institutions (assets over \$1 billion) most frequently reported the use of outside consultants (93 per cent in 2004 compared with 77 per cent in 2003), while 79 per cent (63 per cent in 2003) of smaller foundations (assets worth \$50–\$100 million) do so. Community foundations most often use a consultant (90 per cent) compared with 73 per cent of independent/private foundations and 85 per cent of operating charities. Measured in FTEs, community foundations also report smaller staff (0.8 FTEs) than their counterparts and appear to have greater reliance on consultants. Many foundations require a conflict of interest policy for their consultants. For example, these policies preclude consultants from recommending themselves as a manager or any firm from which they receive any type of commission revenue. Almost two thirds (61 per cent) of foundations report having such a policy; but community foundations were more likely to report having conflict of interest policies (72 per cent) than either independent or private foundations.[2]

Thus, investment consultants play a more significant role in the management of endowment assets in the United States. While attitude towards investment consultants may change in UK and Europe, change can quicken if the consultants directed some of their research funding towards investment issues that concern these institutions. As the endowment and foundation world is highly fragmented with very diverse needs, and assets under management are small compared to the rich pickings available in the pension fund and insurance sectors, investment consultants have historically ignored endowments, foundations, and operating charities as a sector.

Use of external investment consultants

More than twice as many Colleges in Oxford than in Cambridge reported using an external investment consultant in managing the endowment's securities portfolio. Some Colleges, with larger allocation to property assets that received no investment guidance from an external consultant in the management of their securities portfolio, employed property consultants for the overall management of their property assets. In one Cambridge College, for example, with a significant property portfolio, the College's property advisers had been employed for over half a century. The College was also engaged in property development, with their external property adviser acting as consultant. But the same College did not have an investment consultant for its residual securities portfolio.

Table 9.1. Extent to which external investment consultants are used

Usage	Oxford	Cambridge	Oxbridge
Yes, use consultants	56	22	41
No, do not use them	44	78	59
Total	**100**	**100**	**100**

Overall, 59 per cent of respondents reported not using an investment consultant in any capacity. The number of Colleges reporting not using an investment consultant may be somewhat misleading, as many of these Colleges use consultants in their property management. However, when asked: 'Do you use any external investment consultants?' the answer was negative. Many of the bursars appear to have associated the question with regard to the use of investment consultants for the securities portfolio alone, but not for the property portfolio. Bearing that in mind, 41 per cent of Oxbridge institutions reported the use of external investment consultants. In reality, a significantly higher proportion of Colleges have access to investment advice than the responses suggest. Table 9.1 summarizes these responses.

Two Colleges in Cambridge and three in Oxford said they were considering employing an investment consultant, with a view to accessing the consultants' private equity fund created for Oxbridge institutions. 'We are in the process of appointing Cambridge Associates as our consultants as that is the only way we can access their private equity vehicle for Cambridge Colleges,' said one bursar. According to another College bursar, 'apart from monitoring the performance of the private equity fund for which they (Cambridge Associates) have been hired, we would also expect them to give us positive input in asset allocation, risk instruction and establishing the benchmark. We are not sure whether we have an appropriate benchmark—at least, the one created by the fund manager. We would expect them (consultant) to turn up for a series of meetings, not necessarily to produce a hefty or complicated report.'

Another Oxford bursar confirmed they would not be using Cambridge Associates for asset allocation or risk advice, but purely for acquiring a private equity portfolio. One Cambridge bursar, who dispensed with the services of their consultant in 2000, was reconsidering that decision, but purely for the sake of accessing investments in alternative strategies:

We did retain Cambridge Associates for 2 years during 1998–2000. They helped us with a fundamental review of our investments, recasting the accounts, setting our spending policy as well as our total return investment/income policy. The other attribute was their ability to introduce us to investment opportunities, which we would not otherwise come across in private equity and hedge fund sector. However, we have not been fully convinced that we would benefit from investing in alternative assets. It now appears we might, as the bubble in the private equity sector, at least, has abated. Also, we prefer the fund-of-funds route to the asset class instead of investing in individual funds, which Cambridge Associates would manage on behalf of Colleges in Cambridge; similar to the Oxford fund.

There was ample evidence to suggest that most of the Colleges employing a consultant, such as Cambridge Associates, did so primarily for the sake of investing in alternative strategies. Even those Colleges that benefited from general investment guidance, such as strategic asset allocation, did not continue with the relationship. The general perception was that investment consultants did not offer good value. This view may have something to do with the dominance of one consultant. A third of institutions in Oxford and Cambridge employed Cambridge Associates as their investment adviser. As one bursar summed it up:

Cambridge Associates provides valuable manager information and access to research on private equity investments. There are several barriers to investing in private equity such as the high-cost of manager research. These investments are both risky and illiquid. Thus, the private equity charity product created by Cambridge Associates for Oxbridge Colleges provides an efficient solution. They have done a good job at selling their expertise in alternative investments. We pay an annual fee that buys access to the company's research (both hard copy and online access), several consultancy hours, quarterly meetings and manager information (particularly in private equity).

We remain sceptical about active fund management; many Colleges have their listed equity in trackers. The herding mentality of fund managers is a major concern, as is the turnover of the managers/analysts. Lack of specialisation among fund managers is also a feature of the market when compared to the US. Lack of adequate information on fund managers is also an issue; the consulting community (including Cambridge Associates) has not risen to the challenge.

Sir Alan Budd, chairman of the Investment Committee of the University of Oxford, during the period of our study, paid the highest compliment to the role played by Cambridge Associates in influencing management: 'I cannot over-estimate the influence of Cambridge Associates on the University's investment policy. Taking a total return approach was brought about as a result of Cambridge Associates in collaboration with members of the University Investment Committee.' Credit is due to Cambridge Associates for encouraging the shift towards 'total return' policies in Oxford; even among Colleges that did not employ Cambridge Associates as a consultant, their influence made a difference not only by introducing these institutions to the concept of total return but also to investments in alternative strategies. At the time of the study about half the institutions in Oxford employed a 'total return' policy compared to about one-third of Colleges in Cambridge. Today, all the Colleges and the two Universities have implemented a total return

Table 9.2. Investment consultants used by Oxbridge Colleges

Consultant	Oxford	Cambridge	Oxbridge
Cambridge Associates	47	15	33
Other advisers*	9	7	8
No consultant	44	78	59
Total	**100**	**100**	**100**

* Includes Edward Jewson (2), Bacon and Woodrow (1), Chiswell Associates (1), and Mercer (1).

approach in their endowment management. About half these institutions also have some investment in alternative strategies.

Table 9.2 summarizes the use of investment consultants among institutions in Oxford and Cambridge. Forty-one per cent of respondents reported having an investment consultant, most of whom employed Cambridge Associates.

Among the five Colleges that employ 'other' investment consultants—such as Edward Jewson (2), Mercer (1), Bacon and Woodrow (1), and Chiswell Associates (1)—two of the consultants (Mercer and Bacon & Woodrow) were employed on a one-off basis, primarily for manager selection, and secondarily for advice on asset allocation. Not included among 'other' consultants were asset management companies, such as Morgan Stanley, Baring, or Schroders, that offered asset allocation and risk management advice, though there was yet no formal relationship between the Colleges and the private client departments of these investment firms.

Investment management firms typically offer investment advice with the hope of securing a mandate. In the case of Chiswell Associates, it also acted as the fund manager for the College that previously employed Cambridge Associates as their investment consultant for a couple of years. This College switched from an external consultant to its newly appointed fund manager for investment advice. Many Colleges in Oxford and Cambridge traditionally employed their investment manager on the basis of the quality of advice. There was no way of knowing how such advice was assessed by these institutions. Like clients in the pension fund sector, the assessment of consultant's input remains an area of concern, even among those institutions that employ the services of investment consultants.

In the case of Edward Jewson, for example, one Oxford College planned to appoint this firm as a general investment consultant, while another Cambridge College reported using the firm for performance measurement and analysis rather than for asset allocation or risk analysis. 'We use Edward Jewson for performance measurement and analysis, not so much for asset allocation. If we were to select new fund managers, it is possible we could take the assistance of consultants to facilitate that process, as we did recently when we chose UBS as our fund managers,' explained the bursar of one Cambridge

College. A majority of Colleges in Oxford and Cambridge reported employing a consultant for manager selection. The higher level of activity in this area over the past few years may have contributed to a higher use of consultants in Oxbridge as a result.

The contribution of consultants

The contribution of investment consultants to the asset management process among institutions in Oxford and Cambridge was unevenly distributed. The overall use of consultants was low; 59 per cent of Colleges did not have a consultant. Among institutions that had either used one in the past or engaged one presently, the majority (88 per cent) of respondents indicated manager selection as being the main reason for having a consultant. About two-thirds (65 per cent) of these also said they employed the consultant for easier access to alternative assets, but a similar number (62 per cent) also reported using the consultant for asset allocation.

While a quarter (23 per cent) of Oxbridge institutions reported the involvement of a consultant in setting investment policy, only a small number (11 per cent) of these institutions engaged the consultant in determining investment policy. Just 18 per cent of Colleges in Oxford reported using a consultant to review investment policy compared with 4 per cent of Colleges in Cambridge. In total, 89 per cent of Oxbridge institutions did not use a consultant in setting or reviewing investment policy. One third (33 per cent) of Colleges in Cambridge used their investment manager when reviewing investment policy compared with 18 per cent of Colleges in Oxford.

Despite the high level of investment expertise available within these institutions, there was no formal mechanism for assessing the input of investment managers or consultants. One bursar who suggested they were 'results driven' in their approach towards assessing these matters ended up not renewing their investment consultant's contract after an initial appointment lasting no more than a couple of years, during which period the consultant assisted in asset allocation. The use of consultants in the review of the endowment portfolio, on a one-off basis rather than on an ongoing basis, was acknowledged as being valuable. According to one bursar:

We use Cambridge Associates—on issues such as private equity and hedge funds, sustainable spending rules and manager selection. We perceive their US operation as being distinctly more impressive than the UK base. We also perceive the best fund managers as being more prepared to work with sophisticated clients on generic issues to the same (or higher) standards as the consultants. In the UK, the role of consultant is too often that of hand holder/responsibility-spreading mechanism for the trustees who themselves have a very variable grasp of the issues involved. When the investment banks were dealing with a monolithic balanced

239

mandate institutional market the consultants were critical middlemen. As that market shifted to more specific mandates the best larger managers understand that they have to be as flexible as the best boutiques and also offer the advantages of wider coverage or they will lose business.

I have been pushing Cambridge Associates to run a paper portfolio that would allow quantification of their long-term asset allocation strategy, added value from short term tactical allocation if any, and which fund managers they would use to implement that strategy so that it is more than a theoretical exercise and captures transaction cost etc. However, they have been very reluctant to do so because they perceive themselves to be in an impregnable market position and do not want to take on the extra cost or business risk. This will only change if their client base wakes up or if other convincing suppliers fill the vacuum.

The dominance of Cambridge Associates in investment consulting within the educational endowment sector can be traced back to its roots in the United States. The firm invested in developing research capability in the endowment and foundation sector in the United States, where demand existed and the sector was more evolved. Transitioning that expertise to the UK, particularly to Oxford and Cambridge, has not been simple. The challenge is inherent in the sector itself where individual objectives vary widely. The sector also employs some very bright and opinionated individuals. Oxbridge Colleges also employ some of the more original thinkers in the country, if not in the world. These individuals are not easily led; they need to be convinced why they must follow the example set by Harvard, Yale, Stanford, or Princeton; particularly when their own investment experience has been distinctly different. The objectives of these institutions are first and last educational, and the endowment, which is not an independent entity, exists to support the institutional objective.

Length of appointment of consultants

Among institutions in Oxford and Cambridge that employ investment consultants and advisers in the overall endowment management process, only 10 per cent of institutions had received regular investment advice from consultants stretching over a decade. As illustrated in Table 9.3, one-third of Oxbridge Colleges (33 per cent) reported using consultants for over 5 years but less than 10 years; most of these institutions were in Oxford. Another third of institutions reported such access ranging over 3 years but less than 5 years; more Colleges in Cambridge reported such appointments. About a quarter (24 per cent) of Colleges has been using external consultants for less than 2 years.

The use of investment consultants in the management of endowment assets in Oxford and Cambridge has risen steadily over the past decade, accelerating

Table 9.3. Length of appointment of investment consultants

Duration	Oxford	Cambridge	Oxbridge
1–2 years	27	17	24
3–5 years	27	50	33
5–10 years	40	17	33
>10 years	7	17	10
Total	**100**	**100**	**100**

over the past five years. The move to total return policies started about a decade ago. The two University investment committees were the first to hire consultants. It took the Colleges a few years to make that shift, which involved changing College Statutes in most cases. Several institutions employed consultants to assist in this transitioning. Thus, much of the recent rise in the use of consultants among institutions in Oxford, and to some extent Cambridge, can be attributed to the move towards total return investing among Colleges.

The success of Cambridge Associates can also be attributed to this move away from investing for income only. The traditional model, based on income, did not require the expertise of consultants. Asset allocation was left to the asset manager who was required to deliver the requisite income. With the introduction of the total return approach, however, the responsibility of determining the strategic asset allocation shifted to the institutions, away from their managers. Such a radical change in approach necessitated the input of investment consultants who had some experience of doing this for similar institutions in the US. Cambridge Associates were well placed to transfer their expertise within the United States endowment sector, except that institutions in the United States had moved away from income only investing a long time ago, and no longer owned any sizeable investments in property. Thus, there was no real need for consultants to have expertise in property as an asset class.

Conclusion

Unlike the pension fund sector, where trustees are obliged to take external expert advice in investment matters, there is no regulatory requirement imposed on educational endowments in the UK to obtain such advice. The absence of investment consultants in the asset management process among institutions in Oxford and Cambridge may partly account for the lack of herding among the Colleges when making asset allocation decisions. The level of diversity manifest in all aspects of Oxbridge endowment management, except in the alternative assets area where the presence of Cambridge Associates has resulted in greater cohesion and pooling of investments, is something that the

Colleges value and would like to retain. As one external observer commented, 'Cambridge Associates seems to be making a killing advising colleges separately; pooling of endowments will generate considerable economies of scale.'

The trust deeds of the Colleges, going back several hundred years, may make pooling difficult at the outset though not impossible. Some Colleges have already made a start with setting up an investment partnership, Oxford Investment Partners, offering greater pooling of assets and services. It is a small step taken by five colleges in Oxford. Only time will tell whether such an experiment will succeed. Ownership of property assets tends to generate more passion. While Colleges welcome the development of the REIT market in the UK and Europe, pooling of property investments among Colleges appears a distant possibility. There exists scope for these institutions to establish such an investment vehicle while retaining ownership of their assets.

Diversity makes for more efficient portfolios and markets. Whether the high level of diversity manifest in investment approaches in Oxbridge endowment portfolios is necessary or desirable, taking into account the overall size of endowment assets under management is an interesting question. While the Colleges clearly value their independence, one of the questions that engage all the Colleges is: 'Is there an ideal asset allocation for truly long-term investors such as educational endowments?' The asset allocation strategies of Ivy League institutions are examined regularly but not emulated. There exists a degree of scepticism of alternative strategies; also investment opportunities within such strategies remain limited for Oxbridge institutions. Historically, the lack of consultant use among these institutions was responsible for their very individual asset allocation biases. In spite of the collegiate status of Colleges, there exists a healthy competitive environment in Oxbridge resulting in individual decision-making.

Going forward, if the ethos within Oxbridge changes as a result of the appointment of investment bursars with professional backgrounds in asset management, and these individuals are more willing to hire investment consultants in determining strategic asset allocation, it is possible that Colleges end up with fairly similar portfolios, making asset pooling a more desirable response. However, there is no evidence to suggest that will indeed be the case. There is no evidence either to suggest that the Colleges today possess a clear investment edge, apart from their unusual allocation to property, which was a historical construct. It can be assumed that the high level of dispersion manifest in their current asset allocation policies will be eroded with greater influence of consultants on overall investment policy.

To what extent investment consultants will have an impact on the asset management process among institutions in Oxford and Cambridge also depends on the degree to which investment consultants are able and willing to invest in researching the very specific needs of the endowments within the educational sector. The common perception among the bursars today is that the interests of the Colleges and their consultants are far from aligned.

Differences in aims and outcomes exist between endowments and foundations and their external managers or advisers. These include issues surrounding intergenerational equity, investment horizon, tax matters, and risk, which concern endowments more intimately than other group of investors. Agency issues pervade the relationship between advisers and investors. Investment consultants such as Mercer, Watson Wyatt, and Bacon Hewitts among others are developing their expertise in endowment asset management. There is a growing community of advisers specializing in the industry, not to mention dedicated asset managers within the sector.

As institutions within the endowment world adopt a more 'professional' approach to their asset management, as seen in the rise of the appointment of ex-investment bankers who in turn are most likely to hire investment consultants, their collective impact on future practices within foundations and endowments is set to rise. What endowments need to bear in mind is that long-term improvement in investment performance is higher than total costs incurred. As is typically the case, calculating costs and risks is far more challenging compared with computing returns.

10

Manager selection and monitoring

Introduction

The selection and supervision of fund managers is among the key tasks of any investment committee. In identifying external managers, investors have the task of seeking out individual managers with a sound performance record. Identifying good performance is only part of the solution; the real challenge lies in finding individuals or firms with whom the institution can build a long-term relationship. Institutions hiring managers with an understanding and respect for institutional goals and objectives are in a better position to build and maintain such relationships.

'Fiduciaries must ensure that active management leads to higher expected portfolio returns, not just higher investment manager job satisfaction,'[1] notes Swensen. Achieving higher expected portfolio returns on a consistent basis involves not just resources and ability, but also long-term commitment. Analysing the sources of a manager's alpha, defined as the return measured relative to an agreed benchmark, requires a certain level of disclosure by the manager, and vigilance on the part of fiduciaries to examine all information objectively. It is critical to find a manager willing to align the firm's interest with that of the client.

Manager selection is one area of investment activity where most institutions in Oxford and Cambridge sought guidance from a consultant. Several Oxbridge Colleges reported asset manager changes over the past few years; many adding to their roster of managers, while others seeking to enlist managers specializing in alternative strategies. The greatest challenge for investors is to identify in advance managers who can add alpha to their portfolio. This challenge is magnified in the alternative assets sector where the performance differential between the below-median manager and the top-quartile one is significantly larger than in more traditional asset classes.

Research and thorough knowledge of the sector is critical in identifying superior managers, particularly those specializing in alternative strategies.

By the time an emerging manager's performance record becomes apparent, management boutiques with a small group of talented individuals may change ownership or structure. It may not always be the best time to commit funds to a manager at the peak of the firm's performance cycle. One of the reasons why identifying emerging managers is critical is that top-performing teams tend to break up once they have made their personal fortunes. And, if they don't do so, the growth process itself can disturb the dynamics that resulted in a team effort at the outset.

Identifying winning active strategies involve great skill and a certain amount of good luck. In the complex, competitive world of investing, pursuing low-cost passive strategies is often the most efficient solution. Identifying a portfolio that just beats the market is not enough; managers need to identify investments that generate returns greater than the sum total of costs involved in the investment process, which include transaction costs, management fees, and market impact. Beating the market means index returns plus costs. Balancing the active management costs against performance is a formidable challenge. The policy portfolio is thus responsible for generating risk-adjusted returns that must comfortably exceed costs. But appointing the best investment managers to do the job involves selecting for the long-term a group of individuals whose collective vision best represents the aspirations of the trustee.

Investment policy statements therefore tend to describe a variety of guidelines that reflect an institution's investment philosophy. Such statements of investment principles typically include issues relating to investment objectives, asset allocation, spending policies, investment constraints, and performance benchmarks. In addition, the investment policy statement may address risks in the investment pool, rebalancing criteria, and considerations in hiring and retaining investment managers.

Institutions in Oxford and Cambridge address some of these management issues in either their statement of investment principles and/or investment management agreement with the manager. But, among the Colleges surveyed, there were no formal policy statements on hiring and retaining asset managers. Most Colleges either had no such defined policy or at best had informal ones. Among educational endowments in the United States, 71 per cent of institutional investment policy statements feature such considerations. Only 8 per cent had no policy on manager selection, and 21 per cent of institutions reported informal policies in hiring and retaining investment managers. Perhaps because they have internal professional staff to do this job, some of the largest US institutions, with assets over $1 billion, were most likely (57.8 per cent) not to have disclosed formal policies; this group is followed by independent institutions (69.1 per cent) in not reporting formal policies applied in hiring and retaining investment managers.[2]

Endowment assets managed externally

The majority of institutions in Oxford and Cambridge determine the endowment's strategic asset allocation, delegating day-to-day management of the portfolio to the investment bursar and the appointed external manager/s. One-quarter of Colleges used the investment manager in reviewing investment policy; and about one-third (31 per cent) of Colleges depended on the investment manager to review asset allocation. In Cambridge, about half (48 per cent) the Colleges involve the fund manager in asset allocation review. In a third of cases, the contribution of the manager to the asset allocation review process was rated reasonably highly, at 25–50 per cent. External fund managers play an important role in endowment asset management in Oxford and Cambridge and assist in serving institutional objectives.

Only three Colleges (one in Oxford, two in Cambridge) manage their endowment assets internally; the College bursar does the management with help from the broker. In general, two-thirds (64 per cent) of Colleges manage the bulk (>90 per cent) of endowment assets externally. About half (49 per cent) of these institutions confirmed that their endowment assets were managed externally; significantly more Colleges in Cambridge (59 per cent) reporting that to be the case compared with Colleges in Oxford (41 per cent). In the final analysis, strategic investment decision is typically made by the investment committee; it is then communicated to the external fund manager/s for implementation. With property, investment decisions are also made by the investment committee or the property subcommittee, and executed with the assistance of the property adviser or consultant.

It is worth noting that answers given by some bursars in response to various questions were limited to the securities portion of the endowment portfolio. For example, one bursar with a high exposure to property in the endowment suggested that 25 per cent of assets were managed externally. The answer could be interpreted in relation to all the assets; or in relation to the 25 per cent of the endowment held in financial assets like equities, fixed income, and cash, managed by external managers. The 75 per cent in property, managed by the College with the assistance of the appointed property agents, was not taken into account in the response.

The alternative interpretation could be that the College considers its property management as internal, though it is assisted in the process by external agents. Such a bias was evident among several Colleges with large exposure to property assets in their portfolio. At least, 20 per cent of Colleges excluded property investments when responding to the questionnaire. Such an interpretation could be viewed severally—for example, Colleges failed to view the endowment as consisting of both financial and property assets; or the responses assumed a limitation in the study, which itself is possibly influenced by the Colleges' experience of investment consultants and their

Table 10.1. Percentage of endowment assets managed externally

% Managed	Oxford	Cambridge	Oxbridge
All	41	59	49
90–99%	21	7	15
80–90%	12	—	7
70–80%	6	4	5
60–70%	3	—	2
50–60%	6	4	5
40–50%	6	7	7
30–40%	—	7	3
20–30%	3	—	2
10–20%	—	4	2
1–10%	—	—	—
None	3	7	5
Total	**100**	**100**	**100**

lack of inclusion of property-related matters in their overall analysis. Thus, when asked about the names of fund managers employed, at least 10 Colleges (5 each in Oxford and Cambridge) failed to include the names of their property managers in their responses. It is also possible that institutions in Oxford and Cambridge had never been engaged in such a study before; and thus failed to give it due consideration.

Table 10.1 summarizes the information provided by institutions in Oxford and Cambridge indicating the proportion of endowment assets managed externally.

An analysis of the relationship between the size of endowments assets and the proportion of assets managed externally reveals that Colleges with smaller endowments were more likely to manage their assets externally. Over five times as many Colleges in Oxford and Cambridge with assets under £50 million reported 100 per cent of their endowment assets being managed by external fund managers compared to those with larger endowments. Whether this indicated a lack of investment expertise within the Colleges with smaller endowments or the opposite, that is a greater willingness to take risks by appointing appropriate external managers, is not evident. The lack of resources among smaller Colleges is considered the most likely determining factor in their decision to outsource the management of assets.

A further 15 per cent of Colleges with assets under £50 million reported the use of external managers for investing between 75–99 per cent of their endowment assets. Thus, over half (56 per cent) the Colleges with endowment assets under £50 million, used external managers for investing the bulk (>75 per cent) of their assets, while only 18 per cent of the wealthier Colleges reported doing so. Just 7 per cent of Colleges with larger endowments, those with assets over £100 million, appointed external managers to manage 50–75 per cent of their endowment assets.

Table 10.2 provides a breakdown of responses of the participating institutions.

In total, one-third (31 per cent) of richer Colleges reported the use of external managers compared to over two-thirds (69 per cent) of the less wealthy ones. Richer Colleges appear to manage more of their assets internally, which suggests they have better resources to do so efficiently. However, the information provided by the richer institutions tends to exclude property investments. If such assets were included, the reported percentage of assets managed externally would be higher as many of these Colleges have higher allocation to property in the endowment.

Among educational endowments in the United States, the percentage of investment assets that were managed internally has been declining, indicating the widespread practice of external asset management. The full sample dollar-weighted average of assets managed internally, reported by the 2004 NACUBO Endowment Study (NES), fell from 18.3 per cent in 2001 to 11.0 per cent in 2004. The largest proportional average decrease in internally managed assets from 2003 to 2004 occurred with institutions whose endowment assets were less than or equal to $25 million, while institutions with endowment assets greater than $25 million to less than or equal to $50 million reported an average increase of less than 1 per cent—the only asset sized category to report an increase in internally managed assets.[3]

On average, some 89 per cent of institutional assets were managed externally in 2004 compared with 81.7 per cent in 2001. Endowments with assets valued over $500 million and up to $1 billion were the most likely to follow this strategy, and 97.2 per cent of their assets were externally managed. Institutions with assets worth between $100 million and $500 million were also higher users of external services, and 95.2 per cent of their assets were externally managed. Public institutions were also more inclined to hire outside managers (93.1 per cent of their assets being managed externally), as compared to independent institutions (with 87.4 per cent).

Table 10.3 shows the dollar-weighted distribution of internally and externally managed assets in the endowment investment pool of 735 educational institutions in the US participating in the 2004 NES.

Selection of asset managers

External asset managers are usually selected and employed by the investment committees of Oxbridge institutions, sometimes with the assistance of consultants or other advisers, including alumni and friends. The investment committee is responsible for manager selection in over half (59 per cent) the Colleges. About one-quarter (23 per cent) of institutions reported using a consultant in the manager selection process. Five per cent of respondents

Table 10.2. Size of endowment and assets managed externally, in per cent

% External	>£100 m	£75–100 m	£50–75 m	All >£50 m	£25–50 m	£10–25 m	<£10 m	All <£50 m	Total
All	2	2	5	8	13	13	15	41	49
75–99%	5	3	2	10	7	8	—	15	25
50–75%	2	2	3	7	2	—	—	2	8
25–50%	3	—	2	5	7	—	—	7	11
10–25%	—	2	—	2	—	—	—	—	2
>10%	—	—	—	—	—	—	—	—	
None	—	—	—	—	2	3	—	5	5
Total	**11**	**8**	**11**	**31**	**30**	**25**	**15**	**69**	**100**

Table 10.3. US educational endowments: distribution of assets managed internally versus externally (dollar-weighted)

Endowment	External management	Internal management
> $1,000 m	83.3	16.7
$500–1,000 m	97.2	2.8
$100–500 m	95.2	4.8
$50–100 m	93.1	6.9
$25–50 m	93.5	6.5
< $25 m	94.7	5.3
Public	93.1	6.9
Independent	87.4	12.6
Full Sample Average	**89.0**	**11.0**

Source: 2004 NACUBO Study.

engaged 'old members' or 'friends' of the College. 'We use our advisor network and contacts to identify promising managers, and then do the due diligence ourselves,' commented one bursar. In one case, the manager was recommended by the outgoing manager 'who had to let go all of their institutional private clients as a result of an internal restructuring within the organisation.'

A few (7 per cent) of the bursars reported 'inheriting' their fund managers; half of the bursars in such a position were not satisfied with the manager's performance and reported plans to alter such arrangements within the foreseeable future. As one such bursar explained, the College endowment assets were being managed, on a segregated basis, by the external fund manager. The manager then switched the assets from a segregated portfolio to units in an internally managed charity investment pool (commonly referred to as an OEIC or open-ended investment company), with the consent of the College. The manager's recent performance was poor. The bursar was of the opinion that they would have been better off in tracker funds, saving on management cost as active management had not been a winning strategy. Such views, by no means common, were gaining favour among the Colleges.

By avoiding high fees and transaction costs, passive strategies typically provide long-term results that represent the most efficient investment option for investors lacking the resources to pursue active strategies. As the costs associated with active strategies tend to be higher, investors pursuing such strategies need to ensure their risk-adjusted returns compensate them for that extra cost and time spent in monitoring managers. But, in spite of clear evidence showing that active managers are more likely to fail to deliver risk-adjusted excess returns, investors continue to choose active management. In addition, when managers' performance proves to be consistently poor, investors do not switch to indexed products; they incur further costs by switching assets to another active manager most likely at the peak of its investment performance cycle.

Table 10.4. Responsibility for selection of assets managers

Group responsible	Oxford	Cambridge	Oxbridge
Investment Committee	53	67	59
IC and Consultant	32	11	23
IC and Old College Member	9	—	5
IC and previous manager	3	—	2
Current manager inherited	—	15	7
No external fund manager	3	7	5
Total	**100**	**100**	**100**

Poor manager performance was cited by one College, with no policy of reviewing its manager formally, for conducting such a review. This process assisted the College in defining its investment objective, and the manager in changing its investment process. While the College did not switch to an indexed strategy as a result of poor manager performance, at least the College decided not to incur the additional cost involved in switching to another active manager. While Oxbridge institutions generally prefer active management styles, Colleges reasonably satisfied with the overall performance and service of their managers were less keen on reviewing them regularly, compared with those Colleges less satisfied with the manager, particularly if the relationship was not an established one.

Table 10.4 summarizes the responses given by Oxbridge institutions with reference to their manager selection process.

Apart from a few Colleges in Oxford and Cambridge that manage their assets in-house (5 per cent) and those that inherited their asset manager (7 per cent), the remaining (88 per cent) institutions reported that the College Investment Committee was involved in the manager selection process, with 59 per cent of investment committees assuming full responsibility for that decision. In Cambridge, 67 per cent of College investment committees reported full responsibility for manager selection. Also, the majority of Cambridge institutions did not use an investment consultant in the manager selection process compared with Colleges in Oxford.

Overall, 23 per cent of institutions in Oxford and Cambridge employed an investment consultant for manager selection with the consultant's contribution to the process varying between 25 and 50 per cent. Higher use of consultants in the manager selection process was evident among Oxford institutions (32 per cent) compared with those in Cambridge (11 per cent). Oxford Colleges were also ahead of Cambridge institutions in moving to total return investment policies, which involved a comprehensive review of asset allocation and accompanying manager selection. Investment consultants may thus have played a significant role in transforming endowment asset management in Oxford compared with Cambridge, where institutions were slower in implementing total return strategies. The consultant most widely cited in Oxford was Cambridge Associates, whose most important contribution was cited as the introduction of alternative strategies to these institutions. Cambridge Associates also played a role in assisting the institutions in defining investment objective, spending rule in addition to asset allocation and manager selection.

Monitoring manager performance

Monitoring and assessing the performance of asset managers is as critical a role for fiduciaries as selecting the manager. The Trustee Act in the UK places trustees under a duty to review the arrangements under which management of the charitable institution's investments are delegated. Trustees are required to review the actions of the investment manager, whether the manager was appointed under the powers contained in the Act, or under any other power, for example in the institution's governing document. Such a review does not necessarily involve a competitive re-tendering for the position of the investment manager. The statutory requirement to review does not apply where the manager has not been appointed under the powers in the Trustee Act, which is the case with institutions in Oxford and Cambridge. It is, however, good practice to keep the performance of an investment manager under review.

The Charity Commission's guidance on such matters makes it clear that:

The statutory review duty means that Trustees must consider periodically the suitability of the terms under which the investment manager is acting, and how the manager is performing. Does the manager remain a suitable person to carry out the function? Do the terms of the appointment remain appropriate? Trustees are required specifically to consider whether the manager is complying with the policy statement, and the continued suitability of the policy which is expressed in that statement.

This review duty should, of course, be carried out independently of the investment manager, and it should be a properly informed review. If trustees feel that they are unable to make a proper assessment without some expert assistance, they can, at the expense of the charity, employ someone who is independent of their investment manager to provide that assistance.

The duty to 'keep under review' does not oblige trustees to review the arrangements at specific intervals or in a particular way. The way in which this duty should be discharged will depend upon what is reasonable in the circumstances. For example, the duty to review may be triggered by evidence of inadequate performance emerging from a report which the investment manager has sent to the trustees.

The review may throw up concerns about the suitability of the terms under which the investment manager is acting, and/or how the manager is performing. The trustees have to consider using any powers of intervention that they have under the written agreement between themselves and the investment manager or under general law. They may, for example, have the right to give instructions to the manager on certain matters. They may be able to negotiate a change to the agreement. Or they may terminate it.[4]

The Charity Commission in the UK obliges trustees to act in the best interest of the institutions they represent. While Colleges in Oxford and Cambridge are not under the direct supervision of the Charity Commission, these institutions in general also act in the best interests of the institutions they represent, and wish to embrace best practice. A significant number (66 per cent) of institutions in Oxford and Cambridge reported monitoring their asset managers directly, via a combination of manager reports, which are received quarterly and annually, and meetings with the manager, which are held several times a year. About one-quarter (21 per cent) of respondents reported monitoring the performance of the manager vis-à-vis an agreed benchmark—thereby reducing the need for frequent contact with the manager.

In the United States, 88.5 per cent of educational endowments included investment performance benchmarks formally in their institutional investment policy features.[5] A similar number (87 per cent) of institutions in Oxford and Cambridge executed the task of monitoring their asset managers, though there were no formal policies in place with regard to manager review. It is typically left to the College bursar to conduct such a review and present his report to the investment committee. Ultimately, manager review is the bursar's responsibility. Less than 10 per cent of Colleges in Oxford and Cambridge involved an investment consultant or any other firm or individual with special expertise in monitoring the performance of external asset managers.

For Colleges with assets invested in indexed strategies, meetings with external managers were infrequent as such investment of time was unlikely to add value to the overall management process compared with the monitoring of active managers, particularly in the private equity and hedge fund sector. Even in the case of alternative strategies, manager meetings were held more for the sake of due diligence as several strategies involved the investment being locked in for several years. A strategic shift in investment policy could take several years to implement. Such a constraint applies to all classes of investors with assets that may be illiquid in nature, ranging from property to private equity.

One of the attractions of using indexed strategies is not only the reduced burden of monitoring the performance of the manager, but also in terms of liquidity and associated costs involved. In the words of one bursar: 'We scarcely meet our fund managers, Barclays Global Investors (BGI). As long as

Table 10.5. Oxbridge manager monitoring process

Process	Oxford	Cambridge	Oxbridge
Regular manager reports and meetings	59	74	66
Benchmark and manager meetings	29	11	21
Consultant involved in the process	9	7	8
Portfolio managed in-house	3	7	5
Total	**100**	**100**	**100**

they fulfil their brief, there is very little to discuss in meetings. We also get regular reports from all our managers, and that more or less takes care of our need to know. In the case of our private equity investments, we hold six-monthly reviews; but we are locked into them. Not much we can do except to keep ourselves informed.' What the bursar did not emphasize was the low costs involved when trading such products.

Table 10.5 provides a summary of responses to the question: 'How do you monitor the performance of your fund managers?'

Monitoring the performance of external asset managers is a key task of every Investment Committee, though the number of managers and the strategies used may involve a high degree of responsibility for the individual concerned, particularly the investment bursar with a wide range of other College responsibilities. Most (98 per cent) investment committees in Oxford and Cambridge reported being highly engaged in the manager monitoring process, with 80 per cent claiming full responsibility. The level of involvement of the investment committee reported in Cambridge was higher, with 89 per cent of institutions claiming 100 per cent engagement in the manager monitoring process. However, one Cambridge College also reported self-monitoring by the asset manager, while another allocated the task to its retired Senior Bursar. Overall use of a consultant in manager supervision was low; only one institution in Oxford relied entirely (100 per cent) on its investment consultant to monitor its array of asset managers.

Frequency of asset manager review

In endowment asset management, the relationship between sponsor, consultant, and asset manager is often complex; problems may arise in the form of an appropriate investment horizon, business risk, and benchmark. Selecting individuals of high integrity helps to reduce the fiduciary gap that may arise between trustees, advisers, and managers. Sponsors often select individuals known to them; loyalty playing an integral part in the relationship, encouraging long-term thinking to influence decision-making. If a relationship is stable, all parties can concentrate on delivering the best solution for achieving the long-term objective. While such arrangements do not exclude reviewing the manager or the consultant, the understanding that relationships are for the long term reinforces a sense of ownership.

Relationships between fiduciaries and managers come to an end for all sorts of reasons; some compelling, others are more trivial. Investment committees consider changing managers with great caution as it involves significant costs. A patch of poor performance may not be a good reason for firing a manager. In the words of one Oxbridge bursar: 'There is no formal review period. Performance is the key indicator, although it is not clear what will result in termination—apart from very clear violation of trust.' Reasons cited for changing managers in Oxford and Cambridge varied from consistently poor performance to persistent breaches in investment guidelines. The overall quality of manager service was also cited as a reason for changing managers: 'We changed managers as our previous manager could no longer offer us custody; they were taken over by a larger firm and we became a small client in a very big firm. They lost one of their top managers, too. We thought it was time to move.'

Most manager relationships in Oxford and Cambridge are long term. Over one-quarter (28 per cent) of institutions had not recently held and did not plan a review of their manager; over a third (37 per cent) of Colleges in Cambridge reported informal reviews compared with less than one-quarter (21 per cent) of Colleges in Oxford. Some institutions switched from active to passive management, which made short-term manager reviews unnecessary. According to one bursar who switched from active to passive management, there was no need 'to monitor the variance too closely unless it is high enough for us to address the issue. We are mainly concerned with assessing whether passive strategy is suitable for our requirements under prevailing market conditions.'

Frequency of manager review, as cited in Table 10.6, varied among institutions, from annual reviews to those conducted over periods of 3–5 years, or even longer investment cycles in some cases. One-quarter (25 per cent) of respondents said they conducted annual reviews (twice as many institutions in Oxford as in Cambridge), 10 per cent reviewed their manager every 3 years, and a further 10 per cent did so over a 3–5 year period. Over one-quarter (28 per cent) of institutions did not specify a review period agreed between their manager and themselves.

Where bursars 'inherited' the fund manager and the manager's performance following the transition was poor, a formal manager review assisted in either changing the manager or ensuring that the Investment Committee was fully satisfied with the reasons for which the manager failed to deliver. Lack of an established relationship can be a reason for changing managers if the manager also fails to deliver at the early stages of a new relationship. Thus, investment performance remains the key to a long-term relationship. According to one

Table 10.6. Frequency of asset manager review

Frequency	Oxford	Cambridge	Oxbridge
3 months	3	—	2
6 months	6	7	7
1 year	32	15	25
2 years	—	4	2
3 years	12	7	10
3–5 years	9	11	10
5 years	9	7	8
5–10 years	3	—	2
10 years	3	4	3
No review period specified	21	37	28
Self review by manager	3	7	5
Total	**100**	**100**	**100**

College bursar, the fund manager had been with the College for over 12 years: 'We recently reviewed some managers (including our current manager) and decided to stay with our current one as changing managers is expensive and we could not find any major reason for changing managers as we found our existing manager to be quite competitive.' The cost of changing managers was cited as a major reason for staying with the existing manager.

Frequency of changes in asset managers

When asked: 'How many asset managers have you changed or added over the last three years, and are you thinking of making any changes within the next 2–3 years?' About two-thirds (63 per cent) of Colleges in Oxford and Cambridge reported changing asset managers over the past 3 years, or were considering making such changes within the next 3 years. Several of the manager changes recorded were in the alternative assets category. According to one bursar: 'We added 6 new managers (of specialised allocations) in the last three years; a similar rate of addition is likely in the future following our diversification policy.' It is interesting that at the time of our interviews for this study, the remaining 37 per cent of institutions indicated not having changed any managers over the past 3 years, nor did they anticipate any changes over the next few years. The range of responses is recorded in Table 10.7.

For the sake of convenience, all the responses have been broken down into three panels: Panel A refers to Colleges that changed managers over the last three years; Panel B refers to Colleges that had not made any changes recently but were considering changes over the next few years; and Panel C refers to Colleges where manager changes had not been made over the past two to three years and where there were no changes planned for the foreseeable future.

Table 10.7. Changes in the appointment of asset managers

Panel	Expected changes	Oxford	Cambridge	Oxbridge
A: Colleges that	Manager changes made over last 3 years	6	7	7
changed	Manager changes taking place currently	9	—	5
manager	Switched to indexation	12	4	8
over last	No further changes planned	21	7	15
3 years	Further changes planned	3	4	3
	Total	**50**	**22**	**38**
B: No recent	Manager changes due over next 3 years	18	7	13
changes but	Manager review due within 3 years	—	11	5
considering	Thinking of switching to indexation	3	—	2
future change	Seeking alternative strategy managers	9	—	5
	Total	**29**	**19**	**25**
C: No past and	No manager changes over past 3 years	18	15	16
no planned	No changes anticipated	3	44	21
changes	**Total**	**21**	**59**	**37**
	Grand Total	**100**	**100**	**100**

As illustrated, over one-third (38 per cent) of Colleges reported changing asset managers over the last 3 years; of which a significant proportion (15 per cent) expressed no plans to make any further changes within the next 3 years; only 3 per cent indicated further changes in the pipeline. Eight per cent of institutions reported switching from active to passive management, and 5 per cent indicated manager changes were in the process of implementation. One-quarter (25 per cent) of Colleges (Section B) reported no manager changes during the past few years, but indicated that some changes were imminent. The remaining 37 per cent of institutions (Section C) reported no manager changes in the past 3 years, nor did they have any plans for changes in the next 3 years.

In Section B, among Colleges reporting no changes over the past 3 years but considering changes over the next 3 years, 13 per cent of respondents anticipated changes over the next few years; 5 per cent reported considering changes and/or conducting a manager review, though such a review may not translate to a formal change of manager. As expressed by one bursar: 'We have not had a formal review for some time. There is a recognition that we need to review our brokers, and we intend to do so within the next few years. When we conduct the review, we may end up changing our brokers. But, there is no plan to do so currently.' Another bursar pointed out: 'Yes, we have some reservations about our current fund manager. These reservations have to do with their investment style, track record and new corporate structure. But there is no great urgency about transferring to another manager, as there are costs associated with that process.'

A third bursar, in Oxford, reinforced the point succinctly: 'Modern investment management practices tend to emphasise activity and change. It's almost become gospel that a portfolio has to be tweaked every now and then, and a manager changed, just to show that the trustees are doing their job. I've always thought that not to be the case; that a lot of time and expense is wasted, at all levels in the investment industry, by this attitude. I guess what I'm saying is that stable, long-term relationships with managers are no bad thing.' Only one Oxbridge bursar reported: 'No change has been made in our asset managers for over 15 years. I would like as a matter of principle to make a change.'

Section C in Table 10.7 shows that about one-quarter (21 per cent) of Colleges in Oxford and Cambridge did not anticipate any manager change. Reasons given for such a decision varied from cost considerations to time constraints. 'We have not done a formal review,' explained one bursar, adding: 'As we have a huge development programme ongoing, there isn't enough time on the College agenda to conduct a formal review or change our managers.' Some Colleges have had the same fund manager for decades. The University of Cambridge's endowment is well known for having its fund manager in place for a record length of time. Such practices typically existed among Colleges where an individual adviser or broker played a key role in assisting the bursar in managing the endowment.

The importance of personal relationships and knowing your manager is as important for Colleges in Oxford and Cambridge as it is for the asset manager to know the client. While appointments are regularly made on such recommendation, in one instance the College followed an individual manager, moving with the manager as he changed firms, over the past three decades. 'We suspect we are very untypical in this respect,' commented the bursar. In another case, the fund manager had been in place for over 30 years and so it appears had the bursar; but poor manager performance and several changes in bursarial appointments finally resulted in the appointment of a new fund manager for this Cambridge College. While changing managers frequently can be harmful, not reviewing managers, their performance, and philosophy over time is equally damaging.

Asset manager analysis

Currently there is no requirement on the part of Oxford and Cambridge Colleges to disclose the names of their external asset managers in their annual reports and accounts. Some institutions, however, do so voluntarily. An attempt was made to gather some information on the subject. Colleges were requested to supply the names of their appointed asset managers. Most of the respondents provided the information; a few indicated the numbers of managers employed, for example, in the alternative assets arena where the manager count was significantly higher. In addition, there existed significant sensitivities in such disclosure. Colleges, for example, did not wish to disclose the names of their hedge fund managers or their private equity partnerships, except the ones in which several Colleges participated like the Fauchier or Cambridge Associates partnerships.

Some Colleges failed to provide a complete list of managers appointed; only reporting those involved in the management of listed securities such as equities and bond or cash, but not their property managers. Ten Oxbridge institutions did not provide the names of their property managers, though they gave the names of their non-property managers. As most of these institutions also hold large property portfolios, the number of managers indicated in our overall count may be understated as a result. As eight Colleges did not participate in the study, it also affects the total manager count as some of these institutions own large endowments and would reasonably appoint a number of fund managers.

In the newly published annual reports and accounts of Colleges in Oxford and Cambridge, disclosing the names of asset managers was not a requirement. For 2003–4, over half (53 per cent) the Colleges in Cambridge included such information in their reports compared to less than one-third (31 per cent) of Colleges in Oxford. The two universities were more transparent, though there was no obligation on their part to make it publicly available. Cambridge University's endowment was managed by F&C Asset Management, and their property manager was LaSalle Investment Management. In total, 41 per cent of institutions in Oxford and Cambridge provided the name of their asset managers and advisers in their annual reports and accounts for the financial year ending 2004.

Our analysis is based on information gathered during the course of our study as the rate of participation was higher. More Colleges were willing to disclose such information in a study that was non-attributable than include such information in their annual accounts. Several changes in manager appointments have inevitably taken place since our interviews were conducted. Our analysis therefore does not aim to provide the exact picture of managers employed currently, only to give us an idea of what was reported in 2002–3. While some consolidation may have occurred since then, anecdotal evidence suggests that more manager hires had taken place.

Table 10.8 summarizes the information provided by institutions in Oxford and Cambridge that participated in the study. It is estimated that the 61 participating institutions employed over 224 managers. This figure does not reflect the number of mandates per manager. The greatest numbers of asset managers reported were employed in private equity management consisting of almost half the total manager count. These managers were also the least likely to have several Oxbridge mandates. Managers of alternative strategies were mostly recent hires, and the numbers of individual mandates involved in alternative strategies were high reflecting the nature of the industry where

Table 10.8. Number of asset managers

Manager style	Number of managers
Equities—active	52 (23%)
Equities—passive	8 (4%)
Bonds—active	11 (5%)
Bonds—passive	1 (0%)
Cash	12 (5%)
Property	19 (8%)
Hedge funds	11 (5%)
Private equity	110 (49%)
Total*	**224 (100%)**

* Excluding property managers in five Oxford Colleges and five Cambridge Colleges along with the eight Colleges that declined to participate in the study.

managers tend to be niche players, not asset gatherers. It is not surprising that there were more than twice the number of partnerships involved in the management of private equity assets compared to more traditional investments in publicly traded securities.

The average of 3.7 asset managers per institution in Oxford and Cambridge masks the fact that about half (48 per cent) the Colleges employed a single investment manager with a balanced mandate, compared to an average of 12.0 investment managers per institution in the United States, where managers are generally appointed for their specialist skills. As the allocation to alternative strategies is higher among US educational endowments, it also results in a higher manager count. Institutions in Oxford and Cambridge were at the cusp of change when our study was conducted in 2002–3. Income-based asset allocation strategies were common, allocation to alternative strategies were also insignificant. As Colleges increase their allocation to hedge funds and private equity, even to the 5 per cent level, it would be reasonable to expect that the number of managers per College would also increase.

The complexity of endowment portfolios is a function of size, and ultimately the driver of the number of managers used. According to the *Commonfund Benchmarks Study: Educational Endowment Report,* 2005, among the largest US endowments with assets over $1 billion, an average of 68.4 investment managers is used compared with 81.0 reported a year ago. At the other end of the scale, the smallest institutions reported using an average of 1.9 managers compared with 2.1 a year ago. Further analysis of a matched sample of the largest institutions, comparing the number of separate investment management firms that reported in both 2003 and 2004 by institutions in this size group, revealed that the average number of managers in 2003 was 77.4 and the average for 2004 was 79.5, showing a modest increase in the number of managers used.

Table 10.9. Number of asset managers for US educational endowments, 2003 and 2004

Endowment	FY 2004 (N = 707)	FY 2003 (N = 657)
> $1,000 m	68.4	81.0
$500–1,000 m	29.4	30.0
$100–500 m	15.6	14.1
$50–100 m	8.6	8.7
$10–50 m	5.4	5.2
< $10 m	1.9	2.1
Average	**12.0**	**12.5**

N = Number of Institutions.
Source: Commonfund Benchmarks Study: Educational Endowment Report, 2005.

Table 10.9 shows the number of asset managers used by US educational institutions participating in the fiscal years 2003 and 2004 of the *Commonfund Benchmarks Study*.[6] All size groups of endowments in the United States reported they used a greater number of alternative strategies managers than any other type. Within their allocation to alternative strategies, they indicated a significant concentration of managers used in the hedge funds sector. Overall, 73 per cent of assets invested in hedge funds are invested directly via a fund-of-funds, and an average of 7.9 managers are used. The larger institutions used an average of 18.4 managers while the smaller ones reported 3.0 hedge fund managers.[7]

The *Commonfund Benchmarks Study* also revealed that the largest institutions added to their domestic equity manager rosters over the year, while all other size groups reduced the number of managers used for this asset class. The smallest institutions actually cut the number for all asset classes, while mid-sized institutions added to the number of international equity managers and added or held stable the number of fixed income managers. Overall, endowments planned to use an average of 11.4 asset managers in 3 years' time.[8]

Taking into account the smaller size of endowments in Oxford and Cambridge, comparing the average number of managers employed shows that these institutions appear to be efficient in their use of external asset managers. The lower allocation to alternative strategies combined with a higher allocation to property assisted in keeping manager numbers manageable. Though the number of asset managers employed by Oxbridge institutions is understated, it does provide an indication of average numbers involved. Over 224 managers were engaged in managing endowment assets of 61 institutions in Oxford and Cambridge; these assets were valued around £3.8 billion in 2003. Of the 224 managers, 49 per cent were hired for investments in private equity assets alone, 23 per cent in long-only active equity, 8 per cent in

Table 10.10. Number of mandates cited

Manager style	Oxford	Cambridge	Oxbridge
Equities—active	61 (15%)	32 (8%)	93 (23%)
Equities—passive	18 (5%)	9 (2%)	27 (7%)
Bonds—active	12 (3%)	6 (2%)	18 (5%)
Bonds—passive	1 (0%)	1 (0%)	2 (1%)
Cash	29 (7%)	30 (8%)	59 (15%)
Property*	28 (7%)	34 (9%)	62 (16%)
Hedge funds	22 (6%)	3 (1%)	25 (6%)
Private equity	103 (26%)	7 (2%)	110 (28%)
Total	274 (**69**%)	122 (**31**%)	396 (**100**%)

* Excluding property managers in five Oxford Colleges and five Cambridge Colleges along with the Colleges that declined to participate in the study.

property; 5 per cent each in cash, bonds, and hedge funds with the remaining 4 per cent in passive strategies.

An analysis of the number of mandates allocated to asset managers by institutions in Oxford and Cambridge reveals a slightly different picture. For example, 52 managers (see Table 10.8) were employed in long-only, active equity management. Some of these managers had more than one mandate. The 93 mandates reported by Colleges in both Oxford and Cambridge (see Table 10.10) in traditional long-only active equity management were split between 52 managers. Similarly in property, 19 managers were responsible for 62 mandates. It is only in private equity that the number of mandates and managers were the same, as several Colleges provided the number of private equity partnerships in their portfolio instead of the names of individual partnerships. Table 10.10 provides a breakdown of the numbers of mandates cited by Oxbridge institutions. It shows that 396 individual management contracts were spread among 224 asset managers.

Of the total number of mandates, over a third (34 per cent) consisted of alternative strategies, and just 3 per cent of these hires were by Cambridge Colleges. One of the wealthier Colleges in Oxford, for example, reported 26 Private Equity General Partnership investments in its endowment portfolio, which accounted for 76.5 per cent of that institution's total external asset manager hires, and about a quarter (23.6 per cent) of the 110 private equity partnerships reported by all the institutions in Oxford and Cambridge. Among these institutions, there is increased investment in alternative strategies.

The average number of managers used, based on asset class, reflects the asset allocation choices of endowments in both the United States and the UK, revealing the growing emphasis that has been placed on alternative strategies over recent years. Such allocation and manager usage is pronounced among the largest endowments in the United States, where an average of 54.3 alternative strategies managers per institution was reported in 2004 among institutions with assets over $1 billion. The average for all 707 institutions reporting number of managers employed in 2004 was 13.5 managers for alternative strategies.[9] When asked the number of managers by asset class that institutions in Oxford and Cambridge expected to use in the future, several Colleges reported their intention to add to their alternative strategies manager roster. Considering that these institutions were starting from a low base of exposure to the asset class, the intention to hire additional managers in the alternative strategies sector is not unusual.

While the increased diversification into alternative strategies among endowment portfolios in the United States has had a generally positive effect on performance, it has also led most endowments to increase the number of managers hired over the past decade, creating a problem of resources allocation as they attempt to conduct proper due diligence, monitoring, and risk management. As reported by *Commonfund Benchmarks Study*: 'The continued move to alternatives, and particularly to hedge funds, has heightened this demand, as many of these strategies tend to be capacity-constrained, creating the need for more managers for a given allocation. These managers are often less transparent, are smaller, have less infrastructure, and use more leverage, requiring even more sophisticated oversight capability on the part of endowment professional staffs and their boards.'[10] In fact, among the largest endowments, the number of managers used in alternative strategies declined from an average of 64.6 in 2003 to 54.3 in 2004; some endowments using fund of fund managers in addition to direct investments in single hedge funds.

The rise in the use of managers in alternative strategies, particularly hedge funds, not only results in higher costs but adds to the portfolio risk management effort. By comparison, the allocation to property assets among institutions in Oxford and Cambridge appears more efficient. Investing in direct property assets as these institutions typically do may be more expensive than investing passively in equity assets. But ownership of property enhances portfolio diversification and brings in income. Nor is the management of such assets considered overtly risky, as the Colleges have held these properties over long periods, and are fully cognizant of the associated risks. What the Colleges have not done is to leverage that asset base to lower their overall costs. While investment banks have been busy structuring all sorts of financial products for pension funds, insurance companies and the corporate sector; they have not been innovative in catering to the needs of foundations and endowments. As the size and the ability of the sector in investing innovatively for the long term is increasingly recognized, that may yet change.

As the number of managers employed is typically correlated to the size of fund, an attempt was made to analyse such distribution among institutions in Oxford and Cambridge. Table 10.11 illustrates the number of asset managers Oxbridge institutions used, depending on size of endowment assets. Analysis suggests that over half the Colleges (51 per cent) used less than five managers per institution, but there was no clear link between size of endowment assets

Table 10.11. Number of managers versus endowment value

No. of managers	>£100 m	£75–100 m	£50–75 m	All >£50 m	£25–50 m	£10–25 m	<£10 m	All <£50 m	Total
>25	2	2	—	3	—	—	—	—	3
20–24	—	—	—	2	2	—	—	2	3
15–19	2	2	—	3	—	—	—	—	3
10–14	—	2	—	2	2	2	—	3	5
5–9	7	2	7	15	10	8	2	20	34
<5	2	0	5	7	16	15	13	44	51
Total	**11**	**8**	**11**	**31**	**30**	**25**	**15**	**69**	**100**

and number of managers employed. It is worth noting that for over half a century one of the largest endowments, Cambridge University, allocated the bulk of its non-property assets to a single active balanced manager. Such concentration of active fund manager risk is unheard of today. The two University endowments of Cambridge and Oxford employed between them 22 non-property managers (four by Cambridge and 18 by Oxford; responses from the University of Oxford did not include the names of their property managers).

The Oxford University Investment Committee was in the process of making several manager changes over the period of our study; the number of managers reported by the Oxford University endowment was set to rise. While changes in the management of the Cambridge University endowment has been announced, we do not know what those changes will amount to with reference to investment policy, asset allocation, investments in alternative strategies, the number of specialist managers to be engaged, etc. However, the total number of managers employed by Cambridge University to manage its sizeable endowment will no doubt rise significantly.

Over half (51 per cent) the Colleges in Oxford and Cambridge managed their endowment assets with less than 5 managers per College; 7 per cent of the larger endowments (with assets over £50 million) employed less than five asset managers compared with 44 per cent of Colleges with endowment assets worth less than £50 million. About a third (34 per cent) of institutions used over five managers but less than 10, the richer Colleges accounted for 15 per cent of this total. Five per cent of Colleges employed over 10 but less than 15 asset managers per institution. Only 3 per cent of Colleges engaged over 15 but less than 20 managers each, all among the richer Colleges. No College with endowment assets below £50 million employed over 15 managers. A further 3 per cent of Colleges used over 20 but less than 25 managers per institution; only one Oxford College with endowment assets below £50 million was in this category, as a result of its high exposure to alternative strategies. The remaining 3 per cent of institutions employed more than 25 managers each, and both the Colleges had endowments assets worth over £75 million.

Cambridge Associates, the consultant most widely used in Oxford and to a lesser extent in Cambridge, established a private equity investment fund of funds (Oxford Limited Partnership) for the University of Oxford and some of the Colleges. Similar additional private equity partnerships already existed among some of the Colleges and other firms specializing in private equity asset management.

In the hedge funds sector, the Oxford Absolute Return Partnership with Fauchier Partners included the University of Oxford and some 15 Colleges invested in the product, which is structured in such a way that these institutions benefit from such a partnership. The fund charges are 1 per cent of costs with no performance fees; its volatility since inception has been 3.5 per cent and beta 0.11. The hedge fund of funds is quoted in pounds and not in dollars and offers exposure to about 30 positions in half as many strategies. It is surprising that more Colleges had not invested in such a partnership. Compared with institutions in Oxford, the Cambridge partnership with Fauchier Partners at the time of our study was limited to just two Colleges, one of whom (Gonville and Caius) had 3.7 per cent of its endowment invested in the Fauchier fund.

Taking into account the concentration of managers used in traditional assets, the number of managers used in cash management was unusual. There were almost as many managers engaged in cash management as in the management of property, and twice as many cash managers as hedge fund managers. As most of the Colleges invested in the hedge fund of funds managed by Fauchier Partners in Oxford (though three other colleges—All Souls, Christ Church, and Magdalen—had separate mandates with Fauchier), that may have accounted for the lower number of managers in the hedge fund sector. Thus, the pooling of assets in hedge fund investments was innovative on the part of these institutions, particularly when their exposure to such strategies was low.

Compared to hedge funds and the considerable creativity manifested by these institutions, an analysis of cash management revealed that 44 per cent of Colleges managed their cash balances in-house, which meant that cash was deposited either in a Bank or Building Society account, and was not managed actively by a fund manager. Less than one-quarter (23 per cent) of Colleges reported investing cash in the pooled fund managed by the University, though the number of Colleges doing so was significantly higher in Oxford. Had it not been for the Universities' pooled cash funds, the number of external fund managers involved in cash management for Oxbridge institutions could easily have been higher.

Table 10.12 shows the distribution of mandates among asset managers managing the endowment assets of institutions in Oxford and Cambridge.

Though the average number of managers employed by Colleges in Oxford and Cambridge was significantly lower than the average reported by US educational endowments, an analysis of the number of mandates per asset manager indicates there is scope for greater efficiencies of scale among these institutions, particularly in the management of cash and listed securities. Colleges in Oxford and Cambridge hired 35 asset managers, each with a single mandate in the traditional long-only active equities sector. A total of 151 managers, each with a single mandate across various asset classes and strategies, were hired at the time of the survey. There were 21 managers with two mandates, and just five managers with over 10 mandates many of which were pooled funds such as the Charity Property Fund, the University Cash Deposit Pool, the Cambridge Associates private equity partnership, and the Fauchier Partners' hedge fund of funds partnership.

Table 10.12. Number of mandates per asset manager

No. of mandates	Equities		Bonds		Cash	Property	Alternatives		Total
	Active	Passive	Active	Passive			HF	PE	
1	35	2	8	—	16	11	9	70	151
2	9	3	1	1	1	2	1	3	21
3	2	—	—	—	2	1	—	2	7
4	1	2	2	—	—	2	—	1	8
5	1	—	—	—	1	1	—	1	4
6	3	—	—	—	1	1	—	—	5
7	1	—	—	—	—	—	—	—	1
8	—	—	—	—	—	1	—	—	1
9	—	—	—	—	—	—	—	1	1
10	—	—	—	—	—	—	—	1	1
11	—	1	—	—	1	—	—	—	2
12	—	—	—	—	—	—	—	—	—
13	—	—	—	—	1	—	—	—	1
14	—	—	—	—	—	—	1	—	1
15	—	—	—	—	—	—	—	—	—
16	—	—	—	—	—	—	—	—	—
17	—	—	—	—	—	1	—	—	1
Total	**52**	**8**	**11**	**1**	**23**	**20**	**11**	**79**	**396**

HF = Hedge funds; PE = Private equity.

Taking into account the asset allocation distribution among these institutions, the most efficient sector was property where 8 per cent of managers used appear to be responsible for advising and managing on average 26 per cent of total assets invested in property. As these numbers are incomplete (10 major institutions did not include the names or numbers of property managers employed), one needs to adjust the data accordingly. Even if one were to double the number of property managers, the ratio of managers to assets would still be more attractive than that for active equity investments, where 27 per cent of managers were responsible for 53 per cent of assets invested in the asset class. Fixed income management also appears to be reasonably efficient as 5 per cent of managers were responsible for over 12 per cent of assets. Table 10.13 compares the breakdown of managers and asset distribution among the endowments in Oxford and Cambridge.

Table 10.13. Number of managers versus asset allocation

Asset	No. of managers	Average asset allocation
Equities	27	53.2
Fixed Income	5	12.2
Cash	5	7.1
Property	8	26.1
Hedge Funds	5	0.7
Private Equity	49	0.5
Total	**100**	**100**

While the high number of managers per se does not cause concern, it is the lack of any clear evidence that the costs involved justified the number of managers hired. Our inability to obtain reliable long-term data on costs and investment returns from the Colleges constrains our overall conclusions. It has not been possible to assess whether asset allocation strategies and corresponding manager hires were optimal or not. Data on risk allocation were also hard to come by. Thus, it was not possible to know how the Colleges distributed their investments in their search for alpha. Anecdotal evidence suggested that in several instances the Colleges could have benefited from investing passively, as far as traditional equity investments were concerned. Common sense also suggests that economies of scale could be achieved in pooling assets, especially in sectors such as active equity, cash management, and perhaps in private equity investments as well, taking into account that the average asset allocation to private equity was 0.5 per cent while the Colleges reported over 110 partnerships.

Such analysis is flawed due to lack of more reliable data. Nevertheless, it reflects trends in the employment of managers among Oxbridge institutions. The five active equity investment managers with the largest number of mandates in Oxford and Cambridge during 2002–3 were: HSBC Investment Management with seven mandates, Sarasin Chiswell (formerly Chiswell Associates), Newton Asset Management, UBS Laing and Cruickshank with six mandates each (with UBS Laing and Cruickshank serving as broker as well as fund manager), and Cazenove with five Oxbridge clients.

Conclusion

There is increasing recognition of the scope for better diversification in investment strategies and corresponding manager appointments among institutions in Oxford and Cambridge. Cambridge University, for example, has established an investment office and pooled its endowment assets into a single fund. There is some pooling of assets evident among Oxford Colleges with the launch of Oxford Investment Partners. Other examples of pooling in the management of cash, property, and alternative strategies were already in place in Oxford and to a lesser extent in Cambridge.

The Charity Property Fund, specifically set up to provide access to organizations within the charitable sector for diversification of investments into the property sector, was used by 17 Colleges in Oxford and Cambridge (most of whom did not have direct property holdings in their endowment portfolios). The Oxford Absolute Return Partnership with Fauchier Partners had the University of Oxford and 15 Oxford Colleges invested in the product. The Cambridge Associates' Private Equity Amalgamated Fund for Oxford Colleges also had several Colleges signed up, while the Oxford University Cash Deposit

Pool had some 15 Colleges as clients. Despite evidence of pooling in the management of some assets, there exists considerable opportunity for further consolidation in manager hires.

The independence exercised by Oxford and Cambridge institutions in their asset allocation and manager selection is worthy of note. Yet few of these institutions formally covered issues relating to the hiring and retaining of managers in their investment policy statements. Increasingly asset managers were being employed after a formal beauty parade, sometimes with the aid of a consultant. Colleges also reported the use of personal contacts and recommendations in their appointment of managers. Finding appropriate managers in the alternative strategies sector was reported to be the greatest obstacle to investing in the asset class. As a result, it was also the sector where greater pooling in addition to hiring on the basis of personal recommendation was most in evidence. The fund-of-funds route was also perceived as a safer way of investing in alternative strategies, though the added costs were a disincentive for others. Smaller endowments in Oxford and Cambridge used fewer managers; smaller endowments also invested more in pooled products, funds, and fund-of-funds.

The lack of transparency in measuring investment performance and associated costs remains the Achilles heel of endowment asset management in Oxford and Cambridge. These institutions need to make their cost-adjusted investment performance more transparent. One way of achieving that would be to employ collectively an external, independent investment performance measurement firm, whereby overall performance and costs could be assessed. Such arrangements would enable the Colleges to secure economies of scale and achieve the sort of asset allocation they desire, but which are elusive because of constraints in endowment size or organizational structure. As a third of Oxbridge assets are invested in property, and the cost of managing property is among the highest in terms of overall investment management costs, the Colleges could benefit by pooling their assets and expertise in that sector. While such transition will take time and consideration, the Colleges are in a unique position to map their future.

11

Socially responsible investment

Introduction

In the UK, an amendment to the Pensions Act 1995 requiring trustees to indicate their approach to socially responsible investment (SRI) strategy was significant in terms of its potential influence on corporate behaviour. The appointment of a Minister for Corporate Social Responsibility demonstrated the Government's increasing concern about SRI issues. On 3 July 2000, an amendment made to the Pensions Act 1995 required all pension fund trustees to record in their Statement of Investment Principles (SIP) 'the extent (if at all) to which social, environmental and ethical considerations are taken into account in the selection, retention and realisation of investments' and 'their policy (if any) in relation to the exercise of rights (including voting rights) attaching to investments.'[1]

In its Report, 'Private Action: Public Benefit', the Cabinet Office's Strategy Unit recommended that the trustees of larger charities should be required to make similar disclosures in their annual reports. They also expressed the view that it would be good practice for all charities to make such disclosures even where not required to do so. While there is, at present, no legal requirement on any charity trustees to do this, it is considered good practice to include such information in the annual report.[2]

In the United States, the Department of Labor Interpretative bulletin relating to statements of investment policy, clearly stipulates the fiduciary obligations of managing plan assets that are shares of corporate stock. This bulletin, issued in 1994, spells out clearly the fiduciary obligations of prudence and loyalty to plan participants and beneficiaries.[3] SRI issues are therefore included in the fiduciary obligations of plan sponsors and managers. However, institutional endowments in the United States are not required to include social responsibility criteria in their investment management policy. According to the 2004 NES, some three-quarters, or 73.4 per cent, of the reporting institutions do not consider such criteria when making investment decisions, although 8.2 per cent will when required by donors.[4]

270

In the UK, occupational pension schemes are now accountable for their ethical and voting policy as much as for their fund's financial performance. The legislation does not remove the requirement that trustees must also make decisions that are in the best interests of the plan beneficiaries. John Denham, the Labour government minister who first proposed that pension funds be required to disclose their SRI policies, stated: 'As the law stands, nothing can detract from the primary responsibility of pensions trustees, to place the financial interests of the beneficiaries first.'[5] The law endorses the primacy of preserving the financial interests of beneficiaries and the Court regards trustees of a charitable corporation as being subject to the principles of charity law concerning investment.

Socially responsible investment or ethical investment is a wide phrase which is used to cover diverse approaches to investment strategy. An ethical investment policy or SRI may involve looking for companies which demonstrate best practice in areas like environmental protection, employment, and human rights, or for companies whose businesses contribute directly to a cleaner environment or healthier society. It may also involve actively engaging with companies with a view to influencing their ethical policies. Socially responsible investment may also involve negative screening, to avoid investments in a particular business or sector. Many ethical investors and ethical investment funds adopt a combination of positive and negative criteria. While SRI and ethical investment are used to describe a particular ethical approach towards investments, both need to be distinguished from social investment, which *is not* investment in the ordinary financial sense of the term at all. Ethical investment *is* investment in the financial sense, and trustees are bound by law to act appropriately.

The governing document of a charity sometimes imposes ethical restrictions on the scope of that institution's general power of investment. Such restrictions must, of course, be observed by trustees. More commonly, it will be the trustees themselves who decide to adopt an ethical investment policy. In doing so, the Charity Commission stipulates:

They (trustees) need to keep in mind the underlying principle that their power of investment has to be used to further the purposes of the trust, and that those purposes will normally be best served by seeking the maximum return consistent with commercial prudence. As the Judge put it in the case of *Harries (Bishop of Oxford) v Church Commissioners* [1992] 1 WLR 1241 (commonly known as the Bishop of Oxford case), 'most charities need money; and the more of it there is available, the more the trustees can seek to accomplish.'[6]

An ethical investment policy is thus entirely consistent with the investment principle of seeking the best returns. There is an increasingly held view that companies which act in a socially responsible way are more likely to flourish and to deliver the best long-term balance between risk and return. Trustees

271

are free to adopt any ethical investment policy which they reasonably believe will provide the best balance of risk and reward for their charity. As with any other investment strategy, they must be careful to discharge their duties; in particular, they must consider the need for diversification and must take advice where appropriate.

Thus, investors within the charity sector aim to invest their assets in a socially and environmentally responsible manner reflecting their long-term investment objectives. The ethical investment policy of Clare Hall, Cambridge, for example, as outlined in its published accounts states: 'In relation to Socially Responsible Investment, the Investment Committee believe that the interests of the College are in general best served by seeking to obtain the best financial return from investments consistent with commercial prudence.'[7]

Socially responsible investment strategy typically takes into account the ethical, social, and environmental record of the company invested in, incorporating that assessment into its long-term financial performance. Investors recognize there is a corporate governance dividend attached to firms; they command a higher market valuation, have cheaper access to capital and benefit from a strong shareholder base. Historically, this premium has been lower in developed countries compared with emerging market economies, but companies globally are more aware of their branding in terms of corporate governance, their policy towards social and environmental issues as much as financial ones. For corporations and shareholders, adherence to superior ethical business principles is important, it reflects on their overall performance. Investors increasingly demand greater transparency from companies about their governance principles as well as their environmental policies and practices, their record of protecting human rights and their record of involvement in the local communities they operate in.

Whether investors opt to screen out offending companies (as is the case, e.g., with the Church Commissioners who avoid investing in companies whose income is derived from businesses associated with armaments trading, alcohol, tobacco, or gambling) or engage actively with the management of the companies they own shares in (as is the case with various funds managed by the Hermes group), the investment process in the UK pension fund sector has been irrevocably altered.

Traditionally, shareholder actions have been classified into two categories: corporate governance issues and corporate social responsibility. Corporate governance resolutions address issues such as the composition of the board, confidential voting, independence of non-executive directors, compensation of directors, and executives, and so on. Social responsibility resolutions encompass corporate policy issues on environment, health, safety, gender, sweatshops, and other human right issues. Most large corporations as well as investment firms today have an officer responsible for SRI issues.

Though institutions in Oxford and Cambridge do not formally apply SRI criteria to their investment process, this does not imply the Colleges are not conscious of, or do not wish to engage in SRI issues. As one bursar summarized their approach: 'We do not generally concern ourselves with SRI as we wish our managers to be free to make economic decisions. We believe that in the long run the companies that perform well will follow SRI policies themselves. Thus, the best companies are those that manage to increase profitability while advancing the well being of society.' This view was widely endorsed. According to another bursar:

We do not have an SRI policy, but socially unacceptable investments feature at the stock selection level. We have a Quality of Business Checklist and no investments that pass through that internal screening process can enter our investment universe. We would regard companies with SRI issues as those with unsustainable revenue/growth profiles. So they would not feature as candidates for investment. SRI is a sub-set of our investment philosophy, but we are not do-gooders at all. We quite like the Hermes Focus Funds' philosophy of investing, for example, where investors make a difference in the company's valuation via better governance.

Most Colleges in Oxford and Cambridge follow the guidance provided by the Charity Commission. One bursar defined their ethical stance in the following words: 'Any decision by the trustees or their agents to invest ethically by avoiding certain investments, or certain institutions, must be centred on the interests of the charity. If they are satisfied that a particular range of invest-ments would directly impede the furtherance of the objects of the charity or be of financial detriment then they may exclude that range. They should decline to invest in a particular company if it carries out activities which are directly contrary to the Charity's purposes, and therefore against its interests and those of its beneficiaries.'

Some institutions reported subscribing to the Good Corporation Charter: 'Our policy is to endorse the approach contained within the Good Corpo-ration Charter (a set of statements developed with the help of the Institute of Business Ethics) and instruct fund managers to pursue the adoption of the principles contained within the Charter when speaking to companies in which they invest,' clarified another bursar, who explained that '[We] ask the Investment Advisory Committee to explore opportunities for achieving the investment objective by investing in ethical funds.'

There are not many Colleges in Oxford and Cambridge with a formal SRI policy in place. Those that do, typically implement such policies by instruct-ing their managers to avoid investing in certain stocks and sectors, while others prefer to engage with the company to influence its SRI policy and thus aim to align the interests of the different agencies involved. Usually Colleges believe their interest is best served by leaving the manager free to implement

SRI policies that protect the long-term value of the investments. Downing College, in Cambridge, with an active SRI stance included in its published accounts for the fiscal year 2003–4 describes how it switched its ethical policy from engaging with companies to one of exclusion as a result of a change in manager:

The College keeps its duty in regard to the ethical investment of its funds under review. It currently does not have direct holdings in tobacco companies. This exclusion, which pre-dates the findings of the Harries (*Bishop of Oxford* v. *Church Commissioners,* 1992) case, does not have a material impact on financial return.

The College had adopted a policy of requiring its discretionary fund manager to include ethical, social, and environmental issues in its analysis of companies, to engage with the management of companies on these issues, and, when necessary, to censure management through voting. The College received quarterly reports on the social, ethical and corporate governance of companies in which it held stock, together with details of voting. The new fund managers are differently organised, and the College will operate a policy of exclusions rather than engagement. The College is currently assessing the financial impact of a series of exclusions of types of investment considered by the Governing Body not to be in line with the College's charitable objectives.[8]

Sometimes, an ethical investment policy based on stock exclusion alone can have a detrimental impact on performance. While all serious investors take into account the impact of a company's SRI record on its performance, it can be said that institutions in Oxford and Cambridge like their counterparts in the United States do not typically consider socially responsible criteria when making their strategic asset allocation decisions. Such considerations may arise at the stock selection level. As institutions in Oxford and Cambridge typically do not engage actively in stock selection, they expect their invest- ment managers to adopt policies that reflect such concerns. The few Colleges that manage their assets directly include such criteria in their stock selection process. This is more as a part of the financial assessment of the prospects of the company they invest in rather than adopting any specific ethical bias in their investment approach.

A comparison with US practice within the endowment sector shows that independent institutions as well as institutions with smaller endowments are most likely to consider social responsibility criteria in their investment management policies, while institutions with the largest endowments are least likely to do so. Overall, more than one-quarter (26.4 per cent) of institutions with endowment assets less than or equal to $25 million reported consid- ering socially responsible criteria in their investment management policies compared with an average of 18.5 per cent of institutions operating in the sector. Also, 22.2 per cent of independent institutions reported including such

Table 11.1. Extent to which SRI issues influence allocation, in per cent

Response	Oxford	Cambridge	Oxbridge
Clear influence	26	30	28
Limited influence	21	—	11
No influence	53	70	61
Total	**100**	**100**	**100**

criteria compared with 10.3 per cent of public institutions. Such practice is more applicable to some investments and strategies than others, but institutions adopting SRI policies may also face greater obstacles in continuing such practices while endeavouring to improve investment performance.[9]

Does SRI influence asset allocation?

When asked if SRI criteria were formally addressed in endowment management, particularly in asset allocation, more than half (61 per cent) the institutions in Oxford and Cambridge indicated SRI issues had no influence. Over one quarter (28 per cent) of institutions reported including ethical criteria in their asset allocation process, and 11 per cent of respondents said it affected their asset allocation 'to some extent'. Table 11.1 summarizes the response of Oxbridge institutions to the question: 'Do SRI issues influence your asset allocation?'

Institutions in Oxford and Cambridge appear to be relatively more socially responsible as investors compared with their counterparts in the United States where the averages reported by educational endowments and foundations in the 2003 *NACUBO Endowment Study*, indicated that three-quarters (75.1 per cent) of endowments did not consider social responsibility criteria as part of their investment management policies, although 7.6 per cent were prepared to do so when required by donors. Just 17 per cent of the 2003 survey respondents considered social responsibility criteria in their investment management policies.[10]

This response represented an increase from 61.4 per cent of institutions in 2001 reporting no socially responsible criteria influencing investment management decisions to 75.1 per cent of institutions doing so in 2003; in 2004, reported averages declined slightly to 73.4 per cent of institutions not considering SRI criteria in their endowment asset management. Larger US institutions were also more likely not to consider social responsibility criteria in their investment management policies. Eighty per cent of endowments with assets over $1 billion did not do so, and 78.8 per cent of institutions with assets over $500 million and under $1 billion also ignored such issues in their decision-making. Eighty-three per cent of public institutions also did not take SRI into account in their asset management.[11]

Over one-quarter (28 per cent) of institutions in Oxford and Cambridge reported including SRI issues in their investment decision-making. But these Colleges typically implemented such policies via their fund manager by instructing the manager to effect an ethical or SRI policy. Very few Colleges instructed their managers not to invest in certain types of sectors and companies. The emphasis on ethical investments by these institutions was mainly to manage their investments in such a way that their SRI stance was not detrimental to securing their stated investment returns. The Colleges remain pragmatic in their approach; one College's SRI policy states: 'So far as is practicable, and to the extent that return is optimised, an ethically sound investment policy shall be pursued. No direct investment shall be made in companies whose primary business is the manufacture of arms or tobacco products.' Such an ethical stance is aligned with the guidance provided by the Charity Commission on how to establish such policies.

The key for charitable institutions in the UK is to make a judgement in light of their own circumstances, rather than trying to conform to a supposedly homogeneous 'public opinion'. Here are some pointers for those responsible in decision-making, as outlined by the Charity Commission:

- Consider the aims and objectives of the charity.
- Keep in mind the fundamental principle of maximizing return. If an ethical policy is adopted, it should be set out in writing and should be clear both on positive aims and any exclusions.
- If companies or sectors are excluded, the reasons for exclusion should be clearly thought through. The more restrictive the policy (in terms of exclusions), the greater may be the risk to returns.
- Trustees need to evaluate the effect which any proposed policy may have on potential investment returns, and this will usually require expert advice.
- If a proposed policy increases the risk of lower returns, this must be balanced against the risk of alienating support and damage to reputation. This cannot be an exact calculation. It is just one of many areas where trustees have to identify and manage risk.
- Trustees are unlikely to be criticized for adopting a particular policy if they have considered the correct issues, taken appropriate advice and reached a rational result.[12]

Such guidance also assists institutions in dealing with pressure groups and other interests. As students tend to be more active in SRI issues, educational institutions are often most exposed to such demands from their own community. Recent action by students in Oxford and Cambridge appears not to be a serious constraining factor in the endowment asset management among the Colleges. A small group of Colleges (11 per cent), all in Oxford, indicated the inclusion of ethical or SRI criteria to some extent in their investment management process, primarily as a result of pressure from the student community. According to one such College bursar: 'There may be some embargoes as student pressure is strong in this area, such as in the tobacco sector. Otherwise, there is very little SRI influence on asset allocation. We invest in funds rather than in individual companies, and so we do not have an active SRI policy.'

In two Oxford Colleges, for example, the presence of student representatives in the Investment Committee was responsible for introducing SRI issues into the investment process. The bursar of one of these Colleges explained: 'As we have a JCR (Junior Common Room) member in the Management Executive Team, SRI issues feature in our discussions from time to time. The College's view is that we do not take any particular stance in these matters.' In another College where there was no direct student representation, 'it (SRI) was driven to some extent by students,' explained the bursar, adding 'In any case, we have not been investing directly in tobacco or defence sectors for some time now.' Thus, Colleges pre-empt student objections by adopting some form of SRI policy themselves.

In the words of another bursar: 'We do have concerns regarding SRI from the student body from time to time. I am not aware of any serious concerns from Fellows of the College. It is not because they are not socially responsible. I think, they simply delegate this aspect of the College's affairs to those better informed on the subject. With the move to passive management, I suppose it has become difficult for those who may be concerned to actively raise such issues.' Some Colleges resolve such issues by not making their investment portfolio public: 'We do not make our portfolio public, and thereby avoid any issues that may arise. We do, of course, discuss such issues from time to time and address them individually.'

Colleges in general believe that disclosure of relevant information is essential in assessing the effectiveness of an enterprise's corporate governance and SRI policy, and that such transparency in turn promotes efficient capital markets. Colleges also consider that any necessary action is the responsibility of the investment manager. Two Colleges (one each in Oxford and Cambridge) reported exploring the performance of ethical funds for investment purposes; one of these Colleges (in Oxford) had taken a step in that direction, primarily student-led, by making a small investment in a collective investment vehicle managed by the Ethical Investors Group, an investment firm specializing in ethical investing.

Another College in Cambridge was also in the process of monitoring the performance of SRI funds 'to see what their performance was. Otherwise, we are not particularly into SRI, although our students are reasonably active in the field. With a passive strategy, SRI is not a big concern,' explained this bursar. As passive managers are also actively 'engaging' with companies on SRI matters, adopting an SRI policy is no longer incompatible with implementing passive strategies in asset management. Maximizing investment returns being a major concern, the majority of bursars shared the view that a financially successful company was more likely to be an ethically sound company. Taking into account the constraints under which they (bursars) operate—in terms of resources available for the extensive monitoring of companies the fund managers invest in—endorsing an overly restrictive SRI policy is not efficient. One bursar expressed the College's view as follows: 'We prefer to spend our money ethically rather than exclude companies in our portfolio.'

Further analysis of the influence of SRI criteria on the asset management process, with a view to exploring where and how SRI management strategy was applied if at all, reveals that among 80 per cent of institutions in Oxford and Cambridge, it did not feature in any measurable or meaningful way. An overwhelming 88 per cent of institutions in Oxford, compared with 70 per cent of colleges in Cambridge, did not consider SRI criteria in their investment management. Over twice as many institutions in Cambridge reported discussing or reviewing SRI matters in their investment meetings as in Oxford.

Table 11.2 gives a breakdown of responses with regard to addressing SRI criteria in the overall endowment asset management process.

For some Oxford Colleges, SRI issues did not feature in their asset management process as they employed passive strategies in managing their listed securities portfolios, though some issues may still arise in property management. One bursar said: 'With trackers and absolute returns strategies in place, there are no stock exclusions.' For another: 'The students have never pressed us on these issues. We do not have any stocks that are blacklisted as a result. We do have issues raised on the environment and countryside issues, thanks to our property holdings. On the equity side, we do not give any specific SRI instructions to our managers.'

As over one-third (36 per cent) of Colleges had varying rates of exposure to indexed strategies (47 per cent of Colleges in Oxford had switched to trackers compared with 22 per cent in Cambridge), these institutions preferred to

Table 11.2. Extent to which SRI features in the asset management process, in per cent

Response	Oxford	Cambridge	Oxbridge
Discussed or reviewed	12	30	20
SRI does not feature	88	70	80

adopt 'engagement' as the chosen SRI option instead of stock screening or exclusion. For those institutions invested in pooled funds, their SRI stance reflected that of the fund. 'We are moving away from direct holdings to pooled funds; not all are in-house products. We still do have individual holdings in Vodafone, Diageo, GlaxoSmithKline. But, the aim is to move into pooled funds. So, we are as ethically responsible as the funds we invest in,' commented one bursar.

While many of the Colleges indicated an openness to review any such concerns as they arose from time to time, the cost associated with implementation and monitoring inhibited an active SRI process. According to the chairman of a large endowment in Oxford:

As far as SRI policy goes, we do not apply any constraint on the sort of companies in which we can invest, although some student members and some faculty think we should. Given that we make significant use of tracker funds, we do not know how exactly that could be implemented. However, we have signed up to the Good Corporation Charter and have instructed our fund managers accordingly. I suppose, the only constraint we have is that other than our tracker funds, we do not invest in tobacco companies.

Implementation of SRI policy in endowment asset management

The implementation of SRI policy in endowment management in Oxford and Cambridge varies from institution to institution. Socially responsible investment considerations take into account the social and ethical record of a company and incorporate that into its long-term financial performance. Stock exclusions are not the best form of SRI policy management; about a quarter (21 per cent) of Oxbridge institutions reported employing such a method, if they had a SRI policy. Exclusion of investments in sectors, such as tobacco, armaments, pornography, animal testing, global warming, and so on, is increasingly gaining favour among philanthropic institutions as these are also the sectors that concern investors, including the students, most.

Engaging to improve a company's social and ethical policy is considered a superior strategy by some SRI investors. While active managers and investors in private equity can 'engage' with companies with regard to their social and ethical policy, other investment styles—such as passive and absolute return strategies—are not easily open to such engagement strategies. Over one-third (38 per cent) of Colleges in Oxford and Cambridge did not include any stock exclusion criteria in their instructions to the fund manager on the subject, while a quarter (26 per cent) reported engaging with the companies concerned. Increasingly, asset management companies offering passive strategies are also including engagement in the SRI process within their own institutions with a view to reflecting the concerns of their clients, while enhancing the long-term performance of investments held within their portfolios.

Exclusion of some sectors and companies was also reported among Colleges in Oxford and Cambridge. 'Broadly speaking, the College would not expect investments in tobacco, defence or similar sectors where SRI issues are clear.' Such was the view of one bursar who had no formal SRI policy in managing the College endowment funds. For another bursar: 'While we have imposed no restrictions whatsoever on our managers, they do not hold now, and we would prefer that they do not ever hold, tobacco stocks or munitions suppliers. Were they to consider such a purchase in the future, they would check with the bursar.' For a third bursar, in Cambridge: 'The College does not invest directly in companies in the tobacco sector or those deriving more than 15 per cent of their total income from the sale of weapons or arma-ments. While being mindful of their duties, the Investments Committee also reserves the right from time to time to exclude other companies whose envi-ronmental policies are deemed to be inconsistent with the College's overall aims.'

Among Colleges that do not mechanically exclude companies from their portfolio, SRI criteria are intrinsically linked to the stock selection process: 'We attempt to make long-term decisions and do not screen stocks on an SRI basis. The way we see it, investing in companies whose major source of income is from tobacco, pornography or child labour is not a good long-term financial investment anyway. So, we aim to achieve best long-term total return consis-tent with prudence dictated by a small endowment,' said one bursar. Thus, some Colleges subscribe to an ethical stance in their investment policy by excluding companies deriving the bulk of their revenue from arms or tobacco, although other issues such as child labour, pornography, or environment are potential concerns. The exclusion decision is based on financial criteria as much as ethical ones.

Table 11.3 provides a breakdown of responses with regard to different approaches to the implementation of SRI policy.

Table 11.3. Methods for implementing SRI policy in Oxbridge Colleges, in per cent

Method	Oxford	Cambridge	Oxbridge
No stock exclusions	53	19	38
Fund manager engages with companies	18	37	26
Stock exclusions (tobacco and arms)	18	26	21
Follow Charity Commission guidelines	3	7	5
Invested in pooled vehicles	3	7	5
Funds managed passively	3	4	3
Bursar manages fund on SRI principles	30	—	2
Total	**100**	**100**	**100**

In most instances, the College bursar is responsible for monitoring SRI issues. Fund managers are expected to include in their quarterly reports any relevant SRI concerns. Managers are also expected to raise such matters at the quarterly investment meetings. As one bursar explained:

We do not have an SRI policy as such. We have left it to the fund manager who includes an SRI statement in the reports. In accordance with our fund manager's SRI policy, their investment process includes research into the social, environmental and ethical stance of companies. Every quarter the fund manager meets with companies, and these meetings are focused on social and environmental risk across their businesses. Companies are encouraged to integrate their SRI risk within central risk management rather than manage it in separate departments.

Our fund manager subscribes to the Association of British Insurer Guidelines, which aims to improve shareholder value by identifying both emerging threats and opportunities. Another topic is biodiversity, on which the fund manager has worked with a number of brokers to encourage awareness. The quarterly review also provides the College with a record of voting on various issues in the companies invested in. However, the College does not follow any particular line in SRI strategy.

Among institutions that follow an active SRI policy, most employ a policy of exclusion. Only one bursar in Cambridge who also directly manages the College endowment indicated engaging directly with the companies concerned: 'We use FTSE4Good as a guide when investing in UK companies. We also engage with the company, if required, to address our SRI concerns instead of disinvesting on the first sign of any problem.' According to another investment bursar, the performance of the fund manager is linked to the companies in which he invests, and thus such action is left to the fund manager:

[SRI] is incorporated into the investment objectives. But, we do not exclude any category of assets. In terms of voting rights, it is delegated to the fund manager. They believe that companies that do not behave in a socially responsible way are also more liable to face financial problems as a consequence. The fund's policy on the exercise of voting rights is that the rights should be exercised by the fund manager, whose primary interest is the financial outcome of the investments.

The implementation of this policy is delegated to the fund manager whose view is that a greater awareness of social responsibility among companies makes for good investment returns over the long term. They think that companies that work against the tide of public opinion are likely to face social sanctions and/or punitive legislation that may lead to poor returns. Our manager encourages companies to research public opinion on social responsibility and follow it in so far as management considers it to be appropriate.

In the words of another Oxford bursar: 'the College concerns itself with SRI issues from time to time—for example, we excluded South Africa in the past. We are aware of SRI issues, but we do not exclude companies from our investment universe *per se*. We expect our fund manager to engage actively in the companies they invest in—i.e. we expect our fund manager to factor in the SRI implications of their investment decision.' Similarly, for another bursar: 'The College has been concerned with such issues in the past—for example, its "no-South Africa policy" some time ago when the College closed its account with Barclays.' But currently the same College does not have any SRI policy in place, though some exclusion could be introduced if the issue aroused sufficient disapproval of the student body as well as the Fellows.

A comparison with US practice among educational institutional endowments that include socially responsible criteria in their investment management shows that a wide range of issues are covered by these institutions. The most prevalent criteria identified by US institutions were companies that do not produce or market tobacco products (69.9 per cent average), followed by companies that do not produce or market alcoholic beverages (47.1 per cent average) and companies that do not engage in commercial gambling or gaming businesses (44.9 per cent average).

Table 11.4 shows which social responsibility criteria were of most concern to US institutions.

Though the practice of including social responsibility criteria is more common among independent institutions than public ones in the United States, there appears to be little difference in their considerations of environmental or social issues. Public colleges and universities are less likely to have an investment policy that precludes them from investing in 'sin' stocks compared to their independent counterparts. For example, only 26.1 per cent of responding public institutions did not invest in companies that produce or market

Table 11.4. US endowments: Social responsibility criteria followed, in per cent

Endowment	A	B	C	D	E	F	G
>$1,000 m	—	—	—	—	87.5	—	12.5
$500–1,000 m	16.7	16.7	16.7	33.3	66.7	33.3	16.7
$100–500 m	15.8	34.2	5.3	36.8	60.5	36.8	28.9
$50–100 m	27.8	22.2	—	61.1	77.8	50.0	22.2
$25–50 m	24.1	20.7	6.9	62.1	72.4	51.7	17.2
<$25 m	27.0	29.7	8.1	51.4	70.3	56.8	29.7
Public	21.7	21.7	17.4	26.1	60.9	21.7	30.4
Independent	21.2	26.5	3.5	51.3	71.7	49.6	23.0
Full Sample Average	**21.3**	**25.7**	**5.9**	**47.1**	**69.9**	**44.9**	**24.3**

A: Adhere to sound environmental policies and practices.
B: Have no significant involvement in weapons manufacturing.
C: Do not produce nuclear energy.
D: Neither produce nor market alcoholic beverages.
E: Neither produce nor market tobacco products.
F: Do not engage in commercial gambling or gaming businesses.
G: Do not violate US child labour law or standards in either domestic or foreign operations.
Source: 2004 NACUBO Study.

alcoholic beverages compared to 51.3 per cent of responding independent institutions.[13]

Conclusion

For trustees of occupational pension schemes in the UK who have been accountable for their ethical and voting policy as much as for their fund's financial performance, the new legislation on SRI does not remove the requirement that trustees must also make decisions that are in the best interests of the plan beneficiaries. Trustees that adopt formal SRI policies therefore face the issue of funding the cost of achieving their SRI goals without breaching their fiduciary duty to treat the interests of beneficiaries as paramount. Apart from actively engaging with companies they invest in, it is not clear how SRI policy legislation can alter the way in which pension fund trustees and their fund managers determine asset allocation and stock selection. Endowments and foundations inevitably have a role to play in this arena. Institutions in Oxford and Cambridge expect their managers to factor in the SRI implications of their investment decision. Many Colleges by simply following the guidelines set out by the Charity Commissioners fulfil their SRI obligations.

In constructing portfolios, endowments and foundations aim to maximize return at any given level of risk. In doing so, they also fulfil their fiduciary duty. While return objectives are easier to define and measure, there is a lack of consensus among investors in all sectors with regard to the definition of risk. Risk is invariably defined more individually. Also, investors are generally happy to incorporate SRI criteria into their investment policy as long as it does not result in lowered expected returns. Despite the rising power of shareholders in influencing corporate policy, major institutional investors prefer to engage with companies in a way that does not impact on their performance.

The undisputed focus for asset managers is on ways of securing superior investment return. Companies with poor corporate governance records could be excluded on financial grounds alone, not because of their weak policies on the environment or society. Also, directing the fund manager to engage in improving a company's social, environmental and corporate practices is considered a superior SRI investment strategy compared to ethical screening as the latter policy can result in the exclusion of a range of companies and may even lead to a bias towards medium and smaller capitalization companies. While SRI strategies are better suited to private equity investments, they are more difficult to implement with absolute return strategies. Index managers also prefer to engage with companies. Thus, engagement is widely recognized as part of any respectable analyst's or investor's responsibility.

12

Performance measurement

Introduction

An integral aspect of asset management is measuring the overall investment performance of the endowment portfolio. The efficient management of relationships between the sponsoring institution and their appointed asset managers is critical. Once managers are appointed, monitoring their performance assists in ensuring that the endowment's investment objectives are met. To that extent, defining the investment objective in clear terms and agreeing with the manager the terms of assessment helps in the monitoring process, simply because different evaluation methods arise from different performance objectives. As long as the fund's investment objectives remain unaltered, it is important for fiduciaries to be disciplined in monitoring manager performance vis-à-vis the established benchmark.

The guidance provided by the Charity Commission in the UK states:

The precise nature of the benchmarks and targets by which the performance of the manager will be judged by the trustees will depend on the size of the investment assets, on the terms of the investment policy which the trustees have formulated, and on the extent of the powers which have been delegated to the manager. It is for individual bodies of trustees to decide what system of benchmarking is appropriate for their charity, and what targets should be set for the manager by reference to the benchmark. In this connection, trustees may wish to take expert advice from someone who is independent of the manager, to enable them to formulate such a system. But some rational system of performance measurement should be devised, and the manager should be made aware of what it is through the policy statement.[1]

According to the data submitted for this study, about half (48 per cent) the institutions in Oxford and Cambridge employed the services of a single asset manager, with a balanced mandate, for the management of the endowment portfolio. Thus, determining a rational basis for measuring the performance of the portfolio should not have posed too difficult a task, even after accounting for direct investments in property. Yet the disclosure of endowment performance among institutions in both Oxford and Cambridge suggests otherwise. The issue is complicated when some of the bursars point out the existence of historical information, albeit not in the public domain, suggesting an institutional reluctance to publicize endowment investment performance or lack of concern for such analysis as a potentially critical tool in endowment asset management.

In the published accounts for 2003–4, for example, 46 per cent of Colleges in Oxford disclosed their annual endowment return compared with 40 per cent of Cambridge Colleges. Those institutions that provided annual performance data were not necessarily the Colleges with a single investment manager. There exists a combination of factors why measurement of the performance of the endowment among institutions in Oxford and Cambridge is not conducted similarly to institutions in the pension fund sector, for example. External performance management consultants are perceived to be expensive by Colleges; such an expense is not seen to add any value to the investment process.

Historically, Oxbridge institutions along with other charitable organizations invested for income. Monitoring the capital value of investments was less important than knowing the investment's expected yield. Property was valued every five years; sometimes valuations were done over even longer periods, every decade or so. Annual valuations were unheard of until recently. There was no advantage in knowing how much property you own if you were not going to sell it. All you needed to know was how much income such assets were likely to yield annually. It was equally irrelevant to know if your securities had appreciated or depreciated if all you needed from it was a certain amount of income.

The move to total return, where annual valuation of investment performance is critical, is a recent development. While Oxbridge institutions have formally moved to total return investing, investment thinking among many remained fixed on income. The high allocation to property is considered desirable, not just for diversification, but for its income-bearing properties. Very few Colleges in Oxford or Cambridge, for example, reported selling a portion of their endowment capital to raise the necessary level of income for operations. Colleges sold property, and retained some of the cash raised for income. But that was more an investment decision; the need to reduce high exposure to property. Some of the gifts to Colleges are accounted for as income. Spending or income from the endowment was principally via dividends, interest, and rental income. Spending 4 per cent of the endowment for these institutions did not imply they sold 4 per cent of their assets annually to raise that amount.

Even among Colleges with a high allocation to hedge funds and private equity, several maintained a large investment in property. As Colleges build up more sophisticated portfolios of private equity and hedge fund investments that mature over a predetermined cycle, annual disposals will result. Currently, most of the income needs of the Colleges are met without resorting to such trading activity. There are always exceptions, of course. It is relevant to note, however, that the ability to raise funds from endowment capital frees up the asset allocation decision-making process.

Not many institutions in Oxford and Cambridge employ an external performance measurement firm. Auditors employed by Oxbridge institutions typically report to the Governing Body, the report is prepared solely for that purpose, in accordance with the Statutes of the College. The Governing Body of each institution in turn is responsible for preparing its report and financial statements in accordance with the provisions of Statutes made by the relevant university under the Universities of Oxford and Cambridge Act 1923 and of the regulations of that College in preparing the annual accounts. Reporting the annual performance of the endowment is not the responsibility of auditors, nor is it part of their due diligence when reporting that the financial statements give a true and fair view, and are prepared in accordance with relevant statutes. As distinct from pension funds, College accounts are not required to comply with Global Investment Performance Standards (GIPS). Oxbridge Colleges are not required to report specifically about the performance of their endowments. The fact that they do so indicates their willingness to adhere to good practice.

Endowment performance measurement

Even among institutions that routinely hire performance measuring services, maintaining a balance between quantitative and qualitative analysis is perceived as the key in evaluating performance. Measuring the performance of any investment enables the relevant investor or committee to review its own processes carefully. Thus, portfolio return data from the external asset managers serve as major inputs in the overall performance assessment process. Though quantitative analysis assists in attributing performance and understanding the sources of risk and return, such analysis appears not to be commonly applied by institutions in Oxford and Cambridge to their own assessment. The majority of Oxbridge institutions measure their investment performance informally and often adopt a qualitative, soft approach rather than use quantitative methods. As a result, weak manager performance alone does not result in manager changes. Other qualitative considerations play an important part. The higher allocation to property among these institutions is also a determining factor.

Three-quarters (75 per cent) of participating Colleges reported informal assessment procedures, with 20 per cent of respondents using the fund manager's report for such analysis, particularly those with single external

Table 12.1. Organization responsible for undertaking performance measurement

Measurer	Oxford	Cambridge	Oxbridge
College	65	89	75
Fund manager	29	7	20
Consultant	6	4	5
Total	**100**	**100**	**100**

managers. A significantly higher number (29 per cent) of Colleges in Oxford used the manager's performance data as the basis of their internal analysis compared with Colleges in Cambridge, where just 7 per cent of institutions reported doing so. Eighty-nine per cent of Cambridge institutions reported analysing investment performance internally. Only three institutions in Oxford and Cambridge (5 per cent of respondents) reported employing external consultants for performance measurement. Table 12.1 summarizes these responses with regard to performance measurement.

As with the hiring of managers, qualitative factors dominate performance evaluations. For example, the sense of partnership between the College and the external manager is rated highly. A diminished sense of partnership, as a result of changes in people or investment philosophy, is more likely to trigger a change in asset manager than indifferent performance for a year or two. Similarly, diminished commitment on the part of the manager is more likely to trigger a reassessment of the relationship with the manager than poor performance. However, formal portfolio analysis or quantitative attribution analysis does not commonly feature in the performance appraisal process.

A large number of institutions in both Oxford and Cambridge measure investment performance of the endowment portfolio internally. An overwhelming 90 per cent of respondents suggested measuring the performance of each asset class in the portfolio against a given benchmark. St John's College, Oxford, for example, reported its investment performance for 2003–4 as follows:

During the year markets have been very difficult: the indices show an increase of 7.1% in the FTSE all share index and an increase in 6.4% in the JPM Global Govt Bond index. The College's UK managed investments showed a total return of 7.3% for the year ended 31st July 2004. Each asset class held produced positive returns, with the exception of overseas bonds where the portfolio recorded a return of −0.8%. For UK equities, the portfolio return of 14.7% was 3.9% ahead of the return of the FTSE All Share Index. Overseas, the FTSE World ex-UK produced a return of 3.9% during the year, whereas the College's portfolio achieved a combined return of 8.6%. The property portfolio shows a total return of 19.9% against the reported IPD return of 16.6%.

St John's College, Oxford, provided details of the performance of its constituent holdings but did not provide the total return achieved by the endowment as a whole. Similarly in 2004–5, the College reported the performance of its various constituent investments as follows: 'The College's UK investment managers reported a total return of 24.3%. The UK equities portfolio return was 28.8% which was 4.1% ahead of the FTSE All Share Index, whereas the overseas equities produced a return of 37.6% against a FTSE World Ex UK index of 23.8%. Overseas Bonds have returned 24.0% against a JP Morgan Global Bond Ex UK Index of 10.7%. Index Linked bonds have achieved lower returns of 13.9% which were nevertheless still ahead of the relevant index. Property has again performed strongly and this asset class shows a total gross return of 33.0% against the IPD index of 18.0%.'

Some Colleges report investment performance without reference to any benchmark return, reporting only the return achieved in various asset classes though not the total return of the endowment. In an entry under 'Investment Performance', St Peter's College, in Oxford, reported: 'The College's policy of making provision not only for the present but also for the future led the Investment Committee to recommend, for the future, a total return policy in favour of one geared to investment income. That fund yielded income of 3.1% and showed capital growth of 3.5%. Cash on the money market produced an income increasing during the year from 3.5% to 4.5%, and income from the University Deposit Pool of 4.1% with capital growth of further 3.4%.' The total annual return of the endowment was not given.

Colleges, such as Trinity and Lincoln in Oxford, indicated a spending rate (3 per cent in both cases) as a return target, but did not specify the actual endowment return. Others, such as Robinson College, in Cambridge, specified the benchmark—'WM Income Constrained Charity Median Return subject to achieving a minimum yield of 1% over the gross yield on the FTSE All Share'— but did not mention the actual return achieved in their published accounts for 2003–4. Similarly, Clare College, Cambridge, stated that 'the College aims to achieve a total return of 7.5 per cent (including inflation) over the long-term,' but did not provide any information on actual returns achieved by its endowment investments.

Clare Hall and Downing College, both in Cambridge, provide extensive information on their investments and performance. Downing's endowment portfolio was in the midst of major restructuring during 2003–4, and these are all recorded in the accounts of the College for the year. For 2004–5, Downing College reported a total return of 13.33 per cent. Some explanation is provided for the relatively lacklustre performance for the year during which the management of the fund was transferred to Morgan Stanley Private Wealth Management. The College in disclosing its detailed asset allocation revealed that it invested in a more diversified portfolio that included equities, fixed income, hedge funds, private equity, property, gold, and cash. Clare Hall and Downing are exceptions rather than the rule in providing asset allocation, total return, and benchmark data. Their performance attribution analysis is far from comprehensive, yet Downing makes an attempt to explain that the 'reduction in UK equities from 58% to 7.08% of the total fund' was a strategic asset allocation decision that may have led to its lower overall return.[2] In the case of Clare Hall, its 17 per cent gross return compared with its customized benchmark return of 16.6 per cent does not give us any information on costs. As benchmarks do not have costs attached, it is not possible to compare the net return on the fund which definitely incurs costs.

Even when accounts of Colleges in Oxford and Cambridge include information on investment performance, they may not indicate the benchmark. Thus, Churchill College in Cambridge gives us a total return figure of 16.5 per cent for 2004–5 for its endowment investments, but no comparable benchmark return. Nor is it clear that the total return is gross or net of costs. Performance numbers may also not be comparable as Colleges account for their performance differently. Sometimes, a College may actually explain how the returns are measured as was the case with Jesus College in Cambridge. The College's annual account for 2004–5 informs us:

There are various ways of calculating the total return made from an investment portfolio. A method commonly used by Cambridge colleges is to express the aggregate of actual investment income and capital gains during the year as a percentage of the average value of the investment assets during the year, net of debt incurred to acquire the assets in question and net of the related finance costs. On this basis the total return during 2004/05 was 18.2%, compared with 12.4% in 2003/04.[3]

While it is reassuring to know the methodology, we are not aware of the College's 'investment objectives' or provided with any comparable benchmark returns; nor are we given a breakdown of investments except the information that the 'College's investments consisted primarily of UK and World Ex-UK Equities, fixed interest funds, funds of hedge funds, commercial property (offices, industrial and retail) (managed by Bidwells) and agricultural property (managed by Savills).' The notes on endowment asset allocation refer to freehold buildings (60.2 per cent), quoted equities (26.9 per cent), quoted fixed income (7.5 per cent), unquoted securities— equities (0.24 per cent), cash with investment managers (0.23 per cent), and Other (4.8 per cent).[4] There is no information relating to the benchmark, if any, for the endowment portfolio. Nor are we told that there is no benchmark. It is very likely such information exists though it is not included in the accounts. However, Jesus is not the only College in this position. Very few Oxbridge institutions provide comprehensive information on all aspects of asset management, simply because they are not required to do so. Those that do disclose some information deserve encouragement for their attempt to be open and transparent in their reporting.

The range of reported benchmarks used for endowment performance measurement varies considerably, extending from market-index-oriented ones to inflation-adjusted rates of return. Returns-based and factor-based style analysis is still in its infancy within the endowment universe in Europe. Benchmarks typically include market indices and universes of comparable investor groups. Creating an appropriate benchmark is perhaps the most important decision that fiduciaries face as the benchmark or the policy portfolio is really the index that captures the active management decisions of the Investment Committee.

One investment bursar explained their performance measurement process in the following words: 'The fund's investment performance is measured on a rolling three-year basis. Performance is compared with the FTSE All Share and FTSE World Indices and the WM Charities Universe. Performance of the geographical sectors is measured against their local indices. When evaluating the performance of the Fund Manager, the Investments Sub-Committee reserves the right also to take into account such other factors as they deem appropriate from time to time.' Further investigation with regard to benchmarks and indices used as well as investment consultants employed in the evaluation process revealed that about one quarter (23 per cent) of institutions employ internally customized benchmarks for such analysis; twice as many Colleges in Oxford as in Cambridge reported the use of customized benchmarks.

While market indices reflect the potential return from the relevant market over any given period, peer group comparisons also provide an insight into the sort of real returns achieved by other active investors. While peer group comparisons have their limitations, if used as an indicator of asset allocation, along with market indices they do provide a guide to returns achieved by other players in the field. Short-term asset allocations can influence performance; hence most institutions use long-term performance data. Performance comparison with its institutional peer group for Oxford and Cambridge poses some obstacles due to the lack of long-term performance data for these institutions.

As there is no external performance measurement service provider for these institutions, nor do the Colleges follow similar standards in reporting performance, an Oxbridge endowment performance benchmark does not exist. Oxford and Cambridge, universities and colleges, consider themselves as being sufficiently distinct in their approaches to endowment asset management as rejecting the term 'Oxbridge' to reflect their collective stance. Clearly the information exists in the archives of individual institutions. But from what we gathered in the course of our exchanges with various bursars, the Colleges have not found an efficient way of accounting for the investment performance of their endowment funds. Sometimes, consultants and external fund managers provide comparative performance analysis. Typically, such analysis is conducted internally and informally.

The publication of the accounts of Oxford University's Colleges for the year to 31 July 2005 was accompanied by an unprecedented press release on behalf of the Colleges stating that the performance of the endowments collectively had been strong: 'On a starting net balance of £1.81 billion, the Colleges achieved a total return of £413 million, an average gain of 23 per cent over the year.' Oxford Colleges have published aggregate data since they moved to publishing their accounts in the new format in 2002–3. Cambridge Colleges are yet to report in a comparable manner. There is no statutory requirement for the Colleges to do so. Thus, these institutions with an array of demands on their time and resources have not prioritized investment performance measurement, particularly during a period of great change.

The two universities of Oxford and Cambridge, of course, have been publishing the performance of their Endowment annually over the years. The Cambridge University Endowment Fund (the Amalgamated Fund) achieved a total return of 20 per cent for the year ending 2005. Oxford University's Endowment Fund, consisting of the Trust Pool, the Capital Fund and the Deposit Pool, achieved total returns of 19, 17.2, and 4.9 per cent, respectively. The Deposit Pool is the largest pool of endowment assets as it includes deposits made by several Colleges into this vehicle. While Oxford University's aggregate total return is not available, it is worth pointing out that these performance numbers relate to that of the assets managed by the Universities of Oxford and Cambridge and do not include that of their respective constituent Colleges.

Thus to compare Cambridge University's 20 per cent return for 2005 with the 19.2 per cent return achieved by Harvard's General Investment Account net of fees and expenses and including the impact of revenue-sharing agreements with certain fund managers, calculated on a time-weighted basis, is not the same thing. Similarly, Yale Endowment's return for 2005 of 22.3 per cent is not strictly comparable with that of the University endowments of Oxbridge, which exclude that of the constituent Colleges. Also, currency factors come into play when returns are measured in different currencies. While in the very long term currency factors do not play a significant role, in the short term they influence performance. For example, between 30 June 2002 and 30 June 2004, the US dollar depreciated by 19 per cent against Sterling. For UK-based investors without any currency hedging in place the impact of such movements would have been quite different from that experienced by US-based investors also invested in the same asset category.

How is performance measured?

With a total return approach to asset allocation increasing, some 45 per cent of institutions in Oxford and Cambridge reported using the WM Charity Unconstrained index as a peer group benchmark. The WM Charity indices are the only benchmarks available to investors within the charitable sector. The WM Performance Services Company provides two indices for charities: one Constrained (by income) and the other Unconstrained. Investors taking a total return approach normally refer to the 'Unconstrained' index as their preferred benchmark.

The prevalence of property investments in Oxbridge endowment portfolios accounts for the use of the IPD All Property index as among the asset indices used in measuring endowment property performance by 40 per cent of Colleges. It is an index that College bursars monitor, but the nature of their very specific holdings are substantially different from the composition of the IPD index. The illiquid nature of property ownership makes it difficult to change the composition of holdings within a short period as well. Thus, a benchmark that deviates significantly from the mix of assets held by Oxbridge institutions serves simply as a comparator for what other property investors are doing in the field.

Taking into account the very specific nature of their holdings, it is even more surprising that Colleges in Oxford and Cambridge never developed an internally customized benchmark for performance measurement. Several Colleges today have created customized benchmarks, but there is no NACUBO type benchmark as in the United States or any other comparable benchmark for these institutions. Several Colleges use the WM Charity benchmarks. As far as market indices are concerned, the FTSE indices are more widely in use compared to those of other providers such as MSCI. The cited benchmarks and methods of measuring performance as reported by the Colleges in Oxford and Cambridge are illustrated in Table 12.2.

A very small number of institutions in Oxford and Cambridge (less than 10 per cent) employed external consultants for their performance evaluation. Oxbridge Colleges do not usually compare their performance with that of US educational endowments, as their asset allocations vary considerably, though the performance of other investors within the charitable sector in the UK is monitored. About half the Colleges used the WM Charity indices as a benchmark. While no institution in Oxford or Cambridge compared its performance with that of top Ivy League educational endowments in the United States, the overall performance and asset allocation of Harvard, Yale, Princeton, and other comparable institutions are monitored closely; the typical Oxbridge bursar is familiar with the asset allocation and performance of major US educational endowments.

Table 12.2. Criteria for appraising endowment performance

Type of benchmark used	Number of colleges	
	Oxford	Cambridge
Customized	18	9
IPD	12	14
WM Charity Unconstrained	10	14
FTSE	2	9
CAPS	3	1
Consultant (Cambridge Associates)	4	0
WM Charity Unconstrained ex property	1	3
WM Charity Constrained	2	1
MSCI	—	2
WM Total Charity Universe	1	0
None	1	1
Not available	3	4

CAPS = Combined Actuarial Performance Services' Pooled Pension Fund survey; FTSE = Financial Times Stock Exchange indices; IPD = Investment Property Database All Property index; MSCI = Morgan Stanley Capital International indices; WM = WM Performance Services.

NB: Total does not add up to 61 Colleges as some indicated the use, albeit informally, of more than one benchmark; e.g. MSCI (securities) and IPD (property).

Performance measurement remains a key weakness among Oxbridge institutions in endowment management. Colleges are only too aware of this shortcoming. There is recognition of the benefits of developing better performance measurement systems. Colleges could benefit by cooperating in this area of investment activity by collectively hiring an external adviser on performance measurement. While a forum for sharing investment-related information exists among the Colleges in both universities, there is no investment league table of the performance of individual endowment funds. As the rationale for asset allocation among these institutions differs widely, they have not felt the need to compare their performances internally. About half the respondents in Oxford and one-third in Cambridge were unable to supply any performance data. Even among Colleges that provided such information, the data were incomplete—reflecting mainly that of the securities portfolio. Historically, Colleges did not evaluate their property assets annually. Such valuation was conducted periodically, over five-to ten-year intervals, though the performance of the securities portfolio was obtained annually from the fund manager.

For the fiscal year 2002–3, an integrated five-year analysis of the performance of the total endowment portfolio was available from over half the institutions in Oxford and Cambridge. Seventeen Colleges in Oxford (50 per cent of participating institutions) and 18 Colleges in Cambridge (67 per cent) provided investment performance data; not all the data provided included the performance of the property portfolio. The investment performance of

Table 12.3. Percentage total returns reported by Oxbridge colleges

Performance	2002	2001	2000	1999	1998
Oxford average	−12.9	−7.7	9.6	10.3	15.2
Cambridge average	−7.8	−0.2	3.8	11.5	9.5
Oxbridge average	**−10.4**	**−3.9**	**6.7**	**10.9**	**12.3**

the Colleges that supplied such data is shown in Table 12.3. On average, Colleges in Cambridge performed better over this period, particularly after 2000, reflecting their conservative allocation to equities and higher allocation to property assets.

According to the *University of Oxford, Financial Statement of the Colleges, 2002–3*, the Colleges recorded improvement in the performance of their endowment, with positive returns for the financial year ending 2003, following 2 years of negative returns. Endowment assets under management in aggregate for the 36 Colleges in Oxford rose from £1.56 billion in 2002 to £1.71 billion in 2003, an increase of 6.87 per cent. Not all the Colleges reported aggregate performance data; over one-third (13 Colleges out of 36) reported endowment performance numbers for the financial year ending 2003, which is illustrated in Table 12.4.

Table 12.4. Endowment performance of Oxford colleges, FY 2003, in per cent

College	Endowment return	Benchmark return
St John's	12.6	na
St Anne's	9.7	na
Christ Church	9.0	3.4
Hertford	8.4	−2.1
Wolfson	7.7	6.4
Lady Margaret Hall	5.5	5.1
St Edmund Hall	5.2	na
Lincoln	5.0	na
Somerville	4.5	na
Jesus	4.4	na
Magdalen	0.6	na
St Hugh's	−0.1	na
St Catherine's	−2.5	7.4
Average	**5.4**	**na**

Even among Oxford Colleges reporting 2002–3 endowment performance, not all reported their benchmark performance, suggesting that at least a few of these Colleges did not have appropriate benchmarks. Among those reporting both actual return and benchmark return, apart from one College, St Catherine's, the remaining Oxford Colleges appear to have outperformed their chosen benchmarks suggesting a high level of selective disclosure of performance

Table 12.5. Endowment performance of Oxford colleges, FY 2004, in per cent

Oxford	Endowment	Benchmark	Cambridge	Endowment	Benchmark
Harris Manchester	20.0	na	Magdalene	23.0	na
The Queen's	12.5	na	Jesus	16.5	na
St Catherine's	12.0	7.5	Clare Hall	15.2	13.7
Somerville	11.3	7.5	Churchill	14.0	na
Merton	11.3	na	Downing	12.8	na
Hertford	11.3	9.8	Trinity Hall	12.5	na
St Anne's	10.2	na	King's	12.0	na
Templeton	9.8	na	Gonville and Caius	12.0	na
Magdalen	9.6	na	New Hall	11.5	na
LMH	8.1	7.9	St Catharine's	7.4	na
Christ Church	7.0	10.7	Selwyn	3.2	na
Jesus	6.7	na	Peterhouse	3.2	na
Oriel	6.1	na	**Average**	**11.9**	**na**
St Hilda's	5.9	8.0			
St Edmund Hall	5.7	na			
Exeter	5.2	na			
St Hugh's	2.5	3.0			
Wolfson	2.0	2.6			
Average	**8.7**	**na**			

data. Comparable data are not available for Cambridge institutions as they did not publish their accounts in the new RCCA (Recommended Cambridge College Accounts) format for the financial year 2002–3. Such information is available for Cambridge Colleges from financial year 2003 to 2004 when 40 per cent of the Colleges published the performance of their endowment investments.

An analysis of investment performance in the published accounts of Colleges in the financial year 2003–4 in Oxford and Cambridge shows that the Colleges in Cambridge that reported their performance (40 per cent) fared better than the Colleges in Oxford (55.6 per cent) that also reported their performance for that year. More Colleges in Oxford included benchmark performance. The only College in Cambridge, Clare Hall, to provide benchmark return along with actual return on the endowment portfolio also specified it was a customized benchmark, as opposed to an index such as FTSE All Share or a peer group benchmark. Some Colleges included a target level of income or expected rate of return from the endowment for spending purposes, but did not specify the benchmark or its return compared to actual return.

Table 12.5 shows stated investment returns and, wherever provided, benchmark returns of Colleges in Oxford and Cambridge that included such information in their 2003–4 published annual accounts.

To arrive at a rough estimate of the overall performance of all the Oxford and Cambridge College endowments (excluding that of the two universities that employ external consultants for their performance measurement) during financial year 2003–4, an attempt was made using the following calculation.

The investment income received by each College endowment was added to the appreciation or depreciation of the endowment assets over the year. The total was then divided by the endowment value at the beginning of the year, thereby giving us an indication of return on investment assets. While such a method of calculation fails to take into account the annual additions and withdrawals made by the Colleges, it does provide some idea of performance (it is worth noting that additions to the endowments are not large and withdrawals average at 3–4 per cent of the overall value of the endowment).

The average rate of return calculated in such a way showed a return of 13.8 per cent for Cambridge Colleges and 10.6 per cent for Oxford Colleges in 2003–4. This compares with the fiscal year 2004 return for the Harvard endowment (HMC) of 21.1 per cent and the Yale endowment of 19.4 per cent. The 2004 NES results for college and university endowments in the United States showed institutions reporting an annual rate of return of 15.1 per cent.[5] US institutions were better geared for a recovery in equity assets compared to Oxbridge Colleges, whose average allocation to property was over a third of total assets.

The main endowment fund of Trinity College, Cambridge, the largest single fund within the Oxbridge endowment universe, achieved a return of 16.2 per cent in 2004. Performance data provided by the University of Cambridge for 2003–4 show that the University's Amalgamated Fund registered a total return of 17.3 per cent for the year compared to the benchmark (WM Charity Universe Average) return of 17.8 per cent. The Cambridge endowment's performance benefited from stock selection in UK equities and emerging markets equity investments. The portfolio was overweight in UK bonds which depressed performance vis-à-vis the benchmark. Stock selection was a positive contributor to performance in the UK and Continental Europe, and asset allocation was marginally positive due to overweighting of cash. Cambridge University's endowment performance measurement was conducted by the WM Company, while Oxford University's was undertaken by Cambridge Associates. The investment performance of the University of Oxford's endowment, consisting of the Trust Pool, the Deposit Pool, and the Capital Fund (along with investments in some private equity and venture capital funds) for the year ending 31 July 2004, was 7.5 per cent for the Trust Pool. University of Oxford's endowment fared better in 2004–5, when the total return for the Trust Pool was 19 per cent.

While endowment returns for 2002–3 and 2003–4 were positive for institutions in Oxford and Cambridge, they still did not provide the earnings necessary to offset cost increases since 2000. When adjusted for Oxbridge inflation and disappointing returns from the endowment over the previous three years, bursars experienced a challenging time not only in the management of their endowments, but also in curbing the operating expenses of their own Colleges. They had to re-evaluate and modify their investment strategies in response to the potential for lower market returns from equities in future. The awareness that higher educational institutions must also operate in the real commercial world was forced upon them by real declines in income. Both universities, for example, called for big fund-raising campaigns to increase the endowment wealth needed for the universities to become financially more independent, and retain their world-class status.

The result of the last few years in the United States also indicates a reversal in performance trends. For the first time in 3 years, the 2003 NES reported a positive endowment performance with 640 institutions reporting an annual return rate of 3.0 per cent, on average, for the fiscal year ending June 2003. This result was an improvement compared with the same indicator for the prior 2 years ending 30 June 2002 and 2001 when institutions reported average rates of return of negative 6.0 per cent and negative 3.6 per cent, respectively.[6]

After a rough 3 year stretch, college and university endowments in the United States experienced improved returns in fiscal year 2004, fuelled by strong equity performance. In general, institutions with high allocations to publicly traded equities and low allocations to fixed-income assets were among the top performers. As noted previously, the equal-weighted rate of return for 2004 NES participants was 15.1 per cent. This was the highest since 1998, and the dollar weighted return was 17.4 per cent, revealing the tendency of larger endowments to outperform smaller endowments. While colleges and universities have a long way to go to repair and recover from the losses of 2000–3, the positive returns achieved since then represent a welcome shift in direction.

As performance indicators for Oxford and Cambridge institutions are not reliable, and only half the Colleges report their performance, it is not possible to make any meaningful comparisons between Oxbridge endowment investment performance with their US counterparts or with US educational endowments in general. Differences in asset allocation remain a key factor, yet anomalies arise on examining the performance data. Thus, in 2001 the losses reported by educational endowments in the United States were similar to those sustained by reporting institutions in Oxford and Cambridge (−3.6 per cent according to NES and −3.9 per cent for Oxbridge); currency fluctuations notwithstanding.

In 2002, losses reported by institutions in Oxford and Cambridge were −10.4 per cent compared to −6 per cent for US endowments, both measured in local currencies. Between end-June 2001 and end-June 2002, the US dollar lost 8.3 per cent of its value against sterling. With their typically high allocation to property, Oxford and Cambridge Colleges would normally have fared better over this period as equities declined but the property market in the UK held its own. It is possible to argue that Oxford and Cambridge institutions that fared well failed to report. While no data exist for Cambridge Colleges

Table 12.6. Oxford college endowment returns versus size of endowment

Endowment	No. of colleges	Average assets	Average return (%)
>£100 m	5	£142 m	10.7
£50–100 m	7	£72 m	9.6
£25–50 m	10	£33 m	8.4
<£25 m	14	£14 m	4.8

for 2003, the 5.4 per cent achieved by the Colleges reporting performance in Oxford compares well with the 3 per cent reported by the NES. Between end-June 2002 and end-June 2003, the US dollar lost a further 8.4 per cent of its value.

Asset size appears to have some impact on overall investment performance, though some of the highest performing endowment funds in both Oxford and Cambridge were not among the largest in Oxbridge. Table 12.6 provides a breakdown of returns of Oxford Colleges in 2002–3, in terms of size of endowment assets under management.

The average investment return of Oxbridge institutions with endowment assets worth over £100 million was superior (13 per cent for Cambridge and 11 per cent for Oxford) to the average returns achieved by institutions with less than £100 million (12 per cent for Cambridge Colleges and 10 per cent for Oxford Colleges). This differential was significantly higher during 2002–3, when stock markets had not recovered strongly, and Colleges with higher allocations to property assets fared better. The top 5 Colleges in Oxford, in terms of investment performance and with endowments worth over £100 million, achieved significantly higher returns compared to Colleges whose endowments were worth less than £25 million. Differences in asset allocation and the ability to spend more on the investment management process may have influenced the performance of richer institutions in Oxford and Cambridge.

Conclusion

Performance measurement helps to determine whether a manager is able to add value to the investment process. If the value added comes from strategic asset allocation alone, then fiduciaries either need to change managers or invest in trackers. Such decisions depend on the identification of the sources of return in a portfolio. A manager may perform well due to a range of reasons that are external to the decisions taken by the manager. Long-term performance attribution helps in differentiating between skill and luck. As strategic asset allocation is usually determined by the Investment Committee, the appointed fund manager typically adds value by stock selection, some-times by tactical asset allocation. Where there is a single manager involved, the manager is often also responsible for overall asset allocation, in which case it is worth knowing where the skill of the manager lies.

As institutions in Oxford and Cambridge do not rely on external, inde-pendent evaluation of their performance or of their managers, the overall question of performance measurement in the context of total return investing remains a major concern. Given the orientation towards property, lack of consultants in the investment process, institutional fragmentation and lack of a common model, the whole issue of performance measurement is a hot potato. The launch of pooled funds such as OXIP does not resolve this issue. Even if some Colleges allocate let us say 50 per cent of their assets to this fund, the issue of performance measurement is not automatically resolved. It is unlikely that Colleges will opt to invest all their endowment assets in such vehicles; hence measurement issues relating to other assets under management, such as property, will remain in the context of determining the performance of total assets under management.

Colleges should therefore seriously consider pooling their resources in hiring an external consultant to provide such a service, as such evaluation will enable them to assess objectively the returns they are able to achieve compared to their peer group both in the UK and abroad. Current endowment asset management practice among Oxford and Cambridge institutions is far from efficient. There are too many participants in the investment process without any real value addition. As indicated in Chapter 2, the total number of investment committee members reported by the participating institutions was 477. Taking into account the 224 fund managers employed, over 700 individuals were involved in managing endowment assets worth £4.3 billion. During 2003–4, investment returns recorded by Oxford institutions ranged between 2 and 20 per cent and 3 and 23 per cent in the case of Cambridge institutions. While aggregate asset allocation appears to be superior to indi-vidual allocation, the dispersion in the range of investment returns achieved suggests that the current investment management model could be improved.

If each College investment committee in Oxford is considered a specialist fund manager operating within a larger umbrella organization, the Univer-sity, the structure is similar to that of the Capital Group, where individual analysts and portfolio managers have discretion in managing assets. If we then examine the returns achieved by the Colleges and the University, there is not enough value addition to justify the time and expense associated with such activity. In any organization where one manager delivers 12 per cent and another 5 per cent, without any clear differentiation of the scope of the investment universe, the lesser performing manager would have a lot of explaining to do. Unless investment strategies delivering short-term poor returns were very clearly explained, the manager would certainly be fired. It is not clear that the poorly performing Oxbridge institutions put themselves through such scrutiny.

The ones that do are among the top-quartile performers anyway. As stated in Chapter 3, the bursar of Hertford College in Oxford, Roger Van Noorden, who has been managing the endowment over the past 40 years or so, secured 12 per cent annual compound growth on the College endowment investments. When asked about the real rate of return achieved by the endowment over this period, his reply was: 'Our long-term return net of income is 7.75 per cent annually; we could have invested in the index and secured similar returns.' If the difficulty of beating the index and the complexity of the investment process was better appreciated among Oxford and Cambridge institutions, Colleges could have saved significantly on costs and resources expended on the endowment management process.

Effective and fair assessment of the investment manager's performance and that of the investment committee itself is critical to the long-term success of any investment process. It involves the investment committee members in agreeing with the investment manager appropriate benchmarks and targets against which performance would be judged, and having recorded those benchmarks and targets in the policy statement so that manager performance may duly be monitored. Members should also consider comparing the returns achieved on the endowment portfolio in aggregate and assess the success of their own asset allocation policies.

Relatively larger allocation to property should be perceived as a strategic asset allocation decision; it should not be used as an excuse for not making proper performance evaluations. Colleges should regularly assess how the manager has performed against the agreed benchmarks and targets, and they should review their asset allocation decisions based on such analysis. It is encouraging that Oxford and Cambridge institutions have held their own during the recent bear market period. As markets have recovered and uncertainty surrounds future return expectations from traditional asset classes, proper assessment of endowment allocation and performance is more important than before.

13

Endowment management cost

Introduction

One important area for periodic review for all investors is the overall cost incurred in investment management. Monitoring the manager includes such review. Typically, there are two elements: one is the fee charged by the investment manager. In addition, there are other costs that may not always be transparent, such as expenses associated with dealing, research, custody, administration, taxes, and cash management. These costs do not include the market impact of transactions on behalf of the portfolio, though the price pressure from trading is more often associated with larger funds than smaller ones. (These costs may be ameliorated by the lower transaction costs and efficient crossing networks of large investment firms.) Traditionally, the fee charged by the asset manager was related to the value of funds under management rather than to the performance of the asset manager.

The rise of asset classes, such as hedge funds and private equity, the introduction of performance-related fees and the wider use of pooled and/or indexed vehicles as well as ETFs (Exchange Traded Funds) and other derivative instruments, has generated a higher degree of complexity in cost evaluation among investors. Whether the institution is receiving the best value from its investment management arrangements is therefore an area where investment committees of larger endowments and foundations typically seek independent professional advice.

Asset-based compensation arrangements that fail to consider the value-added aspect of investment management may result in the manager losing focus on return generation. It is important for fiduciaries therefore to establish compensation terms that reward managers for delivering higher risk-adjusted returns. As Swensen reminds us, 'Agency issues arise when fee-collecting asset managers profit at the expense of return-seeking investors. . . . Conflicts exist between the goals of principals and agents. Principals [i.e. colleges] wish to pay fair, competitively determined fees for financial services. Agents [i.e. fund managers] prefer larger, less-transparent means of compensation. Sophisticated asset owners engage principal-oriented agents to reduce the impact of conflicts and increase the alignment of interests.'[1]

Investors aiming to beat the odds by pursuing active management strategies face a wide range of obstacles, from manager selection to significantly higher costs in alternative asset investments. Thus, identifying and monitoring the performance of a group of skilled managers with whom long-term relationships can be developed is critical to a successful long-term investment strategy. Distinguishing between manager skill and good fortune not only involves a very clear understanding of the manager's investment philosophy, but also requires regular and close scrutiny of investments and performance evaluation. Most investors have limited access to truly unbiased, independent, and objective analysis and advice.

Identifying high-quality managers with a view to establishing long-term relationships is widely recognized within Cambridge and Oxford as making a significant contribution to investment success. In several cases, low manager turnover has helped in keeping costs down. Regular face-to-face meetings between Oxbridge institutions and their external managers constitute an important tool in measuring performance, particularly when active strategies are employed. Among Colleges investing directly in pooled or mutual funds, the choice can be limited in terms of understanding the true nature of associated costs though investment management companies are increasingly obliged to report all costs and their impact on long-term returns. Intangible costs, such as the market impact of a large buy/sell decision, are more difficult for lay mutual fund investors to keep track of.

Investing imposes costs as agents need to be appointed. It is important therefore to appoint agents that are more likely to behave like owners. Beyond the visible fees, investors have to manage costs associated with asset growth and portfolio turnover; sensible investors therefore seek out high-quality managers that are competitively priced. Inevitably, such a process can be challenging. If there appears to be no such thing as a competitively priced active manager with a good long-term performance record, then passively managed funds typically offer a solution as they are usually cheaper and offer better value compared with active managers that seek to replicate the index. Quite often, investing in indexed funds can be more efficient.

The overall cost of managing endowment assets was reported by the majority of Colleges in Oxford and Cambridge in their published annual accounts for 2003–4. Seventy-eight per cent of Colleges in Oxford disclosed the expenditure incurred in managing the endowment compared with 73 per cent of Colleges in Cambridge. This was an encouraging finding, as understanding and managing the cost of investing the endowment assets is an important skill. Such disclosure is not mandatory in their annual reports and accounts.

It is worth noting that these institutions are more open than they are generally given credit for.

Several Colleges did not include such information in their accounts; a few (six Colleges in Oxford) reported nil endowment management costs. These institutions reported their performance net of fees. Clearly managers do not provide services for free, and Colleges incur costs. As fund managers report cost-adjusted performance, and the Colleges' accounting methods do not require them to identify such costs, they do not appear in the annual accounts. Such a method of reporting is not unique to Colleges in Oxford and Cambridge. Institutions in the United States, such as Harvard and Yale, also do not identify the true cost of endowment management in their annual accounts and reports; only performance net of fees.

Very few institutions in Oxford and Cambridge were able to provide a breakdown of endowment management costs in terms of investment management fees, fees for active and passive management, transaction fees, custodial fees, consultant fees, performance measurement fees along with other internal costs. Not many Colleges report performance-based fees except in relation to investments in private equity and hedge funds. Investments in alternative assets being low in Oxford and Cambridge, the bulk of assets is typically invested in listed securities that incur fees based on the value of assets under management. Property assets are priced very differently and the costs vary among the Colleges. As property is a significant component of their assets, costs associated with the management of these assets have an impact on overall costs of endowment asset management.

The shift to performance-related fees is a recent development within the endowment universe in Europe. The Wellcome Trust, for example, very recently moved away from fixed fees towards performance-related fees for its appointed managers, enabling the Trust to contain its investment management costs, which as a percentage of total assets had doubled during the course of 1996–2003. Over this period the Trust's portfolio was strategically restructured, its exposure to alternative strategies raised, and more funds under management were charged performance-related fees.

Among the two university endowments in Oxford and Cambridge, the financial statements published by the University of Oxford, for example for 2003–4, do not identify costs associated with managing the endowment. The Cambridge University Reporter, on the other hand, includes such costs. While a detailed breakdown of costs was not available for the University of Cambridge's endowment management, the securities portfolio managed for over 48 years by F&C Management Limited cost the University 0.15 per cent of assets inclusive of all costs, while the cost of property assets managed by LaSalle Investment Management Limited was 2 per cent of capital value.

Oxford Colleges: Endowment management costs

Of the 36 Colleges in the University of Oxford whose financial statements are published annually, 28 Colleges reported costs associated with endowment asset management for fiscal year 2003–4. The remaining Colleges (Balliol, Harris Manchester, Keble, Linacre, Mansfield, St Hilda's, St Hugh's, and St Peter's) either did not report costs or indicated their endowment management costs as being nil. These Colleges were not included in our calculations. To derive the cost of endowment asset management as a percentage of assets under management, we divided the reported expenditure for endowment management in 2003–4 by the value of the endowment at the start of the year, that is at the end of financial year 2002–3.

Such analysis revealed that endowment management costs as a percentage of assets varied significantly—from a low of 0.06 per cent for Worcester College to a high of 0.94 per cent for Wadham College. The exception was Templeton College with costs at 6.8 per cent. Further investigation revealed that Templeton's costs did not refer to amounts paid to their fund manager, but other costs associated with fulfilling the purposes of the endowment. According to its annual account for 2003–4, Templeton College reported holding 89 per cent of its endowment in cash on deposit in the money market, for which commercial rates of interest were obtained. The permanent endowment was invested in the Global Growth & Income Fund for charities, managed by Mellon Investment Funds. The annual accounts did not provide any explanation for the high-endowment management costs, nor did they define the nature of these costs. While the cost for investing the endowment appears to have been minimal, alternative costs associated with fulfilling its objectives and purposes were high.

Thus, excluding Templeton College due to its unusual method of accounting, the average cost for the 27 Colleges in Oxford was 0.45 per cent in 2003–4. Richer Colleges had a higher cost structure; 0.6 per cent for Colleges with assets worth more than £60 million compared with 0.38 per cent for Colleges with assets worth less than £60 million. Colleges with higher allocation to property (such as Oriel, Corpus Christi, and Wadham) also reported higher costs, though their total assets under management were less than the average for this group. Richer Colleges with higher exposure to property investments also incurred higher costs. Colleges such as University, Merton, and Christ Church with 49, 47, and 41 per cent respectively invested in land and property holdings registered higher costs as the management of property involves higher management costs. Some of the richer Colleges had higher exposure to alternative strategies, which are also relatively more expensive to manage. Significantly, the College with the highest allocation to alternative strategies in Oxford and Cambridge (St Catherine's College, Oxford) reported

Table 13.1. Oxford endowment management costs, 2003–4, in per cent

College	Costs as % of AUM
All Souls	0.45
Brasenose	0.21
Christ Church	0.77
Corpus Christi	0.86
Exeter	0.48
Hertford	0.47
Jesus	0.37
LMH	0.29
Lincoln	0.26
Magdalen	0.41
Merton	0.80
New	0.43
Nuffield	0.55
Oriel	0.87
Pembroke	0.13
The Queen's	0.38
St Anne's	0.42
St Anthony's	0.18
St Catherine's	0.14
St Edmund Hall	0.42
St John's	0.90
Somerville	0.11
Trinity	0.32
University	0.80
Wadham	0.94
Wolfson	0.22
Worcester	0.06
Average	**0.45**

relatively modest costs in managing its endowment worth £34.7 million in 2003–4.

Table 13.1 summarizes the cost of managing the endowment assets of Oxford Colleges as a percentage of assets under management (AUM) for 2003–4.

As a percentage of total costs incurred by Oxford Colleges, endowment management costs amounted to an average of 4.4 per cent. In general, the richer institutions spent a higher proportion on endowment management compared to less wealthy Colleges. The five Oxford Colleges, with endowments of over £100 million in 2003–4, committed an average 10 per cent of their total expenditure to asset management, while Colleges with endowment assets between £50 million and £100 million spent 5.8 per cent. This compared with 1.4 per cent of total expenditure among Colleges with assets worth under £50 million in 2003–4.

The top five Colleges in Oxford, with endowments worth over £100 million, also achieved significantly higher investment returns compared to Colleges whose endowments were worth less than £25 million. See Table 12.6 for a breakdown of investment returns of Oxford Colleges in 2002–3, in terms of size of endowment assets under management. The performance differential between the Colleges with the largest and smallest sized endowments was noticeable. Differences in asset allocation and the ability to spend more on the investment management process may have influenced the performance of richer institutions in Oxford and Cambridge.

Colleges with higher exposure to property assets also reported higher costs. The 11 Colleges (about one-third, 30.6 per cent) in Oxford with property assets over 40 per cent of endowment assets spent on average over 7 per cent of total costs on endowment management. Colleges with property assets over 10 per cent of endowment assets spent 3.8 per cent of total costs on endowment management. And Colleges with less than 10 per cent of the endowment in property spent less than 1 per cent of total expenditure on endowment management.

Table 13.2 provides a breakdown of the ratio of endowment management costs to total costs of Colleges, the size of the endowment, and the percentage of assets in property, as reported for the fiscal year 2003–4.

There is considerable scope for efficient sharing of information within endowment management among these institutions. From costs to asset allocation, spending rules to investment performance of managers, there could be better pooling of resources among Colleges. While some bursars indicated that a certain amount of information sharing was already taking place, some 60 per cent of respondents indicated having no idea how their own fee structure compared with that of their peer group. About 70 per cent of bursars also indicated that greater access and availability of information on endowment management costs would be a useful tool in their overall investment decision-making. On average, bursars were not too concerned about the costs associated with managing their endowment assets, except with regard to consultancy fees which were perceived as offering inadequate value.

Cambridge Colleges: Endowment management costs

Of the 30 Colleges in the University of Cambridge whose financial statements are published annually, 19 Colleges (63 per cent) reported costs associated with endowment asset management for fiscal year 2003–4. The remaining Colleges (Christ's, Clare Hall, Emmanuel, Jesus, New Hall, Queens', Robinson, St John's, Selwyn, Trinity, and Wolfson) either did not report costs or did not present accounts in the new format. The exclusion of these Colleges from our calculations distorts the overall conclusion as some of the richest Colleges fall into this category. To derive the cost of endowment asset management as a percentage of assets under management, we divided the reported expenditure

Table 13.2. Oxford endowment management costs, 2004, per cent of total expenditure

College	Endowment £ m	Property %	Management cost %
All Souls	155.8	45.0	12.2
Balliol	41.3	8.2	na
Brasenose	62.3	17.9	2.4
Christ Church	180.9	41.1	8.2
Corpus Christi	41.5	49.7	7.8
Exeter	30.1	14.6	3.2
Harris Manchester	2.2	0.0	0.0
Hertford	31.5	0.0	2.5
Jesus	99.5	57.6	5.2
Keble	17.9	0.0	0.0
LMH	20.1	0.0	1.0
Linacre	5.1	0.0	0.0
Lincoln	37.7	55.0	1.8
Magdalen	108.9	17.9	4.9
Mansfield	5.9	0.0	0.0
Merton	96.7	47.8	9.7
New	62.1	35.3	3.1
Nuffield	112.4	40.8	9.0
Oriel	50.3	79.2	6.6
Pembroke	23.3	1.9	0.6
The Queen's	95.6	46.8	5.8
St Anne's	19.7	0.0	1.2
St Anthony's	21.2	1.8	0.9
St Catherine's	34.7	3.5	0.8
St Edmund Hall	18.6	9.6	1.5
St Hilda's	23.7	0.0	0.0
St Hugh's	15.3	0.0	0.0
St John's	210.7	28.3	15.3
St Peter's	16.9	23.6	na
Somerville	27.8	2.0	0.6
Templeton	1.0	0.0	1.5
Trinity	49.4	24.3	3.6
University	67.5	48.7	8.0
Wadham	34.1	45.7	4.5
Wolfson	20.2	20.8	1.3
Worcester	18.1	27.8	0.2

for endowment management in 2003–4 by the value of the endowment at the start of the year, that is at the end of financial year 2002–3.

Such analysis revealed that endowment management costs as a percentage of assets varied significantly—from a low of 0.07 per cent for Newnham College to a high of 1.89 per cent for Lucy Cavendish College. The average cost was 0.56 per cent. Of the two Colleges in Cambridge with endowment assets worth over £100 million, both opted not to disclose in their published annual accounts for 2003–4 the cost associated with endowment management. Of the 10 Colleges in Cambridge with endowment assets worth over £50 million but less than £100 million, two did not report such expenditure. Among Colleges that disclosed endowment management costs, those with the highest costs as a percentage of endowment assets at the start of the year included Gonville and Caius and Corpus Christi. These Colleges are among the wealthier ones; they also had higher allocation to property in their portfolios, 46.2 per cent for Gonville and Caius and 52.5 per cent for Corpus Christi in 2003–4. Of the three Colleges in Cambridge that reported endowment management costs and had assets worth over £60 million, the average cost was 0.71 per cent compared to the average cost for the less wealthy Colleges of 0.53 per cent.

With many of the richer Cambridge Colleges opting not to disclose endowment management costs, it is not possible to infer that Colleges with larger endowments and/or higher allocation to property incurred higher endowment management costs, as was the case in Oxford. Cambridge Colleges, like King's with an endowment portfolio worth £90 million in 2004, of which 23 per cent was invested in property, reported among the lowest endowment management costs in Cambridge. King's was not the exception. Peterhouse, Pembroke, and Trinity Hall with assets worth £75.5 million, £59.6 million, and £65.6 million, respectively in 2003–4, and with relatively higher allocations to property (84 per cent in the case of Peterhouse and 52 per cent for Pembroke though Trinity Hall had only 12.6 per cent) reported lower than average endowment management costs among Cambridge Colleges.

Table 13.3 summarizes the cost of managing the endowment assets as reported by the 19 Cambridge Colleges for 2003–4.

Table 13.3. Cambridge endowment management costs, 2003–4, in per cent

College	Costs as % of AUM
Lucy Cavendish	1.89
Gonville and Caius	1.46
Corpus Christi	1.08
Darwin	0.77
Clare	0.70
Downing	0.70
Fitzwilliam	0.57
Peterhouse	0.50
Sidney Sussex	0.49
Hughes Hall	0.42
St Edmund's	0.31
Churchill	0.31
St Catharine's	0.29
Magdalene	0.27
Pembroke	0.25
Trinity Hall	0.22
Girton	0.21
King's	0.17
Newnham	0.07
Average	**0.56**

Among Colleges with smaller endowments, 28 per cent opted not to disclose endowment management costs in their published annual accounts. For those Colleges that did provide the information, the dispersion of endowment management costs as a percentage of endowment assets varied considerably—from a high of 1.9 per cent of assets to a low of 0.07 per cent. Lucy Cavendish College, with an endowment worth £6.7 million in 2004, of which 5 per cent was in property, reported the highest management cost in Cambridge. Newham College, with £41.6 million of endowment assets in 2004 and 10 per cent invested in property, reported the lowest costs.

The average cost of 0.56 per cent of endowment assets under management as reported by the 19 Cambridge Colleges is higher than the average reported by the Oxford Colleges with the exception of Templeton. The higher exposure to alternative assets among Oxford Colleges should have led to higher costs for these institutions. The fact that they have been able to manage costs while diversifying assets across managers and investment styles suggests that the strategy of pooling assets when investing in alternatives, such as private equity and hedge funds, enabled Oxford Colleges to secure an attractive deal thereby optimizing their cost structure. As investments in alternative strategies were low, even among Oxford Colleges, its cost impact would not have been significant. More Colleges in Oxford reported passive strategies compared to Cambridge, which may account for some of the cost efficiency. Long-term relationships with managers, both in equity and property, also contributed to lower costs. It is worth mentioning that the University of Cambridge's endowment asset management costs have been relatively low, thanks to its long-term relationship with its asset manager, F&C Asset Management.

None of this fully accounts for why Cambridge Colleges spend more on endowment management. While they reported superior investment returns when compared with the returns achieved by Oxford Colleges, the lack of long-term data relating to endowment management cost, asset allocation, investment returns, etc. make it difficult to conclude whether asset allocation decisions implemented by Cambridge Colleges resulted in higher returns. It is difficult, for example, to determine whether higher returns were the result of strategic asset allocation decisions taken by the investment committee or were driven mainly by superior manager selection and/or tactical asset allocation. It is also not possible to suggest that implementing such strategies resulted in higher costs.

As a percentage of total costs, endowment management costs of Cambridge Colleges amounted to an average of 3.4 per cent. This compares with 4.4 per cent for Oxford Colleges. It is worth noting that the average total expenditure among Colleges in Cambridge is higher than that made by Colleges in Oxford; £5.7 million for Oxford in 2003–4 compared with £6.6 million in Cambridge. As several of the Colleges in Cambridge did not disclose their expenditure on endowment management, it is not possible to analyse if richer Colleges in Cambridge also spent a higher proportion of their total expenditure on endowment management as was evident in Oxford. Nor it is clear whether higher allocation to property impacted on endowment management costs.

Twenty per cent of Colleges in Cambridge reporting investment management costs spent more than 5 per cent of their total expenditure on the endowment compared to almost twice as many (39 per cent) Colleges in Oxford. The average for the six wealthier Cambridge Colleges was 8 per cent compared with 8.4 per cent for the 11 Oxford Colleges. There was greater disparity in distribution of costs as well within each group in Cambridge; for example, among the richer Colleges Gonville and Caius spent 14 per cent of its total expenditure on endowment management compared to 10 per cent for St John's, but King's spent only 1 per cent of its total annual expenditure on investment management.

Table 13.4 provides a breakdown of the ratio of the endowment management costs to total costs of Cambridge Colleges along with the size of the

Table 13.4. Cambridge endowment management costs, 2004, per cent of total expenditure

College	Endowment £ m	Property weighting %	Management cost %
Christ's	59.4	na	na
Churchill	31.2	20.0	1.13
Clare	53.1	30.5	6.48
Clare Hall	9.5	10.9	na
Corpus Christi	52.8	52.5	7.64
Darwin	11.0	2.4	3.42
Downing	29.9	40.9	2.13
Emmanuel	78.3	31.7	1.83
Fitzwilliam	16.2	26.6	2.14
Girton	36.1	14.7	0.98
Gonville and Caius	87.8	46.2	13.77
Hughes Hall	2.4	0.0	0.58
Jesus	77.8	53.8	na
King's	90.1	23.0	1.16
Lucy Cavendish	6.7	5.2	5.76
Magdalene	33.6	45.7	2.05
New Hall	22.6	28.3	na
Newnham	41.6	10.1	0.45
Pembroke	59.6	51.6	1.74
Peterhouse	75.5	83.8	4.96
Queens'	42.1	12.0	na
Robinson	11.8	0.0	0.79
St Catharine's	27.8	43.7	0.52
St Edmund's	7.7	0.0	2.26
St John's	232.0	63.7	9.92
Selwyn	17.7	0.0	na
Sidney Sussex	27.6	17.2	3.76
Trinity	649.9	0.0	na
Trinity Hall	65.6	12.6	1.17
Wolfson	5.2	0.0	na

endowment and the allocation to property as reported for the fiscal year 2003–4.

Like their counterparts in Oxford, Cambridge College bursars also do not share much information among themselves on costs. While a few bursars indicated having some knowledge of comparative costs associated with endowment management, an overwhelming 85 per cent of respondents reported having no knowledge of how their own fee structure compared with that of their peer group. Some 88 per cent of Cambridge bursars also said that the availability of comparative information on endowment management costs would be a good thing.

Comparison with the United States

The cost of managing endowment assets among institutions in Oxford and Cambridge is comparable to the costs reported by universities in the United States where the average investment management and custody fees were reported by NACUBO as 0.5 per cent. Some institutions reported additional non-recurring expenses averaging 1.2 per cent.[2] Table 13.5 shows the costs reported by institutions participating in the 2004 NACUBO Endowment Study.

It is worth noting that US academic institutions with endowment assets worth between $500 million and $1 billion reported the highest costs associated with investment management and custody followed by public institutions. The lowest fees were reported by institutions with assets over $50 million but less than $100 million. Institutions with the smallest endowments did not incur high investment management fees, though their non-recurring expenses were significantly higher.

Table 13.5. Endowment management costs for US educational institutions, in per cent

Endowment	Management & custody	Non-recurring expenses
>$1,000 m	0.5	0.5*
$500–1,000 m	0.7	—
$100–500 m	0.5	1.2
$50–100 m	0.4	3.0*
$25–50 m	0.5	3.5
<$25 m	0.5	6.1*
Public	0.6	0.8
Independent	0.5	1.5
Full Sample Average	**0.5**	**1.2**

* Fewer than 10 institutions responding. 695 institutions provided some information on fees. Data are dollar-weighted.
Source: 2004 NACUBO Study.

According to the Commonfund Benchmarks Study of educational endowments, nearly three-quarters (73 per cent) of the institutions participating in the 2005 Study were able to report costs associated with managing their investment programs. The larger institutions (74 per cent) were more able to identify their external management fees compared to their smaller peers (60 per cent), perhaps reflecting the fact that they were able to employ larger staff to track and manage these costs or the fact that more substantial amounts of money are involved. The average cost was 71 basis points (a basis point is equal to 0.01 per cent). The average cost in basis points was not that dissimilar between the largest and the smallest endowments, at 65 and 68 basis points, respectively. Endowments worth over $500 million but under $1 billion were the most likely to incur the highest expenses; this group of institutions reported average costs of 78 basis points. What is included in these fee calculations varied significantly among US endowments. While 96 per cent were able to include investment management fees and 76 per cent custodial fees, just 54 per cent included consulting fees, 47 per cent reported transaction costs, and only 14 per cent included internal costs associated with the investment programme. All costs are, more often, included by larger institutions, and significantly, these institutions were more likely to factor in their internal costs.[3]

Conclusion

At first glance, costs associated with endowment management for Oxford and Cambridge institutions appear to be aligned with that of the industry globally with Oxford reporting greater efficiency in managing such expenditures. Oxbridge costs also compare favourably with that of the philanthropic sector in the UK which averages at 1 per cent of assets per annum among smaller charities, according to one study.[4] Average costs, however, do not reflect asset allocation decisions, the nature of strategies implemented, the level of risk, Sharpe (i.e. reward-to-risk) ratios achieved, or other services delivered to the client.

Taking into account the more traditional approaches to investing within Oxford and Cambridge institutions, a higher level of pooling and/or indexing could reduce costs further; or a higher level of investment service could be secured at the same expense. Colleges currently do not employ any performance measurement consultants; internal pooling in securing such service could address the gap in current practice. The size of the opportunity can be assessed by considering that, for example, the £2 billion currently under fragmented management in Oxford is costing the collegiate University around £10 million per annum, which might be put to greater advantage.

Lowering costs may not be the main objective of these institutional investors that appear to have secured attractive terms with their fund managers over decades. Asset managers have been willing to include such prestigious names in their client list for a competitive fee. One of the reasons why fees have remained low is these institutions have retained the services of their managers over long periods. The low fee charged by F&C Management to the University of Cambridge is a good example; the securities portfolio managed for over 48 years by the asset manager cost the University 0.15 per cent of assets inclusive of all costs. What is not known is the opportunity cost of such an arrangement.

Frequent manager changes would certainly have resulted in fee reviews leading to higher charges. Going forward, Colleges in Oxford and Cambridge could manage investment costs efficiently by introducing performance-related fees with their managers. It may not necessarily lower costs associated with endowment management; it would help to clarify investment objectives and focus manager skills on securing superior investment returns. If Oxford and Cambridge institutions could enhance the overall performance of their endowments at the same cost by acquiring services that equipped them to make better-informed decisions, it would enable them to spend more on their operations.

Successful exploitation of market inefficiencies and timely pursuit of contrarian investment strategies, for example, enabled Yale to create substantial wealth for the University. Over the 10 years ending June 2004, Yale added $5.4 billion to its net wealth thereby enhancing the University's spending power. The story is similar at Harvard, Princeton, and other Ivy League institutions. If Oxbridge institutions enhanced endowment returns by just 1 per cent, that would generate £46.6 million. Currently, these institutions spend around half that sum on endowment management. The question is: Are they getting the best value for money?

14

Fund-raising: Role of gifts

Introduction

Growth in endowment value is achieved through a combination of factors—performance of the policy portfolio, superior performance (enhancing return at same level of risk), spending prudently, and securing new gifts. The endowment's growth and its income stream are therefore reliant on gifts to the endowment in addition to skilled investment management and prudent spending. Unlike academic institutions, whose endowment assets are periodically augmented by alumni and benefactors, not all philanthropic institutions are privileged to boost their asset base via gifts and donations. The Wellcome Trust's assets, for example, are linked directly to the performance of its investment portfolio. The ability of educational institutions to access income from diverse sources also frees them to pursue investment strategies that focus on long-term returns, enabling them to maximize the level of affordable risk.

In the United States, according to the *NACUBO Study*, average endowment growth from gifts was 6.0 per cent while growth from appreciation and investment income was over twice that at 15.6 per cent. As shown in Table 14.1, the gift flow rate, combining individual gifts and bequests with other gifts, was slightly higher for independent institutions than public ones—6.3 per cent versus 5.3 per cent. Public and independent institutions reported similar addition rates for appreciation and investment income—15.9 per cent versus 15.5 per cent. Institutions with endowment assets less than $25 million reported the highest rate of additions from individual gifts and bequests (8 per cent) to the endowment, while institutions with assets greater than $500 million but less than $1 billion, reported the smallest rate (2 per cent) of addition. These institutions also reported the lowest and highest additions respectively from endowment appreciation and investment income (12 per cent vs. 16.8 per cent).

Institutions with larger endowment values delivered higher additions to the investment pool via appreciation and income; while the higher additions registered by institutions with smaller endowments was partly the result of their

Table 14.1. Additions to endowment assets in the United States, 2003, in per cent

Endowment	Appreciation & income	Individual gifts & bequests	Other gifts
>$1000 m	16.1	2.6	0.6*
$500–1000 m	6.8	2.0	3.4*
$100–500 m	14.9	4.3	6.4
$50–100 m	13.8	2.5	3.6
$25–50 m	13.2	3.1	3.6
<$25 m	12.0	8.0	3.7
Public	15.9	2.8	2.5
Independent	15.5	3.1	3.2
Average	**15.6**	**3.0**	**3.0**

* Fewer than 10 institutions responding. 788 institutions provided some information related to additions to the endowment. Data are dollar-weighted and returns are measured over the previous year.
Source: 2004 NACUBO Study.

size as a $1 million gift comprises a larger proportion of the investment pool for a smaller endowment than a larger one.[1] Thus, for institutions with smaller endowments, changes in endowment values from one year to the next are not always indicative of the institution's performance. In 2004, for example, institutions with endowments worth less than or equal to $25 million added 12 per cent to their investment pool via appreciation and investment income. This group of institutions also boosted endowment values by 11.7 per cent via individual gifts, bequests, and other gifts.

According to the *Commonfund Benchmark Study, 2005*, in the United States average endowment growth from gifts was 5.5 per cent compared to growth from reinvested earnings of 9.9 per cent. In fiscal year 2004, gifts amounted to 36 per cent of total growth of endowment assets among the 645 institutions participating in the Study.[2] Institutions with smaller endowments reported higher additions to the investment pool compared to institutions with larger endowments; the largest institutions reporting an increase of 3.1 per cent and the smallest reporting an increase of 12.7 per cent. While larger institutions' gifts as a percentage of endowment assets are lower, annual additions of 3–4 per cent of a significantly larger base of assets sustained over decades makes a substantial difference. Giving can amount to a critical sum, and is today an essential component of planning a long-term endowment strategy among the overwhelming majority of educational institutions in the United States.

The importance of donor support on endowment growth is well illustrated by Swensen in *Pioneering Portfolio Management*, where he cites the experience of Harvard and Yale versus the Carnegie Institution over the course of the twentieth century. Establishing the Carnegie Institution in 1902 with a $10 million gift, Andrew Carnegie increased the endowment by $2 million in 1907 and $10 million in 1911. Carnegie's $22 million endowment nearly equalled

Harvard's 1910 fund balance of $23 million and vastly exceeded Yale's $12 million endowment. Over the course of the next nine decades, the Carnegie Institution's endowment more than kept pace with inflation. At 30 June 1998, it was worth $420 million, comfortably ahead of the $360 million needed to match the rise in price levels. But it simply did not match the growth achieved by the Harvard endowment, which was valued at $12.8 billion or the Yale endowment at $6.6 billion.

'While differences in investment and spending policies no doubt explain some of the gap,' writes Swensen, 'absence of continuing gift inflows constitutes the fundamental reason for Carnegie's failure to keep pace with Yale and Harvard. The existence of a substantial source of external financial support constitutes a significant difference between the endowment funds supporting universities and foundations.'[3] He also emphasized the impact of new gifts to the Yale endowment's value; 'in the absence of new gifts over the past forty-eight years, Yale's endowment would likely total only about one third of today's value.'[4] Most institutions today appreciate the impact of gifts to their overall management strategy. Efficient endowment management also assists in the fund-raising strategy. While investment strategy may not be influenced by an institution's fund-raising strategy, there is increasingly greater recognition of the symbiotic relationship between the two.

Oxford and Cambridge: Recent trends in fund-raising

In the UK, as in the rest of Europe, the balance among funding sources for the academic sector is significantly biased toward Government; only Cambridge and Oxford have significant endowments in the UK. According to Professor Alison Richard, Vice-Chancellor of Cambridge University: 'During the last fifty years philanthropy has played little part in the finances of most universities, discouraged until recently by the tax laws in place and the notion that "the state will provide".... Thus, the overall picture in the UK is indeed one of heavy dependence on a single funding source, Government, with successive Governments holding strong and conflicting views about the purposes and value of universities.' Professor Richard goes on to point out that 'further changes in the tax laws would both help and encourage the University to exercise even more energetically a freedom we already have—to raise funds through philanthropy. Collegiate Cambridge already received generous support from benefactors, and the 800th anniversary in 2009 offers a unique opportunity to increase that support further. The goal of the 800th Anniversary Campaign is to raise £1 billion in additional funds across collegiate Cambridge, with many gifts directed toward endowment.'[5]

The collegiate endowments of Oxford and Cambridge have increased in value over the centuries, both through benefactions and capital appreciation.

Historically, some of the benefactions were in the form of land. Offsetting the benefactions to the Colleges over the centuries have been great expenditures on the College buildings and estates, and on providing bursaries and scholarships to poor students. While the pattern of giving has changed in recent decades, the expectation that Government will fund education has discouraged Colleges from actively fund-raising and alumni and friends from giving. As the level of government funding per student declined, there has been greater pressure on Colleges to work their investments harder while exploring new ways of raising money. Fund-raising may not be a recent development among these institutions, but establishing Development offices with a mandate to raise additional annual funds for operations is.

'Significantly, following the government's involvement in university financing, there has been only one notable benefaction to Peterhouse. If the Government is going to support universities, why should benefactors? It's a major problem for universities today,' commented Murison. While Peterhouse's development office has been in existence for several years, and the College receives donations and gifts annually, the amounts received have been small compared to its overall sources of income and/or new additions to endowment capital. This is not unique to Peterhouse; other Colleges have similar fund-raising histories. It is worth noting that over the past few years, approaches to fund-raising among Oxbridge institutions is changing. The investments being made into fund-raising and development will bear fruit in 5–10 years' time.

The number of Colleges reporting the existence of a fund-raising programme rose from 79 per cent in 2002–3 to virtually 100 per cent today. Both the Universities of Oxford and Cambridge are individually committed to major fund-raising campaigns over the next several years. So are the constituent Colleges. During 2002–3, when the interviews with College bursars and University finance officers and treasurers were held, 79 per cent of respondents indicated the existence of fund-raising programmes in place; the remaining Colleges did not have any such plans. Today, with the exception of All Souls and Nuffield, all the Colleges in Oxford reported receiving some new additions to their endowment in the form of gifts or donations. The amounts may be insignificant, as in the case of St John's in Oxford, and the fund-raising campaigns may not be efficient; but fund-raising as an essential aspect of institutional activity is firmly in the agenda.

In the published accounts for 2003–4 of the Oxford Colleges, income from donations and benefactions as a proportion of total income was £9.2 million, or 4.4 per cent of total income for the year, compared to £6.9 million or 3.5 per cent of overall income the previous year. These amounts exclude funds received by the University of Oxford. Among Colleges in Cambridge that provide such information, income from donations and benefactions amounted to £11.6 million in 2003–4 compared to £10.7 million the previous year. The amount raised by Cambridge is understated as Colleges like Trinity, St John's, Queens', Emmanuel, and Christ's did not disclose such information in their published annual accounts. Donations as a percentage of overall income of the above mentioned Colleges may not be significant, but lack of information does limit our analysis. Income from donations for those Cambridge Colleges that reported such data represented 8.3 per cent of total income for 2003–4. It is also worth noting that the data as disclosed in the published accounts may not be accurate as the Colleges do not report similarly.

In addition to income from benefactions, Colleges also reported new gifts and donations to endowment assets. In 2003–4, such additions to the endowment amounted to £24 million for Cambridge Colleges and £21.8 million for Oxford Colleges, representing less than 2 per cent of endowment assets. Total gifts received were £35.8 million for the 25 Cambridge Colleges that reported data on fund-raising in 2003–4, and £31 million for the 36 Colleges in Oxford, also representing less than 2 per cent of the value of endowment assets reported for the same year. The more successful Colleges in Oxford and Cambridge raised on average £2 million, the average for all the Colleges was about £1 million; older Colleges were able to raise more funds compared with Colleges established more recently. Women's Colleges reported receiving more in the form of legacies compared to men's Colleges.

Meaningful analysis of Oxford and Cambridge Colleges' fund-raising strategy is not possible due to the lack of information on the subject; only five Colleges in Cambridge reported comprehensive data on fund-raising in 2003–4 and two Colleges in 2002–3. Some of the wealthier Colleges in Oxford such as All Souls, Nuffield, or St John's did not have any significant fund-raising initiatives in place. All Souls College reported budget deficits for both fiscal years 2004 and 2003; so did Nuffield. But there was no collegiate strategy for fund-raising to address the shortfall. As these Colleges are among the wealthiest in Oxbridge, it provides some explanation for their not 'asking' for funds regardless of annual operational deficits. The response would be to balance the budget rather than raise funds. For example, St John's College in Oxford, among the wealthiest in Oxbridge, reported an operational deficit in 2003. But it soon turned round its deficit to a small surplus in 2004; the deficit was nearly £1 million in 2003, but the College reported a small surplus (£0.2 million) in 2004.

Oxford Colleges with lesser endowments appear to have been more successful in their fund-raising efforts. As depicted in Table 14.2, according to data published in the annual accounts of the Colleges in 2003–4, those with endowments worth less than £25 million on average raised 7.7 per cent of the value of their endowment by fund-raising compared with just 0.7 per cent for Colleges with endowment assets worth over £100 million.

Colleges with smaller endowments also raised larger sums in absolute terms than Colleges with larger endowments during 2003–4. Thus, Colleges with

Table 14.2. Distribution of Oxford Colleges' funds raised, 2004, as percentage of endowment assets

Endowment size	No. of colleges	Funds raised % of endowment (Avg)	Endowment assets (Avg) £ m
>£100 m	5	0.7	153.8
£50 m–£100 m	7	1.1	76.3
£25m–£50 m	9	2.5	36.4
<£25 m	15	7.7	15.3
Total/Average	**36**	**1.7**	**51.7**

less than £25 million of endowment assets raised £1.2 million on average compared to £1.1 million raised by the wealthiest Colleges, with assets over £100 million. As three of the wealthiest Colleges in Oxford (All Souls, Nuffield, and St John's) did not have any fund-raising strategy in place during 2003–4, it explains partly why total funds raised by institutions with larger endowments were relatively smaller compared with sums raised by Colleges with lesser endowments that were more actively engaged in fund-raising. The two remaining rich Colleges in Oxford, for example, raised £5.2 million between them or £2.6 million per College. If the other three Colleges start actively fund-raising, they would most likely be successful in matching funds raised by their counterparts. While the ratio of funds raised to endowment assets would still remain low for the richer Colleges, the absolute amount of funds raised would be significantly higher.

In 2004–5, for the first time some 44 universities in the UK put together a survey of gift revenue and fund-raising costs as a means of measuring the 'philanthropic health' of each institution, following the conventions applied by the Council for Advancement and Support of Education (CASE) in the United States. CASE Europe was set up to enable educational institutions in Europe to develop a systematic, integrated method of managing relationships in order to increase an educational institution's support from its key outside constituents, including alumni and friends, government policymakers, the media, members of the community, and philanthropic entities of all types. As part of the recent overhaul of university funding, participation in the survey is a precondition of eligibility for university funding. As a result, the development offices of the universities of Oxford and Cambridge, among others, aggregated information for the first time on funds raised and costs incurred in such process by the Colleges and the Universities. Due to the complex structure of these collegiate universities, such information prior to financial year ending 2005 was not compiled, though the information exists in the archives of these institutions.

According to Oxford University's Development Office, philanthropic gifts to the Colleges and the University amounted to £110.4 million in

2004–5; £31.2 million (28 per cent) of which comprised gifts to the constituent Colleges in Oxford. Of the £110.4 million in gifts, 45 per cent was in
the form of realized cash income, not pledges or future income; 8.5 per cent
was received in the form of legacies. Oxford's total philanthropic gifts received
in 2004–5 did not include the £69 million donation made by James Martin;
only the interest on that gift. Oxford has been rather successful in raising
funds in the first year of its participation in the UK CASE survey.

The amount of new funds, defined as new cash and non-legacy pledges but
excluding pledged payments from past years, raised by the Colleges and the
University of Cambridge in 2004–5 was £75.4 million. In 2002–3, Cambridge
raised £72.6 million and in 2003–4 total new funds raised were £55.2 million.
Previous years' fund-raising data for collegiate Oxford are not available. In
recent years, Cambridge has attracted more funds, compared with Oxford,
partly as a result of Cambridge's bias towards the sciences, technology, and
engineering. In 2004–5, for example, the amount of total philanthropic cash
income (not pledges) received by Cambridge was £60.5 million compared
with Oxford's £49.7 million. As the two collegiate universities gear up for
their planned major fund-raising initiatives, it is anticipated that their ability
to attract larger gifts and grants will increase substantially.

Harvard University, for example, received from alumni and friends the total
sum of gifts of $592 million in 2004. Endowment gifts totalled $258 million,
current use gifts were $154 million, and grants for research as well as gifts
for loans, facilities, and life income funds consisted of the remaining $180
million. In the 2004 fiscal year, Yale's operating budget revenue was boosted
by $76 million (5 per cent) from gifts. Taking into account the lack of an
established tradition of annual giving to one's Alma Mater in the UK, the
amounts received by collegiate Oxford and Cambridge as gifts are not insignificant when compared with funds raised by their Ivy League counterparts.

Cost of raising funds

Total funds received in the form of gifts and donations and new annual additions to endowment capital as disclosed in the *University of Oxford: Financial
Statements of the Colleges* for financial years 2002–3 and 2003–4 shows that
the Colleges in aggregate raised £26.2 million and £31.0 million respectively.
The cost of raising such funds was £3.7 million and £4.2 million respectively,
representing 14 per cent of funds raised for both years. Individual expense
ratios varied significantly, with some Colleges reporting costs substantially
exceeding funds raised; the highest reported being 179 per cent for one
College in 2002–3 and 66 per cent for another in 2003–4. The reverse was
also evident with some six Colleges reporting donations received without any
expenditure incurred.

Small gifts and typically legacies were often left to Colleges without any significant fund-raising activity on their part. Some Colleges received small amounts of gifts, but did not report any expenses. Jesus College, for example, reported receiving £251,650 as gifts for 2003–4 but no fund-raising cost was included in its annual account. Similarly, St John's College reported a small new addition to its endowment (£134,136 in 2004) without any expenditure being incurred for the year.

New College in Oxford reported fund inflows of over £0.5 million in 2004 without matching fund-raising expenses in its accounts. This is because fund-raising for New College is carried out by the New College Development Fund, an independent charitable trust set up by the College. The College receives donations from the Development Fund, which was valued at £7.4 million in 2004; but as an independent trust, registered as a charity with the Charity Commission, the assets of the fund are not consolidated in the financial statements of the College.

Using these ratios to draw any direct comparison among the Colleges can be misleading as variations in accounting practice, funding structures and one-off large donations can impact on the statistics that institutions report. Short-term figures on costs associated with fund-raising therefore need to be treated with caution and pose difficulty in comparing one institution with another. However, the fact that most of the Colleges in Oxford report costs associated with fund-raising shows that, at the very least, these institutions are thinking about these issues and can defend themselves against criticism. Comparison of fund-raising ratios can to that extent also help donors in assessing the efficiency of their recipient organizations.

The average cost of fund-raising, as reported by Oxford Colleges, at 14 per cent of funds raised, compares favourably with the philanthropic sector. According to the last cost of fund-raising study conducted by CASE in 1990, it cost 16 cents to raise $1 in the United States.[6] Universities such as Cambridge and Oxford, Harvard and Yale, with their long established record in education and research can build on their past achievements when it comes to investing in fund-raising.

Philanthropic entities with less established histories typically find costs associated with fund-raising to be higher. According to some reports, in America raising $100 can eat up anything from $22 to $43.[7] In Britain, according to a 1998 Charities Aid Foundation (CAF) report, fund-raising costs as a percentage of the voluntary income of the top 500 charities varied from 0 to 123 per cent, and the mean performance was 14 per cent.[8] Data published by CAF for 2003–4 indicate that the ratio of expenditure on fund-raising and publicity to the voluntary income of the top 500 charities monitored by CAF was 15.3 per cent.[9]

According to Iain More Associates, commissioned by Oxford University's Development office to conduct an internal study of College fund-raising and

costs, over a five-year period spanning 2000–5, the 28 Colleges that participated in the Oxford College Benchmarking Study received a total income of
£131.2 million from fund-raising activities, and spent a total of £16.1 million.
Staff costs amounted to 59.6 per cent of fund-raising expenditure. The overall
costs in this study included alumni relations activity of the Colleges. The ratio
of total costs to funds raised for Oxford Colleges during this five-year period
was 7.4 per cent, almost half the expense ratio (14 per cent) reported by the
Oxford Colleges for 2003–4 and 2002–3. It is possible that expenditure on
fund-raising rose towards the end of the five-year period compared to the first
three years of this study.

An examination of overall costs to funds raised for collegiate Oxford, as
disclosed in the CASE survey, shows that Oxford spent £6.2 million (63
per cent of which was staffing costs) in raising £110.4 million in 2004–5; the
resulting expense ratio of just 5.6 per cent appears to be highly competitive.
Historical data for Oxford were not available; hence, it is not possible to
comment whether such a low rate of spending in relation to funds raised
is sustainable.

Collegiate Cambridge raised new funds worth £72.6 million in 2002–3
spending £5.3 million, with an expense ratio of 7.3 per cent. In 2003–4,
Cambridge raised £55 million at an expense ratio of 11.8 per cent, in 2004–
5 new funds raised were £75.4 million at an expense ratio of 9.3 per cent.
The average ratio of costs to funds raised for collegiate Cambridge over this
three-year period was 9.5 per cent.

As per the CASE survey guidelines Cambridge excluded costs associated with
alumni relations but included 50 per cent of database costs for the Colleges
and the University's development office in America—a 20 person office in
New York that works for both the Colleges and the central University. Oxford
also has a substantial office in New York, and one in Japan, for the purposes
of fund-raising and maintaining alumni relations. An expense ratio of less
than 10 per cent is attractive by global standards. The low cost ratio for these
institutions suggests their significant competitive advantage in fund-raising
activity. Of course, additional fund-raising should be undertaken as long as
there is a marginal gain from incremental development effort; so as these
institutions accelerate their fund-raising efforts, an increased expense ratio
could still be acceptable.

Conclusion

The Oxford and Cambridge endowments are the result of centuries of benefactions, donations, bequests, and legacies. In the majority of cases, benefactions
were in the form of land. In principle, when institutions receive a gift, to
provide true permanent support they also incur expenditures in maintaining

that gift. Thus, offsetting benefactions in the form of land were associated costs of maintaining buildings and estates. Similarly with financial donations, institutions are obliged to maintain the inflation-adjusted income from gifts. While gifts enlarge the scope of activities, it implies that institutions must factor in additional costs into their annual budgets to be able to deliver the same set of activities initially supported by the gift.

The average amount raised by an Oxford College was almost £1 million in 2004–5 compared to £0.7 million in 2002–3. Lack of published data on donations and gifts received by the Higher Education sector as a whole in the UK make it difficult to assess the accomplishment of Cambridge and Oxford. Anecdotal evidence suggests that gifts and donations received by the UK's Higher Education sector were insignificant. Cambridge and Oxford retain their pre-eminence as academic institutions, and benefit significantly from gifts and donations from alumni, philanthropists, and donors. While tax incentives for giving in the UK are better than before, as Professor Alison Richard points out there is scope for improvement.

According to the 2004 NACUBO Endowment Study (NES), participating institutions in the United States reported gifts and bequests averaging $7.2 million (compared to $5.7 million in 2003), similar to the $7.3 million recorded in 2002. It is worth noting that 'Other Gifts' averaged $7.3 million. Institutions with endowment assets larger than $1 billion reported receiving gifts and bequests averaging $43 million, while institutions with endowments worth less than $25 million reported receiving gifts and bequests averaging $1.1 million.[10] According to the 2003 NES, institutions with endowment assets larger than $1 billion reported receiving gifts and bequests averaging $34 million, and institutions with endowments worth less than $25 million reported receiving gifts and bequests averaging $0.84 million.[11] Table 14.3 shows additions to the endowment pools of US institutions for 2004.

Table 14.3. Additions to endowment assets among US educational institutions

Endowment	Appreciation & income	Individual gifts & bequests	Other gifts
>$1000 m	305.4	43.0	8.2*
$500–1000 m	110.6	22.6	21.0*
$100–500 m	31.3	8.9	13.0
$50–100 m	9.1	3.3	2.3
$25–50 m	4.5	1.8	1.2
<$25 m	1.6	1.1	0.5
Public	32.7	9.4	5.4
Independent	34.0	6.2	8.6
Average	**33.6**	**7.2**	**7.4**

* Fewer than 10 institutions responding. 711 institutions provided some information related to additions to the endowment. Data are dollar-weighted.

Source: 2004 NACUBO Study.

The rebound in the value of endowments was not just the result of market gains over the past year, but was helped by the flow of gifts and donations. Institutions in Oxford and Cambridge might find the prospect of raising such large gifts challenging, but developing a tradition of 'asking' may involve a different approach altogether. US institutions have been engaged in cultivating their alumni and friends with a view to 'asking' for annual gifts and donations for several decades now. Significant investment of time and funds are typically made at the initial stages of development activity. It cannot be said that Oxbridge institutions have missed out on such benefactions; they have done well under the circumstances. As income from gifts and donations among Oxford and Cambridge institutions is currently rather low, compared with the sums raised by their peer group in the United States, it may nevertheless be easier to enhance that intake without excessive additional cost.

To sustain a long-term fund-raising strategy, Colleges have to refocus their marketing strategies, invest in building relationships, both with Alumni and Friends. As institutions of higher education in the UK become focused on fund-raising as a means of building a diversified, more secure income base, they also have to compete with other philanthropic organizations for funds. Amounts raised by Oxford and Cambridge may look respectable today in terms of what other universities in the UK are able to garner, in the new era of philanthropy where giving is becoming more business-like, these institutions have to compete for funds like any other institutions in the philanthropic sector.

15

Concluding observations

Introduction

Unlike pension funds whose investment objectives may be interpreted as being similar, endowment purposes vary considerably. One philanthropic institution might choose to spend its entire endowment within a defined period while another has the fiduciary obligation to ensure that spending today does not prejudice future generations of beneficiaries. Even within the educational sector, where endowment purposes are ostensibly similar, differences in approaches to investments and fund-raising play a crucial role. In this sector, the indeterminate nature of liabilities means that a successful investment policy sustains the flow of funds to the operating budget and assists in fulfilling institutional goals. A clearly defined objective, on which investment policy is based, therefore acquires greater significance.

Oxford and Cambridge endowments comprise funds generally regarded as for the long term, and which fundamentally underpin and sustain the operation of the institutions at their desired level of activity. This definition of an endowment was historically interpreted differently among Colleges in Oxford and Cambridge resulting in the free transfer of funds between endowment and reserves, between operational and non-operational assets. Removal of internal tax incentives to increase or decrease the value of the endowment will help in curbing such transfers, which have proven to be detrimental to the long-term preservation of its capital. The process of reform has begun; going forward it is anticipated that institutions will fully recognize them as essentially inefficient in securing their long-term objectives.

Oxbridge institutions have collectively embraced major change over the last few years by implementing total return investment strategies. They simultaneously made the shift from spending policies that encouraged income-generating investments towards establishing sensible spending rules that freed up asset allocation decisions. Such changes in investment approaches have consequences in terms of determining appropriate governance, choice of assets, identifying skilled managers, monitoring their performance, understanding the sources of value-addition and cost analysis, and setting many other aspects of endowment policy. As such transitions take a long time to implement many of the institutions are in the process of managing that change.

The practice of borrowing from the endowment at nil rates of interest not only depleted endowment capital, but inhibited investment policy. While borrowing from the endowment is relatively uncommon today, such a method of financing capital expenditure was fairly common in the recent past among Colleges. As a consequence, investment policy decisions were secondary to operational considerations, which effectively dictated endowment asset allocation leading to lower investment returns for the endowment. Under such constraints, it is impressive that endowment income in Oxford and Cambridge today contributes over a third of total income of the Colleges and thus plays a critical role in sustaining operations.

Lack of endowment independence resulting in weak implementation of appropriate investment and spending policies, not to mention capital outflows from the endowment and the lack of a tradition of fund-raising, all contributed to eroding long-term endowment growth. While Ivy League institutions built up substantial endowments over the past few decades, Oxbridge institutions suffered. Comparisons with the size of endowment assets of top universities in the United States are typically made to illustrate the lack of resources available to UK institutions. Size of assets under management is material, as it influences some aspects of decision-making. For example, an endowment's size may restrain its ability to invest in alternative assets and strategies, which tend to be illiquid in nature and carry a higher element of risk. Income requirements have a far greater influence on asset allocation decisions of a smaller endowment than a larger one. An endowment's ability to afford independent investment advice and performance analysis may also be a limiting factor. An institution with less than £10 million of assets under management simply cannot afford to replicate the sort of investment strategies pursued by institutions with assets above £500 million under management.

Universities in the UK have also had to deal with real cuts in higher education funding over the past decades. A significant factor influencing overall quality of output is the difference in spending between Oxford and Cambridge and their counterparts in America. The British government and the academic institutions fully recognize the challenges of globalization; new partnerships, methods of funding, assessment are all part of the way forward in establishing greater plurality of funding support. From 2006–7, for example, universities have the power to vary the fees they charge directly to students, up to a maximum of £3,000 per year in the UK. Changes in the funding of research in meeting new economic and social challenges, including investing in physical infrastructure, issuing debt, among other initiatives, are afoot.

In spite of significant funding gaps between the top US and UK institutions, it is encouraging that the combined endowment assets per FTE student in Oxford and Cambridge are considerably higher today than those at wealthier public universities in the United States. In round numbers, the 2004–5 endowment assets per FTE student in Oxford were $269,000. At Cambridge, the aggregation of the different endowments into a centralized fund meant that endowment assets per FTE student rose to $296,000, resulting in Cambridge and Oxford trailing behind Princeton ($1.6 million), Yale ($1.4 million), Harvard ($1.3 million), Stanford ($0.8 million), and MIT ($0.7 million). In reality, endowment assets per student vary considerably among the Colleges; for example, a student in Trinity College (Cambridge) would be significantly well off, having access to superior facilities compared with a student from a less well-off College in the same University.

Oxford and Cambridge currently receive a large percentage of their income from public sources; the government will continue to be the major source of funding for universities. This should be seen as an opportunity for institutions when determining asset allocation and in leveraging the stability of their diverse sources of funding. What Oxford and Cambridge need is not to forgo income from public sources, but to increase their private income substantially. To do so they must be able to demonstrate not just their pre-eminence as academic institutions but that their endowments are performing efficiently. Donors like to be assured that their gifts are well spent—either in directly supporting academic purposes of the Colleges today and/or in the future. Thus, to attract gifts and donations, Oxford and Cambridge must maintain their status as among the best educational institutions in the world.

Endowment governance and management structure

The collegiate structure of Oxford and Cambridge is unique, its tutorial system unparalleled in terms of delivering excellence in teaching. The Colleges, independent and self-governing institutions, form a core element of each University, to which they are related in a federal system. Students at Oxbridge are members of their College and the University; such an arrangement has proven to be beneficial in fulfilling the primary objective of these institutions—that is the pursuit of education.

The focus on the primary purpose of Colleges is reflected in their annual account and report, which makes no specific reference to 'investment objectives'. Investment performance too is typically described without reference to any stated investment objective. Institutions could benefit from clearer enunciation of the investment objective. As in the United States, they could address how endowment return relates to spending policy, performance benchmark, risk analysis, and issues relating to portfolio rebalancing to maintain the asset allocation target; they could also comment on considerations in hiring and retaining investment managers and consultants. Such information is not uniformly supplied in the United States; nor are these topics always defined quantitatively. But the level of disclosure by educational endowments in the UK, in the form of annual reports or accounts, is lower, there being no requirement on their part to do so.

The primacy of educational objectives should not deter these world-class institutions from investing their endowment portfolios efficiently. In the final analysis, asset allocation involves the appropriate allocation of risk. While bursars acknowledge that risk management remains an area of concern, and the definition of risk associated with individual Colleges inevitably vary, there is no agreement on how to examine these issues formally; none, at least, that we were able to assess during the course of our study. Broadly speaking, risk for these institutions is the inability of the endowment to generate a certain level of income to support their primary educational objective. Therefore, investment objectives need to be clearly defined by these institutions and their endowments allowed the freedom to prosper.

It is worth noting that while the Colleges are independent, self-governing institutions, their endowments are not. Oxbridge investment committees serve largely in an advisory capacity. Investment policy is recommended by the Investment Committee, either via the Finance Committee or directly to the Governing Body of the College. The Investment Committee acts as an adviser to the Governing Body in determining appropriate policies for the management of the endowment assets. Lack of independence of the Endowment has long-term consequences, critically for the institutions if they lose out in terms of superior investment returns. Thus, government and management structures matter, if they can improve asset allocation decisions resulting in superior long-term performance.

This is not to suggest that the universities of Harvard and Yale, for example, do not oversee their investments; they do. But the HMC is responsible for managing the Endowment. Harvard Management Company is a wholly-owned subsidiary of Harvard University; it was founded in 1974 to manage the University's endowment, pension assets, working capital, and deferred giving accounts. Harvard Management Company is governed by a Board of Directors appointed by the President and Fellows of the University. The Yale Investment Office is likewise responsible for investing the Yale Endowment. The collegiate structures of Oxford and Cambridge make it difficult to emulate, for example, the Harvard or Yale management structure. The individual size of the endowment within Colleges is too small to have an impact. The size and contribution of the two Oxbridge University endowments also do not measure up. The establishment of an Investment Office in 2006, with a CIO, for the management of Cambridge University's endowment and the investments of its related bodies therefore marks a new direction. As the Colleges are not part of this University's Investment Office initiative, it illustrates how governance and management considerations influence investment applications.

Similarly, a few Oxford Colleges established a collective investment partnership, OXIP, to meet the specific requirements of educational endowments. Investing 10 per cent of the endowment in such a fund does not lighten the asset allocation burden on the Investment Committees of Colleges. Other existing partnerships for investments in private equity and hedge funds were set up to secure greater economies of scale. While fees paid to external managers currently do not appear to be onerous, it is not clear that the investment performance justifies those costs. If higher cost-adjusted returns could be achieved, then Colleges and Universities should seriously consider amalgamating their resources. Analysis of investment performance is perhaps the greatest weakness in the overall investment process. A centralized fund would help in assessing costs versus performance.

If improved performance can be achieved by investment decisions that emanate from new ways of structuring the governance of some of Oxbridge institutions, such as the question of the independence of the endowment, it is worth scrutiny and implementation. While long-term performance of endowment investments in Oxford and Cambridge is not available, there is a consensus that it does not compare favourably with that consistently achieved by Yale and Harvard over the past 20 years. While combined endowment assets in Oxford or Cambridge are small by comparison with Ivy League institutions, an improvement of even 1 per cent in Oxbridge annual return would boost endowment wealth and assist in the fund-raising effort. Streamlining management arrangements will ensure that the Investment Committee is responsible for determining the strategic investment decisions, which include asset allocation, manager selection, risk, and performance analysis. Currently, Oxbridge institutions are not rigorous in assessing the latter aspects of their endowment asset management.

The recent trend towards finance and investment professionals joining the UK endowment sector is encouraging; today, an increasing proportion of Colleges have professional investment bursars. Only time will tell what their real contribution will be to the collective endowment asset management process. Compared with their US counterparts, Oxbridge institutions appear to have smaller investment committees. But, taking into account the size of assets under management and investment strategies employed, the number of individuals involved in the process is high. Greater effort at pooling assets and strengthening investment expertise could help in efficient management of costs and performance. While the use of investment consultants remains patchy, and several of these hires were limited to advice on manager selection or entry to private equity and absolute return strategies, the use of consultants in performance measurement would complement the effort on making good asset allocation decisions.

While in aggregate there are a large number of people in the investment committees, our study shows that several Colleges are managing with limited professional and support staff, with the Bursar often being the only person responsible for a varied number of investment and non-investment related tasks. The challenge of managing the available resources in support of the College's overall objectives cannot be emphasized enough. Greater independence of the Endowment would benefit the Investment Committees in Oxford and Cambridge in appointing members with greater investment expertise. The Investment Committee's role in determining and being responsible for prudent endowment management needs bolstering. As the contribution of the endowment in sustaining long-term institutional objective is widely acknowledged, investing judiciously in the management structure remains critical.

Spending policy

The concept of a spending policy, prevalent among major endowments and foundations in the United States, is relatively new to Oxford and Cambridge institutions. The link between investment objective, rate of spending, investment return target, and asset allocation is also in the early stages of development. Until recently, Oxford and Cambridge institutions were able to spend only income; not unlike Yale and Harvard in the 1960s when those universities also limited their endowment's annual contribution to the operating budget to investment yield: interest, dividend, and rental income.

Today, determining a sustainable spending rate is among the key decisions that the Governing Body of an Oxbridge College is responsible for. An average 4 per cent spending rate among Oxbridge institutions is a more conservative strategy than at corresponding US institutions, which have spent on average 5 per cent over the past decade. Under a quarter of institutions in Oxford and Cambridge spend more than 5 per cent of the previous year's endowment value, the range of spending varying from less than 2 per cent to a high of 13 per cent. Rates of spending higher than 5 per cent are difficult to sustain in the long-term as generating real returns of more than 5 per cent is not achievable, unless the College is comfortable with taking on significant risk exposure.

A target spending-rate serves as a guide in determining an endowment's ability to maintain intergenerational equity, with higher rates indicating a bias towards the current generation of students and faculty, and lower rates favouring future generations. While some foundations can opt to favour current beneficiaries, educational institutions have a fiduciary responsibility towards protecting the future as much as the present. If an institution places emphasis on its current academic operations alone, then distributions from the endowment may not be adjusted for fluctuations in the market value of investments. At the other extreme, focusing on endowment preservation may mean that funds over and above the rate of inflation alone would be made available for current spending. Setting a sustainable spending rule assists in greater fiscal discipline.

In determining spending policy among educational institutions, it is important to consider not only the needs of current beneficiaries but also those of future generations. The per cent of annual drawdown from the endowment is as important as the need to maximize investment returns at any given level of risk. The methodology used in making such withdrawal is therefore critical. Using a fixed annual withdrawal formula simply transmits the market volatility into the operating budget assumptions. Most US institutions use, for example, a rolling 3-year average market value approach resulting in the spending of 5 per cent of the endowment value. About half the institutions in Oxbridge also apply a rolling 3-year average market value criterion.

The move towards adopting 'total return' investment policies in Oxford and Cambridge is a welcome development as Colleges implement asset allocation strategies that focus on long-term returns rather than income. Total return strategies offer opportunities as well as challenges; inappropriate allocation of assets can prove equally detrimental to preserving the real value of the endowment while providing a stable source of income. It is worth noting that the transition to a total return policy among several Oxbridge Colleges was facilitated by their high weighting in property assets that provide the necessary source of income during this period of transition. Real estate not only provided the necessary diversification but also generated a stable source of income. This was something that several bursars pointed out—that without the stable revenue from property, the path to implementing total return investment policies would have been challenging. Also, the property market cycle assisted in this reconfiguration; if the property market had been in a reverse, correctional cycle, the responses would not have been so tilted in favour of the asset class.

Asset allocation

One of the challenges for endowment managers is how to maximize spending today while preserving the purchasing power of the endowment for posterity. Higher expected returns may resolve the conflict between providing for operations today while preserving real value. At the same time, vulnerability to inflation directs investments away from fixed income towards equity. Institutional portfolios with very long-term investment horizons, such as endowments, are therefore best invested in assets capable of generating equity-like returns, including public and private equity, and strategies that aim to deliver absolute returns. To mitigate equity risks, portfolios may incorporate fixed income, real estate, and other assets such as commodities or natural resources. Non-traditional assets are not only strong diversifiers; they can also serve to enhance returns. Alternative assets tend to be less efficiently priced than traditional marketable securities, providing an opportunity to enhance returns through active management.

While Yale and Harvard have been exploiting illiquid, less efficient markets such as venture capital, leveraged buyouts, oil and gas, timber, and hedged strategies for some time, the salient feature of Oxford and Cambridge endowment portfolios is their investment in property assets, which at an average of over 30 per cent, is among the highest among any group of professional institutional investors, apart from specialist property investors. Property investments span a range of assets from equity to debt as well as assets combining debt and equity-like characteristics. Property can also be privately owned with infrequent valuations or be publicly quoted as any other marketable security. If one were looking for an Oxbridge consensus with regard to asset allocation, it can be suggested that the Colleges (not the Universities) regard real estate as a core investment.

According to the accounts of the Oxford Colleges, the aggregate average allocation to property in 2004–5 had risen to 45 per cent compared with 31 per cent in 2003; this was the result of appreciation in the value of property as well as new investments in the asset class. Cambridge Colleges, for which data are unavailable, would also have benefited from their high allocation to the asset class. The average property holding in Oxbridge today is more likely to be over one-third of endowment assets. By comparison, the educational endowment sector in the United States invested 2.7 per cent in real estate assets while the not-for-profit sector in the UK held 3.4 per cent in the asset class. Oxbridge property allocation is similar to ownership of fixed-income assets among US college endowments. The fixed-income-like characteristics of property were cited as a determining factor among Oxford and Cambridge institutions when investing in the asset class. Oxbridge Colleges with smaller-sized endowments were the least likely to hold property assets in their endowments. About one quarter of Colleges reported not owning any property assets in the endowment. The wealthier Colleges invested less in domestic (UK) equity, fixed income, and cash; richer Colleges were significantly overweight in property, but less so in alternative assets when compared with their peer group in the United States.

Less wealthy institutions in Oxbridge invested significantly more in domestic equity assets compared with the richer Colleges. Poorer Colleges also invested less in absolute return strategies; but they did not necessarily use passive strategies such as indexed products. One of the advantages of indexing, apart from reducing diversifiable risk, is avoiding the risk of poor manager selection. In general, those less well-endowed Colleges in Oxford and Cambridge that did not invest in property, or in absolute return strategies, also reported lower investment returns. Many of them employed a single balanced manager, and were overweight in domestic equity assets. There was under-diversification across asset classes, investment strategies, and specialist managers. However, exposure to property, unlisted securities, or hedge funds does not automatically guarantee superior returns. Non-traditional assets offer opportunities for those who know how to exploit them; equally, they pose a challenge to those who do not have the expertise. Manager selection is therefore a greater risk in active strategies than in passive ones, while market inefficiency is what passive investors have to contend with.

The need to support the operating budget provides the key to under-standing asset allocation decisions among Oxbridge institutions. Colleges seek a certain level of income from their endowments. Generating efficient portfolios did not appear to be the primary focus for those managing the endowment; generating a certain level of income was. At the same time, it would be unfair to suggest that investment bursars were not vexed by the concept; they did not know what an efficient portfolio meant. It was the single most important issue raised among Oxbridge bursars: 'Is there an ideal asset allocation for long-term investors such as educational endowments?' For Colleges with a reasonable contribution of income from property assets, it was relatively easier to generate more efficient portfolios or more diversified ones. Property is seen as a relatively low-risk investment among institutions that have owned such assets for centuries. From the standpoint of some Colleges, even indexed equity investments are not as safe as property in yielding the desired level of income.

Oxford and Cambridge institutions are not averse to investing in absolute return strategies; a major deterrent in expanding such exposure was finding appropriate fund-of-funds managers. The risk of getting the manager selection wrong in hedge funds and private equity partnerships is higher than in ordinary active equity managers, the average return of a manager in the upper quartiles being significantly higher than in the lower quartiles where returns can be negative. The ability to identify such managers early enough in their investment cycle is crucial, and there is concern about the specific risk arising from high exposure to a few managers.

Over one-third of Colleges in Oxford and Cambridge did not invest in alternative strategies at all, particularly hedge funds, as this was perceived as being too risky. The aggregate exposure to alternative strategies is unavailable, but there is evidence to suggest it has increased significantly over this period, albeit from a low base. The increasing professionalism evident in investment approaches among Oxbridge institutions, by way of superior diversification strategies embracing assets and investment styles and leading to a rise in the appointment of specialist managers, illustrates what can be achieved within a relatively short time frame.

Approaches to risk

For experienced investors, a central aspect of asset management is risk control. Thus, understanding the risk profile of the overall portfolio lies at the heart of any assessment of investment alternatives. At the same time, risk is defined individually by every investor, and it is difficult to generalize, except in absolute terms. Though individual perceptions of risk may vary, better diversification can improve the risk-return profile of a portfolio by enabling investors to achieve higher returns for their preferred level of risk or lower risk for a target level of return.

The concept of risk among Oxford and Cambridge investment professionals is interesting because a theoretical definition of risk is often of little use to these individuals; what they are more comfortable with is the range of outcomes that may be experienced in their own institutions. For example, many investors within this sector believe that market volatility is of little consequence to the portfolio as long as income is unaffected. The major risk for them is the failure to secure the required income from the endowment. In an ideal world, these investors would like a sustainable source of income, inflation protected, and not have to worry about how exactly to secure that. This way of conceptualizing risk is also the reason why Colleges frequently think of property as a core asset. It can be argued that Oxbridge's diversity in approaches to asset allocation is largely attributable to their property holdings. Their policies may not be based on quantitative analytical models, but over the centuries, income from property has provided these institutions with an insight into the importance of income diversification.

There is also great diversity in approaches towards risk; investment policies appear to have a more qualitative basis, rarely being driven quantitatively. However, some institutions may have taken inappropriate, ill-informed risk exposures, and may not have been appropriately compensated for that risk. While it is assumed they evaluated investment alternatives, rarely was such analysis conducted systematically and at the level of the whole portfolio. It is quite likely that the level of inadvertent or unintended risks inherent in some College portfolios could drown the potential gains from superior investment skill, thereby leaving the endowment with a higher than intended volatility and a negative contribution to return. This is not to suggest that quantitatively driven investment decisions are superior. Investment decisions are in many organizations more qualitative in nature, but they need to be backed by rigorous quantitative analysis. Risk analysis and risk-adjusted performance were not apparent in more than a small handful of Oxford and Cambridge institutions. Bursars are deeply conscious of such a deficit and wish to address the problem; the question that engages them most is how best to do so.

As the major risks to the Colleges are those that would prevent them from carrying out their charitable objectives permanently, sustaining (if not

increasing) the contribution of the endowment to the Colleges' total operating budget is critical. Focusing on endowment asset management should
therefore be a major objective of the Colleges in their overall risk management. None of the institutions formally covers issues relating to the
degree of risk in their investment pool. At best, risk is managed through
diversification—in terms of asset classes, though not always through investment strategies and fund managers. Diversification is perhaps the least expensive way for institutions with relatively small-sized endowments to manage
portfolio risk, and it is encouraging that many bursars have expressed a strong
interest in how best to diversify their holdings. Nevertheless, for an endowed
institution, there is more to risk management than simply ensuring a spread
of assets in the portfolio.

Performance measurement

The lack of transparency in measuring investment performance and associated
costs remains the Achilles heel of endowment asset management in Oxford
and Cambridge. These institutions need a deeper understanding of their
sources of risk-adjusted performance ('alpha') as well as the risks involved in
attaining that performance. They need to comprehend both asset allocation
decisions (typically guided by the Investment Committee) and stock selection
(generally made by the asset managers). They also need to infer whether
investment returns were achieved as a result of superior decision-making
or were random and non-replicable outcomes—that is, they need to seek
evidence of skill. Needless to say, costs and fees feature in this analysis; when
we refer to performance, it is after-costs performance that matters.

One way to secure comprehensive performance analysis is to employ an
independent performance measurement firm. Outsourcing to an external firm
would secure economies of scale as well as consistency in the choice of
analytical method. Currently, performance analysis is fraught with limitations. Efficient asset allocation decisions cannot realistically be taken without
adequate information on the investment portfolios' aggregate profile on a
range of subjects, such as the asset mix, risk profile, costs, and performance
attribution. It is essential that these institutions address these issues urgently.

Analysis of the annual accounts of the Colleges in Oxford and Cambridge
that do disclose information on investment performance raises an array of
issues. For a start, there is no common standard for reporting investment
performance; no consistent basis for the measurement of performance, comparable analysis of benchmarks, or asset allocation. Long-term analysis of asset
allocation versus investment performance is not possible as neither set of data
is in the public domain. Some Colleges report investment performance without any actual reference to returns as illustrated in the following examples:

- The continued recovery in stock markets is reflected in the growth in the value of the College portfolio. Cash balances invested in the University Deposit Pool continued to earn a competitive interest rate (Linacre College, Oxford).

- The College's Investment Advisory Group (IAG) actively monitors the performance of the professional investment advisers retained by the College, and ensures that an appropriate allocation of asset types is maintained and monitored to pre-agreed benchmarks. The objective of the College is to maximize investment returns over the medium to long-term, taking into account such risk and liquidity factors as appropriate. The current structure is principally a mix of equity, bond and property holdings, while cash investments provide the College's working capital and assist in the management of operational cash flow.

  The College is fortunate in having a high quality commercial property and real estate base to its investment portfolio. In addition, the recovery in investment returns from equities and gilt-edged securities has been beneficial to the College's overall financial position over the course of the year (Corpus Christi College, Cambridge).

Others expressed investment performance in the following terms:

- College investments at the year end were valued at £32.34 million. They included investment properties valued at £4.75 million and non-marketable investments. The College's investment securities portfolio rose in value over the year from £22.63 million to £27.23 million. The increase mainly reflected the improvements in stock market values, but included new gifts that were added to the College's trust and special funds portfolio in the course of the year (Sidney Sussex College, Cambridge).

- The College's investments performed well for a second consecutive year. Outside the operational buildings of the College, which make up 66.1 per cent of its fixed assets, the College has commercial properties valued at £6,240,000 and yielding £540,386 in income, together with a number of equity and fixed interest holdings yielding income amounting to £717,033. These showed a total return (income and capital gain) of 16.51 per cent (Churchill College, Cambridge).

- The Investment Subcommittee manages the College's investment portfolio for total return and it should be noted that the actual endowment income receivable in any particular year as shown on the Income and Expenditure Account is only one component of the endowment return, and may fluctuate significantly from year to year. The benchmark for investment performance since 1 July 2003 has been set at a long term real return of 4.5 per cent. Investment performance is measured by calendar quarters and the total return on quoted endowment securities and cash was 13.2 per cent in the year to 30 June compared with 7.4 per cent for the benchmark. The College's trailing three year investment performance is 23.6 per cent which compares with 18.7 per cent for the benchmark. The total return on the FTSE All Share index over the three years was 25.3 per cent. The Subcommittee's general direction from the Governing Body and its Finance Committee is to provide for a prudent and sustainable percentage of the expected long run return on endowment to fund the College's objectives while at the same time aiming for some growth in real endowment capital. The Subcommittee believes that its sustainable spending target should range between 3 per cent and 4 per cent (St Catherine's College, Oxford).

There are about as many formats for reporting investment performance as there are Colleges. Lincoln College in Oxford, for example, under the heading 'Investment Performance' provided the following information in its financial statements for the year ended 31 July 2005:

The College's investments are under the direction of the Governing Body which acts on the recommendations of the Finance Committee. The Finance Committee is chaired by the Rector and benefits from the advice of two Committee members who are alumni of the College and who have special experience in investment and general financial matters. The College has continued to follow the investment plan formulated initially in October 2001. Investment strategy for financial assets is based on the maintenance of a core portfolio (UK and international equities and cash) supplemented by selected additional investments in specialist areas (private equity, hedge funds etc). During the latest year the College increased its private equity exposure by becoming a founding participant in the Oxford University Fund LP; and reinforced the 'core specialist' strategy by taking an exposure to global commodities, via Goldman Sachs Commodities Index certificates. The core financial asset portfolio is managed by JP Morgan Fleming Asset Management and the specialist investments by a variety of investment managers. The College's portfolio of commercial, agricultural and (non-student) residential properties is overseen by Laws and Fiennes of Broughton, Banbury.

For the purposes of operational budgeting a yield of 3% is assumed to be drawn down on a sustainable basis from the College's endowment assets. The actual yield on the College's investment portfolio was in excess of 3% in 2003–4.

Lincoln College has actually provided a significant amount of information relating to its endowment asset management arrangements, but not much on its actual asset allocation or investment performance.

Even Colleges that are relatively transparent may not disclose total return information in their annual account. All Souls College in Oxford, for example, for the year ending July 2005, reported its asset distribution: 22 per cent in UK-listed equities, 17 per cent in international equities, 3 per cent in private equity, 6 per cent in absolute return investments, 5 per cent in bonds and cash, and the remainder (47 per cent) in a diversified property portfolio. But, total return or individual asset class returns were not available for its endowment, valued at £182.8 million.

St John's College, in Oxford, on the other hand, does not give a detailed breakdown of its endowment asset allocation, except an indication of its broad allocation: listed equities (33.6 per cent), unlisted equities (4.2 per cent), listed fixed income stock (29.8 per cent), cash (3.3 per cent), and property (29.1 per cent). The College generated a return of 28.8 per cent from its UK equities portfolio, 37.6 per cent from its overseas equities holdings; overseas bonds returned 24 per cent; domestic Index-Linked bonds returned 13.9 per cent and property returns were 33 per cent. Each asset category comfortably outperformed its respective benchmark. While a total return figure for the endowment portfolio, worth £257.4 million, is not available, estimates suggest they were higher than the 22.3 per cent achieved by the Yale endowment in 2004–5 during which period the decline of the US dollar over the previous 3 years was reversed, albeit by a narrow margin.[1] Like the Yale endowment, St John's endowment benefited from its broad diversification, though the asset distributions were very dissimilar. Unlike Yale, we do not have access to long-term data to compare the merits of investment strategies pursued by these institutions.

To provide another example of higher returns achieved by a College with a high equity orientation is Somerville College in Oxford, which secured a return of 25 per cent in 2004–5 by holding 66 per cent of its endowment portfolio in equities, 28 per cent in bonds and cash, 4 per cent in unlisted securities, and 2 per cent in property. Somerville's endowment was valued at £32.6 million. Somerville endowment's performance benefited from its high equity allocation. Thus, property was not always the performance driver over the last few years, though Colleges with a high allocation to both property and equities generally did well.

As listed equity investments performed well in 2004–5, it is difficult to understand why Colleges such as Wolfson and St Anne's, in Oxford, with 67 per cent and 70 per cent respectively in listed equities, reported returns of 7.5 per cent and 16.25 per cent respectively when the FTSE All Share rose 24.7 per cent over that period. Wolfson's endowment included 15 per cent in property, 11 per cent in unlisted securities and 7 per cent in bonds and cash in addition to the 67 per cent in equity assets. Wolfson's endowment was worth £22.2 million; but there is no clear explanation for its poor return. St Anne's endowment (70 per cent in public equities, 14 per cent in bonds and cash, and 15 per cent in an internal loan to the College) had a similar allocation to equity assets, and it reported returns twice those reported by Wolfson. Without standardized portfolio reporting, it is hard to establish how and why different Colleges' endowments (some with similar allocations) performed differently.

Even Downing College in Cambridge that provided comprehensive information on its endowment asset allocation, its total, and benchmark return for 2004–5, failed to account fully for its rather lacklustre performance of 13.3 per cent total return for the year. We were informed the College portfolio was being restructured but that was not a serious analysis of well below median returns. Similarly, Gonville and Caius's total return of 20 per cent for the 'eleven months' of 2004–5 was better, but we were not given the underlying asset allocation or benchmark for analysing such performance. One of the poorest returns in Oxbridge was reported by Peterhouse; 10.9 per cent in 2004–5 compared with 2.3 per cent in 2003–4. Its endowment asset distribution was 84 per cent in property, 11 per cent in listed equity, and the remaining assets in subsidiary companies, cash and unlisted securities. The accounts provide no comparable benchmark returns or explanation for its paltry returns. The IPD index return was 18 per cent for the year, the FTSE All Share return was 24.7 per cent and overseas equities returned 23.8 per cent. So, it is difficult to understand the sources of Peterhouse's 11 per cent return.

Each of the Colleges cited above followed investment strategies resulting in differing asset profiles. That by itself is not surprising; what is worth noting is the dispersion of returns arising and tolerated within a single collegiate family. The Colleges, though related in a federal system, operate independently implementing asset allocation policies that make sense to each individual institution. But the range of investment returns among these closely knit institutions raises several issues and potential solutions. There is clearly little herding, which can be a good thing as long as it reflects greater independence of decision-making among these institutions resulting in greater competition.

However, performance should be rigorously analysed. There is no evidence to suggest such a process is in place. There could be better pooling of resources in terms of sharing information on returns, managers, costs, asset mix, and investment approach. There is an informal network of course, but individual investment strategies are not scrutinized among the peer group. Apart from providing networking opportunities, without relevant analytical material available to these institutions, the contribution to the decision-making process from peer consultation can be limited.

Colleges in Oxford and Cambridge are often constrained in what they can afford to do in terms of acquiring and using investment related information. As long as they are truly independent in seeking out individual solutions, it may be appropriate for some Colleges to increase their indexed allocation; for others, it could be investing more in alternative assets and absolute return strategies, including property. Blind replication of what the peer group is doing is not an option for a cohort of investors whose investment policies are highly individualized. But there is clearly scope for more pooling of resources. Knowing the peer group asset allocation could be advantageous in terms of overall decision-making, and benefits could be gained initially from a system of internal benchmarking.

As a third of Oxbridge endowments were invested in property, both the cost and performance of this asset class need to be assessed carefully. The cost of managing property is among the highest in total costs of endowment management. While a detailed cost breakdown between property and non-property investments is not available, overall cost analysis suggests that the Colleges are not paying too much for their endowment management. Nevertheless, the size of the opportunity for gaining good value for money may be gauged by considering that, for example, the £2 billion currently under fragmented management in Oxford is costing the collegiate University around £10 million per annum, which might be put to greater advantage.

Institutions within the endowment world have adopted an increasingly professionalized approach to asset management, as witnessed by the rise in employment of ex-investment bankers and finance specialists in the sector. These individuals are, in turn, more likely to hire investment consultants and to exploit new concepts in asset management, and the collective impact on future practices within endowments is set to rise. Future generations are likely to judge today's endowments by their long-term improvement in risk control and investment performance.

Conclusion

If asset allocation decisions, based on careful assessment of individual objectives, are interpreted as being more efficient, then these institutions in behaving independently could be regarded as being on the right path. From defining investment policy to risk management, though they agree broadly on investment issues and are aware of one another's general approaches, there is little herding among them. What they forego is the scope for economies of scale, not to mention greater centralization in decision-making. Such scale economies are hard to achieve because the Cambridge and Oxford Colleges are truly independent bodies, and are not simply departments of a single institution. However, increased transparency can have a similar effect, in that it is likely to support informed decision-making and to mitigate unnecessary risk-taking. The concern that Colleges compete with other endowments is not an argument for opacity. After all, despite considerable public disclosure, the investment strategies of Yale and Harvard are not easily copied.

The limited role of investment consultants in Oxford and Cambridge asset management may also have contributed to the lack of herding among the Colleges. The level of diversity manifest in all aspects of Oxbridge endowment management, except in the alternative assets area where Cambridge Associates and Fauchier Partners have facilitated greater cohesion and pooling of investments, is something that the Colleges value and seek to retain. As one external observer commented to us, 'Cambridge Associates seems to be making a killing advising colleges separately; pooling of endowments will generate considerable economies of scale.'

If consultants were to have a strategic role in asset allocation among institutions in Oxford and Cambridge, they would doubtless move towards more similar portfolios. While there is no hard evidence to suggest that the Colleges today possess a clear investment edge, apart from their expertise in property and their high allocation to the sector, it can be assumed that the substantial dispersion in their current asset allocation policies would be eroded. We do not know how many Colleges might be persuaded that, by following more homogenous strategies (at least for non-property assets), higher risk-adjusted returns could be achieved. But if that conviction were shared among Colleges, there would be increased pressures to pool endowment assets.

The extent to which investment consultants might make a difference to the asset management process among these institutions also depends on the degree to which consultants are willing to invest in researching the specific needs of the sector. The common perception among the bursars today is that the interests of the Colleges and their consultants are far from aligned. Differences in interest exist between an endowment and their external managers as well as their advisers. Problems surrounding investment horizon, intergenerational equity, tax matters, and various forms of risk, for example, concern endowments more intimately than other investors.

Diversity makes for more efficient portfolios and markets. Whether such a high level of diversity in investment approaches is necessary or desirable, taking into account the overall size of endowment assets in Oxford and Cambridge, is an interesting question. While the Colleges clearly value their independence, one of the questions that engaged all the Colleges was: 'Is there an ideal asset allocation for truly long-term investors such as educational endowments?' The asset allocation strategies of Ivy League institutions are examined regularly but not emulated. There exists a degree of scepticism about such strategies, primarily because access to similar investment opportunities remains limited for Oxbridge institutions.

Unlike pension funds in the 1980s and early 1990s, when balanced mandates based on peer group benchmarks were the norm, Oxbridge institutions remain refreshingly original in their investment approach. Such conviction-driven investing may disappear for a host of reasons, including the rise of 'professional' investment bursars and the increasing influence of investment consultants in strategic decision-making. The low penetration of consultants, coupled with an absence of specialized education for foundation and endowment asset managers, has driven a wedge between the endowment practices in Europe and North America. There is now greater awareness of peer group activity, increased impact from a new breed of professional investors in the sector, and a widening range of professional education activities targeted at endowments. For better or worse, it is likely that the current level of individualism revealed by these institutions will gradually disappear.

Notes

Acknowledgements

1. Note that in our tables, entries are rounded and hence may not sum to 100 per cent.

Chapter 1: Endowment definition

1. David F. Swensen, *Pioneering Portfolio Management: An Unconventional Approach to Institutional Investment* (Free Press, USA; 2000) p. 43.
2. 2004 *NACUBO* (National Association of College and University Business Officers) *Endowment Study* (NES) p. 32.
3. *Higher Education Financial Yearbook 2003* and *2005/6* editions.
4. 2004 NES, p. 148.
5. Ibid., p. 32.
6. *Higher Education Financial Yearbook 2005/6*, p. 2.III.
7. 'Costing, Funding and Sustaining Higher Education: A Case Study of Oxford University', Oxford Centre for Higher Education Policy Studies (OxCHEPS) and The Ulanov Partnership (February 2004), p. 2.
8. *Cambridge University Reporter, Accounts of the Colleges and Approved Foundations in the University of Cambridge*, Vol CXXXV, 18 March 2005, p. 159. According to a news item by Bloomberg, 'Cambridge and Oxford Adopt U.S. Methods to Win Alumni Donations', on 1 December 2005: 'At Cambridge it cost £13,500 to educate an undergraduate each year. The University receives £7,500 in state support and student tuition fees, which the government caps at £1,150. That leaves a £6,000 deficit per student per year.'
9. 'Costing . . . Oxford University', OxCHEPS, p. 12.
10. Ibid., p. 25.
11. Ibid., p. 28.
12. *Higher Education Financial Yearbook, 2005/6*.
13. 'Costing . . . Oxford University', OxCHEPS, p. 6.
14. Comparable data were not available for Cambridge as five Cambridge Colleges, including Trinity, opted not to report their accounts in the newly recommended SORP format. The published *Accounts of the Colleges* in the University of Cambridge for the year ending 2004 therefore does not include comparable data for all the Colleges. Total income for the 25 Cambridge Colleges reporting in the SORP format for the year ending 2004 was £139 million compared to Oxford's £210.6 million.

15. 'Oxford's Academic Strategy: A Green Paper', *Oxford University Gazette*, Vol 135 (February 2005), p. 9.
16. *University of Oxford: Financial Statements of the Colleges, 2003–2004*, New College, p. 1.
17. *Cambridge University Reporter, Accounts of the Colleges and Approved Foundations in the University of Cambridge*, Vol CXXXV, 18 March 2005, p. 699.
18. Professor Alison Richard, 'Public and Private: Universities, Government, and Society: The Annual Address of the Vice-Chancellor', 1 October 2005.
19. 'Inaugural Address by Dr John Hood, 5 October 2004.' See http://www.admin.ox. ac.uk/po/vc/hood_speech.pdf
20. See http://ed.sjtu.edu.cn/rank/2005/ARWU2005_Top100.htm. Also, 'The parlous state of European universities', *The Economist*, 25 September 2004, p. 52. Oxford was ranked fourth in the 2005 *Times Higher Education Supplement*'s World University Rankings, second (after Cambridge) in science, and second (after Harvard) in arts and humanities. The rankings name the world's top 200 universities measured on peer review, number of citations per faculty member, ratio of students to staff, number of international students and staff, and the opinion of global recruiters. The top ranking institution overall was Harvard University. Oxford and Cambridge were the only British universities to appear in the top ten rankings.
21. *University of Oxford: Financial Statements of the Colleges, 2002–2003*, Balliol College, p. 1.
22. *Cambridge University Reporter, Accounts of the Colleges*, Vol CXXXV, 18 March 2005, pp. 185, 190.
23. Ibid., p. 267.
24. Ibid., p. 743.
25. David F. Swensen, *Pioneering Portfolio Management* (The Free Press, US; 2000) pp. 36–7.
26. 2003 NES, p. x.
27. *University of Oxford: Financial Statements of the Colleges, 2002–2003*, New College, p. 1.
28. Ibid.
29. 'Special Report Higher Education', *The Economist*, 26 February 2005, pp. 77–9.
30. 2004 NES, p. xxxii.
31. Ibid., p. 42.
32. James Tobin, 'What Is Permanent Endowment Income?' *The American Economic Review*, Vol 64, No 2, Papers and Proceedings of the Eighty-sixth Annual Meeting of the American Economic Association (May 1974), pp. 427–32.
33. Professor Alison Richard, 'Public and Private: Universities, Government, and Society: The Annual Address of the Vice-Chancellor', 1 October 2005.

Chapter 2: The investment committee

1. *University of Oxford: Financial Statements of the Colleges, 2002–2003*, All Souls College, p. 1.
2. *Financial Report To The Board of Overseers of Harvard College, Fiscal Year, 2004–2005*, p. 23.

3. *The Yale Endowment Annual Report, 2004* and *2005*.
4. The WM Charity Fund Universe, established in 1984, is the UK's most representative database of charity fund assets. At the end of 2005, the universe consisted of 290 funds with a market value of £11.6 billion.
5. *Commonfund Benchmarks Study: Foundations and Operating Charities Report* 2005, p. 52. The Commonfund Institute, established in 2000, is responsible for Commonfund's research, education, and publishing activities. With approximately $32 billion in endowment and treasury assets under management, the Commonfund organization is one of the largest active managers of non-profit assets.
6. 2004 NES, p. 28.
7. *Commonfund Benchmarks Study: Educational Endowment Report, 2005*, p. 52.
8. Ibid., p. 78.
9. Ibid., p. 12.
10. Ibid., p. 53.
11. *Commonfund Benchmarks Study: Foundations and Operating Charities Report, 2005*, pp. 48–9.
12. Ibid., p. 13.
13. Ibid., p. 48.
14. Ibid., p. 50.
15. *Commonfund Benchmarks Study: Educational Endowment Report, 2005*, pp. 51–2.
16. 2004 NES, p. 28.

Chapter 3: Investment objective

1. *Wellcome Trust Annual Report and Financial Statements, 2005*, p. 14.
2. The Charity Commission, *Investment of Charitable Funds: Detailed guidance* (Version February 2003), p. 22. (See http://www.charity-commission.gov.uk/supportingcharities/cc14full.asp)
3. *Cambridge University Reporter, Accounts of the Colleges*, Vol CXXXV, 18 March 2005, p. 280.
4. Ibid, p. 50.
5. *Commonfund Benchmarks Study: Foundations and Operating Charities Report*, 2005, pp. 17–19.
6. *Financial Report to the Board of Overseers of Harvard College, Fiscal Year, 2003–2004*, p. 22.
7. *The Yale Endowment Annual Report, 2004*, pp. 4–5.
8. Elroy Dimson, Paul Marsh, Mike Staunton, *Triumph of the Optimists: 101 Years of Global Investment Returns* (Princeton University Press, 2002), pp. 149–62.
9. Ibid., pp. 150–1.
10. *Commonfund Benchmarks Study: Educational Endowment Report, 2005*, pp. 31–2.
11. *Cambridge University Reporter*, March 2005, pp. 17–18.
12. Ibid., p. 51.
13. Ibid., p. 164.
14. 2004 NES, p. 22–4.
15. James M. Litvack, Burton G. Malkiel, and Richard E. Quandt. 'A Plan for the Definition of Endowment Income', *The American Economic Review*, Vol 64, No 2, Papers

and Proceedings of the Eighty-sixth Annual Meeting of the American Economic Association (May 1974), pp. 433–7.

Chapter 4: Spending policy

1. Swensen, *Pioneering Portfolio Management*, p. 26.
2. Watson Wyatt Worldwide, *UK Charity Trustees' Survey, 2004*, pp. 8–9.
3. 2004 NES, p. 15.
4. *Commonfund Benchmarks Study: Educational Endowment Report* 2005, p. 30.
5. Swensen, *Pioneering Portfolio Management*, p. 37.
6. Yale University, *Report of the Treasurer*, 1965–6, ser. 62, no. 19 (New Haven, 1966), pp. 6–7.
7. *The Yale Endowment Annual Report, 2004*, p. 8.
8. 2004 NES, p. xxvi.
9. *Commonfund Benchmarks Study: Educational Endowment Report, 2005*, p. 26.
10. Ibid., p. 27.
11. *Commonfund Benchmarks Study: Foundations and Operating Charities Report, 2005*, p. 34.
12. Ibid., p. 37.
13. *Financial Report To The Board of Overseers of Harvard College, Fiscal Year, 2003–2004*, p. 42.
14. 2004 NES, p. 21.
15. *Commonfund Benchmarks Study: Educational Endowment Report, 2005*, p. 28.
16. 2003 NES, p. xi.
17. *Commonfund Benchmarks Study: Educational Endowment Report, 2005*, p. 35.
18. 2004 NES, pp. 397–430.
19. *Commonfund Benchmarks Study: Educational Endowment Report, 2005*, p. 28.
20. 2003 NES, p. xiii.

Chapter 5: Asset allocation

1. See Gary P. Brinson, Brian D. Singer, and Gilbert L. Beebower, 'Determinants of Portfolio Performance II: An Update', *Financial Analysts Journal* 47, No. 3 (1991), 40–8. This article builds on Gary P. Brinson, L. Randolph Hood, and Gilbert L. Beebower, 'Determinants of Portfolio Performance', *Financial Analysts Journal* 42, No. 4 (1986), 39–44.
2. Refer to Elroy Dimson, Paul Marsh, and Mike Staunton, *Triumph of the Optimists* (Princeton University Press, 2002).
3. 2003 NES, pp. 9, 33.
4. Ibid., p. x.
5. Ibid., p. xi.
6. Ibid.
7. See websites:
   http://vpf-web.harvard.edu/annualfinancial/pdfs/2002discussion.pdf
   http://www.yale.edu/investments/Yale_Endowment_02.pdf
8. 2004 NES, p. xxiii.

9. *Commonfund* Benchmarks *Study: Educational Endowment Report, 2005*, p. 16.
10. *The Yale Endowment Annual Report, 2004*, p. 5.
11. 2004 NES, p. ix.
12. Ibid., p. 7.
13. *Commonfund Benchmarks Study: Educational Endowment Report, 2005*, p. 16.
14. 2003 NES, p. 34.
15. See Burton G. Malkiel and Atanu Saha, 'Hedge Funds: Risk and Return', *Financial Analysts Journal*, 61, No. 6 (2005), 80–7.

Chapter 6: Investing in property

1. Examples of trading companies in Oxford:

   - Trading activities undertaken by All Souls College's subsidiary company, Chichele Property Company Limited, is liable to corporation tax like any other trading company. Profits made by this company is donated to the College, which in turn distributes them to other charities and worthy causes as determined by All Souls College's General Purposes Committee.

   - Not all subsidiary companies have a similar structure or purpose. St John's subsidiary undertaking, The Lamb and Flag (Oxford) Ltd, for example, is the wholly owned vehicle for the trading activities of Lamb and Flag public house in St Giles', Oxford. The College applies the profits from this business towards the financing of graduate studentships.

   - Magdalen Development Company Limited is a wholly owned trading subsidiary of Magdalen College, and its principal activity is property development.

   - The Merton College Charitable Trust makes grants to the College from donations received for the college while the Merton Enterprises Limited undertakes trading activities on behalf of the college and any profits are paid to Merton College under gift aid.

   - The Jacqueline du Pre Building Limited is the wholly owned vehicle for promoting music at St Hilda's College, and St Hilda's Properties was founded to promote acquisition of residencies for students of the College.

   - Balliol's subsidiary undertaking, the Appeal Trustees' Funds, is an exempt charity engaged in fundraising for education and related facilities at Balliol.

   Examples of trading companies in Cambridge:

   - Churchill College has three wholly owned operating subsidiaries which exist to provide additional revenue to the College and to optimize the use of the College infrastructure. These three companies are all registered and their accounts filed at Companies House. They are:

     - Churchill Residencies II Ltd—which develops property on the College site on behalf of the College.

     - The Møller Centre for Continuing Education Ltd—which operates facilities on the College site to provide a venue for training and staff development, including some conferences. It also runs some training and educational courses.

- Churchill Conferences Ltd—which markets the main College facilities as a conference venue.
- Fitzwilliam College reported two subsidiary companies; Fitzwilliam College Services Limited and Kawakawa Bay Limited.
- Girton College Property Services is the wholly owned trading subsidiary of Girton College.
- Caius Property Services Limited is the wholly owned subsidiary company of Gonville and Caius College; its principal activity is student accommodation development.
- Wolfson College reported three subsidiary companies; Lee Library Ltd., Wolfson College Cambridge Properties Ltd., and Wolfson Developments Ltd.

2. Swensen, *Pioneering Portfolio Management*, p. 219.

Chapter 7: Issues in portfolio management

1. David F. Swensen, *Unconventional Success: A Fundamental Approach to Personal Investment* (Free Press, USA; 2005), p. 185.
2. Swensen, *Pioneering Portfolio Management*, p. 135.
3. Burton Malkiel and Paul Firstenberg, *Managing Risk in an Uncertain Era: An Analysis for Endowed Institutions* (Princeton, NJ; Princeton University Press, 1976).
4. *Commonfund Benchmarks Study: Educational Endowment Report, 2005*, pp. 22–3.
5. Ibid., p. 23.
6. Swensen, *Pioneering Portfolio Management*, pp. 137–8, 297.
7. *Commonfund Benchmarks Study: Educational Endowment Report, 2005*, p. 23.
8. Swensen, *Pioneering Portfolio Management*, p. 248.

Chapter 8: Portfolio risk

1. The Charity Commission, *Investment of Charitable Funds: Detailed guidance* (Version February 2003), p. 14.
2. 2004 NES, p. 23.
3. Swensen, *Unconventional Success*, p. 14.
4. *Commonfund Benchmarks Study: Educational Endowment Report, 2005*, p. 22.
5. The Charity Commission, *Investment of Charitable Funds: Detailed Guidance* (Version February 2003), p. 25.
6. Swensen, *Pioneering Portfolio Management*, p. 249.

Chapter 9: Consultant selection and monitoring

1. 2004 NES, p. 28 and 2003 NES, p. 30.
2. *Commonfund Benchmarks Study: Foundations and Operating Charities Report, 2005*, p. 44.

Chapter 10: Manager selection and monitoring

1. Swensen, *Pioneering Portfolio Management*, p. 250.
2. 2004 NES, p. 23.
3. Ibid., p. 29.
4. The Charity Commission, *Investment of Charitable Funds: Detailed Guidance* (Version February 2003), pp. 27–8.
5. 2004 NES, p. 23.
6. *Commonfund Benchmarks Study: Educational Endowment Report* 2005, p. 47.
7. Ibid., p. 49.
8. Ibid., p. 48.
9. Ibid., p. 49.
10. Ibid., p. 50.

Chapter 11: Socially responsible investment

1. See Paul Myners, *Institutional Investment in the UK: A Review* (HM Treasury, UK; March 2001), p. 92.
2. The Charity Commission, *Investment of Charitable Funds: Detailed guidance* (Version February 2003), p. 18.
3. Interpretative bulletin relating to statements of investment policy, including proxy voting policy or guidelines, *Code of Federal Regulations* Table 29 Chapter XXV, 2509. 94–2, 1994.
4. 2004 NES, p. 25.
5. The Right Honourable John Denham, 'Building a Better World: The Future of Socially Responsible Pensions', Lecture at the UK Social Investment Forum, Annual General Meeting, 9 July 1998.
6. Charity Commission, *Investment of Charitable Funds: Detailed Guidance* (Feb. 2003), p. 17.
7. *Cambridge University Reporter*, p. 77.
8. Ibid., p. 165.
9. 2004 NES, p. 25.
10. 2003 NES, p. 5.
11. 2004 NES, p. 25.
12. Charity Commission, *Investment of Charitable Funds: Detailed Guidance* (Feb. 2003), p. 18.
13. 2004 NES, p. 26.

Chapter 12: Performance measurement

1. The Charity Commission, *Investment of Charitable Funds: Detailed guidance* (Version February 2003), p. 26.
2. 2004 NES, p. vii.
3. *Cambridge University Reporter, Accounts of the Colleges and Approved Foundations in the University of Cambridge*, Vol CXXXVI, 10 March 2006, p. 370.
4. Ibid.

5. 2003 NES, p. x.
6. 2004 NES, p. ix.

Chapter 13: Endowment management cost

1. Swensen, *Unconventional Success*, pp. 220–1.
2. 2004 NES, p. 17.
3. *Commonfund Benchmarks Study: Educational Endowment Report, 2005*, pp. 50–1.
4. Sarasin Chiswell, 'The Cost of Investment Management', *Charity Investment Matters*, January 2006, Issue 36, p. 5.

Chapter 14: Fund-raising: Role of gifts

1. 2004 NES, pp. 15–16.
2. *Commonfund Benchmarks Study: Educational Endowment Report, 2005*, pp. 36–7.
3. Swensen, *Pioneering Portfolio Management*, p. 43.
4. Ibid., pp. 36–7.
5. Professor Alison Richard, 'Public and Private: Universities, Government, and Society: The Annual Address of the Vice-Chancellor', 1 October 2005.
6. *Expenditures in Fund Raising, Alumni Relations, and Other Constituent (Public) Relations*, (Item Number 24502, CASE Books; 1990).
7. 'The Business of Giving: A Survey of Wealth and Philanthropy', *The Economist*, 25 February 2006, p. 16.
8. Adrian Sargeant and Juergen Kaehler, *Benchmarking Charity Costs* (CAF Research Programme, Research Report 5, UK; 1998).
9. Charities Aid Foundation, Charity Trends 2005.
10. 2004 NES, p. 18.
11. 2003 NES, p. 43.

Chapter 15: Concluding observations

1. $/£ exchange rates as at end-June: 2000 (1.51); 2001 (1.41); 2002 (1.52); 2003 (1.65); 2004 (1.81); 2005 (1.79); 2006 (1.85).

Bibliography

Acharya, S. (2002). *Asset Management: Equities Demystified*. UK: John Wiley & Sons.

Bernstein, P. L. (1997). 'What Rate of Return Can You Reasonably Expect... or What Can the Long Run Tell Us About the Short Run?', *Financial Analysts Journal*, 53 (2): 20–8.

Bodie, Z. (1995). 'On the Risk of Stocks in the Long Run', *Financial Analysts Journal*, 51 (3): 18–22.

Bolton, M. (2005). 'Foundations and Social Investment: Making Money Work Harder in Order to Achieve More', Esmée Fairbairn Foundation, The Ashden Trust, Charities Aid Foundation.

Brinson, G. P., Singer, B. D., and Beebower, G. L. (1991). 'Determinants of Portfolio Performance II: An Update', *Financial Analysts Journal*, 47 (3): 40–8.

—— Hood, L. R., and Beebower, G. L. (1986). 'Determinants of Portfolio Performance', *Financial Analysts Journal*, 42 (4): 39–44.

Cabinet Office Strategy Unit (2002). *Private Action, Public Benefit: A Review of Charities and the Wider Not-for-Profit Sector*. UK: The Cabinet Office.

CaritasData Limited (2004, 2005, 2006). *Higher Education Financial Yearbook*.

CASE Books (1990). Expenditures in Fund Raising, Alumni Relations, and Other Constituent (Public) Relations.

Charity Commission (2003). Investment of Charitable Funds: Detailed guidance.

Coiner, H. M. (1992). 'How Large a Fraction of University Endowment May Be Safely Spent?' *Journal of Higher Education Management*, 8 (1): 57–67.

Commonfund Institute (2004, 2005). Commonfund Benchmarks Study: Foundations and Operating Charities Report.

—— (2003, 2004, 2005). 'Commonfund Benchmarks Study': Educational Endowment Report.

Department for Education and Skills, UK (2003). The Future of Higher Education.

Dimson, E., Marsh, P., and Staunton, M. (2002). *Triumph of the Optimists: 101 Years of Global Investment Returns*. Princeton, NJ: Princeton University Press.

—————— (2003, 2004, 2005, 2006). *Global Investment Returns Yearbook*. ABN AMRO/London Business School.

The Economist

'The Business of Giving: A Survey of Wealth and Philanthropy', 25 February 2006.

'Universities as Global Businesses', February 26–4 March 2005, 77–9.

'The Parlous State of European Universities', 25 September–1 October 2004, 52.

'A Golden Age of Philanthropy?', 31 July–6 August 2004, 61–3.

'Philanthropy and the Arts', 18–24 August 2001, 75–7.

European Foundation Centre (2003, 2004, 2005). *Annual Report and Financial Statement*.

The Financial Times 'Breakaway Warning by Oxford College Head', 6 October 2004.

The Ford Foundation Advisory Committee on Endowment Management (1969, 1972), Managing Educational Endowments.

Garland, J. P. (2005). 'Long-Duration Trusts and Endowments', *The Journal of Portfolio Management*, 31 (3): 44–54.

Greenwich Associates (2004, 2005). Endowment and Foundation Asset Size, Asset Mix, and Spending Policies.

Harvard University (2003, 2004, 2005). Financial Report to the Board of Overseers of Harvard College.

Litvack, J. M., Malkiel, B. G., and Quandt, R. E. (1974). 'A Plan for the Definition of Endowment Income', *American Economic Review*, 64 (2): 433–7.

Malkiel, B. G. and Firstenberg, P. B. (1976). *Managing Risk in an Uncertain Era: An Analysis for Endowed Institutions*. Princeton, NJ: Princeton University Press.

—— and Saha, A. (2005). 'Hedge Funds: Risk and Return', *Financial Analysts Journal* 61 (6): 80–7.

Merton, R. C. (1991). 'Optimal Investment Strategies for University Endowment Funds', *National Bureau of Economic Research Working Paper No. 3820*, 39–40.

—— (1992). *Continuous-Time Finance*, Chapter 21. Oxford, UK: Basil Blackwell.

—— (1993). 'Optimal Investment Strategies for University Endowment Funds', in C. Clotfelter and M. Rothschild (eds.), *Studies of Supply and Demand in Higher Education*. Chicago, IL: University of Chicago Press.

Murison, A. (2005). Presentation to UK SIP, London.

Myners, P. (2001). 'Institutional Investment in the UK: A Review', HM Treasury, UK.

National Association of College and University Business Officers, USA (2003, 2004, 2005). *NACUBO Endowment Study*.

Olson, R. L. (1999). *The Independent Fiduciary*. USA: John Wiley & Sons.

—— (2003). *Investing in Pension Funds and Endowments: Tools and Guidelines for the New Independent Fiduciary*. USA: McGraw Hill.

Oster, S. M. (2003). 'The Effect of University Endowment Growth on Giving: Is There Evidence of Crowding Out?', *New Directions for Institutional Research*, 119: 81–92.

Oxford Centre for Higher Education Policy Studies (OxCHEPS) and The Ulanov Partnership (February 2004). 'Costing, Funding and Sustaining Higher Education: A Case Study of Oxford University'.

Richard, Professor Alison (2005). 'Public and Private: Universities, Government, and Society': The annual address of the Vice-Chancellor (1 October).

Russell, Chris (2006). *Trustee Investment Strategy for Endowments and Foundations*. UK: John Wiley & Sons.

Sarasin Chiswell
Annual Review (2004, 2005).
Compendium of Investment for Charities (2004, 2005).

Schneider, W., Dimeo, R., and Cluck, D. R. (1997). *Asset Management for Endowments and Foundations*. USA: McGraw-Hill.

Siegel, L. B. (2001). *Investment Management for Endowed Institutions*. The Ford Foundation.

Sparks, R. (1995). *The Ethical Investor*. UK: Zondervan Press.

—— (2002). *Socially Responsible Investment: A Global Revolution*. UK: John Wiley & Sons.

Steuerle, E. (1976). Distribution Requirements for Foundations, *U.S. Treasury Department, Office of Tax Analysis*, Paper 12.

Swensen, D. F. (2000). *Pioneering Portfolio Management: An Unconventional Approach to Institutional Investment*. New York: Free Press.

—— (2005). *Unconventional Success: A Fundamental Approach to Personal Investment*. New York: Free Press.

The Sutton Trust (March 2003). University Endowments—A US/UK Comparison.

Tobin, J. (1974). 'What Is Permanent Endowment Income?', *The American Economic Review*, 64 (2): 427–32.

The University of Connecticut Foundation Incorporated (2004). Reassessing Your Asset Allocation Strategy after a Reassuring 2003: Optimal Allocation to Achieve a Return that Supports a 5% Distribution (Does It Exist?).

University of Cambridge (2005, 2006). Accounts of the Colleges and Approved Foundations in the University of Cambridge.

University of Oxford

  'Oxford's Academic Strategy: A Green Paper', *Oxford University Gazette* (February 2005).

  Financial Statements (2003–4, 2004–5).

  Financial Statements of the Colleges (2003–4, 2004–5).

  Oxford Today: The University Magazine, various issues.

Watson Wyatt Worldwide (2004). *UK Charity Trustees' Survey 2004*.

Williamson, J. P. (1974). 'Endowment Funds: Income, Growth and Total Return', *The Journal of Portfolio Management*, 1 (1): 74–9.

WM Performance Services (2004, 2005). *WM Annual Review: UK Charity Funds*.

Yale University (2002, 2003, 2004, 2005). *The Yale Endowment Annual Report*.

Index

absolute return strategies 188, 190, 197, 213, 225, 279, 332
  virtually nonexistent 212
Academic Bursars 64
academic fees 19, 20, 23, 25
  agreement to reduce 29
academic pay, *see* salaries
accountability 226, 227, 230, 232
ACT (Advance Corporation Tax) 30, 34, 83
advisers 171, 173–4, 210, 213–14, 233
  key 65, 68
  see also consultants
agricultural property 172
All Souls College (Oxford) 14, 17, 51, 93, 96, 266, 337
  access to direct partnerships 145
  collective responsibility for maintenance of buildings 170
  endowment income distribution 117
  Estates and Finance Committee 50, 209
  fund-raising initiatives 317, 318, 319
  General Purposes Committee 163, 209
  Investment and Property Sub-Committees 50, 209
  operational deficit 25
  risk assessment 209
  trading activities by subsidiary company 163
allocation to property 130, 150–4, 163–8, 171, 213, 215, 235, 296, 300
  aggregate 159, 332
  high 125, 126, 139, 160, 170, 175, 181, 190, 216–17, 248, 285, 294, 297, 304, 308, 310, 338
  overweight 130, 132
  significant 122
  spread in 129
alternative assets 122, 125, 127, 128, 129, 131, 135, 136, 138, 143–50, 178, 237
  access to 133, 213, 239
  allocation to 261
  collective funds for 162
  higher exposure to 304
  low or no allocation to 192
  no exposure to 166
  pooling of investments in 162

property a substitute for 160
  reason for not investing in 151
  rebalancing in 194
  safer way of investing in 269
alumni 42, 45, 233, 317
  as advisers 68
  cultivating 324
  cultural differences in giving 29
  gifts from 320
  goodwill and investment expertise of 55
  maintaining relations 322
annual deficits 22, 23, 24, 25
appreciation 295, 316
arbitrage 200
aristocracy 181–2
Asia 7
asset allocation 2, 7, 47, 104, 121–59, 165, 188, 197, 233, 234, 331–3
  ability to alter 10
  advice on 238
  aggregate 299
  allocation of risk 328
  appropriate 79
  astute policies 41
  benchmark 71
  changes in 59, 116, 203
  clearly defined spending policy decisions 102
  detailed 288–9
  dictated by needs of annual operating budget 102
  allocation differences in 232, 297, 306
  efficient 190, 335
  expected return target 79
  exploring new policies 116
  high exposure to property in 179
  ideal 333
  immense possibilities 185
  impact of property on 176–81
  influences on 13, 99, 104
  information on 95
  key advisers to formulate policy 65, 68
  lack of standardization in 205
  liquidity influence on 216
  long-term 102, 213, 240
  major issues in 168

asset allocation (*Cont.*)
  marginally positive 296
  policy formally defined 96
  positive input in 236
  property holdings excluded from 176, 177,
    178
  rebalancing and 54
  scepticism with regard to 197
  search for an ideal 215
  short-term 290
  spending policy did not affect 105
  split 167
  SRI issues and 275–9
  tactical 196, 200, 240, 298
  target 168
  total return approach to 87
  unshackling from income constraints 84
  very concentrated, risks associated with 168
  wide bands of 197
  widespread improvements in 70
  see also allocation to property; strategic asset
    allocation
asset management 162
  analysis 258–68
  changes in 256–8
  expenditure to 305
  few institutions provide comprehensive
    information on 290
  review 254–6
  selection 248–52
Associated Trusts 11
Association of British Insurer Guidelines 281
Atlantic Philanthropies 2
auditors 210, 286

Bacon and Woodrow 238
Bacon Hewitts 243
Balliol College (Oxford) 44
  Appeal Trustees Fund 10–11
  endowment management costs 304
  Governing Body 34
  property assets 139, 152, 162, 168, 207
  Specific Trust Funds 8
  substantial deficit 34
bank deposits 155
bank loans 183
Barclays 282
Barings 64, 214, 238
bear markets 101, 102, 104, 113, 142, 144, 161
  recovery after 213
benchmarks 70, 95, 96, 97, 174, 226, 229, 245,
  253, 284, 287, 288
  asset allocation 71
  clearly formulated 200
  composite 224
  customized 196, 214, 289, 290, 292, 295
  depressed performance vis-à-vis 296

  establishing 236
  internally established 175
  mutually agreed 230
  outperformed 294
  peer-group 128, 129, 214, 292, 295
  performance falls short of or consistently
    above 230
  pre-agreed 336
  risk management 225
  risk relative to 213–15
  see also Commonfund Benchmarks Study
benefactions 316–17, 323
bequests 8, 31, 39, 185, 323
  unrestricted 34
Berkeley (University of California) 22, 24
Bermuda 2
best practices 50, 96, 167, 183, 209
  risk management 226
BGI (Barclays Global Investors) 253–4
Bidwells 289
Bill and Melinda Gates Foundation 2
Bishop of Oxford case (1992) 271, 274
blacklisted stocks 278
block grants 29
board and lodging charges 21, 23
bonds 24, 133, 155, 173, 262, 338
  index linked 288
  overseas 288
  property a substitute for 162
  risky 190
  unanticipated inflation damages 161
borrowing 183–4, 326
  external 24
brokers 226, 246, 268
Buckmaster & Moore 10
Budd, Sir Alan 5, 237
Buffet, Warren 2
Building Societies 155
bull markets 113
bursars:
  asset allocation 123, 125, 128, 146, 147–8,
    149, 161
  brokers and 226, 246
  comparative information on costs 311
  curbing operating expenses 296
  female 64–5
  health and safety issues 210
  'inheriting' fund managers 250
  investment objectives 74–5, 76, 80, 87, 91,
    92, 100
  market risk 211, 213
  professional background 229
  property investment 160–2, 167–9, 171–80,
    201, 214–15
  senior 224
  spending policy 102, 105, 106, 110,
    113–16

willingness to use financial instruments 204
see also Academic Bursars; Domestic Bursars;
    Estates Bursars; Finance Officers;
    Investment Bursars; Property Bursars

Calls and Puts 204
Cambridge Associates 87, 145, 147, 148, 207,
    215, 223, 233–4, 236, 239, 259, 296
  dominance in investment consulting 240
  influence on investment policy 237
  most widely cited in Oxford 252
  private equity 197, 237, 265, 266, 268
  success of 241
Cambridge University:
  accounts 295, 302
  aggregate income from public sources 20
  Anniversary Campaign (800th) 29, 316
  annual endowment return disclosure 285
  capital project expenditures 24
  cash holdings 216, 217
  distribution of endowment income 20–1,
    113, 125
  endowment management costs 306–11
  equity culture 139
  expenditure 25, 26
  female bursars 64–5
  gifts 320
  housing undergraduate students 37
  income from donations and benefactions 317
  investment consultants 61, 67, 233–40
  investment decision-making 9
  investment strategy 189, 190
  Ivy League funding comparison versus 26–32
  less well-endowed Colleges 132
  losses reported 297
  median annual salary for full professor 22
  non-property managers 265
  older Colleges better able to attract gifts and
    donations 41
  pooling of investments in alternative
    assets 162
  portfolio changes 199
  rebalancing process 197, 198
  recent trends in fund-raising 316–20
  richer Colleges 41, 132, 142, 144, 150, 308,
    310
  risk factors 209, 211, 216, 217, 219, 221
  total return approach 87
  wealthiest Colleges 151
Cambridge University Colleges, *see* Christ's;
    Churchill; Clare; Downing; Emmanuel;
    Girton; Gonville and Caius; Homerton;
    Hughes Hall; King's; Lucy Cavendish; New
    Hall; Newnham; Pembroke; Peterhouse;
    Queen's; Robinson; St John's; Selwyn;
    Sidney Sussex; Trinity; Trinity Hall;
    Wolfson

Cambridge University institutions/offices:
  Board of Scrutiny 4
  Council 4
  Deposit Pool 11, 155
  Development Office 319, 322
  Endowment Fund (Amalgamated Fund) 10,
    11, 60, 291, 296
  Finance Committee 4
  Fitzwilliam Museum 39
  Investment Board 51–2, 146
  Investment Office 10, 11, 29, 44, 328
  Learning and Examination Scheme
    (Cambridge Assessment) 11
  Regent House 4
*Cambridge University Reporter, Accounts of the
    Colleges (2003–4)* 86, 94, 210, 303
capacity constraint 148
capital 317
  better access to 179
  boosting inflows 2
  depleted 326
  development programmes 38
  expendable 9
  growth 288
  out-flows from endowment 326
  projects 24
  share 228
capital appreciation 39, 93
capital gains 166
Capital Group 299
capital losses 166, 184, 225
capital markets:
  global 143
  volatility and downward trend 217
CAPS (Combined Actuarial Pension Service)
    data 174
Carnegie, Andrew 2, 315
Carnegie Institution 3, 315–16
Carr Sheppards Crosthwaite Savills Fund
    Management 173
CASE (Council for Advancement and Support
    of Education) 319, 320, 321, 322
cash 124, 128, 131, 132, 135, 136, 143, 167,
    216, 228, 262, 338
  allocation of 154–6
  balances managed in-house 266
  income to meet liabilities 166
  money market 288, 303
  overweighting of 296
  predictable return on incremental equity
    165
cash flow:
  discounted 173
  problem with 24
  reduction in 30
  sufficient 217
catastrophic event scenario 167, 168

Cazenove 268
Chancellor 5
charities 1, 5, 10, 11, 36, 55, 131
    amount recoverable in respect of tax credits
        on ordinary dividends 30
    biomedical, world's largest 69, 109, 195
    internally managed investment pool 250
    investment committee demographics
        among 59
    larger, likely to employ investment
        consultant 111
    larger, trustees of 270
    obligations of trustees 70
    obliged to invest for income 205
    optimal rate of disbursement 98
    profits distributed to 163
    recent changes in the regulation of 221
    smaller, unlikely to employ investment
        consultant 111
    withdrawal of ACT relief from 30
Charities Act (1993) 5
Charities Aid Foundation report (1998) 321
Charities Bill (2006) 7
Charity Commission (UK) 5, 7, 71, 98, 208,
    221–2, 252, 253, 271, 273, 276, 284, 321
Charity Property Fund 152, 169, 170, 173, 175,
    178, 266, 268
Chartered Colleges 5
Chichele Property Company Limited 163
Chiswell Associates 238
    See also Sarasin Chiswell
Christ Church (Oxford) 14, 17, 44, 266, 304
    expenditure 25
    property assets 181
    Specific Trust Funds 8
Christ's College (Cambridge) 6, 306
    endowment income distribution 117
    information on donations 318
    significant investments in hedge funds 145
Christ's Hospital 90
Church Commissioners 272
Churchill College (Cambridge) 163, 289, 336
    Investment Advisory Committee 94
CIOs (Chief Investment Officers) 5, 10, 44, 52,
    54, 62, 66, 138, 196, 328
Clare College (Cambridge) 288–9, 295, 306
    aims and objectives 72–3
    ethical investment policy 272
    SIP 94–5
collective funds 197, 225, 226, 231
College Contributions scheme 36, 42–3
College Fee reduction 43
Columbia University 13
commercial development 20
commercial property 162, 164, 172, 289
commercialisation 31
Commoners 1

Commonfund Benchmarks Study (2005) 55–6, 58,
    59, 63, 65, 77, 88, 108–9, 112, 117, 119,
    136, 142, 198, 235, 260, 261, 263, 311–12,
    314
Companies Act (1985) 163
compensation arrangements 301
Conference of Colleges in Oxford 23
conservatism 203–4, 210
consolidated accounts 163
construction projects 24
consultants 61, 65, 67, 98, 171, 186, 209, 329
    absence in strategic asset allocation 205
    contribution of 239–40
    lack of, in property 299
    length of appointment 240–1
    low usage of 111
    most widely cited in Oxford 252
    responsible for rebalancing 197
    selection and monitoring 233–43
    stochastic asset-liability model 196
    see also Cambridge Associates; Fauchier
        Partners
contracts 28
corporation tax 36, 163
    see also ACT
Corpus Christi College (Cambridge) 308, 336
Corpus Christi College (Oxford) 304
Council 4, 9, 55
Council funds 19, 20
CPI (Consumer Price Index) 79
CUP (Cambridge University Press) 6, 11
currency hedging 204, 291

Dawson, Oliver 10
debt 24, 162
    unsecured 200
deflation 161
Denham, John 271
departmental heads 210
Deposit Pools 10, 11, 155, 266, 268–9, 288,
    291, 296
depreciation 40, 290, 295
derivatives 189, 203–4, 229, 301
    guidelines regarding the use of 227
Diageo 279
disclosure 6, 271, 284–5, 288, 302, 307–8, 328
    selective 294
diversification 9, 121, 122, 128, 140–1, 146,
    162, 180, 335
    alternative assets there to provide 149
    avoiding exposure to catastrophic event
        scenario 167
    determined by objectives of the investor 161
    fund manager 173
    implementation of strategies 225
    income 206
    manager appointments 223

opportunity for 176
overall 149
portfolio 213
property contributes to 160
risk managed through 232
scope for better 268
strategies for 138
strong 167
superior strategies 333
time for 168
uncorrelated assets and strategies 210
dividends 29, 30, 42, 50, 73, 95, 99, 285
abolition of tax credits on 84
reinvested 85
Domestic Bursars 64
female 65
Domestic Committees 210
domestic staff 210
donations 2, 21, 27, 31, 41, 320, 324
annual 3, 324
financial 323
income from 317, 318, 324
large, one-off 321
older Colleges better able to attract 41
surpluses from 23
undesignated or general 102
unrestricted 34
Downing College (Cambridge) 39, 288–9,
    338–9
active SRI stance 274
Governing Body 274
Investment Committee role in setting asset
    allocation 95
published accounts (2003–4) 274
SIP 95
drawdown 38
due diligence 147, 156, 213, 250, 286

earnings power 165
impeccable 166
eBay 2
economies of scale 232, 242, 268
Economist, The 45
eleemosynary corporations 1
El-Erian, Mohamed 53
Emerging Markets 190, 296
need to avoid investments in 203
Emmanuel College (Cambridge) 117, 306,
    318
endowment management:
costs 301–13
governance structure 327–30
engagement strategies 274, 279
equity allocation 123–4, 132, 138–43, 146, 152,
    211–12
Estates Bursars 64, 115
ETFs (Exchange Traded Funds) 301

ethical investment policy 71, 271, 272, 274,
    276, 277, 279
Ethical Investors Group 277
Europe/EU countries 7, 29, 55
enlargement 161, 182
expected returns 79, 83, 104, 115, 141
long-term 152

F&C (Foreign & Colonial) Asset
    Management 10, 223, 259, 303, 309
factor-based style analysis 290
farmland holdings 164
Fauchier Partners 145, 147, 197, 259, 265–6,
    268
fees 19, 20, 21, 25, 92, 213
gap between cost of education and 23, 34
higher 23–4, 27, 41
loss of income 43
performance-related 301, 303
publicly-funded 30
top-up 29
variable 29
see also academic fees; tuition fees
Fellows 1, 4, 51, 64, 148, 170, 172
costs 92
need to achieve consensus among 217
Fellows Housing Scheme 175
fiduciary issues 255
institutional principals 226
obligations 2, 122, 270, 325
risk 156, 218–19, 223
Finance Committees 50, 64, 172, 209, 328, 337
Finance Officers 64, 175
financial aid 26
Financial Delegates 210
financial instruments 204
financial markets 185
risks associated with 219
Fitzwilliam Museum (Cambridge) 39
fixed-income assets 124, 125, 126, 130, 131,
    132, 133, 135, 136, 139, 142
exotic products 188
low allocations to 297
fixed-income management 267
foreign equity 133, 135, 141
foundations 1, 7, 9, 31, 58, 78
extensive research on 215
investment committee demographics
    among 59
largest/larger 2, 59, 234, 301
many older ones do not accept gifts 3
smaller 56, 59
spending rules 108–9
wealthier 59
see also Bill and Melinda Gates; Commonfund
    Benchmarks Study; James Martin
France 29

Franklin W. Olin College of Engineering 15
fraud prevention/detection 210
FTEs (full time equivalent) students 14–18, 22, 47, 65, 235, 327
FTSE indices 81, 190, 290, 292
   All Share 113, 123, 141, 213, 217, 225, 287, 288, 295, 336, 338, 339
   FTSE4Good 281
   World 290
   World ex-UK 287, 288
fund managers 123, 143, 146, 149, 173, 196, 199–200, 203, 238
   ability to gain exposure to the best 150
   best 239, 240
   bursar typically the point of contact for 226
   competence of 220
   credibility of new breed 150
   external 223, 224, 231
   failure to deliver income 220
   good, difficult to identify 148
   herding mentality of 237
   high cost of changing 221
   IMA with 223
   lack of specialisation among 237
   overall asset allocation 299
   relationships between Colleges and 147
   return targets for 225
   risk instructions to 224
   selection and supervision of 244–69
   stock selection 298
fund-of-funds managers 333
fund-raising 29, 31
   cost of 320–2
   recent trends 316–20

Gates Trust (Cambridge) 6, 11
   see also Bill and Melinda Gates Foundation
gender 64
General Accounting Standards 40
General Endowments 7–8
General Funds, see Unrestricted Funds
General Purposes Committees 50, 163, 209
Germany 29
gifts 2, 8, 25, 27, 31, 41, 102, 336
   annual 3
   Colleges that historically received land as 170
   directed towards endowment 29
   donors frequently specify a particular purpose for 9
   leveraging the value of 24
   many older foundations do not accept 3
   older Colleges better able to attract 41
   permanent support towards specific activity 102
   role of 314–24

gilts 217
   long-dated 202
GIPS (Global Investment Performance Standards) 286
Girton College (Cambridge) 9, 39, 40
'Giving-while-Living' 2, 3
Glaxo Wellcome 30
GlaxoSmithKline 279
Global Growth & Income Fund 304
globalization 19, 45, 143
Goldman Sachs Commodities Index certificates 337
Gonville and Caius College (Cambridge) 217, 266, 308, 310
   Annual Report and Accounts (2003–4) 72
   endowment asset worth 14
   hedge funds and private equity 7, 145
   Perse Trust 11
   Specific Trust Funds within Consolidated Trust Fund 8
   total return 339
Good Corporation Charter 273, 279
Governing Bodies 1, 4, 30, 34, 36, 50, 51, 52, 149, 153, 204, 209, 274, 337
   bursars build important relationships with 65–6
   Investment Committee as adviser to 328
   key decisions 120, 330
   preserving endowment assets 102
   recommendations on Investment Committee membership 55
   responsibilities 72, 210, 286
   stable membership 55
government:
   decision to abolish tax credit on dividends 29
   failure to provide full cost of operating 26
   funding 19, 31, 49
   transfer of resources from 2
Graduate Houses 36
graduate studentships 35
grant-making institutions 3, 98
grants:
   block 29
   private 21
   research 19, 20, 28
   surpluses from 23
Green College (Oxford) 5
Grigson, R. S. G. 128

Harris Manchester College (Oxford) 6, 96, 304
Harvard University 3, 7, 13, 17, 18, 46, 187, 240, 315, 316, 327, 329, 330
   admission based entirely on merit 26
   asset allocation 135, 141, 142, 154, 161
   capital project expenditures 24
   cost of attending 22

cost of endowment management 303
distribution policies 109–10
expenditure 25, 26
exploitation of illiquid, less efficient
    markets 332
FTE students 15, 16
fund-raising initiatives 320, 321
high allocations to alternative strategies 215
investment in wider range of assets 114
investment objective 78
largest source of nongovernmental
    income 47
major contributory factor in generating
    wealth 41
major redevelopment 38
median annual salary for full professor 22
operating budget 99
overall performance and asset allocation 292
revenue sources 27
risk-taking 160
specific funds 8–9
spending rate 109
total revenue 28
wealth of students 14
Harvard University institutions/offices:
Endowment 89, 139
General Investment Account 52, 53, 55, 78,
    290
Policy Portfolio benchmark 78
see also HMC
Heads of College 1, 4, 56
health and safety issues 210
hedge funds 7, 122, 125, 127, 136, 143, 162,
    182, 197, 231, 236, 239, 262, 265–6
allocation to 146, 191, 285
concern over 213
credibility of new breed of managers 150
difficulties associated with 226
growth of the sector 188
information on 148
institutions not heavily exposed to 217–18
managers 225
preference for 147, 148–9
risk of 146, 147, 190
significant investments in 145
successful, identifying 146
Hedley, Barry 217
Henry II, King of England 5
Henry III, King of England 5
HEPPI (Higher Education Pay and Prices
    Index) 81, 95, 115, 117, 175
herding 214, 232, 237, 241
Hermes group 272, 273
Hertford College (Oxford) 21, 81, 115,
    300
Higher Education Act (2006) 24, 45
Higher Education Financial Yearbook (2005–6) 18

Higher Education Funding Council for
    England 4, 19, 20
HMC (Harvard Management Company) 52, 53,
    78, 109
Annual Report 79–80
Board of Directors 328
cornerstone for management of investments
    of 71
fiscal year return (2004) 296
Policy Portfolio 133, 135
target policy portfolio 167
Homerton College (Cambridge) 5
Hood, John 31, 43–4
housekeepers 36
housing 175
student 203
HSBC Investment Management 268
Hughes Hall (Cambridge) 6, 40
human rights 272

IAG (Investment Advisory Group) 336
Iain More Associates 321–2
illiquid investments 146, 152, 167, 194, 237,
    253
lack of information relating to 218
property 217
IMAs (investment management
    agreements) 221, 222, 223
characteristics of 226–32
immigration policy 161
Imperial College London 31
in-house management 155, 187, 251, 266
income-only spending policies 104, 105, 111,
    114
income tax 181
indexation 187–8, 189, 193, 204
top three allocations to 192
individualism 205, 214, 232
inflation 37, 71, 80, 81, 94, 95, 99, 219, 296
costs ahead of 45
fees not keeping pace with 43
secure hedge against unexpected changes
    in 160
spending and 84, 102, 103, 104, 109, 114–17
unanticipated 161
inflation vulnerability to 79, 139, 331
wage 75, 76
inflationary pressures 102, 115
infrastructure 19, 263
long-term underinvestment in 25
lower investments in 22
optimizing use of 163
Institute of Business Ethics 273
institutional investors 121, 122, 139, 143
Intel 2
interest rates 161
commercial 304

intergenerational equity 69
international equity 145
  see also foreign equity
international scholarship programme 11
Investment Advisory Committee 273
investment assets 39
investment banks 239–40
investment behaviour 162
Investment Bursars 6, 53–4, 62, 63–6, 81, 155,
    254
  direct investment in property 123
  efficient portfolios 333
  management of property assets 171–2
Investment Committees 5, 6, 10, 11, 29,
    50–68, 99, 123, 147, 208, 223, 288, 328–9,
    330
  active management decisions 290
  asset allocation policy 196
  collaboration with 237
  expertise within 233
  first to hire consultants 241
  key task of 254
  larger endowments and foundations 301
  manager selection/monitoring process 251,
    254
  rebalancing responsibility 197
  risk averse and conservative 203–4
  strategic asset allocation usually determined
    by 298
investment objectives 69–97, 289, 327, 328
  assisting institutions in defining 252
  income-driven 105
Investment Sub-Committees 146, 149, 290,
    336–7
investment trusts 173
  real estate 122, 123
IPD (Investment Property Database) index 174,
    175, 287, 288, 339
  All Property 292
IPOs (initial public offerings) 85
Ireland 2
IRS (US Internal Revenue Service) 108–9
Isaac Newton Trust, The 11
Ivy League 41, 205
  asset allocation strategies 242
  funding comparison with Oxbridge 26–32
  Investment Committees 62
  salaries 21
  wealth of Colleges 182
  see also Columbia; Harvard; Princeton; Yale

James Martin 21st Century Foundation 11
Japan 203, 322
JCR (Junior Common Room) 277
Jesus College (Cambridge) 151, 306
  annual account (2004–5) 289
  gifts and legacies 321

Jesus College (Oxford) 6, 14, 181, 183
  operational deficit 25
  property investment 151
Jewson (Edward) 238
Jiao Tong University 31
JP Morgan Fleming Asset Management 337
JP Morgan Global Bond Ex UK Index 288
JPM Global Govt Bond index 287

Keble College (Oxford) 163, 304
Kellogg College (Oxford) 5
Keynes, John Maynard 39, 153
King's College (Cambridge) 39, 310
  endowment asset worth 14, 308
  expenditure 25
  First Bursar 153
  operational deficit 25
Kyoto University 25

Lady Margaret Hall (Oxford) 94
Lamb and Flag (Oxford) Ltd., The 35
Lambert review (2003) 23
land agents 171, 172–3
LaSalle Investment Management Limited 259,
    303
Laws and Fiennes 337
lawyers 223
legacies 31, 318, 320, 321
Lehman Aggregate Bond Index 78
leverage 263
Levin, Richard 62
liabilities 166, 196
  indeterminate nature of 325
Linacre College (Oxford) 304
Lincoln College (Oxford) 288, 337
Liontrust Asset Management 147
liquidity:
  and associated costs 253
  constraints 149
  good 183
liquidity risk 179, 216–18
listed buildings 34
  Grade I 35, 38, 170, 174
Litvack, J. M. 97
Local Education Authorities 19, 29
London:
  Albany, Piccadilly 161, 164
  Harley Street 162
  West 40, 172
London School of Economics 27, 90
Lucy Cavendish College (Cambridge) 6, 39,
    307, 309

Magdalen College (Oxford) 6, 14, 182, 266
  Development Trust 11
magister scolarum Oxonie 5
Malkiel, B. G. 97, 194

management structure 52–4
manager selection 10, 333
Manciples 210
Mansfield College (Oxford) 304
market equilibrium 161
market liberalization 143
market-timing strategies 194, 211
Martin, James 320
Masters 5, 55
meals 37
Mellon Investment Funds 304
Mercer 238, 243
Merton College (Oxford) 14, 93, 304
Meyer, Jack 53
Michigan University 22
MIT (Massachusetts Institute of
    Technology) 13, 16, 327
money market:
    cash on 288, 303
    fixed-term deposits 155
Moore, Gordon and Betty 2
Morgan Stanley 238
    Private Wealth Management 95, 288
Morris, William Richard, 1st Viscount
    Nuffield 41
moving average approach 104, 107, 109, 110,
    112, 113, 114
MSCI indices 143, 213, 292
Murison, Andrew 22, 38, 92, 122–3, 128, 153,
    164–5, 166, 181, 317

National Insurance Contributions 34
NES (NACUBO Endowment Study 2004) 18, 42,
    57, 66, 96, 100, 107, 112, 119, 130, 131,
    133, 136, 137, 143, 195, 248, 275, 296, 297,
    311, 314, 323
New College (Oxford) 93, 321
    functional estate 39–40
New College Development Fund 11, 39, 43,
    321
New Hall (Cambridge) 17, 306
New York 322
Newnham College (Cambridge) 307, 309
    Specific Trust Funds 8
Newton Asset Management 268
Nominations Committee 55–6
non-EU students 27
Norrington League Table 38
Norwegian Petroleum Fund 69–70
Nuffield College (Oxford) 41, 42, 317, 318,
    319
    endowment asset worth 14
    operational deficit 25

OECD (Organization for Economic
    Cooperation and Development) 29
OEIC (open-ended investment company) 250

older Colleges 41, 42, 149, 151–2
    average property holding 152–3
Omidyar, Pierre 2
operational assets 81, 169, 181
    accounting for endowment and 35–9
    transferring investment assets into 33
Ordinance 4
Oriel College (Oxford) 181, 183, 304
OUP (Oxford University Press) 6, 11
overseas equity 141, 142, 199–200, 228
    see also foreign equity
overseas students 200
    higher fees payable by 27
oversight 213
oversupply 161
Oxford Absolute Return Partnership 265–6, 268
Oxford and Cambridge Act (1571) 5
    see also Universities of Oxford and Cambridge
    Act
Oxford City:
    Cornmarket Street 183
    Lamb & Flag public house, St Giles 35
Oxford College Benchmarking Study 322
Oxford Investment Management Company 68
Oxford Limited Partnership 265
Oxford Science Park 182
Oxford University:
    accounts 23, 291, 295, 302, 317
    aggregate income from public sources 20
    alternative assets and cash 166–7
    annual endowment return disclosure 285
    capital project expenditures 24
    cash holdings 216
    disparities of wealth among Colleges 180
    distribution of endowment income 20, 21,
        113, 125
    endowment management costs 304–6
    equity culture 139
    expenditure 25, 26
    female bursars 64–5
    gifts and donations 41, 320
    governance structure 4
    housing undergraduate students 37
    investment consultants 61, 67, 233–40
    investment decision-making 9
    investment strategy 190
    Ivy League funding comparison versus 26–32
    losses reported 297
    non-property managers 265
    operational surplus 24
    overseas marketing 45
    passive investment strategies 189
    portfolio changes 199
    rebalancing process 197, 198
    recent trends in fund-raising 316–20
    richer Colleges 41, 132, 142, 144, 150, 151,
        154

Oxford University (*Cont.*)
  risk factors 209, 211, 216, 217, 219, 221
  starting salaries for lecturers 22
  total return approach 87
  tutorial system 34
  wealthier Colleges 318, 319
Oxford University Colleges, *see* All Souls;
    Balliol; Christ Church; Green; Harris
    Manchester; Hertford; Jesus; Keble; Kellogg;
    Lady Margaret Hall; Linacre; Magdalen;
    Mansfield; Merton; New; Nuffield; Queen's;
    St Catherine's; St Cross; St Edmund Hall; St
    Hilda's; St Hugh's; St John's; St Peter's;
    Somerville; Templeton; Trinity; University;
    Wadham; Worcester
Oxford University Fund LP 337
Oxford University institutions/offices:
  Capital Fund 290, 296
  Cash Deposit fund 155
  Cash Deposit Pool 266, 268–9, 288, 291, 296
  Congregation 4
  Council 4
  Development Office 319
  Endowment 223, 291
  Income and Expenditure Accounts 87
  Investment Committee 223, 265, 288
  Staff Pension Scheme 34
  Statutes and Regulations 4
  Trust Pool 10, 11, 155, 290, 296
OXIP (Oxford Investment Partners) 44, 162,
    242, 268, 299, 328

Paris, University of 5
passive strategies 187, 189, 190, 191, 192, 193,
    250, 255, 262, 279, 332
  ascendance of 188
  low-cost 245
Pembroke College (Cambridge) 37, 151, 308
pension funds 30, 188, 205, 214
  required to disclose SRI policies 271
  trustees 270
Pensions Act (UK 1995) 270
performance measurement 284–300, 335–40
  see also benchmarks
Permanent Private Halls 65
Perse Trust 11
Peterhouse College (Cambridge) 38, 92–3,
    308
  development office 317
  Governing Body 153
  operational deficit 25
  paltry returns 339
  property investment 122–3, 128, 151, 153,
    161, 164–5, 166
  Tuition Fund 22
pledges 31
  cash and non-legacy 320

pooling 9, 10, 11, 203, 231, 266, 268, 269, 279,
    299, 329
  wider use of 301
poorer backgrounds 24
poorer Colleges 32, 33, 327, 332
portfolio management issues 185–207
portfolio risk 208–32
Princeton University 3, 7, 240, 327
  endowments 13, 16, 17, 18, 22, 46
  high allocations to alternative strategies 215
  overall performance and asset allocation 292
  tuition costs 22
  wealth of students 14
Private Action: Public Benefit (UK Cabinet Office
    2002) 270
private equity 7, 122, 123, 125, 127, 131, 133,
    135, 138, 139, 143, 144, 145, 160, 162, 173,
    185, 197, 236, 239, 261, 296
  access to research on 237
  allocation to 146, 148, 191, 268
  barriers to investing in 237
  fund-of-funds 197, 237, 265
  General Partnership investments 262
  high allocation to 285
  information on 148
  institutions not heavily exposed to 217–18
  monitoring the performance of 215
  partnership agreements 231
  perceived as highly risky 190
  preference for 147, 148–9
  risk of getting manager selection wrong
    in 147
  six-monthly reviews 254
private funding 24
Privy Council 217
property 35, 37, 40, 80, 84, 126, 130–1, 133,
    202
  collectivization of 173
  consultants appear not to know very much
    about 233
  cost of managing 339
  direct holdings 212
  endowment income derived from 168–70
  fixed-income-like characteristics of 332
  high exposure to 149, 214–15
  holding on 139
  impact on asset allocation 176–81
  investing in 160–84
  large direct investments 187–8
  management of 170–6
  preferred to alternative assets 147
  prime assets 122
  seen as a relatively low-risk investment 333
  viewed as quintessential long-term
    investment 149
  see also allocation to property
Property Bursars 64, 171

'prudence' concept 219
Prudential Assurance Company Ltd. 182
public equity 138, 139, 142, 144, 149
  managed passively 190
public funding 24, 29
  students not eligible for 30
public scrutiny 7
purchasing power:
  long-term 115
  preserving 98, 102, 104, 121

Quality of Business Checklist 273
Quandt, R. E. 97
Queen's College, The (Oxford) 14, 94
Queens' College (Cambridge) 6, 306, 318
  endowment income distribution 117

RCCA (Recommended Cambridge College
    Accounts) 40, 295
real estate 122–3, 150, 152, 160, 174, 175, 332
  prevailing inefficiencies in the market 173
  see also REITs
rebalancing 54, 193–203
REITs (real estate investment trusts) 122, 123,
    162, 163, 173, 176, 177, 242
rents 35, 83, 175, 200
  collection of 172
  commercial 181
  economic 43, 181
  ground 162
  income derived from 169
  market-based 36, 181
  subsidized 37, 43
  uneconomic 184
research grants 19, 20, 28
residential charges 35
Restricted Funds 7–11
return-to-risk ratio 78
returns on investment 9, 23, 77, 95
  benchmark 295
  determining 122
  dispersion in range of 299
  failure to deliver 150
  higher-than-market 189
  improving 31
  indication of 296
  inflation-adjusted 290
  long-term 122, 155, 175
  risk-adjusted 53, 245, 250, 301
  see also expected returns; total return
    approach
Rhodes Trust (Oxford) 6, 11
Richard, Alison 29, 31, 43, 48–9, 87, 316, 323
richer Colleges 25, 33, 41–2, 76, 107, 319
  asset allocation to property 132, 142, 144,
    145, 150, 151
  cost structure 304, 305, 308, 310

external managers 248
  stronger position to subsidize rents 37
risk 187, 200, 220
  acceptable 75, 77, 80, 139, 175
  affordable 314
  approaches to 333–5
  appropriate 78
  avoidable 194
  balance between return, volatility and 9
  control of 194, 208
  counterparty 208
  diversification of 188
  downside 229, 230, 232
  fiduciary 156, 218–19, 223
  higher element of 13
  inappropriate, ill-informed 192
  individual manager 213
  instructions given to investment
    manager 221–6
  interest rate 143
  irrational 160
  liquidity 179, 216–18
  manager 224
  market 211–13, 224
  minimizing 77
  operational or business 213
  potential 146
  spreading 225
  stock specific 224
risk analysis:
  BARRA 224
  quantitative 196
risk assessment 209, 210, 233
risk aversion 203, 210
risk management 71, 165, 189, 211, 232, 328
  advice on 238
  benchmarks used for 225
  best practice 226
  delegated 209, 224
  macro level 226
risk profile 194
  change in 203
  understanding 208
risk-return characteristics 168, 194
Robinson College (Cambridge) 288, 306
Rockefeller, John D. 2
Rockefeller University, The 15
Rowntree, Joseph 2
Royal Academy of Music 90
Royal Charters 4, 5
RPI (Retail Price Index) 34, 76, 81, 114, 116
  costs which rise faster than 115
Russell Index 78, 142–3

St Anne's College (Oxford) 338
St Catherine's College (Oxford) 44, 94, 294,
    304–5, 337

St Cross College (Oxford) 5
St Edmund Hall (Oxford) 17, 94
St Hilda's College (Oxford) 304
St Hugh's College (Oxford) 163, 304
St John's College (Cambridge) 12, 14, 17, 306, 310
  donations 318, 321
  endowment income distribution 117
  expenditure 25
St John's College (Oxford) 35, 287–8, 317, 318, 319
  broad allocation 337–8
  endowment asset worth 12, 14
  expenditure 25
St Peter's College (Oxford) 288, 304
salaries 21, 37, 115
  full professor 22
  lower 25
  starting 22
  tutors 81–3
  younger academics 116
S&P (Standard & Poor's) Index 78
Sarasin Chiswell 268
Savills 289
Scholar, Sir Michael 23
Scholars 1
Schroders 238
securitization 163
Selwyn College (Cambridge) 306
Senior Bursars 254
Shanghai 31
Sharpe, William F. 189
Sidney Sussex College (Cambridge) 30, 336
  Keynes bequest 39
SIP (Statement of Investment Principles) 71, 94–5, 270
Somerville College (Oxford) 338
  Specific Trust Funds 8
SORP (Statement of Recommended Practice) 6, 25, 66, 70, 117, 170
Specific Funds, see Restricted Funds
speculation 164, 166
spending policy 98–120, 330–1
spending rate 98, 99–100, 102–6
  and inflation 114–17
  and size of endowment 106–10
  smoothing mechanism applied in determining 110–14
  target 330
spending rules 108–9
  annual 111
  assisting institutions in defining 252
  consistent 217
  income-only 83
  sustainable 239
spin outs 20

SRI (socially responsible investment) 8, 75–6, 95, 270–83
stabilization reserves 113
staff costs 34, 322
staffing levels 65
Stanford University 3, 240, 327
  endowment assets per FTE student 16
  endowment size 13
  high allocations to alternative strategies 215
Statement of Investment Principles 226
  See also SIP
Statutes:
  College 217, 241, 286
  University 5, 36
Steinberg, Gary 138
Sterling 291
stock exclusions 274, 276, 278, 279, 280
stock markets 118, 152, 173, 194
  downturn 185, 201
  failure to deliver 161
  fall in 34
  hedging 143
  improvements in values 336
  private equity companies acquire listing 218
  uncertainty 46
stock selection 296, 298, 335
strategic asset allocation 161, 195, 199, 233, 237, 274, 289
  absence of consultants in 205
  determining 241, 242, 246
  usually determined by Investment Committee 298
student accommodation 23, 32, 37, 40
subsidiary trading companies 20, 35, 36, 163
Swensen, David 41, 52, 53, 62, 98, 146, 173, 194, 199, 205, 213, 226, 243, 244, 301, 315, 316

talented students 23
tangible assets 36
tax credits 29, 30
  abolition of 43, 84
tax incentives 9, 24, 31, 323
  removal of 46
taxation 36
  exemption 9, 24
  favourable status 2
  sensitivity 213
teaching costs 23
Templeton College (Oxford) 50, 117, 303
Texas, see University of Texas System
Tobin, James 48, 69
Tokyo University 25, 31
total return approach 8, 10, 86, 104, 105, 111, 114, 175, 176, 178, 229, 251, 331
  accounting, essential transition to 217
  encouraging the shift towards 237

income versus 83–7
  spending policies 113
tracking error 224, 225, 229, 230, 232
  guidelines regarding the use of 227
traded options 204
trading subsidiaries 35, 36
transparency 213, 272
Treasury Committee 50
trend following 194
Trinity College (Cambridge) 12, 14, 17, 18,
    180, 182, 296, 327
  endowment income distribution 117
  endowment management costs 306
  expenditure 25
  information on donations 318
  Isaac Newton Trust 11
  main endowment fund 296
  property investment 151
  Senior Bursar appointment 62, 64
  superior facilities 327
Trinity College (Oxford) 94, 288
Trinity Hall (Cambridge) 308
  Bursar's Report (2004) 40
  windfall profits 40
  Wychfield accommodation project 40
Trust Funds 8, 10–11, 87
Trustee Act (UK 2000) 10, 83, 84, 221, 222,
    252
trustees 50, 98, 208, 221, 239, 276, 284
  fiduciary responsibilities 219
  obligations 70, 122
  pension fund 196, 270
TUCS (Trust Universe Comparison Service)
    Median 53
tuition fees:
  cost-based 26
  payable by students 21
tuition income 23

UBS (Union Bank of Switzerland) 238
UBS Laing and Cruickshank 268
undergraduates:
  capitation fee 34
  cost 22
  funding 26
United Kingdom:
  consultant role 239
  equity market 85
  fiduciary responsibilities of trustees 219
  funding of higher education 19–26
  income-only spending rules 83
  investment committees 58–62
  largest foundation in 95, 109
  not-for-profit 332
  obligations of charity trustees 70
  philanthropic institutions 85, 185

publicly quoted real estate market 173
occupational pension schemes 271
United States 2, 12, 13, 14, 18, 44, 55–6
  alternative strategies managers 261
  asset allocations 130, 133, 135–6, 142, 144,
      154, 262
  asset managers 245
  consultants 67, 234, 235, 240
  contemporary practice 7
  cost-based tuition fees 26
  Department of Labor Interpretative
      bulletin 270
  endowment management cost comparison
      with 311–12
  external asset management 248
  fiduciary responsibilities of trustees 219
  foundations pay out percentage of assets
      every year 98
  gifts/bequests/donations 323, 324
  higher return strategies 143
  institutional policy 95, 96
  investment approach 85
  investment committees 58–62
  investment objective 77–8
  investment performance benchmarks 253
  investment thinking 187
  operating budgets funded by endowment
      income 88
  passive strategies 193
  performance trends reversal 297
  private universities 45
  real estate assets 332
  rebalancing 198
  research on endowments and
      foundations 215
  safe investments by banks 24
  salaries at top universities 25
  spending policies 100, 101–2, 108, 109, 111,
      112
  student indebtedness 45
  top endowments 160
  total return approach 84
  wealthier public universities 16
  wealthier universities 327
  see also Ivy League; also under Berkeley;
      Commonfund Benchmarks; Franklin W. Olin;
      Michigan; MIT; NES; Rockefeller; Stanford;
      Texas
Universities and College Estates Act (1925,
    amended 1964) 8
Universities of Oxford and Cambridge Act
    (1923) 5, 286
University College London 31
University College (Oxford) 94, 151,
    304
University Equation 103

University of Oxford: Financial Statement of
  the Colleges
  (2002–3) 34, 43, 51, 93, 170, 183, 209, 294,
    321
  (2003–4) 86, 93, 321
University of Texas System 13, 14, 52
  FTE students 15
University Officers 4
unlisted securities 228
Unrestricted Funds 7–11
US dollar depreciation 291

valuations 173, 211
  annual 285
  infrequent 332
Van Noorden, Roger 21, 81, 300
Van Noorden index 115, 129
venture capital funds 296
Vodafone 279
voting rights 270, 281

Wadham College (Oxford) 304
Wardens 51, 170, 209
Watson Wyatt 98, 243
wealthier Colleges 37, 38, 41, 80, 132, 133,
    151, 308, 332
  Colleges fund-raising 318, 319
wealthier universities 327
Wellcome, Henry 2
Wellcome Trust 30, 69, 106, 138, 195–6
  assets linked directly to performance 314
  investment objective 71
  move towards performance-related fees 303
withdrawals 296, 331
WM Company/Charity indices 53, 76, 84, 130,
    288, 290, 292, 296
Wolfson College (Cambridge) 96, 306

Wolfson College (Oxford) 338
Womack, Joanna 5
women's Colleges 318
Worcester College (Oxford) 304

Yale Corporation Investment Committee 52,
    58, 103–4
Yale Endowment 53, 58, 139, 154, 296, 316
  actual allocation 133, 135
  expected real return from 104
  investment policy objective 71
  responsibility for investing 328
  return (2005) 291
  review of investment policy (2004) 79
Yale Investment Office 328
Yale University 3, 7, 13, 17, 18, 43, 46, 62, 187,
    240, 315, 329, 330
  asset allocation 135, 141, 142, 154, 161
  cost of endowment management 303
  exploitation of illiquid, less efficient
    markets 332
  FTE students 15, 16
  high allocations to alternative strategies 215
  investment objective 78
  largest source of nongovernmental
    income 47
  major contributory factor in generating
    wealth 41
  management structure 52, 53
  median annual salary for full professor 22
  operating budget 99
  overall performance and asset allocation 292
  revenue sources 27
  risk-taking 160
  specific funds 8–9
  spending policy 102, 103, 110, 114
  total revenue 28
  wealth of students 15